www.wadsworth.com

www.wadsworth.com is the World Wide Web site for Thomson Wadsworth and is your direct source to dozens of online resources.

At *www.wadsworth.com* you can find out about supplements, demonstration software, and student resources. You can also send e-mail to many of our authors and preview new publications and exciting new technologies.

www.wadsworth.com
Changing the way the world learns®

Classics in American Government

Third Edition

Jay M. Shafritz and Lee S. Weinberg
Graduate School of Public and International Affairs
University of Pittsburgh

AUSTRALIA • CANADA • MEXICO • SINGAPORE • SPAIN • UNITED KINGDOM • UNITED STATES

Classics in American Government, Third Edition
Jay M. Shafritz/Lee S. Weinberg

Publisher: *Clark Baxter*
Executive Editor: *David Tatom*
Associate Development Editor: *Rebecca Green*
Editorial Assistant: *Cheryl Lee*
Senior Marketing Manager: *Janise Fry*
Marketing Assistant: *Teresa Jessen*
Marketing Communications Manager: *Kelley McAllister*
Production Assistant: *Jennifer Kostka*
Senior Print Buyer: *Mary Beth Hennebury*
Senior Permissions Editor: *Joohee Lee*
Production Service/Compositor: *International Typesetting and Composition*
Cover Designer: *Jeanette Barber/Silver Valley Graphic Design*
Cover/Text Printer: *Webcom, Ltd.*

© 2006 Thomson Wadsworth, a part of The Thomson Corporation. Thomson, the Star logo, and Wadsworth are trademarks used herein under license.

ALL RIGHTS RESERVED. No part of this work covered by the copyright hereon may be reproduced or used in any form or by any means—graphic, electronic, or mechanical, including photocopying, recording, taping, web distribution, information storage and retrieval systems, or in any other manner—without the written permission of the publisher.

Printed in Canada
1 2 3 4 5 6 7 09 08 07 06 05

For more information about our products, contact us at:
Thomson Learning
Academic Resource Center
1-800-423-0563

For permission to use material from this text or product, submit a request online at
http://www.thomsonrights.com

Any additional questions about permissions can be submitted by e-mail to
thomsonrights@thomson.com

Library of Congress Control Number: 2005922182

ISBN 0-534-60271-1

Credits appear on pages 439–441, which constitute a continuation of the copyright page.

Thomson Higher Education
10 Davis Drive
Belmont, CA 94002-3098
USA

Asia (including India)
Thomson Learning
5 Shenton Way
#01-01 UIC Building
Singapore 068808

Australia/New Zealand
Thomson Learning Australia
102 Dodds Street
Southbank, Victoria 3006
Australia

Canada
Thomson Nelson
1120 Birchmount Road
Toronto, Ontario M1K 5G4
Canada

UK/Europe/Middle East/Africa
Thomson Learning
High Holborn House
50–51 Bedford Road
London WC1R 4LR
United Kingdom

Latin America
Thomson Learning
Seneca, 53
Colonia Polanco
11560 Mexico
D.F. Mexico

Spain (including Portugal)
Thomson Paraninfo
Calle Magallanes, 25
28015 Madrid, Spain

Overview Contents

Contents

IX: Mass Media 259

X: The Congress 281

XI: The Presidency 307

Preface

This is a collection of documents, court cases, speeches, articles, and portions of books on American government. They were written by revolutionaries, presidents, U.S. Supreme Court judges, historians, political scientists, journalists, and politicians. The one thing they have in common is widely recognized importance. Each selection is generally acknowledged to be a major statement about some aspect of American government. That is why we have called them classics.

The primary characteristic of a classic in any field is its enduring value. We have classic automobiles, classic works of literature, classic techniques for dealing with legal, medical, or military problems, and so on. Classics emerge and endure through the years because of their continuing ability to be useful. *The Three Musketeers* is as good an adventure story today as it was in 1844 when Alexandre Dumas wrote it. But how many other nineteenth-century pieces of literature have general utility for a twenty-first-century audience? It is no different with the literature of American government. Much has been written, but what is still worth reading today or will be tomorrow? The intent of this collection is to make readily available some of the worthwhile material on American government from the past that will be equally valuable for tomorrow.

To be included, a selection had to be relevant to a main theme of American government. It had to be a basic statement that was consistently echoed or attacked in subsequent years. This leads to our second criterion—significance. The selection had to be generally recognized as a significant contribution. An "unrecognized classic" seems to us to be a contradiction. As a rule of thumb, we asked ourselves, "Should the serious student of American government be expected to be able to identify this author or that court case?" If the answer was yes, it meant that the contribution had long been recognized as a landmark document or court case or as an important theme by a significant writer. The editors can and expect to be criticized for excluding this or that particular article, writer, document, or court case, but we believe it would be difficult to criticize us for our inclusions. The items chosen have been widely quoted and reprinted. The basic idea of this book was simply to bring them together.

The selections, which date from the Mayflower Compact of 1620 to a 2002 speech by George W. Bush, are grouped into fourteen sections that correspond to the way American government courses are typically taught. Within each section they are in chronological order. At the beginning of each selection, a brief introduction summarizes the selection and places it in historical context. Although many of the selections might seem quite old to a student readership, they are not dated. They are considered classics because of their continuing value and significance to each new generation.

What's New to this Edition

This third edition has been able to take advantage of the comments of innumerable colleagues, reviewers, and students. Taking these judgments into account, we have deleted several articles and replaced them with others that both the reviewers and the editors deemed more useful.

Thus, we have added to this edition selections from:

- Woodrow Wilson's classic analysis of congressional government
- Franklin D. Roosevelt's 1935 speech outlining a new definition of liberalism
- Milton Friedman's defense of free markets and "competitive capitalism"
- Harry S. Truman's address explaining the U.S. role in the Cold War
- George W. Bush's 2002 speech offering a rationale for preemptive war

The preceding list is just what is new. When combined with the classic material from the previous edition, we believe we have created the most useful and most readable collection of the classics in American government with which every student should be familiar.

Finally, of course, we want to thank the reviewers: Victor L. Mote, *University of Houston*; Michael Cairo, *Georgetown College*; and Robert Alexander, *Ohio Northern University* for their assistance in revising and improving this collection of classic readings. We also want to acknowledge the assistance of our graduate assistant, William Kulina, and our administrative secretary, Joyce Valiquette, for their help in preparing the materials for publication. We hope instructors and students will find the new edition to be a challenging and stimulating supplement to their study of American government.

About the Authors

Jay M. Shafritz is a professor in the Graduate School of Public and International Affairs at the University of Pittsburgh. Previously he has taught at the University of Colorado in Denver, the University of Houston in Clear Lake City, the State University of New York in Albany, and Rensselaer Polytechnic Institute. He is the author, coauthor, or editor of more than three dozen books on government, including the *HarperCollins Dictionary of American Government and Politics* (1992), the *Dictionary of Twentieth-Century World Politics* (1993), and *The Dictionary of Public Policy and Administration* (2004). Dr. Shafritz received his Ph.D. from Temple University.

Lee S. Weinberg is an associate professor in the Graduate School of Public and International Affairs at the University of Pittsburgh. Dr. Weinberg is coauthor of three books and more than a hundred articles in newspapers and journals. An attorney, Dr. Weinberg is Director of the Administration of Justice and Legal Studies Programs at the University of Pittsburgh. He received both his J.D. and Ph.D. degrees from the University of Pittsburgh.

I

The Constitutional Framework

1. The Mayflower Compact

The Mayflower Compact was the agreement for governing the Plymouth Plantation signed by most of the male passengers of the Mayflower *in 1620. While it has since been idealized as the beginning of American Constitutional thinking, it was just a loose social compact for local government. We have reprinted it in its original diction and spelling to give the reader the true flavor of the original.*

In the name of God, Amen. We whose names are underwritten, the loyall subjects of our dread soveraigne Lord, King James, by the grace of God, of Great Britaine, France, & Ireland king, defender of the faith, &c., haveing undertaken, for the glorie of God, and advancemente of the Christian faith, and honour of our king & countrie, a voyage to plant the first colonie in the Northerne parts of Virginia, doe by these presents solemnly & mutualy in the presence of God, and one of another, covenant & combine our selves togeather into a civill body politick, for our better ordering & preservation & furtherance of the ends aforesaid; and by vertue hearof to enacte, constitute, and fram such just & equall lawes, ordinances, acts, constitutions, & offices, from time to time, as shall be thought most meete & convenient for the generall good of the Colonie, unto which we promise all due submission and obedience. In witnes whereof we have hereunder subscribed our names at Cap-Codd the 11. of November, in the year of the raigne of our soveraigne lord, King James, of England, France & Ireland the eithteenth, and of Scotland the fiftie fourth. Anno: Dom. 1620.

Source: From William Bradford, *History of Plymouth Plantation* (1856).

ABIGAIL ADAMS

2. The First American Feminist

Abigail Adams's forceful letter to her husband, John, reminds us that the struggle by women to achieve full political equality in America did not begin with the feminist movement of the 1960s. Nor did it begin with the women's suffrage movement of the early twentieth century. In fact, the struggle began before the Constitution was even adopted. Abigail Adams, in this portion of a 1776 letter to her husband, uses rhetoric one might have expected to hear in the 1970s when she writes that "all Men would be tyrants if they could" and threatens that the women will "foment a Rebellion" if her husband and the other founding fathers fail to give women a voice in the new government.

I long to hear that you have declared an independancy—and by the way in the new Code of Laws which I suppose it will be necessary for you to make I desire you would Remember the Ladies, and be more generous and favourable to them than your ancestors. Do not put such unlimited power into the hands of the Husbands. Remember all Men would be tyrants if they could. If perticuliar care and attention is not paid to the Laidies we are determined to foment a Rebellion, and will not hold ourselves bound by any Laws in which we have no voice, or Representation.

That your Sex are Naturally Tyrannical is a Truth so thoroughly established as to admit of no dispute, but such of you as wish to be happy willingly give up the harsh title of Master for the more tender and endearing one of Friend. Why then, not put it out of the power of the vicious and the Lawless to use us with cruelty and indignity with impunity. Men of Sense in all Ages abhor those customs which treat us only as the vassals of your Sex. Regard us then as Beings placed by providence under your protection and in immitation of the Supreem Being make use of that power only for our happiness.

Source: From Charles Frances Adams, *Letters of Mrs. Adams, the Wife of John Adams* (1848).

3. THE DECLARATION OF INDEPENDENCE

Drafted primarily by Thomas Jefferson during the Second Continental Congress, the Declaration of Independence remains the classic statement of human rights constantly invoked by social and political reformers in the United States and by advocates of human rights all over the world.

The Declaration begins with a philosophic discussion of the nature of law and the rights of men. Jefferson then offers a theoretical justification for breaking with England's tyrannical king. This is followed by a long list of the king's abuses and a statement of how the colonists constantly petitioned for redress with no effect. Then the "Representatives of the United States of America" declare their independence and "mutually pledge to each other our lives, our fortunes, and our sacred honor." The Declaration, which was approved by the convention in July 1776, was the first significant political—as opposed to philosophical—statement that the people of a nation had a right to choose their own government.

When in the course of human events, it becomes necessary for one people to dissolve the political bands which have connected them with another, and to assume among the Powers of the earth, the separate and equal station to which the Laws of Nature and of Nature's God entitle them, a decent respect to the opinions of mankind requires that they should declare the causes which impel them to the separation.

We hold these truths to be self-evident, that all men are created equal, that they are endowed by their Creator with certain unalienable Rights, that among these are Life, Liberty and the pursuit of Happiness. That to secure these rights, Governments are instituted among Men, deriving their just powers from the consent of the governed. That whenever any Form of Government becomes destructive of these ends, it is the Right of the People to alter or abolish it, and to institute new government, laying its foundation on such principles and organizing its powers in such form, as to them shall seem most likely to effect their Safety and Happiness. Prudence, indeed, will dictate that Governments long established should not be changed for light and transient causes; and accordingly all experience hath shown, that mankind are more disposed to suffer, while evils are sufferable, than to right themselves by abolishing the forms to which they are accustomed. But when a long train of abuses and usurpations, pursuing invariably the same Object evinces a design to reduce them under absolute Despotism, it is their right, it is their duty, to throw off such Government, and to provide new Guards for their future security.—Such has been the patient sufferance of these Colonies; and such is now the necessity which constrains them to alter their former Systems of Government. The history of the present King of Great Britain is a history of repeated injuries and usurpations, all having in direct object the establishment of an absolute tyranny over these States. To prove this, let Facts be submitted to a candid world.

He has refused his Assent to Laws, the most wholesome and necessary for the public good.

He has forbidden his Governors to pass Laws of immediate and pressing importance, unless suspended in their operation till his Assent should be obtained; and when so suspended, has utterly neglected to attend to them.

He has refused to pass other Laws for the accommodation of large districts of people, unless those people would relinquish the right of Representation in the Legislature, a right inestimable to them and formidable to tyrants only.

He has called together legislative bodies at places unusual, uncomfortable, and distant from the depository of their Public Records, for the sole purpose of fatiguing them into compliance with his measures.

He has dissolved Representative Houses repeatedly, for opposing with manly firmness his invasions on the rights of the people.

He has refused for a long time, after such dissolutions, to cause others to be elected; whereby the Legislative Powers, incapable of Annihilation, have returned to the People at large for their exercise; the State remaining in the meantime exposed to all the dangers of invasion from without, and convulsions within.

He has endeavoured to prevent the population of these States; for that purpose obstructing the Laws of Naturalization of Foreigners; refusing to pass others to encourage their migrations hither, and raising the conditions of new Appropriations of Lands.

He has obstructed the Administration of Justice, by refusing his Assent to Laws for establishing Judiciary Powers.

He has made Judges dependent on his Will alone, for the tenure of their offices, and the amount and payment of their salaries.

He has erected a multitude of New Offices, and sent hither swarms of Officers to harass our people, and eat out their substance.

He has kept among us, in times of peace, Standing Armies without the Consent of our legislatures.

He has affected to render the Military independent of and superior to the Civil Power.

He has combined with others to subject us to a jurisdiction foreign to our constitution, and unacknowledged by our laws; giving his Assent to their acts of pretended Legislation:

For quartering large bodies of armed troops among us:

For protecting them, by a mock Trial, from Punishment for any Murders which they should commit on the inhabitants of these States:

For cutting off our Trade with all parts of the world:

For imposing taxes on us without our Consent:

For depriving us in many cases, of the benefits of Trial by Jury:

For transporting us beyond Seas to be tried for pretended offences:

For abolishing the free System of English Laws in a neighbouring Province, establishing therein an Arbitrary government, and enlarging its Boundaries so as to render it at once an example and fit instrument for introducing the same absolute rule into these Colonies:

For taking away our Charters, abolishing our most valuable Laws, and altering fundamentally the Forms of our Governments:

For suspending our own Legislatures, and declaring themselves invested with Power to legislate for us in all cases whatsoever.

He has abdicated Government here, by declaring us out of his Protection and waging War against us.

He has plundered our seas, ravaged our Coasts, burnt our towns, and destroyed the lives of our people.

He is at this time transporting large armies of foreign mercenaries to compleat the works of death, desolation and tyranny, already begun with circumstances of Cruelty & perfidy scarcely paralleled in the most barbarous ages, and totally unworthy the Head of a civilized nation.

He has constrained our fellow Citizens taken Captive on the high Seas to bear Arms against their Country, to become the executioners of their friends and Brethren, or to fall themselves by their Hands.

He has excited domestic insurrections amongst us, and has endeavoured to bring on the inhabitants of our frontiers, the merciless Indian Savages, whose known rule of warfare, is an undistinguished destruction of all ages, sexes and conditions.

In every stage of these Oppressions We have Petitioned for Redress in the most humble terms: Our repeated Petitions have been answered only by repeated injury. A Prince, whose character is thus marked by every act which may define a Tyrant, is unfit to be the ruler of a free people.

Nor have We been wanting in attentions to our British brethren. We have warned them from time to time of attempts by their legislature to extend an unwarrantable jurisdiction over us. We have reminded them of the circumstances of our emigration and a settlement here. We have appealed to their native justice and magnanimity, and we have conjured them by the ties of our common kindred to disavow these usurpations which, would inevitably interrupt our connections and correspondence. They too have been deaf to the voice of justice and of consanguinity. We must, therefore, acquiesce in the necessity, which denounces our Separation, and hold them, as we hold the rest of mankind, Enemies in War, in Peace Friends.

We, therefore, the Representatives of the united States of America, in General Congress, Assembled, appealing to the Supreme Judge of the world for the rectitude of our intentions, do, in the Name, and by authority of the good People of these Colonies, solemnly publish and declare, That these United Colonies are, and of Right ought to be Free and Independent States; that they are Absolved from all Allegiance to the British Crown, and that all political connection between them and the State of Great Britain, is and ought to be totally dissolved; and that as Free and Independent States, they have full power to levy War, conclude Peace, contract Alliances, establish Commerce, and to do all other Acts and Things which Independent States may of right do. And for the support of this Declaration, with a firm reliance on the Protection of Divine Providence, we mutually pledge to each other our Lives, our Fortunes and our sacred Honor.

John Hancock
(Massachusetts)

NEW HAMPSHIRE

Josiah Barlett
William Whipple
Matthew Thornton

MASSACHUSETTS

Samuel Adams
John Adams
Robert Treat Paine
Elbridge Gerry

DELAWARE

Caesar Rodney
George Read
Thomas McKean

NEW YORK

William Floyd
Philip Livingston
Francis Lewis
Lewis Morris

NEW JERSEY

Richard Stockton
John Witherspoon
Francis Hopkinson
John Hart
Abraham Clark

NORTH CAROLINA

William Hooper
Joseph Hewes
John Penn

MARYLAND

Samuel Chase
William Paca
Thomas Stone
Charles Carroll of Carrollton

SOUTH CAROLINA

Edward Rutledge
Thomas Heywood, Jr.
Thomas Lynch, Jr.
Arthur Middleton

RHODE ISLAND

Stephen Hopkins
William Ellery

CONNECTICUT

Roger Sherman
Samuel Huntington
William Williams
Oliver Wolcott

PENNSYLVANIA

Robert Morris
Benjamin Rush
Benjamin Franklin
John Morton
George Clymer
James Smith
George Taylor
James Wilson
George Ross

VIRGINIA

George Wythe
Richard Henry Lee
Thomas Jefferson
Benjamin Harrison
Thomas Nelson, Jr.
Francis Lightfoot Lee
Carter Braxton

GEORGIA

Button Gwinnett
Lyman Hall
George Walton

4. The Constitution of the United States

The Constitution of the United States is the oldest written constitution continuously in force and serves as an example to many other states of the benefits and effectiveness of such a well-crafted document. As James Madison put it in Federalist No. 57, "the aim of every political constitution is, or ought to be, first to obtain for rulers men [and women] who possess most wisdom to discern, and most virtue to pursue, the common good of society; and in the next place, to take the most effectual precautions for keeping them virtuous whilst they continue to hold their public trust."

When the fifty-five delegates began to struggle with the problems of government under the Articles of Confederation (1781–1787), they quickly realized that they needed to draft an entirely new constitution rather than simply modify the existing one. While everyone at the convention agreed that a national government derived its authority from the people and that the powers of that government must be limited, there was disagreement on how governing institutions should best represent the people.

The large states preferred representation based on population while the smaller ones preferred equal representation for each state regardless of size. The compromise that broke the deadlock was proposed by the Connecticut delegation; it called for one house, the Senate, to represent the states equally, while the other, the House of Representatives, would be based on population.

When ratified in 1788, the Constitution did not contain explicit guarantees of individual rights. In 1791 ten amendments—known as the Bill of Rights—were approved by Congress and ratified by the states. The Bill of Rights originally restricted only the actions of the federal government; unless prohibited by their own state constitutions, state and local governments could infringe on individual liberties in situations where the federal government could not.

When the Fourteenth Amendment was adopted in 1868, it asserted that no state may "deprive any person of life, liberty, or property without due process of law." A long series of Supreme Court decisions beginning in 1927 (Gitlow v. New York) *have interpreted these words so as to ensure that most of the Bill of Rights now also limits the actions of state governments.*

We the people of the United States, in Order to form a more perfect Union, establish Justice, insure domestic Tranquility, provide for the common defense, promote the general Welfare, and secure the Blessings of Liberty to ourselves and our Posterity, do ordain and establish this Constitution for the United States of America.

ARTICLE I

Section 1

All legislative Powers herein granted shall be vested in a Congress of the United States, which shall consist of a Senate and House of Representatives.

Section 2

The House of Representatives shall be composed of Members chosen every second Year by the People of the several States, and the Electors in each State shall have the Qualifications requisite for Electors of the most numerous Branch of the State Legislature.

No person shall be a representative who shall not have attained to the Age of twenty five Years, and been seven Years a Citizen of the United States, and who shall not, when elected, be an Inhabitant of that State in which he shall be chosen.

Representatives and direct Taxes shall be apportioned among the several States which may be included within this union, according to their respective Numbers, which shall be determined by adding to the whole Number of free Persons, including those bound to Service for a Term of Years, and excluding Indians not taxed, three fifths of all other Persons. The actual Enumeration shall be made within three Years after the first Meeting of the Congress of the United States, and within every subsequent Term of Ten Years, in such Manner as they shall by Law direct. The Number of Representatives shall not exceed one for every thirty Thousand, but each State shall have at Least one Representative; and until such enumeration shall be made, the State of New Hampshire shall be entitled to chuse three, Massachusetts eight, Rhode-Island and Providence Plantations one, Connecticut five, New York six, New Jersey four, Pennsylvania eight, Delaware one, Maryland six, Virginia ten, North Carolina five, South Carolina five, and Georgia three.

When vacancies happen in the Representation from any State, the Executive Authority thereof shall issue Writs of Election to fill such Vacancies.

The House of Representatives shall chuse their Speaker and other Officers; and shall have the sole Power of Impeachment.

Section 3

The Senate of the United States shall be composed of two Senators from each State, chosen by the Legislature thereof, for six Years; and each Senator shall have one Vote.

Immediately after they shall be assembled in Consequence of the first Election, they shall be divided as equally as may be into three Classes. The Seats of the Senators of the first Class shall be vacated at the Expiration of the second Year, of the second Class at the Expiration of the fourth Year, and of the third Class at the Expiration of the sixth Year, so that one third may be chosen every second Year; and if Vacancies happen by Resignation, or otherwise, during the Recess of the Legislature of any State, the Executive thereof may make temporary Appointments until the next Meeting of the Legislature, which shall then fill such Vacancies.

No Person shall be a Senator who shall not have attained to the Age of thirty Years, and been nine Years a Citizen of the United States, and who shall not, when elected, be an Inhabitant of that State for which he shall be chosen.

The Vice President of the United States shall be President of the Senate, but shall have no Vote, unless they be equally divided.

The Senate shall chuse their other Officers, and also a President pro tempore, in the Absence of the Vice President, or when he shall exercise the Office of the President of the United States.

The Senate shall have the sole Power to try all Impeachments. When sitting for that Purpose, they shall be on Oath or Affirmation. When the President of the United States is tried, the Chief Justice shall preside; And no Person shall be convicted without the Concurrence of two thirds of the Members present.

Judgment in Cases of Impeachment shall not extend further than to removal from Office, and disqualification to hold and enjoy any Office of honor, Trust or Profit under the United States: but the Party convicted shall nevertheless be liable and subject to Indictment, Trial, Judgment and Punishment, according to law.

Section 4

The Times, Places and Manner of holding Elections for Senators and Representatives, shall be prescribed in each State by the Legislature thereof; but the Congress may at any time by Law make or alter such regulations, except as to the Places of chusing Senators.

The Congress shall assemble at least once in every Year, and such Meeting shall be on the first Monday in December, unless they shall by Law appoint a different Day.

Section 5

Each House shall be the Judge of the Elections, Returns and Qualifications of its own Members, and a Majority of each shall constitute a Quorum to do Business; but a smaller Number may adjourn from day to day, and may be authorized to compel the Attendance of absent Members, in such Manner, and under such Penalties as each House may provide.

Each House may determine the Rules for its Proceedings, punish its Members for disorderly Behaviour, and, with the Concurrence of two thirds, expel a Member.

Each House shall keep a Journal of its Proceedings, and from time to time publish the same, excepting such Parts as may in their Judgment require Secrecy; and the Yeas and Nays of the Members of either House on any question shall, at the Desire of one fifth of those Present, be entered on the Journal.

Neither house, during the Sessions of Congress, shall, without the Consent of the other, adjourn for more than three days, nor to any other Place than that in which the two Houses shall be sitting.

Section 6

The Senators and Representatives shall receive a Compensation for their Services, to be ascertained by Law, and paid out of the Treasury of the United States. They shall in all Cases, except Treason, Felony and Breach of the Peace, be privileged from Arrest during their Attendance at the Session of their respective Houses, and in going to and returning from the same; and for any Speech or Debate in either House, they shall not be questioned in any other Place.

No Senator or Representative shall, during the Time for which he was elected, be appointed to any civil Office under the Authority of the United States, which shall have been created, or the Emoluments whereof shall have been encreased during such time; and no Person holding any Office under the United States, shall be a Member of either House during his Continuance in Office.

Section 7

All Bills for raising Revenue shall originate in the House of Representatives; but the Senate may propose or concur with Amendments as on other Bills.

Every Bill which shall have passed the House of Representatives and the Senate, shall, before it become a Law, be presented to the President of the United States; If he approve he shall sign it, but if not he shall return it, with his Objections to that House in which it shall have originated, who shall enter the Objections at large on their Journal, and proceed to reconsider it. If after such Reconsideration two thirds of that House shall agree to pass the Bill, it shall be sent, together with the Objections, to the other House, by which it shall likewise be reconsidered, and if approved by two thirds of that House, it shall become a Law. But in all such Cases the Votes of both Houses shall be determined by Yeas and Nays, and the Names of the Persons voting for and against the Bill shall be entered on the Journal of each House respectively. If any Bill shall not be returned by the President within ten Days (Sundays excepted) after it shall have been presented to him, the Same shall be a Law, in like Manner as if he had signed it, unless the Congress by their Adjournment prevent its Return, in which Case it shall not be a Law.

Every Order, Resolution, or Vote to which the Concurrence of the Senate and House of Representatives may be necessary (except on a question of Adjournment) shall be presented to the President of the United States; and before the Same shall take Effect, shall be approved by him, or being disapproved by him, shall be repassed by two thirds of the Senate and House of Representatives, according to the Rules and Limitations prescribed in the Case of a Bill.

Section 8

The Congress shall have Power To lay and collect Taxes, Duties, Imposts and Excises, to pay the Debts and provide for the common Defence and general Welfare of the United States; but all Duties, Imposts and Excises shall be uniform throughout the United States;

To borrow Money on the credit of the United States;

To regulate Commerce with foreign Nations, and among the several States, and with the Indian Tribes;

To establish a uniform Rule of Naturalization, and uniform Laws on the subject of Bankruptcies throughout the United States;

To coin Money, regulate the Value thereof, and of foreign Coin, and fix the Standard of Weights and Measures;

To provide for the Punishment of counterfeiting the Securities and current Coin of the United States;

To establish Post Offices and post Roads;

To promote the Progress of Science and useful Arts, by securing for limited Times to Authors and Inventors the exclusive Right to their respective Writings and Discoveries;

To constitute Tribunals inferior to the supreme Court;

To define and punish Piracies and Felonies committed on the high Seas, and Offences against the Law of Nations;

To declare War, grant Letters of Marque and Reprisal, and make Rules concerning Captures on Land and Water;

To raise and support Armies, but no Appropriation of Money to that Use shall be for a longer Term than two Years;

To provide and maintain a Navy;

To make Rules for the Government and Regulation of the land and naval Forces;

To provide for calling forth the Militia to execute the Laws of the Union, suppress Insurrections and repel Invasions;

To provide for organizing, arming, and disciplining, the Militia, and for governing such Part of them as may be employed in the Service of the United States, reserving to the States respectively, the Appointment of the Officers, and the Authority of training the Militia according to the discipline prescribed by Congress;

To exercise exclusive Legislation in all Cases whatsoever, over such District (not exceeding ten Miles square) as may, by Cession of particular States, and the Acceptance of Congress, become the Seat of the Government of the United States, and to exercise like Authority over all Places purchased by the Consent of the Legislature of the State in which the Same shall be for the Erection of Forts, Magazines, Arsenals, dock-Yards, and other needful Buildings;—And

To make all Laws which shall be necessary and proper for carrying into Execution the foregoing Powers, and all other Powers vested by this Constitution in the Government of the United States, or in any Department or Officer thereof.

Section 9

The Migration or Importation of such Persons as any of the States now existing shall think proper to admit, shall not be prohibited by the Congress prior to the Year one thousand eight hundred and eight, but a Tax or duty may be imposed on such Importation, not exceeding ten dollars for each Person.

The Privilege of the Writ of Habeas Corpus shall not be suspended, unless when in Cases of Rebellion or Invasion the public Safety may require it.

No Bill of Attainder or ex post facto Law shall be passed.

No Capitation, or other direct, Tax shall be laid, unless in Proportion to the Census or Enumeration herein before directed to be taken.

No Tax or Duty shall be laid on Articles exported from any State.

No Preference shall be given by any Regulation of Commerce or Revenue to the Ports of one State over those of another; nor shall Vessels bound to, or from, one State, be obliged to enter, clear, or pay Duties in another.

No Money shall be drawn from the Treasury, but in Consequence of Appropriations made by Law; and a regular Statement and Account of the Receipts and Expenditures of all public Money shall be published from time to time.

No Title of Nobility shall be granted by the United States; And no Person holding any office of Profit or Trust under them, shall, without the Consent of the Congress, accept of any present, Emolument, Office, or Title, of any kind whatever, from any King, Prince, or foreign States.

Section 10

No State shall enter into any Treaty, Alliance, or Confederation; grant Letters of Marque and Reprisal; coin Money; emit Bills of Credit; make any Thing but gold and silver Coin a Tender of Payment of Debts; pass any Bill of Attainder, ex post facto Law, or Law impairing the Obligation of Contracts, or grant any Title of Nobility.

No State shall, without the Consent of the Congress, lay any Imposts or Duties on Imports or Exports, except what may be absolutely necessary for executing its inspection Laws; and the net Produce of all Duties and Imposts, laid by any State on Imports or Exports, shall be for the Use of the Treasury of the United States; and all such Laws shall be subject to the Revision and Control of the Congress.

No State shall, without the Consent of Congress, lay any Duty of Tonnage, keep Troops, or Ships of War in time of Peace, enter into any Agreement or Compact with another State, or with a foreign Power, or engage in War, unless actually invaded, or in such imminent Danger as will not admit of delay.

ARTICLE II

Section 1

The executive Power shall be vested in a President of the United States of America. He shall hold his Office during the Term of four Years, and, together with the Vice President, chosen for the same term, be elected, as follows:

Each State shall appoint, in such Manner as the Legislature thereof may direct, a Number of Electors, equal to the whole Number of Senators and Representatives to which the State may be entitled in the Congress; but no Senator or Representative, or Person holding an Office of Trust or Profit under the United States, shall be appointed an Elector.

The Electors shall meet in their respective States, and vote by Ballot for two Persons, of whom one at least shall not be an Inhabitant of the same State with themselves. And they shall make a List of all the Persons voted for, and of the Number of Votes for each; which List they shall sign and certify, and transmit sealed to the Seat of the Government of the United States, directed to the President of the Senate. The President of the Senate shall, in the Presence of the Senate and House of Representatives, open all the Certificates, and the Votes shall then be counted. The Person having the greatest Number of Votes shall be the President, if such Number be a Majority of the whole Number of Electors appointed; and if there be more than one who have such Majority, and have an equal Number of Votes, then the House of Representatives shall immediately chuse by Ballot one of them for President: and if no Person have a Majority, then from the five highest on the List the said House shall in like Manner chuse the President. But in chusing the President, the Votes shall be taken by States, the Representation from each State having one Vote; A quorum for this Purpose shall consist of a Member or Members from two thirds of the States, and a Majority of all the States shall be necessary to a Choice. In every Case, after the Choice of the President, the Person having the greatest Number of Votes of the Electors shall be the Vice President. But if there should remain two or more who have equal Votes, the Senate shall chuse from them by Ballot the Vice President.

The Congress may determine the Time of chusing the Electors and the Day on which they shall give their Votes; which Day shall be the same throughout the United States.

No Person except a natural born Citizen, or a Citizen of the United States, at the time of the Adoption of this Constitution, shall be eligible to the Office of President; neither shall any Person be eligible to that Office who shall not have attained the Age of thirty five Years, and been fourteen Years a Resident within the United States.

In Case of the Removal of the President from Office, or of his Death, Resignation, or Inability to discharge the Powers and Duties of the said Office, the Same shall devolve on the Vice President, and the Congress may by Law provide for the Case of Removal, Death, Resignation or Inability, both of the President and Vice President, declaring what Officer shall then act as President, and such Officer shall act accordingly, until the Disability be removed, or a President shall be elected.

The President shall, at stated Times, receive for his Services a Compensation, which shall neither be encreased nor diminished during the Period for which he shall have been elected, and he shall not receive within that Period any other Emolument from the United States, or any of them.

Before he enter on the Execution of his Office, he shall take the following Oath or Affirmation:—"I do solemnly swear (or affirm) that I will faithfully execute the Office of President of the United States, and will to the best of my Ability, preserve, protect and defend the Constitution of the United States."

Section 2

The President shall be Commander in Chief of the Army and Navy of the United States, and of the Militia of the several States, when called into the actual Service of the United States; he may require the Opinion, in writing, of the principal Officer in each of the executive Departments, upon any Subject relating to the Duties of their respective Offices, and he shall have Power to grant Reprieves and Pardons for Offences against the United States, except in Cases of Impeachment.

He shall have Power, by and with the Advice and Consent of the Senate, to make Treaties, provided two thirds of the Senators present concur; and he shall nominate, and by and with the Advice and Consent of the Senate, shall appoint Ambassadors, other public Ministers and Consuls, Judges of the supreme Court, and all other Officers of the United States, whose Appointments are not herein otherwise provided for, and which shall be established by Law; but the Congress may by Law vest the Appointment of such inferior officers, as they think proper, in the President alone, in the Courts of Law, or in the Heads of Departments.

The President shall have Power to fill up all Vacancies that may happen during the Recess of the Senate, by granting Commissions which shall expire at the End of their next Session.

Section 3

He shall from time to time give to the Congress Information of the State of the Union, and recommend to their Consideration such Measures as he shall judge necessary and expedient; he may, on extraordinary Occasions, convene both Houses, or either of them, and in Case of Disagreement between them, with Respect to the Time of Adjournment, he may adjourn them to such Time as he shall think proper; he shall receive Ambassadors and other public Ministers; he shall take Care that the Laws be faithfully executed, and shall Commission all the officers of the United States.

Section 4

The President, Vice President and all civil Officers of the United States, shall be removed from Office on Impeachment for, and Conviction of, Treason, Bribery, or other High Crimes and Misdemeanors.

ARTICLE III

Section 1

The judicial Power of the United States, shall be vested in one supreme Court, and in such inferior Courts as the Congress may from time to time ordain and establish. The Judges, both of the supreme and inferior Courts, shall hold their Offices during good Behaviour, and shall, at stated Times, receive for their Services, a Compensation, which shall not be diminished during their Continuance in Office.

Section 2

The judicial Power shall extend to all Cases, in Law and Equity, arising under this Constitution, the Laws of the United States, and Treaties made, or which shall be made, under their Authority;—to all Cases affecting Ambassadors, other public Ministers and Consuls;—to all Cases of admiralty and maritime Jurisdiction;—to Controversies to which the United States shall be a Party;—to Controversies between two or more States;—between a State and Citizens of another State;—between Citizens of different States;—between Citizens of the same State claiming Lands under Grants of different States, and between a State, or the Citizens thereof, and foreign States, Citizens or Subjects.

In all Cases affecting Ambassadors, other public Ministers and Consuls, and those in which a State shall be Party, the supreme Court shall have original Jurisdiction. In all other Cases before mentioned, the supreme Court shall have appellate Jurisdiction, both as to Law and Fact, with such Exceptions, and under such Regulations as the Congress shall make.

The Trial of all Crimes, except in Cases of Impeachment, shall be by Jury; and such Trial shall be held in the State where the said Crimes shall have been committed; but when not committed within any State, the Trial shall be at such Place or Places as the Congress may by Law have directed.

Section 3

Treason against the United States, shall consist only in levying War against them, or in adhering to their Enemies, giving them Aid and Comfort. No Person shall be convicted of Treason unless on the Testimony of two Witnesses to the same overt Act, or on Confession in open Court.

The Congress shall have the Power to declare the Punishment of Treason, but no Attainder of Treason shall work Corruption of Blood, or Forfeiture except during the Life of the Person attainted.

ARTICLE IV

Section 1

Full Faith and Credit shall be given in each State to the public Acts, Records, and judicial Proceedings of every other State. And the Congress may by general Laws prescribe the Manner in which such Acts, records, and Proceedings shall be proved, and the Effect thereof.

Section 2

The Citizens of each State shall be entitled to all Privileges and Immunities of Citizens in the several States.

A Person charged in any State with Treason, Felony, or other Crime, who shall flee from Justice, and be found in another State, shall on Demand of the executive Authority of the State from which he fled, be delivered up, to be removed to the State having Jurisdiction of the Crime.

No Person held to Service or Labour in one State, under the Laws thereof, escaping into another, shall, in Consequence of any Law or Regulation therein, be discharged from such Service or Labour, but shall be delivered up on Claim of the Party to whom such Service or Labour may be due.

Section 3

New States may be admitted by the Congress into this Union; but no new State shall be formed or erected within the Jurisdiction of any other State; nor any State be formed by the Junction of two or more States, or Parts of States, without the Consent of the Legislatures of the States concerned as well as of the Congress.

The Congress shall have power to dispose of and make all needful Rules and Regulations respecting the Territory or other Property belonging to the United States; and nothing in this Constitution shall be so construed as to Prejudice any Claims of the United States, or of any particular State.

Section 4

The United States shall guarantee to every State in this Union a Republican Form of Government, and shall protect each of them against Invasion, and on Application of the Legislature, or of the Executive (when the Legislature cannot be convened) against domestic Violence.

Article V

The Congress, whenever two thirds of both Houses shall deem it necessary, shall propose Amendments to this Constitution, or, on the Application of the Legislatures of two thirds of the several States, shall call a Convention for proposing Amendments, which, in either Case, shall be valid to all Intents and Purposes, as Part of this Constitution, when ratified by the Legislatures of three fourths of the several States, or by Conventions in three fourths thereof, as the one or the other Mode of Ratification may be proposed by the Congress; Provided that no Amendment which may be made prior to the Year One thousand eight hundred and eight shall in any Manner affect the first and fourth Clauses in the Ninth Section of the first Article; and that no State, without its Consent, shall be deprived of its equal Suffrage in the Senate.

Article VI

All Debts contracted and Engagements entered into, before the Adoption of this Constitution, shall be as valid against the United States under this Constitution, as under the Confederation.

This Constitution, and the laws of the United States which shall be made in Pursuance thereof; and all Treaties made, or which shall be made, under the Authority of the United States, shall be the supreme Law of the Land; and the Judges in every State shall be bound thereby, any Thing in the Constitution or Laws of any State on the Contrary notwithstanding.

The Senators and Representatives before mentioned, and the Members of the several State Legislatures, and all executive and judicial Officers, both of the United States and of the several States, shall be bound by Oath or Affirmation, to support this Constitution; but no religious Test shall ever be required as a Qualification to any Office or public Trust under the United States.

Article VII

The Ratification of the Conventions of nine States shall be sufficient for the Establishment of this Constitution between the States so ratifying the Same.

Done in Convention by the Unanimous Consent of the States present the Seventeenth Day of September in the Year of our Lord one thousand seven hundred and eighty seven and of the Independence of the United States of America the Twelfth. In witness whereof We have hereunto subscribed our Names.

Go. WASHINGTON
Presid't. and deputy from Virginia

Attest
William Jackson
Secretary

DELAWARE
Geo. Read
Gunning Bedford jun
John Dickinson
Richard Basset
Jaco. Broom

MASSACHUSETTS
Nathaniel Gorham
Rufus King

CONNECTICUT
Wm. Saml. Johnson
Roger Sherman

NEW YORK
Alexander Hamilton

NEW JERSEY
Wh. Livingston
David Brearley
Wm. Paterson
Jona. Dayton

PENNSYLVANIA
B. Franklin
Thomas Mifflin
Robt. Morris
Geo. Clymer
Thos. FitzSimons
Jared Ingersoll
James Wilson
Gouv. Morris

NEW HAMPSHIRE
John Langdon
Nicholas Gilman

MARYLAND
James McHenry
Dan of St. Thos. Jenifer
Danl. Carroll

VIRGINIA
John Blair
James Madison Jr.

NORTH CAROLINA
Wm. Blount
Richd. Dobbs Spaight
Hu. Williamson

SOUTH CAROLINA
J. Rutledge
Charles Cotesworth Pinckney
Charles Pinckney
Pierce Butler

GEORGIA
William Few
Abr. Baldwin

Amendment 1

Congress shall make no law respecting an establishment of religion, or prohibiting the free exercise thereof; or abridging the freedom of speech, or of the press; or the right of the people peaceably to assemble, and to petition the Government for a redress of grievances.

Amendment 2

A well regulated militia, being necessary to the security of a free State, the right of the people to keep and bear arms, shall not be infringed.

Amendment 3

No Soldier shall, in time of peace be quartered in any house, without the consent of the Owner, nor in time of war, but in a manner to be prescribed by law.

Amendment 4

The right of the people to be secure in their persons, houses, papers, and effects, against unreasonable searches and seizures, shall not be violated, and no Warrants shall issue, but upon probable cause, supported by Oath or affirmation, and particularly describing the place to be searched and the persons or things to be seized.

AMENDMENT 5

No person shall be held to answer for a capital, or otherwise infamous crime, unless on a presentment or indictment of a Grand Jury, except in cases arising in the land or naval forces, or in the Militia, when in actual service in time of war or public danger; nor shall any person be subject for the same offense to be twice put in jeopardy of life or limb; nor shall be compelled in any criminal case to be a witness against himself, nor be deprived of life, liberty, or property, without due process of law; nor shall private property be taken for public use, without just compensation.

AMENDMENT 6

In all criminal prosecutions, the accused shall enjoy the right to a speedy and public trial, by an impartial jury of the State and district wherein the crime shall have been committed, which district shall have been previously ascertained by law, and to be informed of the nature and cause of the accusation; to be confronted with the witnesses against him; to have compulsory process for obtaining witnesses in his favor, and to have the Assistance of Counsel for his defense.

AMENDMENT 7

In Suits at common law, where the value in controversy shall exceed twenty dollars, the right of trial by jury shall be preserved, and no fact tried by a jury, shall be otherwise reexamined in any Court of the United States, than according to the rules of common law.

AMENDMENT 8

Excessive bail should not be required, nor excessive fines imposed, nor cruel and unusual punishments inflicted.

AMENDMENT 9

The enumeration in the Constitution, of certain rights, shall not be construed to deny or disparage others retained by the people.

AMENDMENT 10

The powers not delegated to the United States by the Constitution, nor prohibited by it to the States, are reserved to the States respectively, or to the people.

Amendment 11
[Ratified February 7, 1795]

The Judicial power of the United States shall not be construed to extend to any suit in law or equity, commenced or prosecuted against one of the United States by Citizens of another State, or by Citizens or Subjects of any Foreign State.

Amendment 12
[Ratified July 27, 1804]

The Electors shall meet in their respective states and vote by ballot for President and Vice-President, one of whom, at least, shall not be an inhabitant of the same state with themselves; they shall name in their ballots the person voted for as President, and in distinct ballots the person voted for as Vice-President, and they shall make distinct lists of all persons voted for as President, and of all persons voted for as Vice-President, and of the number of votes for each, which lists they shall sign and certify, and transmit sealed to the seat of the government of the United States, directed to the President of the Senate;—The President of the Senate shall, in the presence of the Senate and House of Representatives, open all the certificates and the votes shall then be counted;—The person having the greatest number of votes for President, shall be the President, if such number be a majority of the whole number of Electors appointed; and if no person have such majority, then from the persons having the highest numbers not exceeding three on the list of those voted for as President, the House of Representatives shall choose immediately by ballot, the President. But in choosing the President, the votes shall be taken by states, the representation from each state having one vote; a quorum for this purpose shall consist of a member or members from two-thirds of the states, and a majority of all the states shall be necessary to a choice. And if the House of Representatives shall not choose a President whenever the right of choice shall devolve upon them, before the fourth day of March next following, the Vice-President shall act as President, as in the case of the death or other constitutional disability of the President.—The person having the greatest number of votes as Vice-President, shall be the Vice-President, if such number be a majority of the whole number of Electors appointed, and if no person have a majority, then from the two highest numbers on the list, the Senate shall choose the Vice-President; a quorum for the purpose shall consist of two-thirds of the whole number of Senators, and a majority of the whole number shall be necessary to a choice. But no person constitutionally ineligible to the office of President shall be eligible to that of Vice-President of the United States.

AMENDMENT 13
[RATIFIED DECEMBER 6, 1865]

Section 1

Neither slavery nor involuntary servitude, except as a punishment for crime whereof the party shall have been duly convicted, shall exist within the United States, or any place subject to their jurisdiction.

Section 2

Congress shall have the power to enforce this article by appropriate legislation.

AMENDMENT 14
[RATIFIED JULY 9, 1868]

Section 1

All persons born or naturalized in the United States, and subject to the jurisdiction thereof, are citizens of the United States and of the State wherein they reside. No State shall make or enforce any law which shall abridge the privileges or immunities of citizens of the United States; nor shall any State deprive any person of life, liberty, or property, without due process of law; nor deny to any person within its jurisdiction the equal protection of the laws.

Section 2

Representatives shall be apportioned among the several States according to their respective numbers, counting the whole number of persons in each State, excluding Indians not taxed. But when the right to vote at any election for the choice of electors for President and Vice President of the United States, Representatives in Congress, the Executive and Judicial Officers of a State, or the members of the Legislature thereof, is denied to any of the male inhabitants of such State, being twenty-one years of age, and citizens of the United States, or in any way abridged, except for participation in rebellion, or other crime, the basis of representation therein shall be reduced in the proportion which the number of such male citizens shall bear to the whole number of male citizens twenty-one years of age in such State.

Section 3

No person shall be a Senator or Representative in Congress, or elector of President or Vice President, or hold any office, civil or military, under the United States, or under any State, who, having previously taken an oath, as a member of Congress, or as an officer of the United States, or as a member of any State legislature, or as an executive or judicial officer of any State, to support the Constitution of the United States, shall have engaged in insurrection or rebellion against the same, or given aid or comfort to the enemies thereof. But Congress may by a vote of two-thirds of each House, remove such disability.

Section 4

The validity of the public debt of the United States, authorized by law, including debts incurred for payment of pensions and bounties for services in suppressing insurrection or rebellion, shall not be questioned. But neither the United States nor any State shall assume or pay any debt or obligation incurred in aid of insurrection or rebellion against the United States, or any claim for the loss or emancipation of any slave; but all such debts, obligations and claims shall be held illegal and void.

Section 5

The Congress shall have power to enforce, by appropriate legislation, the provisions of this article.

AMENDMENT 15
[RATIFIED FEBRUARY 3, 1870]

Section 1

The right of citizens of the United States to vote shall not be denied or abridged by the United States or by any State on account of race, color, or previous condition of servitude.

Section 2

The Congress shall have the power to enforce this article by appropriate legislation.

AMENDMENT 16
[RATIFIED FEBRUARY 3, 1913]

The Congress shall have power to lay and collect taxes on incomes, from whatever source derived, without apportionment among the several States, and without regard to any census or enumeration.

AMENDMENT 17
[RATIFIED APRIL 8, 1913]

The Senate of the United States shall be composed of two Senators from each State, elected by the people thereof for six years; and each Senator shall have one vote. The electors in each state shall have the qualifications requisite for electors of the most numerous branch of the State legislatures.

When vacancies happen in the representation of any State in the Senate, the executive authority of such State shall issue writs of election to fill such vacancies: *Provided,* That the legislature of any State may empower the executive thereof to make temporary appointments until the people fill the vacancies by election as the legislature may direct.

This amendment shall not be so construed as to affect the election or term of any Senator chosen before it becomes valid as part of the Constitution.

AMENDMENT 18
[RATIFIED JANUARY 16, 1919]

Section 1

After one year from the ratification of this article the manufacture, sale, or transportation of intoxicating liquors within, the importation thereof into, or the exportation thereof from the United States and all territory subject to the jurisdiction thereof for beverage purposes is hereby prohibited.

Section 2

[The Congress and the several States shall have concurrent power to enforce this article by appropriate legislation.]

Section 3

This article shall be inoperative unless it shall have been ratified as an amendment to the Constitution by the legislatures of the several States, as provided in the Constitution, within seven years from the date of the submission hereof to the State by the Congress.

AMENDMENT 19
[RATIFIED AUGUST 18, 1920]

The right of citizens of the United States to vote shall not be denied or abridged by the United States or by any State on account of sex. Congress shall have the power to enforce this article by appropriate legislation.

AMENDMENT 20
[RATIFIED JANUARY 23, 1933]

Section 1

The terms of the President and Vice-President shall end at noon on the 20th day of January, and the terms of Senators and Representatives at noon on the 3rd day of January, of the years in which such terms would have ended if this article had not been ratified; and the terms of their successors shall then begin.

Section 2

The Congress shall assemble at least once in every year, and such meeting shall begin at noon on the 3rd day of January, unless they shall by law appoint a different day.

Section 3

If, at the time fixed for the beginning of the term of the President, the President elect shall have died, the Vice-President elect shall become President. If a President shall not have been chosen before the time fixed for the beginning of his term, or if the President elect shall have failed to qualify, then the Vice-President elect shall act as President until a President shall have qualified; and the Congress may by law provide for the case wherein neither a President elect nor a Vice-President elect shall have qualified, declaring who shall then act as President, or the manner in which one who is to act shall be selected, and such person shall act accordingly until a President or Vice-President shall have qualified.

Section 4

The Congress may by law provide for the case of the death of any of the persons from whom the House of Representatives may choose a President whenever the rights of choice shall have devolved upon them, and for the case of the death of any of the persons from whom the Senate may choose a Vice-President whenever the right of choice shall have devolved upon them.

Section 5

Sections 1 and 2 shall take effect on the 15th day of October following the ratification of this article.

Section 6

This article shall be inoperative unless it shall have been ratified as an amendment to the Constitution by the legislatures of three-fourths of the several states within seven years from the date of its submission.

AMENDMENT 21
[RATIFIED DECEMBER 5, 1933]

Section 1

The eighteenth article of amendment to the Constitution of the United States is hereby repealed.

Section 2

The transportation or importation into any State, Territory, or Possession of the United States for delivery or use herein of intoxicating liquors, in violation of the laws thereof, is hereby prohibited.

Section 3

This article shall be inoperative unless it shall have been ratified as an amendment to the Constitution by conventions in several States, as provided in the Constitution, within seven years from the date of the submission hereof to the States by the Congress.

AMENDMENT 22
[RATIFIED FEBRUARY 27, 1951]

Section 1

No person shall be elected to the office of the President more than twice, and no person who has held the office of President, or acted as President, for more than two years of a term to which some other person was elected President shall be elected to the office of the President more than once. But this Article shall not apply to any person holding the office of President when this Article was proposed by the Congress, and shall not prevent any person who may be holding the office of President, or acting as President, during the term within which this Article becomes operative from holding the office of President or acting as President during the remainder of such term.

Section 2

This article shall be inoperative unless it shall have been ratified as an amendment to the Constitution by the legislatures of three-fourths of the several States within seven years from the date of its submission to the States by the Congress.

AMENDMENT 23
[RATIFIED MARCH 29, 1961]

Section 1

The District constituting the seat of Government of the United States shall appoint in such manner as the Congress may direct:

A number of electors of President and Vice President equal to the whole number of Senators and Representatives in Congress to which the District would be entitled if it were a State, but in no event more than the least populous State;

they shall be in addition to those appointed by the States, but they shall be considered, for the purposes of the election of President and Vice President, to be electors appointed by a State; and they shall meet in the District and perform such duties as provided by the twelfth article of amendment.

Section 2

The Congress shall have power to enforce this article by appropriate legislation.

AMENDMENT 24
[RATIFIED JANUARY 23, 1964]

Section 1

The right of citizens of the United States to vote in any primary or other election for President or Vice President, for electors for President or Vice President, or for Senator or Representative in Congress, shall not be denied or abridged by the United States or by any State by reason of failure to pay any poll tax or other tax.

Section 2

The Congress shall have power to enforce this article by appropriate legislation.

AMENDMENT 25
[RATIFIED FEBRUARY 10, 1967]

Section 1

In case of the removal of the President from office or of his death or resignation, the Vice President shall become President.

Section 2

Whenever there is a vacancy in the office of the Vice President, the President shall nominate a Vice President who shall take office upon confirmation by a majority vote of both Houses of Congress.

Section 3

Whenever the President transmits to the President pro tempore of the Senate and the speaker of the House of Representatives his written declaration that he is unable to discharge the powers and duties of his office, and until he transmits to them a written declaration to the contrary, such powers and duties shall be discharged by the Vice President as Acting President.

Section 4

Whenever the Vice President and a majority of either the principal officers of the executive department or of such other body as Congress may by law provide, transmit to the President pro tempore of the Senate and the Speaker of the House of Representatives their written declaration that the President is unable to discharge the powers and duties of his office, the Vice President shall immediately assume the powers and duties of the office as Acting President.

Thereafter, when the President transmits to the President pro tempore of the Senate and the Speaker of the House of Representatives his written declaration that no inability exists, he shall resume the powers and duties of his office unless the Vice President and a majority of either the principal officers of the executive department or of such other body as Congress may by law provide, transmit within four days to the President pro tempore of the Senate and the Speaker of the House of Representatives their written declaration that the President is unable to discharge the powers and duties of his office. Thereupon Congress shall decide the issue, assembling within forty-eight hours for that purpose if not in session. If the Congress, within twenty-one days after receipt of the latter written declaration, or, if Congress is not in session, within twenty-one days after Congress is required to assemble, determines by two-thirds vote of both Houses that the President is unable to discharge the powers and duties of his office, the Vice President shall continue to discharge the same as Acting President; otherwise, the President shall resume the powers and duties of his office.

AMENDMENT 26
[RATIFIED JUNE 30, 1971]

Section 1

The right of citizens of the United States, who are eighteen years of age or older, to vote shall not be denied or abridged by the United States or by any State on account of age.

Section 2

The Congress shall have the power to enforce this article by appropriate legislation.

AMENDMENT 27
[RATIFIED MAY 7, 1992]

No law, varying the compensation for the service of the Senate and Representatives, shall take effect, until an election of Representatives shall have intervened.

JAMES MADISON

5. Explaining the Separation of Powers

The most famous set of arguments supporting ratification of the United States Constitution appeared in The Federalist, *a series of newspaper articles written by Alexander Hamilton, James Madison, and John Jay. Their arguments have become classic statements of the philosophy underlying American governance.*

The Federalist, *No. 51, explains how the proposed constitution provided for a "separation of powers" so that no one segment of the government can acquire too much power. This is achieved by "contriving the interior structure of the government as that its several constituent parts may, by their mutual relations, be the means of keeping each other in their proper places."*

The Constitution reflected political compromises and did not completely satisfy either those who feared a strong national government (the anti-federalists) or those who believed that a strong national government was needed. Nonetheless, ratification of the new Constitution required that at least nine of the thirteen states accept it and supporters of the Constitution, led by Madison, Jay, and Hamilton, waged a major political campaign to encourage ratification.

To the People of the State of New York:

To what expedient, then, shall we finally resort, for maintaining in practice the necessary partition of power among the several departments, as laid down in the Constitution? The only answer that can be given is, that as all these exterior provisions are found to be inadequate, the defect must be supplied, by so contriving the interior structure of the government as that its several constituent parts may, by their mutual relations, be the means of keeping each other in their proper places. Without presuming to undertake a full development of this important idea, I will hazard a few general observations, which may perhaps place it in a clearer light, and enable us to form a more correct judgment of the principles and structure of the government planned by the convention.

Source: The Federalist, No. 51 (1788).

In order to lay a due foundation for that separate and distinct exercise of the different powers of government, which to a certain extent is admitted on all hands to be essential to the preservation of liberty, it is evident that each department should have a will of its own; and consequently should be so constituted that the members of each should have as little agency as possible in the appointment of the members of the others. Were this principle rigorously adhered to, it would require that all the appointments for the supreme executive, legislative, and judiciary magistracies should be drawn from the same fountain of authority, the people, through channels having no communication whatever with one another. Perhaps such a plan of constructing the several departments would be less difficult in practice than it may in contemplation appear. Some difficulties, however, and some additional expense would attend the execution of it. Some deviations, therefore, from the principle must be admitted. In the constitution of the judiciary department in particular, it might be inexpedient to insist rigorously on the principle: first, because peculiar qualifications being essential in the members, the primary consideration ought to be to select that mode of choice which best secures these qualifications; secondly, because the permanent tenure by which the appointments are held in that department, must soon destroy all sense of dependence on the authority conferring them.

It is equally evident, that the members of each department should be as little dependent as possible on those of the others, for the emoluments annexed to their offices. Were the executive magistrate, or the judges, not independent of the legislature in this particular, their independence in every other would be merely nominal.

But the great security against a gradual concentration of the several powers in the same department, consists in giving to those who administer each department the necessary constitutional means and personal motives to resist encroachments of the others. The provision for defence must in this, as in all other cases, be made commensurate to the danger of attack. Ambition must be made to counteract ambition. The interest of the man must be connected with the constitutional rights of the place. It may be a reflection on human nature, that such devices should be necessary to control the abuses of government. But what is government itself, but the greatest of all reflections on human nature? If men were angels, no government would be necessary. If angels were to govern men, neither external nor internal controls on government would be necessary. In framing a government which is to be administered by men over men, the great difficulty lies in this: you must first enable the government to control the governed; and in the next place oblige it to control itself. A dependence on the people is, no doubt, the primary control on the government; but experience has taught mankind the necessity of auxiliary precautions.

This policy of supplying, by opposite and rival interests, the defect of better motives, might be traced through the whole system of human affairs, private as well as public. We see it particularly displayed in all the subordinate distributions of power, where the constant aim is to divide and arrange the several offices in such a manner as that each may be a check on the other—that the private interest of every individual may be a sentinel over the public rights. These interventions of prudence cannot be less requisite in the distribution of the supreme powers of the State.

But it is not possible to give to each department an equal power of self-defence. In republican government, the legislative authority necessarily predominates. The remedy for this inconveniency is to divide the legislature into different branches; and to render them, by different modes of election and different principles of action, as little connected with each other as the nature of their common functions and their common dependence on the society will admit. It may even be necessary to guard against dangerous encroachments by still further precautions. As the weight of the legislative authority requires that it should be thus divided, the weakness of the executive may require, on the other hand, that it should be fortified. An absolute negative on the legislature appears, at first view, to be the natural defence with which the executive magistrate should be armed. But perhaps it would be neither altogether safe nor alone sufficient. On ordinary occasions it might not be exerted with the requisite firmness, and on extraordinary occasions it might be perfidiously abused. May not this defect of an absolute negative be supplied by some qualified connection between this weaker department and the weaker branch of the stronger department, by which the latter may be led to support the constitutional rights of the former, without being too much detached from the rights of its own department?

If the principles on which these observations are founded be just, as I persuade myself they are, and they be applied as a criterion to the several State constitutions, and to the federal Constitution, it will be found that if the latter does not perfectly correspond with them, the former are infinitely less able to bear such a test.

There are, moreover, two considerations particularly applicable to the federal system of America, which place that system in a very interesting point of view.

First. In a single republic, all the power surrendered by the people is submitted to the administration of a single government; and the usurpations are guarded against by a division of the government into distinct and separate departments. In the compound republic of America, the power surrendered by the people is first divided between two distinct governments, and then the portion allotted to each subdivided among distinct and separate departments. Hence a double security arises to the rights of the people. The different governments will control each other, at the same time that each will be controlled by itself.

Second. It is of great importance in a republic not only to guard the society against the oppression of its rulers, but to guard one part of the society against the injustice of the other part. Different interests necessarily exist in different classes of citizens. If a majority be united by a common interest, the rights of the minority will be insecure. There are but two methods of providing against this evil: the one by creating a will in the community independent of the majority—that is, of the society itself; the other, by comprehending in the society so many separate descriptions of citizens as will render an unjust combination of a majority of the whole very improbable, if not impracticable. The first method prevails in all governments possessing an hereditary or self-appointed authority. This, at best, is but a precarious security; because a power independent of the society may as well espouse the unjust views of the major, as the rightful interests of the minor party, and may possibly be turned against both parties. The second method will be exemplified in the federal republic of the United States. Whilst all authority in it will be derived from and dependent on the society, the society itself will be broken into so many parts, interests and classes of citizens, that the rights of individuals, or of the minority, will be in little danger from interested combinations of the majority. In a free government the security for civil rights must be the same as that for religious rights. It consists in the one case in the multiplicity of interests, and in the other in the multiplicity of sects. The degree of security in both cases will depend on the number of interests and sects; and this may be presumed to depend on the extent of country and number of people comprehended under the same government. This view of the subject must particularly recommend a proper federal system to all the sincere and considerate friends of republican government, since it shows that in exact proportion as the territory of the Union may be formed into more circumscribed Confederacies, or States, oppressive combinations of a majority will be facilitated; the best security, under the republican forms, for the rights of every class of citizens, will be diminished; and consequently the stability and independence of some member of the government, the only other security, must be proportionally increased. Justice is the end of government. It is the end of civil society. It ever has been and ever will be pursued until it be obtained, or until liberty be lost in the pursuit. In a society under the forms of which the stronger faction can readily unite and oppress the weaker, anarchy may as truly be said to reign as in a state of nature, where the weaker individual is not secured against the violence of the stronger; and as, in the latter state, even the strong individuals are prompted, by the uncertainty of their condition, to submit to a government which may protect the weak as well as themselves; so, in the former state, will the more powerful factions or parties be gradually induced, by a like motive, to wish for a government which will protect all parties, the weaker as well as the more powerful. It can be little doubted that if the State of Rhode Island was separated from the Confederacy and left to itself, the insecurity of rights under the popular form of government within such narrow limits would be displayed by such reiterated oppressions of factious majorities that some power altogether independent of the people would soon be called for by the voice of the very factions whose misrule had provided the necessity of it. In the extended republic of the United States, and among the great variety of interests, parties, and sects which it embraces, a coalition of a majority of the whole society could seldom take place on any other principles than those of justice and the general good; whilst there being thus less danger to a minor from the will of a major party, there must be less pretext, also, to provide for the security of the former, by introducing into the government a will not dependent on the latter, or, in other words, a will independent of the society itself. It is no less certain than it is important, notwithstanding the contrary opinions which have been entertained, that the larger the society, provided it lie within a practical sphere, the more duly capable it will be of self-government. And happily for the *republican cause*, the practicable sphere may be carried to a very great extent, by a judicious modification and mixture of the *federal principle*.

ALEXIS DE TOCQUEVILLE

6. CONTROLLING TYRANNICAL MAJORITIES

Alexis de Tocqueville (1805–1859), the French historian who visited the United States in the 1830s, wrote Democracy in America, *his landmark description of American political culture. While impressed with what he saw in America, de Tocqueville warned about the "tryanny of the majority," whereby minorities are forced to conform with the dictates of the majority. De Tocqueville was the first to observe that "there is hardly a political question in the United States which sooner or later does not turn into a judicial one." This did not disturb him, however, because he believed that the power of American courts to declare statutes to be unconstitutional "forms one of the most powerful barriers that have ever been devised against the tyranny of political assemblies."*

I hold it to be an impious and an execrable maxim that, politically speaking, a people has a right to do whatsoever it pleases, and yet I have asserted that all authority originates in the will of the majority. Am I, then, in contradiction with myself?

Source: Alexis de Tocqueville, *Democracy in America* (New York: D. Appelton and Co., 1839, translated 1899).

A general law—which bears the name of Justice—has been made and sanctioned, not only by a majority of this or that people, but by a majority of mankind. The rights of every people, are consequently confined within the limits of what is just. A nation may be considered in the light of a jury which is empowered to represent society at large, and to apply the great and general law of justice. Ought such a jury, which represents society, to have more power than the society in which the laws it applies originate?

When I refuse to obey an unjust law, I do not contest the right which the majority has of commanding, but I simply appeal from the sovereignty of the people to the sovereignty of mankind. It has been asserted that a people can never entirely outstep the boundaries of justice and of reason in those affairs which are more peculiarly its own, and that consequently full power may fearlessly be given to the majority by which it is represented. But this language is that of a slave.

A majority taken collectively may be regarded as a being whose opinions, and most frequently whose interests, are opposed to those of another being, which is styled a minority. If it be admitted that a man, possessing absolute power, may misuse that power by wronging his adversaries, why should a majority not be liable to the same reproach? Men are not apt to change their characters by agglomeration; nor does their patience in the presence of obstacles increase with the consciousness of their strength. And for these reasons I can never willingly invest any number of my fellow-creatures with that unlimited authority which I should refuse to any one of them.

I do not think it is possible to combine several principles in the same government, so as at the same time to maintain freedom, and really to oppose them to one another. The form of government which is usually termed mixed has always appeared to me to be a mere chimera. Accurately speaking, there is no such thing as a mixed government (with the meaning usually given to that word), because in all communities some one principle of action may be discovered which preponderates over the others. England in the last century, which has been more especially cited as an example of this form of Government, was in point of fact an essentially aristocratic State, although it comprised very powerful elements of democracy; for the laws and customs of the country were such that the aristocracy could not but preponderate in the end, and subject the direction of public affairs to its own will. The error arose from too much attention being paid to the actual struggle which was going on between the nobles and the people, without considering the probable issue of the contest, which was in reality the important point. When a community really has a mixed government—that is to say, when it is equally divided between two adverse principles—it must either pass through a revolution or fall into complete dissolution.

I am therefore of opinion that some one social power must always be made to predominate over the others; but I think that liberty is endangered when this power is checked by no obstacles which may retard its course, and force it to moderate its own vehemence.

Unlimited power is in itself a bad and dangerous thing; human beings are not competent to exercise it with discretion, and God alone can be omnipotent, because his wisdom and his justice are always equal to his power. But no power upon earth is so worthy of honour for itself, or of reverential obedience to the rights which it represents, that I would consent to admit its uncontrolled and all-predominant authority. When I see that the right and the means of absolute command are conferred on a people or upon a king, upon an aristocracy or a democracy, a monarchy or a republic, I recognise the germ of tyranny, and I journey onward to a land of more hopeful institutions.

In my opinion the main evil of the present democratic institutions of the United States does not arise, as is often asserted in Europe, from their weakness, but from their overpowering strength; and I am not so much alarmed at the excessive liberty which reigns in that country as at the very inadequate securities which exist against tyranny.

When an individual or a party is wronged in the United States, to whom can he apply for redress? If to public opinion, public opinion constitutes the majority; if to the legislature, it represents the majority, and implicitly obeys its injunctions; if to the executive power, it is appointed by the majority, and remains a passive tool in its hands; the public troops consist of the majority under arms; the jury is the majority invested with the right of hearing judicial cases; and in certain States even the judges are elected by the majority. However iniquitous or absurd the evil of which you complain may be, you must submit to it as well as you can.

If, on the other hand, a legislative power could be so constituted as to represent the majority without necessarily being the slave of its passions; an executive, so as to retain a certain degree of uncontrolled authority; and a judiciary, so as to remain independent of the two other powers; a government would be formed which would still be democratic without incurring any risk of tyrannical abuse.

I do not say that tyrannical abuses frequently occur in America at the present day, but I maintain that no sure barrier is established against them, and that the causes which mitigate the government are to be found in the circumstances and the manners of the country more than in its laws.

CHARLES A. BEARD

7. An Economic Interpretation of the Constitution

Charles A. Beard (1874–1948) was one of the most influential of all American historians in part because of the sheer number of his books (more than fifty). In The

Source: From Charles A. Beard, *An Economic Interpretation of the Constitution* (New York: Macmillan, 1913).

Supreme Court and the Constitution *(1912), Beard argued that the framers wanted the Supreme Court to have the power of judicial review— that is, to have the authority to judge the constitutionality of legislation. He believed that this authority was consistent with the framers' general intention of protecting the interests of the propertied class.*

This theme provided the basis for Beard's best-known work, An Economic Interpretation of the Constitution, *in which he makes the classic argument that the founders wrote the Constitution largely to protect their own economic interests. While later scholars have criticized his methods, his basic thesis continues to stir scholarly debate. After Beard analyzed the backgrounds of the drafters and the provisions of the Constitution, he concluded: "The Constitution was essentially an economic document based upon the concept that the fundamental private rights of property are anterior to government and morally beyond the reach of popular majorities."*

The requirements for an economic interpretation of the formation and adoption of the Constitution may be stated in a hypothetical proposition which, although it cannot be verified absolutely from ascertainable data, will at once illustrate the problem and furnish a guide to research and generalization.

It will be admitted without controversy that the Constitution was the creation of a certain number of men, and it was opposed by a certain number of men. Now, if it were possible to have an economic biography of all those connected with its framing and adoption,—perhaps about 160,000 men altogether,—the materials for scientific analysis and classification would be available. Such an economic biography would include a list of the real and personal property owned by all of these men and their families: lands and houses, with incumbrances, money at interest, slaves, capital invested in shipping and manufacturing, and in state and continental securities.

Suppose it could be shown from the classification of the men who supported and opposed the Constitution that there was no line of property division at all; that is, that men owning substantially the same amounts of the same kinds of property were equally divided on the matter of adoption or rejection—it would then become apparent that the Constitution had no ascertainable relation to economic groups or classes, but was the product of some abstract causes remote from the chief business of life—gaining a livelihood.

Suppose, on the other hand, that substantially all of the merchants, money lenders, security holders, manufacturers, shippers, capitalists, and financiers and their professional associates are to be found on one side in support of the Constitution and that substantially all or the major portion of the opposition came from the non-slaveholding farmers and the debtors—would it not be pretty conclusively demonstrated that our fundamental law was not the product of an abstraction known as "the whole people," but of a group of economic interests which must have expected beneficial results from its adoption? Obviously all the facts here desired cannot be discovered, but the data presented in the following chapters bear out the latter hypothesis, and thus a reasonable presumption in favor of the theory is created.

Of course, it may be shown (and perhaps can be shown) that the farmers and debtors who opposed the Constitution were, in fact, benefited by the general improvement which resulted from its adoption. It may likewise be shown, to take an extreme case, that the English nation derived immense advantages from the Norman Conquest and the orderly administrative processes which were introduced, as it undoubtedly did; nevertheless, it does not follow that the vague thing known as "the advancement of general welfare" or some abstraction known as "justice" was the immediate, guiding purpose of the leaders in either of these great historic changes. The point is, that the direct, impelling motive in both cases was the economic advantages which the beneficiaries expected would accrue to themselves first, from their action. Further than this, economic interpretation cannot go. It may be that some larger world-process is working through each series of historical events; but ultimate causes lie beyond our horizon. . . .

A survey of the economic interests of the members of the Convention presents certain conclusions:

A majority of the members were lawyers by profession.

Most of the members came from towns, on or near the coast, that is, from the regions in which personalty was largely concentrated.

Not one member represented in his immediate personal economic interests the small farming or mechanic classes.

The overwhelming majority of members, at least five-sixths, were immediately, directly, and personally interested in the outcome of their labors at Philadelphia, and were to a greater or less extent economic beneficiaries from the adoption of the Constitution. . . .

It cannot be said, therefore, that the members of the Convention were "disinterested." On the contrary, we are forced to accept the profoundly significant conclusion that they knew through their personal experiences in economic affairs the precise results which the new government that they were setting up was designed to attain. As a group of doctrinaries, like the Frankfort assembly of 1848, they would have failed miserably; but as practical men they were able to build the new government upon the only foundations which could be stable: fundamental economic interests. . . .

CONCLUSIONS

At the close of this long and and arid survey—partaking of the nature of catalogue—it seems worth while to bring together the important conclusions for political science which the data presented appear to warrant.

The movement for the Constitution of the United States was originated and carried through principally by four groups of personalty interests which had been adversely affected under the Articles of Confederation: money, public securities, manufactures, and trade and shipping.

The first firm steps toward the formation of the Constitution were taken by a small and active group of men immediately interested through their personal possessions in the outcome of their labors.

No popular vote was taken directly or indirectly on the proposition to call the Convention which drafted the Constitution.

A large propertyless mass was, under the prevailing suffrage qualifications, excluded at the outset from participation (through representatives) in the work of framing the Constitution.

The members of the Philadelphia Convention which drafted the Constitution were, with a few exceptions, immediately, directly, and personally interested in, and derived economic advantages from, the establishment of the new system.

The Constitution was essentially an economic document based upon the concept that the fundamental private rights of property are anterior to government and morally beyond the reach of popular majorities.

The major portion of the members of the Convention are on record as recognizing the claim of property to a special and defensive position in the Constitution.

In the ratification of the Constitution, about three-fourths of the adult males failed to vote on the question, having abstained from the elections at which delegates to the state conventions were chosen, either on account of their indifference or their disenfranchisement by property qualifications.

The Constitution was ratified by a vote of probably not more than one-sixth of the adult males.

It is questionable whether a majority of the voters participating in the elections for the state conventions in New York, Massachusetts, New Hampshire, Virginia, and South Carolina, actually approved the ratification of the Constitution.

The leaders who supported the Constitution in the ratifying conventions represented the same economic groups as the members of the Philadelphia Convention; and in a large number of instances they were also directly and personally interested in the outcome of their efforts.

In the ratification, it became manifest that the line of cleavage for and against the Constitution was between substantial personalty interests on the one hand and the small farming and debtor interests on the other.

The Constitution was not created by "the whole people" as the jurists have said; neither was it created by "the states" as Southern nullifiers long contended; but it was the work of a consolidated group whose interests knew no state boundaries and were truly national in their scope.

THURGOOD MARSHALL

8. AN AFRICAN AMERICAN'S PERSPECTIVE ON THE CONSTITUTION

Thurgood Marshall (1908–1993), who retired and was replaced by Clarence Thomas in 1991, was the first African American to serve on the U.S. Supreme Court. Marshall, appointed by President Lyndon Johnson in 1967, was one of the Court's leading liberals and a forceful voice in favor of civil rights. As an attorney, he had directed the NAACP Legal Defense Fund from 1940 to 1961. He was the attorney who argued before the Supreme Court in Brown v. Board of Education *(1954) that laws creating racially segregated schools were unconstitutional.*

On the occasion of the 200th anniversary of the ratification of the Constitution, Marshall gave a speech rejecting the view that Americans should celebrate the Constitution as the source of all that is good in the nation. On the contrary, he said of the founders that "the government they devised was defective from the start, requiring several amendments, a civil war, and momentous social transformation to attain the system of constitutional government, and its respect for individual freedoms and human rights, we hold as fundamental today."

1987 marks the 200th anniversary of the United States Constitution. A Commission has been established to coordinate the celebration. The official meetings, essay contests, and festivities have begun.

The planned commemoration will span three years, and I am told 1987 is "dedicated to the memory of the Founders and the document they drafted in Philadelphia." We are to "recall the achievement of our Founders and the knowledge and experience that inspired them, the nature of the government they established, its origins, its character, and its ends, and the rights and privileges of citizenship, as well as its attendant responsibilities."

Like many anniversary celebrations, the plan for 1987 takes particular events and holds them up as the source of all the very best that has followed.

Source: Thurgood Marshall, "The Constitution's Bicentennial: Commemorating the Wrong Document?" Volume 40, *Vanderbilt Law Review* (1987). Reprinted by permission of *Vanderbilt Law Review.* Footnotes omitted.

Patriotic feelings will surely swell, prompting proud proclamations of the wisdom, foresight, and sense of justice shared by the Framers and reflected in a written document now yellowed with age. This is unfortunate—not the patriotism itself, but the tendency for the celebration to oversimplify, and overlook the many other events that have been instrumental to our achievements as a nation. The focus of this celebration invites a complacent belief that the vision of those who debated and compromised in Philadelphia yielded the "more perfect Union" it is said we now enjoy.

I cannot accept this invitation, for I do not believe that the meaning of the Constitution was forever "fixed" at the Philadelphia Convention. Nor do I find the wisdom, foresight, and sense of justice exhibited by the Framers particularly profound. To the contrary, the government they devised was defective from the start, requiring several amendments, a civil war, and momentous social transformation to attain the system of constitutional government, and its respect for individual freedoms and human rights, we hold as fundamental today. When contemporary Americans cite "The Constitution," they invoke a concept that is vastly different from what the Framers barely began to construct two centuries ago.

For a sense of the evolving nature of the Constitution we need look no further than the first three words of the document's preamble: "We the People." When the Founding Fathers used this phrase in 1787, they did not have in mind the majority of America's citizens. "We the People" included, in the words of the Framers, "the whole Number of free Persons." On a matter so basic as the right to vote, for example, Negro slaves were excluded, although they were counted for representational purposes—at three-fifths each. Women did not gain the right to vote for over a hundred and thirty years.

These omissions were intentional. The record of the Framers' debates on the slave question is especially clear: The Southern States acceded to the demands of the New England States for giving Congress broad power to regulate commerce, in exchange for the right to continue the slave trade. The economic interests of the regions coalesced: New Englanders engaged in the "carrying trade" would profit from transporting slaves from Africa as well as goods produced in America by slave labor. The perpetuation of slavery ensured the primary source of wealth in the Southern States.

Despite this clear understanding of the role slavery would play in the new republic, use of the words "slaves" and "slavery" was carefully avoided in the original document. Political representation in the lower House of Congress was to be based on the population of "free Persons" in each State, plus three-fifths of all "other Persons." Moral principles against slavery, for those who had them, were compromised, with no explanation of the conflicting principles for which the American Revolutionary War had ostensibly been fought: the self-evident truths "that all men are created equal, that they are endowed by their Creator with certain unalienable Rights, that among these are Life, Liberty and the pursuit of Happiness."

It was not the first such compromise. Even these ringing phrases from the Declaration of Independence are filled with irony, for an early draft of what became that Declaration assailed the King of England for suppressing legislative attempts to end the slave trade and for encouraging slave rebellions. The final draft adopted in 1776 did not contain this criticism. And so again at the Constitutional Convention eloquent objections to the institution of slavery went unheeded, and its opponents eventually consented to a document which laid a foundation for the tragic events that were to follow.

Pennsylvania's Gouverneur Morris provides an example. He opposed slavery and the counting of slaves in determining the basis for representation in Congress. At the Convention he objected that

> the inhabitant of Georgia [or] South Carolina who goes to the coast of Africa, and in defiance of the most sacred laws of humanity tears away his fellow creatures from their dearest connections and damns them to the most cruel bondages, shall have more votes in a Government instituted for protection of the rights of mankind, than the Citizen of Pennsylvania or New Jersey who views with a laudable horror, so nefarious a practice.

And yet Gouverneur Morris eventually accepted the three-fifths accommodation. In fact, he wrote the final draft of the Constitution, the very document the Bicentennial will commemorate.

As a result of the compromise, the right of the Southern States to continue importing slaves was extended, officially, at least until 1808. We know that it actually lasted a good deal longer, as the Framers possessed no monopoly on the ability to trade moral principles for self-interest. But they nevertheless set an unfortunate example. Slaves could be imported, if the commercial interests of the North were protected. To make the compromise even more palatable, customs duties would be imposed at up to ten dollars per slave as a means of raising public revenues.

No doubt it will be said, when the unpleasant truth of the history of slavery in America is mentioned during this Bicentennial year, that the Constitution was a product of its times, and embodied a compromise which, under other circumstances, would not have been made. But the effects of the Framers' compromise have remained for generations. They arose from the contradiction between guaranteeing liberty and justice to all, and denying both to Negroes.

The original intent of the phrase, "We the People," was far too clear for any ameliorating construction. Writing for the Supreme Court in 1857, Chief Justice Taney penned the following passage in the *Dred Scott* case, on the issue whether, in the eyes of the Framers, slaves were "constituent members of the sovereignty," and were to be included among "We the People":

> We think they are not, and that they are not included, and were not intended to be included. . . .

. . . .

They had for more than a century before been regarded as beings of an inferior order; and altogether unfit to associate with the white race . . . ; and so far inferior, that they had no rights which the white man was bound to respect; and that the negro might justly and lawfully be reduced to slavery for his benefit.

. . . .

[A]ccordingly, a negro of the African race was regarded . . . as an article of property, and held, and bought and sold as such. . . . [N]o one seems to have doubted the correctness of the prevailing opinion of the time.

And so, nearly seven decades after the Constitutional Convention, the Supreme Court reaffirmed the prevailing opinion of the Framers regarding the rights of Negroes in America. It took a bloody civil war before the thirteenth amendment could be adopted to abolish slavery, though not the consequences slavery would have for future Americans.

While the Union survived the Civil War, the Constitution did not. In its place arose a new, more promising basis for justice and equality, the fourteenth amendment, ensuring protection of the life, liberty, and property of *all* persons against deprivations without due process, and guaranteeing equal protection of the laws. And yet almost another century would pass before any significant recognition was obtained of the rights of black Americans to share equally even in such basic opportunities as education, housing, and employment, and to have their votes counted, and counted equally. In the meantime, blacks joined America's military to fight its wars and invested untold hours working in its factories and on its farms, contributing to the development of this country's magnificent wealth and waiting to share in its prosperity.

What is striking is the role legal principles have played throughout America's history in determining the condition of Negroes. They were enslaved by law, emancipated by law, disenfranchised and segregated by law; and, finally, they have begun to win equality by law. Along the way, new constitutional principles have emerged to meet the challenges of a changing society. The progress has been dramatic, and it will continue.

The men who gathered in Philadelphia in 1787 could not have envisioned these changes. They could not have imagined, nor would they have accepted, that the document they were drafting would one day be construed by a Supreme Court to which had been appointed a woman and the descendant of an African slave. "We the People" no longer enslave, but the credit does not belong to the Framers. It belongs to those who refused to acquiesce in outdated notions of "liberty," "justice," and "equality," and who strived to better them.

And so we must be careful, when focusing on the events which took place in Philadelphia two centuries ago, that we not overlook the momentous events which followed, and thereby lose our proper sense of perspective. Otherwise, the odds are that for many Americans the Bicentennial celebration will be little more than a blind pilgrimage to the shrine of the original document now stored in a vault in the National Archives. If we seek, instead, a sensitive understanding of the Constitution's inherent defects, and its promising evolution through

200 years of history, the celebration of the "Miracle at Philadelphia" will, in my view, be a far more meaningful and humbling experience. We will see that the true miracle was not the birth of the Constitution, but its life, a life nurtured through two turbulent centuries of our own making, and a life embodying much good fortune that was not.

Thus, in this Bicentennial year, we may not all participate in the festivities with flag-waving fervor. Some may more quietly commemorate the suffering, struggle, and sacrifice that has triumphed over much of what was wrong with the original document, and observe the anniversary with hopes not realized and promises not fulfilled. I plan to celebrate the Bicentennial of the Constitution as a living document, including the Bill of Rights and the other amendments protecting individual freedoms and human rights.

SECTION I
REVIEW QUESTIONS

1. How does the current distribution of power among the legislative, executive, and judicial branches of government compare to what James Madison envisioned in *The Federalist,* No. 51?

2. Some early observers, including Alexander Hamilton, predicted that the judiciary would be the "least dangerous" branch of the newly created American government. Which contemporary political groups would agree? Disagree?

3. Alexis de Tocqueville believed that the judicial system would protect minorities against tyrannical majorities. Some argue today that the judicial system undermines democracy by elevating the rights of minorities. Who is right?

4. Do you agree with Charles Beard that the founders were primarily motivated by economic self-interest? If so, does this in any way diminish the value of the constitutional system they designed?

5. After reading Thurgood Marshall's speech, why should black Americans *not* be cynical about the Constitution?

II

Federalism

JAMES MADISON

9. DEFENDING A REPUBLICAN FORM OF GOVERNMENT

When the Constitution was drafted, the founders faced many critics who feared a strong national government and favored a weak confederation of states as existed under the Articles of Confederation. In The Federalist, *No. 39, James Madison answered these criticisms by arguing that the proposed new form of government combined the best aspects of both governmental models. The powers of the national government were limited to those enumerated in the Constitution and the states retained all authority not specifically delegated to the national government. This unique sharing of powers between the states and the national government was the basis for the American federal system.*

But it was not sufficient, say the adversaries of the proposed Constitution, for the Convention to adhere to the republican form. They ought, with equal care, to have preserved the *federal* form, which regards the union as a *confederacy* of sovereign States; instead of which, they have framed a *national* government, which regards the union as a *consolidation* of the States. And it is asked by what authority this bold and radical innovation was undertaken. The handle which has been made of this objection requires, that it should be examined with some precision.

Without enquiring into the accuracy of the distinction on which the objection is founded, it will be necessary to a just estimate of its force, first to ascertain the real character of the government in question; secondly, to enquire how far the Convention were authorised to propose such a government; and thirdly, how far the duty they owed to their country, could supply any defect of regular authority.

First. In order to ascertain the real character of the government it may be considered in relation to the foundation on which it is to be established; to the sources from which its ordinary powers are to be drawn; to the operation of those powers; to the extent of them; and to the authority by which future changes in the government are to be introduced.

Source: The Federalist, No. 39 (1788).

On examining the first relation, it appears on one hand that the Constitution is to be founded on the assent and ratification of the people of America, given by deputies elected for the special purpose; but on the other, that this assent and ratification is to be given by the people, not as individuals composing one entire nation; but as composing the distinct and independent States to which they respectively belong. It is to be the assent and ratification of the several States, derived from the supreme authority in each State, the authority of the people themselves. The act therefore establishing the Constitution, will not be a *national* but a *federal* act.

That it will be a federal and not a national act, as these terms are understood by the objectors, the act of the people as forming so many independent States, not as forming one aggregate nation, is obvious from this single consideration that it is to result neither from the decision of a *majority* of the people of the Union, nor from that of a *majority* of the States. It must result from the *unanimous* assent of the several States that are parties to it, differing no other wise from their ordinary assent than in its being expressed, not by the legislative authority, but by that of the people themselves. Were the people regarded in this transaction as forming one nation, the will of the majority of the whole people of the United States would bind the minority; in the same manner as the majority in each State must bind the minority; and the will of the majority must be determined either by a comparison of the individual votes; or by considering the will of a majority of the States, as evidence of the will of a majority of the people of the United States. Neither of these rules has been adopted. Each State in ratifying the Constitution, is considered as a sovereign body independent of all others, and only to be bound by its own voluntary act. In this relation then the new Constitution will, if established, be a *federal* and not a *national* Constitution.

The next relation is to the sources from which the ordinary powers of government are to be derived. The house of representatives will derive its powers from the people of America, and the people will be represented in the same proportion, and on the same principle, as they are in the Legislature of a particular State. So far the Government is *national* not *federal.* The Senate on the other hand will derive its powers from the States, as political and co-equal societies; and these will be represented on the principle of equality in the Senate, as they now are in the existing Congress. So far the government is *federal,* not *national.* The executive power will be derived from a very compound source. The immediate election of the President is to be made by the States in their political characters. The votes allotted to them are in a compound ratio, which considers them partly as distinct and co-equal societies; partly as unequal members of the same society. The eventual election again is to be made by that branch of the Legislature which consists of the national representatives; but in this particular act, they are to be thrown into the form of individual delegations from so many distinct and co-equal bodies politic. From this aspect of the Government, it appears to be of a mixed character presenting at least as many *federal* as *national* features.

The difference between a federal and national Government as it relates to the *operation of the Government* is supposed to consist in this, that in the former, the powers operate on the political bodies composing the confederacy, in their political capacities: In the latter, on the individual citizens, composing the nation, in their individual capacities. On trying the Constitution by this criterion, it falls under the *national,* not the *federal* character; though perhaps not so compleatly, as has been understood. In several cases and particularly in the trial of controversies to which States may be parties, they must be viewed and proceeded against in their collective and political capacities only. So far the national countenance of the Government on this side seems to be disfigured by a few federal features. But this blemish is perhaps unavoidable in any plan; and the operation of the Government on the people in their individual capacities, in its ordinary and most essential proceedings, may on the whole designate it in this relation a *national* Government.

But if the Government be national with regard to the *operation* of its powers, it changes its aspect again when we contemplate it in relation to the extent of its powers. The idea of a national Government involves in it, not only an authority over the individual citizens; but an indefinite supremacy over all persons and things, so far as they are objects of lawful Government. Among a people consolidated into one nation, this supremacy is compleatly vested in the national Legislature. Among communities united for particular purposes, it is vested partly in the general, and partly in the municipal Legislatures. In the former case, all local authorities are subordinate to the supreme; and may be controlled, directed or abolished by it at pleasure. In the latter the local or municipal authorities form distinct and independent portions of the supremacy, no more subject within their respective spheres to the general authority, than the general authority is subject to them, within its own sphere. In this relation then the proposed Government cannot be deemed a *national* one; since its jurisdiction extends to certain enumerated objects only, and leaves to the several States a residuary and inviolable sovereignty over all other objects. It is true that in controversies relating to the boundary between the two jurisdictions, the tribunal which is ultimately to decide is to be established under the general Government. But this does not change the principle of the case. The decision is to be impartially made, according to the rules of the Constitution; and all the usual and most effectual precautions are taken to secure this impartiality. Some such tribunal is clearly essential to prevent an appeal to the sword, and a dissolution of the compact; and that it ought to be established under the general rather than under the local Governments; or to speak more properly, that it could be safely established under the first alone, is a position not likely to be combated.

If we try the Constitution by its last relation, to the authority by which amendments are to be made, we find it neither wholly *national,* nor wholly *federal.* Were it wholly national, the supreme and ultimate authority would reside in the *majority* of the people of the Union; and this authority would be competent at all times, like that of a majority of every national society, to alter or abolish its established Government. Were it wholly federal on the other hand, the concurrence of each State in the Union would be essential to every alteration that would be binding on all. The mode provided by the plan of the Convention is not founded on either of these principles. In requiring more than a majority, and particularly, in computing the proportion by *States*, not by *citizens*, it departs from the *national*, and advances towards the *federal* character: In rendering the concurrence of less than the whole number of States sufficient, it loses again the *federal*, and partakes of the *national* character.

The proposed Constitution therefore is in strictness neither a national nor a federal constitution; but a composition of both. In its foundation, it is federal, not national; in the sources from which the ordinary powers of the Government are drawn, it is partly federal, and partly national; in the operation of these powers, it is national, not federal; in the extent of them again, it is federal, not national. And finally, in the authoritative mode of introducing amendments, it is neither wholly federal, nor wholly national.

MCCULLOCH V. MARYLAND

10. The "Necessary and Proper" Clause

Fearing the concentration of power in a few people, the framers of the Constitution not only divided powers among the legislative, executive, and judicial branches of the government, but also divided power between the states and the newly formed national government. This system of government in which a national government shares power with subnational or state governments constitutes a "federal" system.

But drawing the lines between state and national functions was not easy because the Constitution itself did not provide clear guidelines. Article 1, Section 8 delegates powers to the Congress. Some of these are specifically or expressly described, while others are implied in that part of Section 8 that gives to the Congress the power to "make all Laws which shall be necessary and proper for carrying into Execution the foregoing Powers. . . . "

Source: U.S. Supreme Court, *McCulloch v. Maryland* (1819).

The U.S. Supreme Court first interpreted the "necessary and proper" clause in McCulloch v. Maryland *in 1819. Congress had established a National Bank, which the State of Maryland tried to tax. Maryland argued that since the power to charter banks was not listed in Article 1, Section 8 among the powers delegated to the Congress, the National Bank was unconstitutional. The Court disagreed and held that the "necessary and proper" clause gave Congress the authority to pass any law needed to further any of the legitimate governmental objectives expressly listed in Section 8. In this case the Court ruled that because Congress was expressly authorized to coin money and levy taxes, it was thereby implicitly authorized to create a National Bank.*

Writing for the Court, Chief Justice John Marshall also ruled that because the National Bank was a creation of Congress, the states could not take any action (such as taxing it) that might undermine its effectiveness. This idea that national laws were always to prevail over state laws in the case of a conflict is found in Article 6 of the Constitution, which states that laws made by the United States government "shall be the supreme Law of the Land."

Chief Justice MARSHALL delivers the opinion of the Court.

In the case now to be determined, the defendant, a sovereign state, denies the obligation of a law enacted by the legislature of the Union, and the plaintiff, on his part, contests the validity of an act which has been passed by the legislature of that state. The constitution of our country, in its most interesting and vital parts, is to be considered; the conflicting powers of the government of the Union and of its members, as marked in that constitution, are to be discussed; and an opinion given, which may essentially influence the great operations of the government. . . .

If any one proposition could command the universal assent of mankind, we might expect it would be this—that the government of the Union, though limited in its powers, is supreme within its sphere of action. This would seem to result necessarily from its nature. It is the government of all; its powers are delegated by all; it represents all, and acts for all. Though any one state may be willing to control its operations, no state is willing to allow others to control them. The nation, on those subjects on which it can act, must necessarily bind its component parts. But this question is not left to mere reason; the people have, in express terms, decided it by saying "this constitution, and the laws of the United States, which shall be made in pursuance thereof," "shall be the supreme law of the land," and by requiring that the members of the state legislatures, and the officers of the executive and judicial departments of the states shall take the oath of fidelity to it. . . .

Among the enumerated powers, we do not find that of establishing a bank or creating a corporation. But there is no phrase in the instrument which, like the articles of confederation, excludes incidental or implied powers; and which requires that everything granted shall be expressly and minutely described. Even the 10th amendment, which was framed for the purpose of quieting the excessive jealousies which had been excited, omits the word "expressly," and declares only that the powers "not delegated to the United States, nor prohibited to the states, are reserved to the states or to the people"; thus leaving the question, whether the particular power which may become the subject of contest has been delegated to the one government, or prohibited to the other, to depend on a fair construction of the whole instrument. The men who drew and adopted this amendment had experienced the embarrassments resulting from the insertion of this word in the articles of confederation, and probably omitted it to avoid those embarrassments. A constitution, to contain an accurate detail of all the subdivisions of which its great powers will admit, and of all the means by which they may be carried into execution, would partake of prolixity of a legal code, and could scarcely be embraced by the human mind. It would probably never be understood by the public. Its nature, therefore, requires, that only its great outline should be marked, its important objects designated, and the minor ingredients which compose those objects be deduced from the nature of the objects themselves. That this idea was entertained by the framers of the American constitution, is not only to be inferred from the nature of the instrument, but from the language. Why else were some of the limitations, found in the ninth section of the 1st article, introduced? It is also, in some degree warranted by their having omitted to use a restrictive term which might prevent its receiving a fair and just interpretation. In considering this question, then, we must never forget that it is a constitution we are expounding.

Although, among the enumerated powers of government, we do not find the word "bank" or "incorporation," we find the great power to lay and collect taxes; to borrow money; to regulate commerce; to declare and conduct war; and to raise and support armies and navies. The sword and the purse, all the eternal relations, and no inconsiderable portion of the industry of the nation, are entrusted to its government. It can never be pretended that these vast powers draw after them others of inferior importance, merely because they are inferior. Such an idea can never be advanced. But it may with great reason be contended, that a government, entrusted with such ample powers, on the due execution of which the happiness and prosperity of the nation so vitally depends, must also be entrusted with ample means for the execution. The power being given, it is the interest of the nation to facilitate its execution. It can never be their interest, as cannot be presumed to have been their intention, to clog and embarrass its execution in withholding the most appropriate means. Throughout this vast republic, from the St. Croix to the Gulf of Mexico, from the Atlantic to the Pacific, revenue is to be collected and expended, armies are to be marched and supported. The exigencies of the nation may require that the treasure raised in the north should be transported to the south, that raised in the east conveyed to the west, or that this order should be reversed. Is that construction of the constitution to be preferred which would render these operations difficult, hazardous, and expensive? Can we adopt that construction (unless the words imperiously require it) which would impute to the framers of that instrument, when granting these powers for the public good, the intention of impeding their exercise by withholding a choice of means? . . .

On what foundation does this argument rest? On this alone: The power of creating a corporation, is one appertaining to sovereignty, and is not expressly conferred on Congress. This is true. But all legislative powers appertain to sovereignty. The original power of giving the law on any subject whatever, is a sovereign power; and if the government of the Union is restrained from creating a corporation, as a means for performing its functions, on the single reason that the creation of a corporation is an act of sovereignty; if the sufficiency of this reason be acknowledged, there would be some difficulty in sustaining the authority of Congress to pass other laws for the accomplishment of the same objects. . . .

But the constitution of the United States has not left the right of Congress to employ the necessary means for the execution of the powers conferred on the government to general reasoning. To its enumeration of powers is added that of making "all laws which shall be necessary and proper, for carrying into execution the foregoing powers, and all other powers vested by this constitution, in the government of the United States, or in any department thereof."

The counsel for the State of Maryland have urged various arguments, to prove that this clause, though in terms a grant of power, is not so in effect; but is really restrictive of the general right, which might otherwise be implied, of selecting means for executing the enumerated powers. . . .

[T]he argument on which most reliance is placed, is drawn from the peculiar language of this clause. Congress is not empowered by it to make all laws, which may have relation to the powers conferred on the government; but such only as may be "necessary and proper" for carrying them into execution. The word "necessary" is considered as controlling the whole sentence, and as limiting the right to pass laws for the execution of the granted powers, to such as are indispensable, and without which the power would be nugatory. That it excludes the choice of means, and leaves to Congress, in each case, that only which is most direct and simple.

Is it true that this is the sense in which the word "necessary" is always used? Does it always import an absolute physical necessity, so strong that one thing, to which another may be termed necessary, cannot exist without that other? We think it does not. If reference be had to its use, in the common affairs of the world, or in approved authors, we find that it frequently imports no more than that one thing is convenient, or useful, or essential to another. To employ the means necessary to an end, is generally understood as employing any means calculated to produce the end, and not as being confined to those single means, without which the end would be entirely unattainable. Such is the character of human language, that no word conveys to the mind, in all situations, one single definite idea; and nothing is more common than to use words in a figurative sense. Almost all compositions contain words, which, taken in their rigorous sense, would convey a meaning different from that which is obviously intended. It is essential to just construction, that many words which import something excessive should be understood in a more mitigated sense—in that sense which common usage justifies. The word "necessary" is of this description. It has not a fixed character peculiar to itself. It admits of all degrees of comparison; and is often connected with other words, which increase or diminish the impression the mind receives of the urgency it imports. A thing may be necessary, very necessary, absolutely or indispensably necessary. To no mind would the same idea be conveyed by these several phrases. This comment on the word is well illustrated by the passage cited at the bar, from the 10th section of the 1st article of the constitution. It is, we think, impossible to compare the sentence which prohibits a state from laying "imposts or duties on imports or exports, except what may be absolutely necessary for executing its inspection laws," with that which authorizes Congress "to make all laws which shall be necessary and proper for carrying into execution" the powers of the general government, without feeling a conviction that the convention understood itself to change materially the meaning of the word "necessary," by prefixing the word "absolutely." This word, then, like others, is used in various senses; and, in its construction, the subject, the context, the intention of the person using them, are all to be taken into view. . . .

We admit, as all must admit, that the powers of the government are limited, and that its limits are not to be transcended. But we think the sound construction of the constitution must allow to the national legislature that discretion, with respect to the means by which the powers it confers are to be carried into execution, which will enable that body to perform the high duties assigned to it, in the manner most beneficial to the people. Let the end be legitimate, let it be within the scope of the constitution, and all means which are appropriate, which are plainly adapted to that end, which are not prohibited, but consist with the letter and spirit of the constitution, are constitutional. . . .

It being the opinion of the court that the act incorporating the bank is constitutional, and that the power of establishing a branch in the state of Maryland might be properly exercised by the bank itself, we proceed to inquire:

2. Whether the state of Maryland may, without violating the constitution, tax that branch?

That the power of taxation is one of vital importance; that it is retained by the states; that it is not abridged by the grant of a similar power to the government of the Union; that it is to be concurrently exercised by the two governments: are truths which have never been denied. But, such is the paramount character of the constitution that its capacity to withdraw any subject from the action of even this power, is admitted. The states are expressly forbidden to lay any duties on imports or exports, except what may be absolutely necessary for executing their inspection laws. If the obligation of this prohibition must be conceded—if it may restrain a state from the exercise of its taxing power on imports and exports—the same paramount character would seem to restrain, as it certainly may restrain, a state from such other exercise of this power, as is in its nature incompatible with, and repugnant to, the constitutional laws of the Union. A law, absolutely repugnant to another, as entirely repeals that other as if express terms of repeal were used.

On this ground the counsel for the bank place its claim to be exempted from the power of a state to tax its operations. There is no express provision for the case, but the claim has been sustained on a principle which so entirely pervades the constitution, is so intermixed with the materials which compose it, so interwoven with its web, so blended with its texture, as to be incapable of being separated from it without rendering it into shreds.

This great principle is, that the constitution and the laws made in pursuance thereof are supreme; that they control the constitution and laws of the respective states, and cannot be controlled by them. From this, which may be almost termed an axiom, other propositions are deduced as corollaries, on the truth or error of which, and on their application to this case, the cause has been supposed to depend. These are, 1st. that a power to create implies a power to preserve. 2d. That a power to destroy, if wielded by a different hand, is hostile to, and incompatible with these powers to create and to preserve. 3d. That where this repugnancy exists, that authority which is supreme must control, not yield to that over which it is supreme. . . .

If we apply the principle for which the state of Maryland contends, to the constitution generally, we shall find it capable of changing totally the character of that instrument. We shall find it capable of arresting all the measures of the government, and of prostrating it at the foot of the states. The American people have declared their constitution, and the laws made in pursuance thereof, to be supreme; but this principle would transfer the supremacy, in fact, to the states. . . .

It has also been insisted, that, as the power of taxation in the general and state governments is acknowledged to be concurrent, every argument which would sustain the right of the general government to tax banks chartered by the states, will equally sustain the right of the states to tax banks chartered by the general government.

But the two cases are not on the same reason. The people of all the states have created the general government, and have conferred upon it the general power of taxation. The people of all the states, and the states themselves, are represented in Congress, and, by their representatives, exercise this power. When they tax the chartered institutions of the states, they tax their constituents; and these taxes must be uniform. But, when a state taxes the operations of the government of the United States, it acts upon institutions created, not by their own constituents, but by people over whom they claim no control. It acts upon the measures of a government created by others as well as themselves, for the benefit of others in common with themselves. The difference is that which always exists, and always must exist, between the action of the whole on a part, and the action of a part on the whole—between the laws of a government declared to be supreme, and those of a government which, when in opposition to those laws, is not supreme.

But if the full application of this argument could be admitted, it might bring into question the right of Congress to tax the state banks, and could not prove the right of the states to tax the Bank of the United States. . . .

We are unanimously of opinion that the law passed by the legislature of Maryland, imposing a tax on the Bank of the United States, is unconstitutional and void.

GIBBONS V. OGDEN

11. INTERPRETING THE "COMMERCE" CLAUSE

Article 1, Section 8, of the United States Constitution gives to the Congress the "power to regulate commerce . . . among the several states." But, like most constitutional language, the meaning of "commerce . . . among the states" is not self-evident. Gibbons v. Ogden *represents the first of many Supreme Court decisions attempting to define the precise scope of federal as opposed to state power to regulate interstate commerce—both foreign and domestic.*

Robert Livingston and Robert Fulton (generally considered the "inventor" of the modem steamboat) had been granted an exclusive right by the state of New York to operate the new steamboats on the waterways of New York. They, in turn, had granted a license to Aaron Ogden. Another steamboat operator, Thomas Gibbons, was operating his business with a license obtained from the federal government. Ogden tried to stop Gibbons from operating his steamboat on the grounds that Ogden had an "exclusive" license from New York. Gibbons argued that a federal license should take precedence over a state license. In the end, the Court ruling invalidated the New York license that had been granted to Aaron Ogden, who was forced out of business and into financial ruin.

The opinion by Justice Marshall defines the commerce clause very broadly. Writing for the Court,

---

Source: U.S. Supreme Court, *Gibbons v. Odgen* (1824).

> *Marshall concludes that the power of Congress to regulate interstate and foreign commerce "is complete within itself, may be exercised to its utmost extent, and acknowledges no limitations, other than are prescribed in the Constitution." Although the Supreme Court backed away from this very broad view of the commerce clause in cases such as* Hammer v. Dagenhart *(1918), where the Court held that Congress could not rely on the commerce clause for authority to ban the interstate shipment of goods made by child labor, the modern view that began in 1941 with* U.S. v. Darby Lumber *(which reversed* Hammer*) is similar to Marshall's original view in* Gibbons v. Ogden. *Thus, there is constitutional justification for congressional action in a wide range of policy areas, including, for example, the enactment of civil rights laws regulating public facilities that serve products transported in interstate commerce (*Heart of Atlanta v. United States, *1964).*

The appellant contends that this decree is erroneous, because the laws which purport to give the exclusive privilege it sustains, are repugnant to the constitution and laws of the United States.

They are said to be repugnant—

1st. To that clause in the constitution which authorizes Congress to regulate commerce. . . .

This instrument contains an enumeration of powers expressly granted by the people to their government. It has been said, that these powers ought to be construed strictly. But why ought they to be so construed? Is there one sentence in the constitution which gives countenance to this rule? In the last of the enumerated powers, that which grants, expressly, the means for carrying all others into execution, Congress is authorized "to make all laws which shall be necessary and proper" for the purpose. But this limitation on the means which may be used, is not extended to the powers which are conferred; nor is there one sentence in the constitution, which has been pointed out by the gentlemen of the bar, or which we have been able to discern, that prescribes this rule. We do not, therefore, think ourselves justified in adopting it. What do gentlemen mean, by a strict construction? If they contend only against that enlarged construction, which would extend words beyond their natural and obvious import, we might question the application of the term, but should not controvert the principle. If they contend for that narrow construction which, in support of some theory not to be found in the constitution, would deny to the government those powers which the words of the grant, as usually understood, import, and which are consistent with the general views and objects of the instrument; for that narrow construction, which would cripple the government, and render it unequal to the object for which it is declared to be instituted, and to which the powers given, as fairly understood, render it competent; then we cannot perceive the propriety of this strict construction, nor adopt it as the rule by which the constitution is to be expounded. As men, whose intentions require no concealment, generally employ the words which most directly and aptly express the ideas they intend to convey, the enlightened patriots who framed our constitution, and the people who adopted it, must be understood to have employed words in their natural sense, and to have intended what they have said. If, from the imperfection of human language, there should be serious doubts respecting the extent of any given power, it is a well settled rule, that the objects for which it was given, especially when those objects are expressed in the instrument itself, should have great influence in the construction. We know of no reason for excluding this rule from the present case. The grant does not convey power which might be beneficial to the grantor, if retained by himself, or which can enure solely to the benefit of the grantee; but is an investment of power for the general advantage, in the hands of agents selected for that purpose; which power can never be exercised by the people themselves, but must be placed in the hands of agents, or lie dormant. We know of no rule for construing the extent of such powers, other than is given by the language of the instrument which confers them, taken in connexion with the purposes for which they were conferred.

The words are, "Congress shall have power to regulate commerce with foreign nations, and among the several States, and with the Indian tribes."

The subject to be regulated is commerce; and our constitution being, as was aptly said at the bar, one of enumeration, and not of definition, to ascertain the extent of the power, it becomes necessary to settle the meaning of the word. The counsel for the appellee would limit it to traffic, to buying and selling, or the interchange of commodities, and do not admit that it comprehends navigation. This would restrict a general term, applicable to many objects, to one of its significations. Commerce, undoubtedly, is traffic, but it is something more: it is intercourse. It describes the commercial intercourse between nations, and parts of nations, in all its branches, and is regulated by prescribing rules for carrying on that intercourse. The mind can scarcely conceive a system for regulating commerce between nations, which shall exclude all laws concerning navigation, which shall be silent on the admission of the vessels of the one nation into the ports of the other, and be confined to prescribing rules for the conduct of individuals, in the actual employment of buying and selling, or of barter.

If commerce does not include navigation, the government of the Union has no direct power over that subject, and can make no law prescribing what shall constitute American vessels, or requiring that they shall be navigated by American seamen. Yet this power has been exercised from the commencement of the government, has been exercised with the consent of all, and has been understood by all to be a commercial regulation. All America understands, and has uniformly understood, the word "commerce," to comprehend navigation. It was so understood, and must have been so understood, when the constitution was framed. The power over commerce, including navigation, was one of the primary objects for which the people of America adopted their government, and must have been contemplated in forming it. The convention must have used the word in that sense, because all have understood it in that sense; and the attempt to restrict it comes too late.

If the opinion that "commerce," as the word is used in the constitution, comprehends navigation also, requires any additional confirmation, that additional confirmation is, we think, furnished by the words of the instrument itself.

It is a rule of construction, acknowledged by all, that the exceptions from a power mark its extent; for it would be absurd, as well as useless, to except from a granted power, that which was not granted—that which the words of the grant could not comprehend. If, then, there are in the constitution plain exceptions from the power over navigation, plain inhibitions to the exercise of that power in a particular way, it is a proof that those who made these exceptions, and prescribed these inhibitions, understood the power to which they applied as being granted.

The 9th section of the 1st article declares, that "no preference shall be given, by any regulation of commerce or revenue, to the ports of one State over those of another." This clause cannot be understood as applicable to those laws only which are passed for the purposes of revenue, because it is expressly applied to commercial regulations; and the most obvious preference which can be given to one port over another, in regulating commerce, relates to navigation. But the subsequent part of the sentence is still more explicit. It is, "nor shall vessels bound to or from one State, be obliged to enter, clear, or pay duties, in another." These words have a direct reference to navigation. . . .

The word used in the constitution, then, comprehends, and has been always understood to comprehend, navigation within its meaning; and a power to regulate navigation, is as expressly granted, as if that term had been added to the word "commerce."

To what commerce does this power extend? The constitution informs us to commerce "with foreign nations, and among the several States, and with the Indian tribes."

It has, we believe, been universally admitted, that these words comprehend every species of commercial intercourse between the United States and foreign nations. No sort of trade can be carried on between this country and any other, to which this power does not extend. It has been truly said, that commerce, as the word is used in the constitution, is a unit, every part of which is indicated by the term.

If this be the admitted meaning of the word, in its application to foreign nations, it must carry the same meaning throughout the sentence, and remain a unit, unless there be some plain intelligible cause which alters it.

The subject to which the power is next applied, is to commerce "among the several States." The word "among" means intermingled with. A thing which is among others, is intermingled with them. Commerce among the States, cannot stop at the external boundary line of each State, but may be introduced into the interior.

It is not intended to say that these words comprehend that commerce, which is completely internal, which is carried on between man and man in a State, or between different parts of the same State, and which does not extend to or affect other States. Such a power would be inconvenient, and is certainly unnecessary.

Comprehensive as the word "among" is, it may very properly be restricted to that commerce which concerns more States than one. The phrase is not one which would probably have been selected to indicate the completely interior traffic of a State, because it is not an apt phrase for that purpose; and the enumeration of the particular classes of commerce, to which the power was to be extended, would not have been made, had the intention been to extend the power to every description. The enumeration presupposes something not enumerated; and that something, if we regard the language or the subject of the sentence, must be the exclusively internal commerce of a State. The genius and character of the whole government seem to be, that its action is to be applied to all the external concerns of the nation, and to those internal concerns which affect the States generally; but not to those which are completely within a particular State, which do not affect other States, and with which it is not necessary to interfere, for the purpose of executing some of the general powers of the government. The completely internal commerce of a State, then, may be considered as reserved for the State itself.

But, in regulating commerce with foreign nations, the power of Congress does not stop at the jurisdictional lines of the several States. It would be a very useless power, if it could not pass those lines. The commerce of the United States with foreign nations, is that of the whole United States. Every district has a right to participate in it. The deep streams which penetrate our country in every direction, pass through the interior of almost every State in the Union, and furnish the means of exercising this right. If Congress has the power to regulate it, that power must be exercised whenever the subject exists. If it exists within the States, if a foreign voyage may commence or terminate at a port within a State, then the power of Congress may be exercised within a State.

This principle is, if possible, still more clear, when applied to commerce "among the several States." They either join each other, in which case they are separated by a mathematical line, or they are remote from each other, in which case other States lie between them. What is commerce "among" them; and how is it to be conducted? Can a trading expedition between two adjoining States, commence and terminate outside of each? And if the trading intercourse be between two States remote from each other, must it not commence in one, terminate in the other, and probably pass through a third? Commerce among the States must, of necessity, be commerce with the States. In the regulation of trade with the Indian tribes, the action of the law, especially when the constitution was made, was chiefly within a State. The power of Congress, then, whatever it may be, must be exercised within the territorial jurisdiction of the several States. The sense of the nation on this subject, is unequivocally manifested by the provisions made in the laws for transporting goods, by land, between Baltimore and Providence, between New-York and Philadelphia, and between Philadelphia and Baltimore.

We are now arrived at the inquiry—What is this power?

It is the power to regulate; that is, to prescribe the rule by which commerce is to be governed. This power, like all others vested in Congress, is complete in itself, may be exercised to its utmost extent, and acknowledges no limitations, other than are prescribed in the constitution. These are expressed in plain terms, and do not affect the questions which arise in this case, or which have been discussed at the bar. If, as has always been understood, the sovereignty of Congress, though limited to specified objects, is plenary as to those objects, the power over commerce with foreign nations, and among the several States, is vested in Congress as absolutely as it would be in a single government, having in its constitution the same restrictions on the exercise of the power as are found in the constitution of the United States. The wisdom and the discretion of Congress, their identity with the people, and the influence which their constituents possess at elections, are, in this, as in many other instances, as that, for example, of declaring war, the sole restraints on which they have relied, to secure them from its abuse. They are the restraints on which the people must often rely solely, in all representative governments.

The power of Congress, then, comprehends navigation, within the limits of every State in the Union; so far as that navigation may be, in any manner, connected with "commerce with foreign nations, or among the several States, or with the Indian tribes." It may, of consequence, pass the jurisdictional line of New-York, and act upon the very waters to which the prohibition now under consideration applies.

JAMES BRYCE

12. DUAL FEDERALISM

Dual federalism, the earliest American version of the federal system, assumed that the functions and responsibilities of the states and the federal government were separate and distinct and that each could perform its

---

Source: From James Bryce, "Working Relationships of the National and the State Governments," *The American Commonwealth* (New York: The Macmillan Company, 3rd Ed., 1907).

role independent from the other. In the following brief selection, James Bryce (1838–1922), a British scholar who visited the United States in the 1880s, offers a concise description of the dual federalism concept of "two governments covering the same ground, yet distinct and separate in their actions." Incidentally, Bryce would later return to the United States as the British Ambassador (1907–1913).

The characteristic feature and special interest of the American Union is that it shows us two governments covering the same ground, yet distinct and separate in their actions. It is like a great factory wherein two sets of machinery are at work, their revolving wheels apparently intermixed, their bands crossing one another, yet each set doing its own work without touching or hampering the other. To keep the National government and the State governments each in the allotted sphere, preventing collision and friction between them, was the primary aim of those who formed the Constitution, a task the more needful and the more delicate because the States had been until then almost independent and therefore jealous of their privileges, and because, if friction should arise, the National government could not remove it by correcting defects in the machinery. For the National government, being itself the creature of the Constitution, was not permitted to amend the Constitution, but could only refer it back for amendment to the people of the States or to their legislatures. Hence the men of 1787, feeling the cardinal importance of anticipating and avoiding occasions of collision, sought to accomplish their object by the concurrent application of two devices. One was to restrict the functions of the National government to the irreducible minimum of functions absolutely needed for the national welfare, so that everything else should be left to the States. The other was to give that government, so far as those functions extended, a direct and immediate relation to the citizens, so that it should act on them not through the States but of its own authority and by its own officers. These are fundamental principles whose soundness experience has approved, and which will deserve to be considered by those who in time to come may have in other countries to frame federal or quasi-federal constitutions. They were studied, and to a large extent, though in no slavish spirit, adopted by the founders of the present constitution of the Swiss Confederation, a constitution whose success bears further witness to the soundness of the American doctrines.

The working relations of the National government to the States may be considered under two heads, viz. its relations to the States as communities, and its relations to the citizens of the States as individuals, they being also citizens of the Union.

The National government touches the States as corporate commonwealths in three points. One is their function in helping to form the National government; another is the control exercised over them by the Federal Constitution through the Federal courts; the third is the control exercised over them by the Federal Legislature and Executive in the discharge of the governing functions which these latter authorities possess. . . .

So far from lamenting as a fault, though an unavoidable fault, of their Federal system, the State independence I have described, the Americans are inclined to praise it as a merit. They argue, not merely that the best way on the whole is to leave a State to itself, but that this is the only way in which a permanent cure of its diseases will be effected. They are consistent not only in their Federal principles but in their democratic principles. "As *laissez aller*," they say, "is the necessary course in a Federal government, so it is the right course in all free governments. Law will never be strong or respected unless it has the sentiment of the people behind it. If the people of a State make bad laws, they will suffer for it. They will be the first to suffer. Let them suffer. Suffering, and nothing else, will implant that sense of responsibility which is the first step to reform. Therefore let them stew in their own juice: let them make their bed and lie upon it. If they drive capital away, there will be less work for the artisans: if they do not enforce contracts, trade will decline, and the evil will work out its remedy sooner or later. Perhaps it will be later rather than sooner: if so, the experience will be all the more conclusive. It is said that the minority of wise and peaceable citizens may suffer? Let them exert themselves to bring their fellows round to a better mind. Reason and experience will be on their side. We cannot be democrats by halves; and where self-government is given, the majority of the community must rule. Its rule will in the end be better than that of any external power." No doctrine more completely pervades the American people, the instructed as well as the uninstructed. Philosophers will tell you that it is the method by which Nature governs, in whose economy error is followed by pain and suffering, whose laws carry their own sanction with them. Divines will tell you that it is the method by which God governs: God is a righteous Judge and God is provoked every day, yet He makes His sun to rise on the evil and the good, and sends His rain upon the just and the unjust. He does not directly intervene to punish faults, but leaves sin to bring its own appointed penalty. Statesmen will point to the troubles which followed the attempt to govern the reconquered seceding States, first by military force and then by keeping a great part of their population disfranchised, and will declare that such evils as still exist in the South are far less grave than those which the denial of ordinary self-government involved. "So," they pursue, "Texas and California will in time unlearn their bad habits and come out right if we leave them alone: Federal interference, even had we the machinery needed for prosecuting it, would check the natural process by which the better elements in these raw communities are purging away the maladies of youth, and reaching the settled health of manhood."

A European may say that there is a dangerous side to this application of democratic faith in local majorities and in *laissez aller*. Doubtless there is: yet those who have learnt to know the Americans will answer that no nation better understands its own business.

MORTON GRODZINS

13. THE "MARBLE CAKE" THEORY OF FEDERALISM

As a consequence of the expanded role of the federal government during the New Deal, thinking about the nature of American federalism began to change. While federal and state officials had always worked together despite their separate and distinct spheres of action, following the New Deal there was even closer cooperation. Morton Grodzins's (1917–1964) 1960 description of this interdependence as resembling a "marble cake" as opposed to a "layer cake" captures the essence of the intermingling relationships among the levels of government in the federal system. In contrast to James Bryce's view of the state and federal governments as separate spheres of activity, Grodzins concludes that "No important activity of government in the United States is the exclusive province of one of the levels, not even what may be regarded as the most national of national functions, such as foreign relations; not even the most local of local functions, such as police and park maintenance."

Federalism is a device for dividing decisions and functions of government. As the constitutional fathers well understood, the federal structure is a means, not an end. The pages that follow are therefore not concerned with an exposition of American federalism as a formal, legal set of relationships. The focus, rather, is on the purpose of federalism, that is to say, on the distribution of power between central and peripheral units of government.

THE SHARING OF FUNCTIONS

The American form of government is often, but erroneously, symbolized by a three-layer cake. A far more accurate image is the rainbow or marble cake, characterized by an inseparable mingling of differently colored ingredients, the colors appearing in vertical and diagonal strands and unexpected whirls. As colors are mixed in the marble cake, so functions are mixed in the American

---

Source: From Morton Grodzins, "The Federal System," in *Goals for Americans,* The Committee on National Goals, pp. 265–282. New York, The American Assembly. Reprinted with permission.

federal system. Consider the health officer, styled "sanitarian," of a rural county in a border state. He embodies the whole idea of the marble cake of government.

The sanitarian is appointed by the state under merit standards established by the federal government. His base salary comes jointly from state and federal funds, the county provides him with an office and office amenities and pays a portion of his expenses, and the largest city in the county also contributes to his salary and office by virtue of his appointment as a city plumbing inspector. It is impossible from moment to moment to tell under which governmental hat the sanitarian operates. His work of inspecting the purity of food is carried out under federal standards; but he is enforcing state laws when inspecting commodities that have not been interstate commerce; and somewhat perversely he also acts under state authority when inspecting milk coming into the county from producing areas across the state border. He is a federal officer when impounding impure drugs shipped from a neighboring state; a federal-state officer when distributing typhoid immunization serum; a state officer when enforcing standards of industrial hygiene; a state-local officer when inspecting the city's water supply; and (to complete the circle) a local officer when insisting that the city butchers adopt more hygienic methods of handling their garbage. But he cannot and does not think of himself as acting in these separate capacities. All business in the county that concerns public health and sanitation he considers his business. Paid largely from federal funds, he does not find it strange to attend meetings of the city council to give expert advice on matters ranging from rotten apples to rabies control. He is even deputized as a member of both the city and county police forces.

The sanitarian is an extreme case, but he accurately represents an important aspect of the whole range of government activities in the United States. Functions are not neatly parceled out among the many governments. They are shared functions. It is difficult to find any governmental activity which does not involve all three of the so-called "levels" of the federal system. In the most local of local functions—law enforcement or education, for example—the federal and state governments play important roles. In what, *a priori,* may be considered the purest central government activities—the conduct of foreign affairs, for example—the state and local governments have considerable responsibilities, directly and indirectly.

The federal grant programs are only the most obvious example of shared functions. They also most clearly exhibit how sharing serves to disperse governmental powers. The grants utilize the greater wealth-gathering abilities of the central government and establish nation-wide standards, yet they are "in aid" of functions carried out under state law, with considerable state and local discretion. The national supervision of such programs is largely a process of mutual accommodation. Leading state and local officials, acting through their professional organizations, are in considerable part responsible for the very standards that national officers try to persuade all state and local officers to accept.

Even in the absence of joint financing, federal-state-local collaboration is the characteristic mode of action. Federal expertise is available to aid in the building of a local jail (which may later be used to house federal prisoners), to improve a local water purification system, to step up building inspections, to provide standards for state and local personnel in protecting housewives against dishonest butchers' scales, to prevent gas explosions, or to produce a land use plan. States and localities, on the other hand, take important formal responsibilities in the development of national programs for atomic energy, civil defense, the regulation of commerce, and the protection of purity in foods and drugs; local political weight is always a factor in the operation of even a post office or a military establishment. From abattoirs and accounting through zoning and zoo administration, any government activity is almost certain to involve the influence, if not the formal administration, of all three planes of the federal system. . . .

A POINT OF HISTORY

The American federal system has never been a system of separated governmental activities. There has never been a time when it was possible to put neat labels on discrete "federal," "state," and "local" functions. Even before the Constitution, a statute of 1785, reinforced by the Northwest Ordinance of 1787, gave grants-in-land to the states for public schools. Thus the national government was a prime force in making possible what is now taken to be the most local function of all, primary and secondary education. More important, the nation, before it was fully organized, established by this action a first principle of American federalism: the national government would use its superior resources to initiate and support national programs, principally administered by the states and localities.

The essential unity of state and federal financial systems was again recognized in the earliest constitutional days with the assumption by the federal government of the Revolutionary War debts of the states. Other points of federal-state collaboration during the Federalist period concerned the militia, law enforcement, court practices, the administration of elections, public health measures, pilot laws, and many other matters.

The nineteenth century is widely believed to have been the preeminent period of duality in the American system. Lord Bryce at the end of the century described (in *The American Commonwealth*) the federal and state governments as "distinct and separate in their action." The system, he said, was "like a great factory wherein two sets of machinery are at work, their revolving wheels apparently intermixed, their bands crossing one another, yet each set doing its own work without touching or hampering the other." Great works may contain gross errors. Bryce was wrong. The nineteenth century, like the early days of the republic, was a period principally characterized by intergovernmental collaboration.

Decisions of the Supreme Court are often cited as evidence of nineteenth century duality. In the early part of the century the Court, heavily weighted with Federalists, was intent upon enlarging the sphere of national authority; in the later years (and to the 1930's) its actions were in the direction of paring down national powers and indeed all government authority. Decisions referred to "areas of exclusive competence" exercised by the federal government and the states; to their powers being "separate and distinct;" and to neither being able "to intrude within the jurisdiction of the other."

Judicial rhetoric is not always consistent with judicial action, and the Court did not always adhere to separatist doctrine. Indeed, its rhetoric sometimes indicated a positive view of cooperation. In any case, the Court was rarely, if ever, directly confronted with the issue of cooperation *vs.* separation as such. Rather it was concerned with defining permissible areas of action for the central government and the states; or with saying with respect to a point at issue whether any government could take action. The Marshall Court contributed to intergovernmental cooperation by the very act of permitting federal operations where they had not existed before. Furthermore, even Marshall was willing to allow interstate commerce to be affected by the states in their use of the police power. Later courts also upheld state laws that had an impact on interstate commerce, just as they approved the expansion of the national commerce power, as in statutes providing for the control of telegraphic communication or prohibiting the interstate transportation of lotteries, impure foods and drugs, and prostitutes. Similar room for cooperation was found outside the commerce field, notably in the Court's refusal to interfere with federal grants in land or cash to the states. Although research to clinch the point has not been completed, it is probably true that the Supreme Court from 1800 to 1936 allowed far more federal-state collaboration than it blocked.

Political behavior and administrative action of the nineteenth century provide positive evidence that, throughout the entire era of so-called dual federalism, the many governments in the American federal system continued the close administrative and fiscal collaboration of the earlier period. Governmental activities were not extensive. But relative to what governments did, intergovernmental cooperation during the last century was comparable with that existing today.

Occasional presidential vetoes (from Madison to Buchanan) of cash and land grants are evidence of constitutional and ideological apprehensions about the extensive expansion of federal activities which produced widespread intergovernmental collaboration. In perspective, however, the vetoes are a more important evidence of the continuous search, not least by state officials, for ways and means to involve the central government in a wide variety of joint programs. The search was successful.

Grants-in-land and grants-in-services from the national government were of first importance in virtually all the principal functions undertaken by the states and their local subsidiaries. Land grants were made to the states for, among other purposes, elementary schools, colleges, and special educational institutions; roads, canals, rivers, harbors, and railroads; reclamation of desert and swamp lands; and veterans' welfare. In fact whatever was at the focus of state attention became the recipient of national grants. (Then, as today, national grants established state emphasis as well as followed it.) If Connecticut wished to establish a program for the care and education of the deaf and dumb, federal money in the form of a land grant was found to aid that program. If higher education relating to agriculture became a pressing need, Congress could dip into the public domain and make appropriate grants to states. If the need for swamp drainage and flood control appeared, the federal government could supply both grants-in-land and, from the Army's Corps of Engineers, the services of the only trained engineers then available.

Aid also went in the other direction. The federal government, theoretically in exclusive control of the Indian population, relied continuously (and not always wisely) on the experience and resources of state and local governments. State militias were an all-important ingredient in the nation's armed forces. State governments became unofficial but real partners in federal programs for homesteading, reclamation, tree culture, law enforcement, inland waterways, the nation's internal communications system (including highway and railroad routes), and veterans' aid of various sorts. Administrative contacts were voluminous, and the whole process of interaction was lubricated, then as today, by constituent conscious members of Congress.

The essential continuity of the collaborative system is best demonstrated by the history of the grants. The land grant tended to become a cash grant based on the calculated disposable value of the land, and the cash grant tended to become an annual grant based upon the national government's superior tax powers. In 1887, only three years before the frontier was officially closed, thus signalizing the end of the disposable public domain, Congress enacted the first continuing cash grants.

A long, extensive, and continuous experience is therefore the foundation of the present system of shared functions characteristic of the American federal system, what we have called the marble cake of government. It is a misjudgment of our history and our present situation to believe that a neat separation of governmental functions could take place without drastic alterations in our society and system of government.

SECTION II
REVIEW QUESTIONS

1. What specific aspects of the proposed Constitution did James Madison point to as providing a good balance between a "federal" and a "national" government? How has this balance changed since Madison first described it in 1788?

2. How did the Supreme Court's interpretation of the "necessary and proper" clause in *McCulloch v. Maryland* affect the power of the Supreme Court? Did Chief Justice Marshall's logic convince you? Can you point to any weaknesses in his argument?

3. What part of the Constitution was at the heart of the Supreme Court opinion in *Gibbons v. Ogden?* What philosophy is expressed by Chief Justice Marshall regarding the power of the Congress? Compare this case with *McCulloch v. Maryland.* Are the two opinions by Chief Justice Marshall consistent in how they view the powers of the federal government?

4. Compare and contrast the views of James Bryce and Morton Grodzins regarding the relationship between the states and the federal government. Which is the more accurate description of federalism today? Can you think of any ways in which the relationship between the states and the federal government might be improved?

III

Civil Liberties

GITLOW V. NEW YORK

14. INCORPORATION OF THE FIRST AMENDMENT

Gitlow v. New York *is a landmark case in the history of civil liberties in the United States because it was the first case in which a part of the Bill of Rights was found to be applicable to the states by means of the Fourteenth Amendment's "due process" clause. In* Gitlow, *the Court ruled that the First Amendment guarantees of freedom of speech and freedom of the press "are among the fundamental personal rights and 'liberties' protected by the due process clause of the Fourteenth Amendment." This was the beginning of a long process that came to be known as incorporation, by which most portions of the Bill of Rights have been construed (incorporated) by the Court as limitations on the actions of state governments.*

Justice SANFORD delivers the opinion of the Court.

Benjamin Gitlow was indicted in the Supreme Court of New York, with three others, for the statutory crime of criminal anarchy. He was separately tried, convicted, and sentenced to imprisonment. . . .

The contention here is that the statute, by its terms and as applied in this case, is repugnant to the due process clause of the Fourteenth Amendment. Its material provisions are: . . .

"Sec. 161. *Advocacy of Criminal Anarchy.* Any person who:

"1. By word of mouth or writing advocates, advises or teaches the duty, necessity or propriety of overthrowing or overturning organized government by force or violence, or by assassination of the executive head or of any of the executive officials of government, or by any unlawful means; or,

"2. Prints, publishes, edits, issues or knowingly circulates, sells, distributes or publicly displays any book, paper, document, or written or printed matter in any form, containing or advocating, advising or teaching the doctrine that organized government should be overthrown by force, violence or any unlawful means, . . .

"Is guilty of a felony and punishable" by imprisonment or fine, or both. . . .

Source: U.S. Supreme Court, *Gitlow v. New York* (1925).

The sole contention here is, essentially, that as there was no evidence of any concrete result flowing from the publication of the Manifesto or of circumstances showing the likelihood of such result, the statute as construed and applied by the trial court penalizes the mere utterance, as such, of "doctrine" having no quality of incitement, without regard either to the circumstances of its utterance or to the likelihood of unlawful consequences. . . .

The statute does not penalize the utterance or publication of abstract "doctrine" or academic discussion having no quality of incitement to any concrete action. It is not aimed against mere historical or philosophical essays. It does not restrain the advocacy of changes in the form of government by constitutional and lawful means. What it prohibits is language advocating, advising or teaching the overthrow of organized government by unlawful means. These words imply urging to action. . . .

The Manifesto, plainly, is neither the statement of abstract doctrine nor, as suggested by counsel, mere prediction that industrial disturbances and revolutionary mass strikes will result spontaneously in an inevitable process of evolution in the economic system. It advocates and urges in fervent language mass action which shall progressively foment industrial disturbances and through political mass strikes and revolutionary mass action overthrow and destroy organized parliamentary government. . . .

For present purposes we may and do assume that freedom of speech and of the press—which are protected by the First Amendment from abridgement by Congress—are among the fundamental personal rights and "liberties" protected by the due process clause of the Fourteenth Amendment from impairment by the States. . . .

It is a fundamental principle, long established, that the freedom of speech and of the press which is secured by the Constitution, does not confer an absolute right to speak or publish, without responsibility, whatever one may choose, or an unrestricted and unbridled license that gives immunity for every possible use of language and prevents the punishment of those who abuse this freedom. . . .

That a State in the exercise of its police power may punish those who abuse this freedom by utterances inimical to the public welfare, tending to corrupt public morals, incite to crime, or disturb the public peace, is not open to question. . . .

By enacting the present statute the State has determined, through its legislative body, that utterances advocating the overthrow of organized government by force, violence and unlawful means, are so inimical to the general welfare and involve such danger of substantive evil that they may be penalized in the exercise of its police power. That determination must be given great weight. Every presumption is to be indulged in favor of the validity of the statute. *Mugler v. Kansas*. . . . And the case is to be considered "in the light of the principle that the State is primarily the judge of regulations required in the interest of public safety and welfare"; and that its police "statutes may only be declared unconstitutional where they are arbitrary or unreasonable attempts to exercise authority vested in the State in the public interest." *Great Northern Ry. v. Clara City* [246 U.S. 434 (1918)]. That utterances inciting to the overthrow of organized government by unlawful means, present a sufficient danger of substantive evil to bring their punishment within the range of legislative discretion, is clear. Such utterances, by their very nature, involve danger to the public peace and to the security of the State. They threaten breaches of the peace and ultimate revolution. And the immediate danger is none the less real and substantial, because the effect of a given utterance cannot be accurately foreseen. The State cannot reasonably be required to measure the danger from every such utterance in the nice balance of a jeweler's scale. A single revolutionary spark may kindle a fire that, smouldering for a time, may burst into a sweeping and destructive conflagration. It cannot be said that the State is acting arbitrarily or unreasonably when in the exercise of its judgment as to the measures necessary to protect the public peace and safety, it seeks to extinguish the spark without waiting until it has enkindled the flame or blazed into the conflagration. It cannot reasonably be required to defer the adoption of measures for its own peace and safety until the revolutionary utterances lead to actual disturbances of the public peace or imminent and immediate danger of its own destruction; but it may, in the exercise of its judgment, suppress the threatened danger in its incipiency. . . .

We cannot hold that the present statute is an arbitrary or unreasonable exercise of the police power of the State unwarrantably infringing the freedom of speech or press; and we must and do sustain its constitutionality.

This being so it may be applied to every utterance—not too trivial to be beneath the notice of the law—which is of such a character and used with such intent and purpose as to bring it within the prohibition of the statute. . . .

In other words, when the legislative body has determined generally, in the constitutional exercise of its discretion, that utterances of a certain kind involve such danger of substantive evil that they may be punished, the question whether any specific utterance coming within the prohibited class is likely, in and of itself, to bring about the substantive evil, is not open to consideration. It is sufficient that the statute itself be constitutional and that the use of the language comes within its prohibition.

It is clear that the question in such cases is entirely different from that involved in those cases where the statute merely prohibits certain acts involving the danger of substantive evil, without any reference to language itself, and it is sought to apply its provisions to language used by the defendant for the purpose of bringing about the prohibited results. There, if it be contended that the statute cannot be applied to the language used by the defendant because of its protection by the freedom of speech or press, it must necessarily be found, as an original question, without any previous determination by the legislative body, whether the specific language used involved such likelihood of bringing about the substantive evil as to deprive it of the constitutional protection. In such case it has been held that the general provisions of the statute may be constitutionally applied to the specific utterance of the defendant if its natural tendency and probable effect was to bring about the substantive evil which the legislative body might prevent. *Schenck v. United States,* [249 U.S. 47 (1919)]; *Debs v. United States,* [249 U.S. 211 (1919)]. And the general statement in the *Schenck* Case, [249 U.S. 47 (1919)], that the "question in every case is whether the words used are used in such circumstances and are of such a nature as to create a clear and present danger that they will bring about the substantive evils,"—upon which great reliance is placed in the defendant's argument—was manifestly intended, as shown by the context, to apply only in cases of this class, and has no application to those like the present, where the legislative body itself has previously determined the danger of substantive evil arising from utterances of a specified character. . . .

Affirmed.

GIDEON V. WAINWRIGHT

15. EXTENDING THE RIGHT TO COUNSEL TO THE STATE COURTS

Prior to the Supreme Court's decision in Gideon v. Wainwright *in 1963, defendants in state criminal trials had substantially fewer rights than they would have had in federal courts. For example, because the Court had not yet incorporated the Sixth Amendment right to counsel into the Fourteenth Amendment due process clause, state courts were not required to provide lawyers for criminal defendants who were unable to afford them except in certain cases such as those in which the death penalty was involved.*

This all changed after Clarence Earl Gideon was convicted of a minor burglary and sentenced to five years in a Florida prison following a trial in which he could not afford to hire a lawyer to defend him. In a handwritten appeal Mr. Gideon convinced the Supreme Court to hear his case. Their decision revolutionized state criminal proceedings by ruling that all persons brought to trial in state courts on felony charges have a right under the Fourteenth Amendment to have a court-appointed lawyer to defend them if they cannot afford to hire their own lawyer. In arguing that the Sixth

Source: U.S. Supreme Court, *Gideon v. Wainwright* (1963).

Amendment right to counsel should be included among the basic rights protected under the Fourteenth Amendment, Justice Black wrote, "reason and reflection require us to recognize that in our adversary system of criminal justice, any person hauled into court, who is too poor to hire a lawyer, cannot be assured a fair trial unless counsel is provided for him. This seems to us to be an obvious truth."

Mr. Justice BLACK delivered the opinion of the Court.

Petitioner was charged in a Florida state court with having broken and entered a poolroom with intent to commit a misdemeanor. This offense is a felony under Florida law. Appearing in court without funds and without a lawyer, petitioner asked the court to appoint counsel for him, whereupon the following colloquy took place.

> "The Court: Mr. Gideon, I am sorry, but I cannot appoint Counsel to represent you in this case. Under the laws of the State of Florida, the only time the Court can appoint Counsel to represent a Defendant is when that person is charged with a capital offense. I am sorry, but I will have to deny your request to appoint Counsel to defend you in this case.
>
> "The Defendant: The United States Supreme Court says I am entitled to be represented by Counsel."

Put to trial before a jury Gideon conducted his defense about as well as could be expected from a layman. He made an opening statement to the jury, cross-examined the State's witnesses, presented witnesses in his own defense, declined to testify himself, and made a short argument "emphasizing his innocence to the charge contained in the Information filed in this case." The jury returned a verdict of guilty, and petitioner was sentenced to serve five years in the state prison. Later, petitioner filed in the Florida Supreme Court this *habeas corpus* petition attacking his conviction and sentence on the ground that the trial court's refusal to appoint counsel for him denied him rights "guaranteed by the Constitution and the Bill of Rights by the United States Government." Treating the petition for *habeas corpus* as properly before it, the State Supreme Court, "upon consideration thereof" but without an opinion, denied all relief. Since 1942, when *Betts v. Brady* . . . was decided by a divided Court, the problem of a defendant's federal constitutional right to counsel in a state court has been a continuing source of controversy and litigation in both state and federal courts. . . .

I.

. . . . Like Gideon, Betts sought release by *habeas corpus*, alleging that he had been denied the right to assistance of counsel in violation of the Fourteenth

Amendment. Betts was denied any relief, and on review this Court affirmed. It was held that a refusal to appoint counsel for an indigent defendant charged with a felony did not necessarily violate the Due Process Clause of the Fourteenth Amendment, which for reasons given the Court deemed to be the only applicable federal constitutional provision. The Court said:

> "Asserted denial [of due process] is to be tested by an appraisal of the totality of facts in a given case. That which may, in one setting, constitute a denial of fundamental fairness, shocking to the universal sense of justice, may, in other circumstances, and in the light of other considerations, fall short of such denial." . . .

Treating due process as "a concept less rigid and more fluid than those envisaged in other specific and particular provisions of the Bill of Rights," the Court held that refusal to appoint counsel under the particular facts and circumstances in the *Betts* case was not so "offensive to the common and fundamental ideas of fairness" as to amount to a denial of due process. Since the facts and circumstances of the two cases are so nearly indistinguishable, we think the *Betts v. Brady* holding if left standing would require us to reject Gideon's claim that the Constitution guarantees him the assistance of counsel. Upon full reconsideration we conclude that *Betts v. Brady* should be overruled.

II.

The Sixth Amendment provides, "In all criminal prosecutions, the accused shall enjoy the right . . . to have the Assistance of Counsel for his defence." We have construed this to mean that in federal courts counsel must be provided for defendants unable to employ counsel unless the right is competently and intelligently waived. Betts argued that this right is extended to indigent defendants in state courts by the Fourteenth Amendment. In response the Court stated that, while the Sixth Amendment laid down "no rule for the conduct of the States, the question recurs whether the constraint laid by the Amendment upon the national courts expresses a rule so fundamental and essential to a fair trial, and so, to due process of law, that it is made obligatory upon the States by the Fourteenth Amendment." . . . In order to decide whether the Sixth Amendment's guarantee of counsel is of this fundamental nature, the Court in *Betts* set out and considered "relevant data on the subject . . . afforded by constitutional and statutory provisions subsisting in the colonies and the States prior to the inclusion of the Bill of Rights in the national Constitution, and in the constitutional, legislative, and judicial history of the States to the present date." . . . On the basis of this historical data the Court concluded that "appointment of counsel is not a fundamental right, essential to a fair trial." . . . It was for this reason the *Betts* Court refused to accept the contention that the Sixth Amendment's guarantee of counsel for indigent federal defendants was extended to or, in the words of that Court, "made obligatory upon the States by the Fourteenth Amendment." Plainly, had the Court concluded that appointment of counsel for an indigent criminal defendant was "a fundamental right, essential to a fair trial," it would have held that the Fourteenth Amendment requires appointment of counsel in a state court, just as the Sixth Amendment requires in a federal court.

We think the Court in *Betts* had ample precedent for acknowledging that those guarantees of the Bill of Rights which are fundamental safeguards of liberty immune from federal abridgement are equally protected against state invasion by the Due Process Clause of the Fourteenth Amendment. This same principle was recognized, explained, and applied in *Powell v. Alabama*. . . . (1932), a case upholding the right of counsel, where the Court held that despite sweeping language to the contrary in *Hurtado v. California*. . . . (1884), the Fourteenth Amendment "embraced" those "fundamental principles of liberty and justice which lie at the base of all our civil and political institutions," even though they had been "specifically dealt with in another part of the federal Constitution." . . . In many cases other than *Powell* and *Betts*, this Court has looked to the fundamental nature of original Bill of Rights guarantees to decide whether the Fourteenth Amendment makes them obligatory on the States. Explicitly recognized to be of this "fundamental nature" and therefore made immune from state invasion by the Fourteenth, or some part of it, are the First Amendment's freedoms of speech, press, religion, assembly, association, and petition for redress of grievances. For the same reason, though not always in precisely the same terminology, the Court has made obligatory on the States the Fifth Amendment's command that private property shall not be taken for public use without just compensation, the Fourth Amendment's prohibition of unreasonable searches and seizures, and the Eighth's ban on cruel and unusual punishment. On the other hand, this Court in *Palko v. Connecticut* . . . (1937), refused to hold that the Fourteenth Amendment made the double jeopardy provision of the Fifth Amendment obligatory on the States. In so refusing, however, the Court, speaking through Mr. Justice Cardozo, was careful to emphasize that "immunities that are valid as against the federal government by force of the specific pledges of particular amendment have been found to be implicit in the concept of ordered liberty, and thus, through the Fourteenth Amendment, become valid as against the states" and that guarantees "in their origin . . . effective against the federal government alone" had by prior cases "been taken over from the earlier articles of the federal bill of rights and brought within the Fourteenth Amendment by a process of absorption. . . .

Ten years before *Betts v. Brady*, this Court, after full consideration of all the historical data [later] examined in *Betts*, had unequivocally declared that "the right to the aid of counsel is of this fundamental character." . . . in 1936, the Court reemphasized what it had said about the fundamental nature of the right to counsel in this language:

> "We concluded that certain fundamental rights, safeguarded by the first eight amendments against federal action, were also safeguarded against state action by the due process of law clause of the Fourteenth Amendment, and among them the fundamental right of the accused to the aid of counsel in a criminal prosecution." . . .

And again in 1938 this Court said:

> "[The assistance of counsel] is one of the safeguards of the Sixth Amendment deemed necessary to insure fundamental human rights of life and liberty. . . . The Sixth Amendment stands as a constant admonition that if the constitutional safeguards it provides be lost, justice will not 'still be done.' " . . .

Not only these precedents but also reason and reflection require us to recognize that in our adversary system of criminal justice, any person hauled into court, who is too poor to hire a lawyer, cannot be assured a fair trial unless counsel is provided for him. This seems to us to be an obvious truth. Governments, both state and federal, quite properly spend vast sums of money to establish machinery to try defendants accused of crime. Lawyers to prosecute are everywhere deemed essential to protect the public's interest in an orderly society. Similarly, there are few defendants charged with crime, few indeed, who fail to hire the best lawyers they can get to prepare and present their defenses. That government hires lawyers to prosecute and defendants who have the money hire lawyers to defend are the strongest indications of the widespread belief that lawyers in criminal courts are necessities, not luxuries. The right of one charged with crime to counsel may not be deemed fundamental and essential to fair trials in some countries, but it is in ours. From the very beginning, our state and national constitutions and laws have laid great emphasis on procedural and substantive safeguards designed to assure fair trials before impartial tribunals in which every defendant stands equal before the law. This noble ideal cannot be realized if the poor man charged with crime has to face his accusers without a lawyer to assist him. . . .

The judgment is reversed and the cause is remanded to the Supreme Court of Florida for further action not inconsistent with this opinion.

Reversed.

MIRANDA V. ARIZONA

16. Custodial Interrogations

Probably the best-known criminal justice decision of the Supreme Court is the case of Miranda v. Arizona. *There, as in* Mapp, *the Supreme Court was faced with the question of how to ensure that individual civil liberties (in this case protected under the Fourth, Fifth, and Sixth*

Source: U.S. Supreme Court, *Miranda v. Arizona* (1966).

Amendments) would actually be meaningful when a person was arrested by the police. The Court held in Miranda *that, in order to be sure that an arrested person about to be questioned by the police is aware of his or her rights, the police must inform the arrested person of these rights.*

As everyone now knows, if only from watching police shows on television, police are required to read "rights" or "Miranda warnings" to arrested persons. The suspect is told: You have the right to remain silent (based on the Fifth Amendment protection against self-incrimination), the right to an attorney (based on the Sixth Amendment right to counsel), the right to a court-appointed attorney if you cannot afford one, and the fact that statements made to the police may be used against you in court.

If the police proceed to question an arrested person without having first read the individual these Miranda rights, any statement or confession that the person might make cannot be introduced by the prosecution at a later trial. Specifically, the Court ruled that "the prosecution may not use statements . . . stemming from custodial interrogation of the defendant unless it demonstrates the use of procedural safeguards effective to secure the privilege against self-incrimination."

Mr. Chief Justice WARREN delivered the opinion of the Court.

The cases before us raise questions which go to the roots of our concepts of American criminal jurisprudence: the restraints society must observe consistent with the Federal Constitution in prosecuting individuals for crime. More specifically, we deal with the admissibility of statements obtained from an individual who is subjected to custodial police interrogation and the necessity for procedures which assure that the individual is accorded his privilege under the Fifth Amendment to the Constitution not to be compelled to incriminate himself.

We dealt with certain phases of this problem recently in *Escobedo v. Illinois,* 378 U.S. 478 (1964). There, as in the four cases before us, law enforcement officials took the defendant into custody and interrogated him in a police station for the purpose of obtaining a confession. The police did not effectively advise him of his right to remain silent or of his right to consult with his attorney. Rather, they confronted him with an alleged accomplice who accused him of having perpetrated a murder. When the defendant denied the accusation and said "I didn't shoot Manuel, you did it," they handcuffed him and took him to an interrogation room. There, while handcuffed and standing, he was questioned for four hours until he confessed. During the interrogation, the police denied his request to speak to his attorney, and they prevented his retained attorney, who had come to the police station, from consulting with him. At his trial, the State, over his objection, introduced the confession against him. We held that the statements thus made were constitutionally inadmissible.

This case has been the subject of judicial interpretation and spirited legal debate since it was decided two years ago. Both state and federal courts, in assessing its implications, have arrived at varying conclusions. A wealth of scholarly material has been written tracing its ramifications and underpinnings. Police and prosecutor have speculated on its range and desirability. We granted certiorari in these cases, 382 U.S. 924, 925, 937, in order further to explore some facets of the problems, thus exposed, of applying the privilege against self-incrimination to in-custody interrogation, and to give concrete constitutional guidelines for law enforcement agencies and courts to follow.

We start here, as we did in *Escobedo,* with the premise that our holding is not an innovation in our jurisprudence, but is an application of principles long recognized and applied in other settings. We have undertaken a thorough reexamination of the *Escobedo* decision and the principles it announced, and we reaffirm it. That case was but an explication of basic rights that are enshrined in our Constitution—that "No person . . . shall be compelled in any criminal case to be a witness against himself," and that "the accused shall . . . have the Assistance of Counsel"—rights which were put in jeopardy in that case through official overbearing. These precious rights were fixed in our Constitution only after centuries of persecution and struggle. And in the words of Chief Justice Marshall, they were secured "for ages to come, and . . . designed to approach immortality as nearly as human institutions can approach it," *Cohens v. Virginia,* 6 Wheat. 264, 387 (1821).

Our holding will be spelled out with some specificity in the pages which follow but briefly stated it is this: the prosecution may not use statements, whether exculpatory or inculpatory, stemming from custodial interrogation of the defendant unless it demonstrates the use of procedural safeguards effective to secure the privilege against self-incrimination. By custodial interrogation, we mean questioning initiated by law enforcement officers after a person has been taken into custody or otherwise deprived of his freedom of action in any significant way. As for the procedural safeguards to be employed, unless other fully effective means are devised to inform accused persons of their right of silence and to assure a continuous opportunity to exercise it, the following measures are required. Prior to any questioning, the person must be warned that he has a fight to remain silent, that any statement he does make may be used as evidence against him, and that he has a right to the presence of an attorney, either retained or appointed. The defendant may waive effectuation of these rights, provided the waiver is made voluntarily, knowingly and intelligently. If, however, he indicates in any manner and at any stage of the process that he wishes to consult with an attorney before speaking there can be no questioning. Likewise, if the individual is alone and indicates in any manner that he does not wish to be interrogated, the police may not question him.

The mere fact that he may have answered some questions or volunteered some statements on his own does not deprive him of the right to refrain from answering any further inquiries until he has consulted with an attorney and thereafter consents to be questioned.

I.

The constitutional issue we decide in each of these cases is the admissibility of statements obtained from a defendant questioned while in custody or otherwise deprived of his freedom of action in any significant way. In each, the defendant was questioned by police officers, detectives, or a prosecuting attorney in a room in which he was cut off from the outside world. In none of these cases was the defendant given a full and effective warning of his rights at the outset of the interrogation process. In all the cases, the questioning elicited oral admissions, and in three of them, signed statements as well which were admitted at their trials. They all thus share salient features—incommunicado interrogation of individuals in a police-dominated atmosphere, resulting in self-incriminating statements without full warnings of constitutional rights.

An understanding of the nature and setting of this in-custody interrogation is essential to our decisions today. The difficulty in depicting what transpires at such interrogations stems from the fact that in this country they have largely taken place incommunicado. From extensive factual studies undertaken in the early 1930's, including the famous Wickersham Report to Congress by a Presidential Commission, it is clear that police violence and the "third degree" flourished at that time. In a series of cases decided by this Court long after these studies, the police resorted to physical brutality—beating, hanging, whipping—and to sustained and protracted questioning incommunicado in order to extort confessions. The Commission on Civil Rights in 1961 found much evidence to indicate that "some policemen still resort to physical force to obtain confessions," 1961 Comm'n on Civil Rights Rep., Justice, pt. 5, 17. The use of physical brutality and violence is not, unfortunately, relegated to the past or to any part of the country. Only recently in Kings County, New York, the police brutally beat, kicked and placed lighted cigarette butts on the back of a potential witness under interrogation for the purpose of securing a statement incriminating a third party. . . .

To highlight the isolation and unfamiliar surroundings, the manuals instruct the police to display an air of confidence in the suspect's guilt and from outward appearance to maintain only an interest in confirming certain details. The guilt of the subject is to be posited as a fact. The interrogator should direct his comments toward the reasons why the subject committed the act, rather than court failure by asking the subject whether he did it. Like other men, perhaps the subject has had a bad family life, had an unhappy childhood, had too much to drink, had an unrequited desire for women. The officers are instructed to minimize the moral seriousness of the offense, to cast blame on the victim or on society. These tactics are designed to put the subject in a psychological state where his story is but an elaboration of what the police purport to know already—that he is guilty. Explanations to the contrary are dismissed and discouraged. . . .

From these representative samples of interrogation techniques, the setting prescribed by the manuals and observed in practice becomes clear. In essence, it is this: To be alone with the subject is essential to prevent distraction and to deprive him of any outside support. The aura of confidence in his guilt undermines his will to resist. He merely confirms the preconceived story the police seek to have him describe. Patience and persistence, at times relentless questioning, are employed. To obtain a confession, the interrogator must "patiently maneuver himself or his quarry into a position from which the desired objective may be obtained." When normal procedures fail to produce the needed result, the police may resort to deceptive stratagems such as giving false legal advice. It is important to keep the subject off balance, for example, by trading on his insecurity about himself or his surroundings. The police then persuade, trick, or cajole him out of exercising his constitutional rights.

Even without employing brutality, the "third degree" or the specific stratagems described above, the very fact of custodial interrogation exacts a heavy toll on individual liberty and trades on the weakness of individuals. This fact may be illustrated simply by referring to three confession cases decided by this Court in the Term immediately preceding our *Escobedo* decision. In *Townsend v. Sain,* 372 U.S. 293 (1963), the defendant was a 19-year-old heroin addict, described as a "near mental defective," id., at 307–310. The defendant in *Lynumn v. Illinois,* 372 U.S. 528 (1963), was a woman who confessed to the arresting officer after being importuned to "cooperate" in order to prevent her children from being taken by relief authorities. This Court as in those cases reversed the conviction of a defendant in *Haynes v. Washington,* 373 U.S. 503 (1963), whose persistent request during his interrogation was to phone his wife or attorney. In other settings, these individuals might have exercised their constitutional rights. In the incommunicado police-dominated atmosphere, they succumbed.

In the cases before us today, given this background, we concern ourselves primarily with this interrogation atmosphere and the evils it can bring. In No. 759, *Miranda v. Arizona,* the police arrested the defendant and took him to a special interrogation room where they secured a confession. In No. 760, *Vignera v. New York,* the defendant made oral admissions to the police after interrogation in the afternoon, and then signed an inculpatory statement upon being questioned by an assistant district attorney later the same evening. In No. 761, *Westover v. United States,* the defendant was handed over to the Federal Bureau of Investigation by local authorities after they had detained and interrogated him for a lengthy period, both at night and the following morning. After some two hours of questioning, the federal officers had obtained signed statements from the defendant. Lastly, in No. 584, *California v. Stewart,* the local police held the defendant five days in the station and interrogated him on nine separate occasions before they secured his inculpatory statement.

In these cases, we might not find the defendants' statements to have been involuntary in traditional terms. Our concern for adequate safeguards to protect precious Fifth Amendment rights is, of course, not lessened in the slightest. In each of the cases, the defendant was thrust into an unfamiliar atmosphere and run through menacing police interrogation procedures. The potentiality for compulsion is forcefully apparent, for example, in *Miranda,* where the indigent Mexican defendant was a seriously disturbed individual with pronounced sexual fantasies, and in *Stewart,* in which the defendant was an indigent Los Angeles Negro who had dropped out of school in the sixth grade. To be sure, the records do not evince overt physical coercion or patent psychological ploys. The fact remains that in none of these cases did the officers undertake to afford appropriate safeguards at the outset of the interrogation to insure that the statements were truly the product of free choice.

It is obvious that such an interrogation environment is created for no purpose other than to subjugate the individual to the will of his examiner. This atmosphere carries its own badge of intimidation. To be sure, this is not physical intimidation, but it is equally destructive of human dignity. The current practice of incommunicado interrogation is at odds with one of our Nation's most cherished principles—that the individual may not be compelled to incriminate himself. Unless adequate protective devices are employed to dispel the compulsion inherent in custodial surroundings, no statement obtained from the defendant can truly be the product of his free choice. . . .

Accordingly we hold that an individual held for interrogation must be clearly informed that he has the right to consult with a lawyer and to have the lawyer with him during interrogation under the system for protecting the privilege we delineate today. As with the warnings of the right to remain silent and that anything stated can be used in evidence against him, this warning is an absolute prerequisite to interrogation. No amount of circumstantial evidence that the person may have been aware of this right will suffice to stand in its stead. Only through such a warning is there ascertainable assurance that the accused was aware of this right.

If an individual indicates that he wishes the assistance of counsel before any interrogation occurs, the authorities cannot rationally ignore or deny his request on the basis that the individual does not have or cannot afford a retained attorney. The financial ability of the individual has no relationship to the scope of the rights involved here. The privilege against self-incrimination secured by the Constitution applies to all individuals. The need for counsel in order to protect the privilege exists for the indigent as well as the affluent. In fact, were we to limit these constitutional rights to those who can retain an attorney, our decisions today would be of little significance. The cases before us as well as the vast majority of confession cases with which we have dealt in the past involve those unable to retain counsel. While authorities are not required to relieve the accused of his poverty, they have the obligation not to take advantage of indigence in the administration of justice. Denial of counsel to the indigent at the time of interrogation while allowing an attorney to those who can afford one would be no more supportable by reason or logic than the similar situation at trial and on appeal struck down in *Gideon v. Wainwright,* 372 U.S. 335 (1963), and *Douglas v. California*, 372 U.S. 353 (1963).

In order fully to apprise a person interrogated of the extent of his rights under this system then, it is necessary to warn him not only that he has the right to consult with an attorney, but also that if he is indigent a lawyer will be appointed to represent him. Without this additional warning, the admonition of the right to consult with counsel would often be understood as meaning only that he can consult with a lawyer if he has one or has the funds to obtain one. The warning of a right to counsel would be hollow if not couched in terms that would convey to the indigent—the person most often subjected to interrogation—the knowledge that he too has a right to have counsel present. As with the warnings of the right to remain silent and of the general right to counsel, only by effective and express explanation to the indigent of this right can there be assurance that he was truly in a position to exercise it.

Once warnings have been given, the subsequent procedure is clear. If the individual indicates in any manner, at any time prior to or during questioning, that he wishes to remain silent, the interrogation must cease. At this point he has shown that he intends to exercise his Fifth Amendment privilege; any statement taken after the person invokes his privilege cannot be other than the product of compulsion, subtle or otherwise. Without the right to cut off questioning, the setting of in-custody interrogation operates on the individual to overcome free choice in producing a statement after the privilege has been once invoked. If the individual states that he wants an attorney, the interrogation must cease until an attorney is present. At that time, the individual must have an opportunity to confer with the attorney and to have him present during any subsequent questioning. If the individual cannot obtain an attorney and he indicates that he wants one before speaking to police, they must respect his decision to remain silent.

This does not mean, as some have suggested, that each police station must have a "station house lawyer" present at all times to advise prisoners. It does mean, however, that if police propose to interrogate a person they must make known to him that he is entitled to a lawyer and that if he cannot afford one, a lawyer will be provided for him prior to any interrogation. If authorities conclude that they will not provide counsel during a reasonable period of time in which investigation in the field is carried out, they may refrain from doing so without violating the person's Fifth Amendment privilege so long as they do not question him during that time.

If the interrogation continues without the presence of an attorney and a statement is taken, a heavy burden rests on the government to demonstrate that the defendant knowingly and intelligently waived his privilege against self-incrimination and his right to retained or appointed counsel. *Escobedo v. Illinois,* 378 U.S. 478, 490, n. 14. This Court has always set high standards of proof for the waiver of constitutional rights, *Johnson v. Zerbst,* 304 U.S. 458 (1938), and we re-assert these standards as applied to in-custody interrogation. Since the State is responsible for establishing the isolated circumstances under which the interrogation takes place and has the only means of making available corroborated evidence of warnings given during incommuicado interrogation, the burden is rightly on its shoulders. . . .

The principles announced today deal with the protection which must be given to the privilege against self-incrimination when the individual is first subjected to police interrogation while in custody at the station or otherwise deprived of his freedom of action in any significant way. It is at this point that our adversary system of criminal proceedings commences, distinguishing itself at the outset from the inquisitorial system recognized in some countries. Under the system of warnings we delineate today or under any other system which may be devised and found effective, the safeguards to be erected about the privilege must come into play at this point.

Our decision is not intended to hamper the traditional function of police officers in investigating crime. See *Escobedo v. Illinois,* 378 U.S. 478, 492. When an individual is in custody on probable cause, the police may, of course, seek out evidence in the field to be used at trial against him. Such investigation may include inquiry of persons not under restraint. General on-the-scene questioning as to facts surrounding a crime or other general questioning of citizens in the fact-finding process is not affected by our holding. It is an act of responsible citizenship for individuals to give whatever information they may have to aid in law enforcement. In such situations the compelling atmosphere inherent in the process of in-custody interrogation is not necessarily present.

In dealing with statements obtained through interrogation, we do not purport to find all confessions inadmissible. Confessions remain a proper element in law enforcement. Any statement given freely and voluntarily without any compelling influences is, of course, admissible in evidence. The fundamental import of the privilege while an individual is in custody is not whether he is allowed to talk to the police without the benefit of warnings and counsel, but whether he can be interrogated. There is no requirement that police stop a person who enters a police station and states that he wishes to confess to a crime, or a person who calls the police to offer a confession or any other statement he desires to make. Volunteered statements of any kind are not barred by the Fifth Amendment and their admissibility is not affected by our holding today.

To summarize, we hold that when an individual is taken into custody or otherwise deprived of his freedom by the authorities in any significant way and is subjected to questioning, the privilege against self-incrimination is jeopardized. Procedural safeguards must be employed to protect the privilege, and unless other fully effective means are adopted to notify the person of his right of silence and to assure that the exercise of the right will be scrupulously honored, the following measures are required. He must be warned prior to any questioning that he has the right to remain silent, that anything he says can be used against him in a court of law, that he has the right to the presence of an attorney, and that if he cannot afford an attorney one will be appointed for him prior to any questioning if he so desires. Opportunity to exercise these rights must be afforded to him throughout the interrogation. After such warnings have been given, and such opportunity afforded him, the individual may knowingly and intelligently waive these rights and agree to answer questions or make a statement. But unless and until such warnings and waiver are demonstrated by the prosecution at trial, no evidence obtained as a result of interrogation can be used against him. . . .

IV.

A recurrent argument made in these cases is that society's need for interrogation outweighs the privilege. This argument is not unfamiliar to this Court. See, e.g., *Chambers v. Florida,* 309 U.S. 227, 240–241 (1940). The whole thrust of our foregoing discussion demonstrates that the Constitution has prescribed the rights of the individual when confronted with the power of government when it provided in the Fifth Amendment that an individual cannot be compelled to be a witness against himself. That right cannot be abridged. . . .

If the individual desires to exercise his privilege, he has the right to do so. This is not for the authorities to decide. An attorney may advise his client not to talk to police until he has had an opportunity to investigate the case, or he may wish to be present with his client during any police questioning. In doing so an attorney is merely exercising the good professional judgment he has been taught. This is not cause for considering the attorney a menace to law enforcement. He is merely carrying out what he is sworn to do under his oath—to protect to the extent of his ability the rights of his client. In fulfilling this responsibility the attorney plays a vital role in the administration of criminal justice under our Constitution.

In announcing these principles, we are not unmindful of the burdens which law enforcement officials must bear, often under trying circumstances. We also fully recognize the obligation of all citizens to aid in enforcing the criminal laws. This Court, while protecting individual rights, has always given ample latitude to law enforcement agencies in the legitimate exercise of their duties. The limits we have placed on the interrogation process should not constitute an undue interference with a proper system of law enforcement. As we have noted, our decision does not in any way preclude police from carrying out their traditional investigatory functions. Although confessions may play an important role in some convictions, the cases before us present graphic examples of the overstatement of the "need" for confessions. In each case authorities conducted interrogations ranging up to five days in duration despite the presence, through standard investigating practices, of considerable evidence against each defendant. Further examples are chronicled in our prior cases.

MAPP V. OHIO

17. EXTENDING THE EXCLUSIONARY RULE TO THE STATE COURTS

The Fourth Amendment protects against unreasonable searches and seizures by federal authorities. However, without some type of enforcement mechanism, that protection has little meaning. Recognizing the problem, the Supreme Court created the "exclusionary rule" in 1914. Under this rule, evidence that has been illegally obtained must be excluded from federal criminal trials. Because the Bill of Rights initially limited only the federal government, illegally obtained evidence was regularly admitted in state criminal prosecutions until the 1961 case of Mapp v. Ohio.

In Mapp, *police officers had broken into a woman's rooming house without a search warrant and seized a number of obscene materials. Following her conviction for possession of these materials, Dollree Mapp appealed all the way to the Supreme Court where the justices ruled that the exclusionary rule, which had long been applied in federal courts, would now be applied as well in all state criminal courts. Thus, the process of "incorporation" into the Fourteenth Amendment of rights previously protected against federal infringement continued.*

Mr. Justice CLARK delivered the opinion of the Court.

On May 23, 1957, three Cleveland police officers arrived at appellant's residence in that city pursuant to information that "a person [was] hiding out in the home who was wanted for questioning in connection with a recent bombing, and that there was a large amount of policy paraphernalia being hidden in the home." Miss Mapp . . . lived on the top floor of the two-family dwelling. Upon their arrival at that house, the officers knocked on the door and demanded entrance but appellant, after telephoning her attorney, refused to admit them without a search warrant. . . .

The officers again sought entrance some three hours later when four or more additional officers arrived on the scene. When Miss Mapp did not come to the door immediately, at least one of the several doors to the house was

---

Source: U.S. Supreme Court, *Mapp v. Ohio* (1961).

forcibly opened and the policemen gained admittance. . . . It appears that Miss Mapp was halfway down the stairs from the upper floor to the front door when the officers, in this high-handed manner, broke into the hall. She demanded to see the search warrant. A paper, claimed to be a warrant, was held up by one of the officers. She grabbed the "warrant" and placed it in her bosom. A struggle ensued in which the officers recovered the piece of paper and as a result of which they handcuffed appellant because she had been "belligerent" in resisting their official rescue of the "warrant" from her person. Running roughshod over appellant, a policeman "grabbed" her, "twisted [her] hand," and she "yelled [and] pleaded with him" because "it was hurting." Appellant, in handcuffs, was then forcibly taken upstairs to her bedroom where the officers searched a dresser, a chest of drawers, a closet and some suitcases. They also looked into a photo album and through personal papers belonging to the appellant. The search spread to the rest of the second floor including the child's bedroom, the living room, the kitchen and a dinette. The basement of the building and a trunk found therein were also searched. The obscene materials for possession of which she was ultimately convicted were discovered in the course of that widespread search.

At the trial no search warrant was produced by the prosecution, nor was the failure to produce one explained or accounted for. At best, "there is, in the record, considerable doubt as to whether there ever was any warrant for the search of defendant's home." . . .

The State says that even if the search were made without authority, or otherwise unreasonably, it is not prevented from using the unconstitutionally seized evidence at trial, . . . "that in a prosecution in a State court for a State crime the Fourteenth Amendment does not forbid the admission of evidence obtained by an unreasonable search and seizure." . . . On this appeal . . . it is urged . . . that we review that holding. . . .

. . . this Court, in *Weeks v. United States* (1914), stated that

> "the Fourth Amendment . . . put the courts of the United States and Federal officials, in the exercise of their power and authority, under limitations and restraints [and] . . . forever secure[d] the people, their persons, houses, papers and effects against all unreasonable searches and seizures under the guise of law . . . and the duty of giving to it force and effect is obligatory upon all entrusted under our Federal system with the enforcement of the laws." . . .

Specifically dealing with the use of the evidence unconstitutionally seized, the Court concluded:

> "If letters and private documents can thus be seized and held and used in evidence against a citizen accused of an offense, the protection of the Fourth Amendment declaring his right to be secure against such searches and seizures is of no value, and, so far as those thus placed are concerned, might as well be stricken from the Constitution. The efforts of the courts and their officials to bring the guilty to punishment, praiseworthy as they are, are not to be aided by sacrifice of those great principles established by years of endeavor and

suffering which have resulted in their embodiment in the fundamental law of the land. . . . "

Finally, the Court in that case clearly stated that use of the seized evidence involved "a denial of the constitutional rights of the accused." . . . Thus, in the year 1914, in the *Weeks* case, this Court "for the first time" held that "in a federal prosecution the Fourth Amendment barred the use of evidence secured through an illegal search and seizure." . . . This Court has ever since required of federal law officers a strict adherence to that command which this Court has held to be a clear, specific, and constitutionally required—even if judicially implied—deterrent safeguard without insistence upon which the Fourth Amendment would have been reduced to "a form of words." . . . It meant, quite simply, that "conviction by means of unlawful seizures and enforced confessions . . . should find no sanction in the judgments of the courts . . ." and that such evidence "shall not be used at all. . . . "

In 1949, 35 years after *Weeks* was announced, this Court, in *Wolfe v. Colorado,* . . . again for the first time, discussed the effect of the Fourth Amendment upon the States through the operation of the Due Process Clause of the Fourteenth Amendment. It said:

"We have no hesitation in saying that were a State affirmatively to sanction such police incursion into privacy it would run counter to the guaranty of the Fourteenth Amendment." . . .

Nevertheless, after declaring that the "security of one's privacy against arbitrary intrusion by the police" is "implicit in the 'concept of ordered liberty' and as such enforceable against the States through the Due Process Clause," . . . and announcing that it "stoutly adhere[d]" to the *Weeks* decision, the Court decided that the *Weeks* exclusionary rule would not then be imposed upon the states as "an essential ingredient of the right." . . .

And only last Term, after . . . carefully re-examining the *Wolf* doctrine in *Elkins v. United States,* . . . the Court pointed out that "the controlling principles" as to search and seizure and the problem of admissibility "seemed clear" . . . until the announcement in *Wolf* "that the Due Process Clause of the Fourteenth Amendment does not itself require state courts to adopt the exclusionary rule" of the *Weeks* case. . . . Today we once again examine *Wolf's* constitutional documentation of the right to privacy free from unreasonable state intrusion, and, after its dozen years on our books, are led by it to close the only courtroom door remaining open to evidence secured by official lawlessness in flagrant abuse of that basic right, reserved to all persons as a specific guarantee against that very same unlawful conduct. We hold that all evidence obtained by searches and seizures in violation of the Constitution is, by that same authority, inadmissible in a state court. . . .

Since the Fourth Amendment's right of privacy has been declared enforceable against the States through the Due Process Clause of the Fourteenth, it is enforceable against them by the same sanction of exclusion as is used against the Federal Government. Were it otherwise, then just as without the *Weeks* rule the assurance against unreasonable federal searches and seizures would be "a form of words," valueless and undeserving of mention in a perpetual charter of inestimable human liberties, so too, without that rule the freedom from state invasions of privacy would be so ephemeral and so neatly severed from its conceptual nexus with the freedom from all brutish means of coercing evidence as not to merit this Court's high regard as a freedom "implicit in the concept of ordered liberty." . . .

The ignoble shortcut to conviction left open to the State tends to destroy the entire system of constitutional restraints on which the liberties of the people rest. Having once recognized that the right to privacy embodied in the Fourth Amendment is enforceable against the States, and that the right to be secure against rude invasions of privacy by state officers is, therefore, constitutional in origin, we can no longer permit that right to remain an empty promise. Because it is enforceable in the same manner and to like effect as other basic rights secured by the Due Process Clause, we can no longer permit it to be revocable at the whim of any police officer who, in the name of law enforcement itself, chooses to suspend its enjoyment. Our decision, founded on reason and truth, gives to the individual no more than that which the Constitution guarantees him, to the police officer no less than that to which honest law enforcement is entitled, and, to the courts, that judicial integrity so necessary in the true administration of justice.

Reversed and remanded.

MASSACHUSETTS V. SHEPPARD

18. The Good Faith Exception

The exclusionary rule, designed to deter police misconduct by excluding evidence illegally obtained, has been widely criticized for its ultimate effect: The criminal may be released because of a police error. In the wake of such criticism, the Supreme Court began to modify the exclusionary rule where it did not seem to serve the purpose of deterring police misconduct.

Source: U.S. Supreme Court, *Massachusetts v. Sheppard* (1984).

A major exception to the exclusionary rule was announced in the 1984 case of Massachusetts v. Sheppard. *There, a police officer investigating a murder found a judge at home on a Sunday afternoon and obtained the judge's signature on a search warrant to be used in a search for evidence. The warrant that the police officer presented to the judge for his signature was on a form that was used to search for drugs and was accompanied by an affidavit in which the officer listed what he was looking for. Before signing it, the judge failed to attach the affidavit and failed to change the part of the warrant indicating that it authorized only a drug search. Consequently, the warrant did not properly state "the persons or things to be seized" as required by the Fourth Amendment, and the Massachusetts Supreme Court ruled that the evidence obtained in that search could not be used against the defendant.*

The Supreme Court reversed and created a "good faith" exception to the exclusionary rule under which illegally obtained evidence could be used in a criminal prosecution if the police officer involved had obtained a search warrant and done everything he could be expected to do in following the Fourth Amendment. If the judge or magistrate signing the warrant made a mistake, neither the public nor the police should be made to suffer for it. The Court reasoned that police misconduct could not be deterred in this type of case because there simply was no police misconduct at all. Rather, a judge had made a mistake. In such cases, evidence that was illegally obtained due to such an error may now be admitted.

Justice WHITE delivered the opinion of the Court.

This case involves the application of the rules articulated today in *United States v. Leon,* ante, p. 897, to a situation in which police officers seize items pursuant to a warrant subsequently invalidated because of a technical error on the part of the issuing judge.

I.

The badly burned body of Sandra Boulware was discovered in a vacant lot in the Roxbury section of Boston at approximately 5 A.M., Saturday, May 5, 1979. An autopsy revealed that Boulware had died of multiple compound skull fractures caused by blows to the head. After a brief investigation, the police decided to question one of the victim's boyfriends, Osborne Sheppard. Sheppard told the police that he had last seen the victim on Tuesday night and that he had been at a local gaming house (where card games were played) from 9 P.M. Friday until 5 A.M. Saturday. He identified several people who would be willing to substantiate the latter claim.

By interviewing the people Sheppard had said were at the gaming house on Friday night, the police learned that although Sheppard was at the gaming house that night, he had borrowed an automobile at about 3 o'clock Saturday morning in order to give two men a ride home. Even though the trip normally took only 15 minutes, Sheppard did not return with the car until nearly 5 A.M.

On Sunday morning, police officers visited the owner of the car Sheppard had borrowed. He consented to an inspection of the vehicle. Bloodstains and pieces of hair were found on the rear bumper and within the trunk compartment. In addition, the officers noticed strands of wire in the trunk similar to wire strands found on and near the body of the victim. The owner of the car told the officers that when he last used the car on Friday night, shortly before Sheppard borrowed it, he had placed articles in the trunk and had not noticed any stains on the bumper or in the trunk.

On the basis of the evidence gathered thus far in the investigation, Detective Peter O'Malley drafted an affidavit designed to support an application for an arrest warrant and a search warrant authorizing a search of Sheppard's residence. The affidavit set forth the results of the investigation and stated that the police wished to search for

> [a] fifth bottle of amaretto liquor, 2 nickel bags of marijuana, a woman's jacket that has been described as black-grey (charcoal) possessions of Sandra D. Boulware, similar type wire and rope that match those on the body of Sandra D. Boulware, or in the above [T]hunderbird. Blunt instrument that might have been used on the victim. Men's or women's clothing that may have blood, gasoline, burns on them. Items that may have fingerprints of the victim.

Detective O'Malley showed the affidavit to the District Attorney, the District Attorney's first assistant, and a sergeant, who all concluded that it set forth probable cause for the search and the arrest. 387 Mass. 488, 492, 441 N.E.2d 725, 727 (1982).

Because it was Sunday, the local court was closed, and the police had a difficult time finding a warrant application form. Detective O'Malley finally found a warrant form previously in use in the Dorchester District. The form was entitled "Search Warrant—Controlled Substance G.L. c. 276 §§ 1 through 3A." Realizing that some changes had to be made before the form could be used to authorize the search requested in the affidavit, Detective O'Malley deleted the subtitle "controlled substance" with a typewriter. He also substituted "Roxbury" for the printed "Dorchester" and typed Sheppard's name and address into blank spaces provided for that information. However, the reference to "controlled substance" was not deleted in the portion of the form that constituted the warrant application and that, when signed, would constitute the warrant itself.

Detective O'Malley then took the affidavit and the warrant form to the residence of a judge who had consented to consider the warrant application. The judge examined the affidavit and stated that he would authorize the search as requested. Detective O'Malley offered the warrant form and stated that he knew the form as presented dealt with controlled substances. He showed the judge where he had crossed out the subtitles. After unsuccessfully searching for a more suitable form, the judge informed O'Malley that he would make the necessary changes so as to provide a proper search warrant. The judge then took the form, made some changes on it, and dated and signed the warrant. However, he did not change the substantive portion of the warrant, which continued to authorize a search for controlled substances; nor did he alter the form so as to incorporate the affidavit. The judge returned the affidavit and the warrant to O'Malley, informing him that the warrant was sufficient authority in form and content to carry out the search as requested. O'Malley took the two documents and, accompanied by other officers, proceeded to Sheppard's residence. The scope of the ensuing search was limited to the items listed in the affidavit, and several incriminating pieces of evidence were discovered. Sheppard was then charged with first-degree murder.

At a pretrial suppression hearing, the trial judge concluded that the warrant failed to conform to the commands of the Fourth Amendment because it did not particularly describe the items to be seized. The judge ruled, however, that the evidence could be admitted notwithstanding the defect in the warrant because the police had acted in good faith in executing what they reasonably thought was a valid warrant. . . . At the subsequent trial, Sheppard was convicted.

On appeal, Sheppard argued that the evidence obtained pursuant to the defective warrant should have been suppressed. The Supreme Judicial Court of Massachusetts agreed. A plurality of the justices concluded that although "the police conducted the search in a good faith belief, reasonably held, that the search was lawful and authorized by the warrant issued by the judge," 387 Mass., at 503, 441 N.E. 2d, at 733, the evidence had to be excluded because this Court had not recognized a good-faith exception to the exclusionary rule. Two justices combined in a separate concurrence to stress their rejection of the good-faith exception, and one justice dissented, contending that since exclusion of the evidence in this case would not serve to deter any police misconduct, the evidence should be admitted. We granted certiorari and set the case for argument in conjunction with *United States v. Leon*, ante, p. 897, 463 U.S. 1205 (1983).

II.

Having already decided that the exclusionary rule should not be applied when the officer conducting the search acted in objectively reasonable reliance on a warrant issued by a detached and neutral magistrate that subsequently is determined to be invalid, ante, at 922–923, the sole issue before us in this case is whether the officers reasonably believed that the search they conducted was authorized by a valid warrant. There is no dispute that the officers believed that the warrant authorized the search that they conducted. Thus, the only question is whether there was an objectively reasonable basis for the officers' mistaken belief. Both the trial court, App. 35a, and a majority of the Supreme Judicial Court, 387 Mass., at 503, 441 N.E. 2d, at 733; id., at 524–525, 441 N.E. 2d, at 745 (Lynch, J., dissenting), concluded that there was. We agree.

The officers in this case took every step that could reasonably be expected of them. Detective O'Malley prepared an affidavit which was reviewed and approved by the District Attorney. He presented that affidavit to a neutral judge. The judge concluded that the affidavit established probable cause to search Sheppard's residence, App. 26a, and informed O'Malley that he would authorize the search as requested. O'Malley then produced the warrant form and informed the judge that it might need to be changed. He was told by the judge that the necessary changes would be made. He then observed the judge make some changes and received the warrant and the affidavit. At this point, a reasonable police officer would have concluded, as O'Malley did, that the warrant authorized a search for the materials outlined in the affidavit.

Sheppard contends that since O'Malley knew the warrant form was defective, he should have examined it to make sure that the necessary changes had been made. However, that argument is based on the premise that O'Malley had a duty to disregard the judge's assurances that the requested search would be authorized and the necessary changes would be made. Whatever an officer may be required to do when he executes a warrant without knowing beforehand what items are to be seized, we refuse to rule that an officer is required to disbelieve a judge who has just advised him, by word and by action, that the warrant he possesses authorizes him to conduct the search he has requested. In Massachusetts, as in most jurisdictions, the determinations of a judge acting within his jurisdiction, even if erroneous, are valid and binding until they are set aside under some recognized procedure. . . . If an officer is required to accept at face value the judge's conclusion that a warrant form is invalid, there is little reason why he should be expected to disregard assurances that everything is all right, especially when he has alerted the judge to the potential problems.

In sum, the police conduct in this case clearly was objectively reasonable and largely error-free. An error of constitutional dimensions may have been committed with respect to the issuance of the warrant, but it was the judge, not the police officers, who made the critical mistake. "[T]he exclusionary rule was adopted to deter unlawful searches by police, not to punish the errors of magistrates and judges." *Illinois v. Gates,* 462 U.S. 213, 263 (1983) (White, J., concurring in judgment). Suppressing evidence because the judge failed to make all the necessary clerical corrections despite his assurances that such changes would be made will not serve the deterrent function that the exclusionary rule was designed to achieve. Accordingly, federal law does not require the exclusion of the disputed evidence in this case. The judgment of the Supreme Judicial Court is therefore reversed, and the case is remanded for further proceedings not inconsistent with this opinion.

It is so ordered.

GRISWOLD V. CONNECTICUT

19. RIGHT TO PRIVACY

The framers and the American people have long believed that governmental interference in our individual private lives must be restricted. The Fourth Amendment, and its subsequent incorporation into the Fourteenth Amendment, reflects this basic value. Nonetheless, the word "privacy" does not appear in the Constitution or in the Bill of Rights.

In fact, until the 1965 decision in Griswold v. Connecticut, *no constitutional right to privacy had ever been announced by the Supreme Court. But when the state of Connecticut convicted a married couple, their doctor, and the director of the local Planned Parenthood organization under a law banning the use or distribution of contraceptives, the Supreme Court announced for the first time that a right to privacy existed in the Constitution. A majority of the court basically found that Connecticut's attempt to regulate the private sexual conduct of a married couple intruded into a protected "zone of privacy" beyond the power of any government. As Justice Douglas put it, "The First Amendment has a penumbra where privacy is protected from governmental intrusion." Although the precise source of the constitutional right of privacy was not clear because there was no reference to it in the Constitution, the* Griswold *decision remains the basis for subsequent controversial Court decisions on abortion and other private aspects of life that are of ongoing debate in U.S. society today.*

Source: U.S. Supreme Court, *Griswold v. Connecticut* (1965).

Justice DOUGLAS delivered the opinion of the Court.

[A Connecticut statute makes it a crime to use contraceptives. Another statute makes it illegal to provide or assist another in using contraceptives. A married couple, their doctor, and the director of Planned Parenthood of Connecticut challenge their convictions under these statutes.]

. . . [W]e are met with a wide range of questions that implicate the Due Process Clause of the Fourteenth Amendment. Overtones of some arguments suggest that *Lochner v. New York* should be our guide. But we decline that invitation. We do not sit as a super-legislature to determine the wisdom, need, and propriety of laws that touch economic problems, business affairs, or social conditions. This law, however, operates directly on an intimate relation of husband and wife and their physician's role in one aspect of that relation.

The association of people is not mentioned in the Constitution nor in the Bill of Rights. The right to educate a child in a school of the parents' choice—whether public or private or parochial—is also not mentioned. Nor is the right to study any particular subject or any foreign language. Yet the First Amendment has been construed to include certain of those rights.

By *Pierce v. Society of Sisters,* the right to educate one's children as one chooses is made applicable to the States by the force of the First and Fourteenth Amendments. By *Myer v. Nebraska,* the same dignity is given the right to study the German language in a private school. In other words, the State may not, consistently with the spirit of the First Amendment, contract the spectrum of available knowledge. The right of freedom of speech and press includes not only the right to utter or to print, but the right to distribute, the right to receive, the right to read and freedom of inquiry, freedom of thought, and freedom to teach, indeed the freedom of the entire university community. Without those peripheral rights the specific rights would be less secure. And so we reaffirm the principle of the *Pierce* and the *Meyer* cases.

In *NAACP v. Alabama,* we protected the "freedom to associate and privacy in one's associations," noting that freedom of association was a peripheral First Amendment right. . . .

The foregoing cases suggest that specific guarantees in the Bill of Rights have penumbras, formed by emanations from those guarantees that help give them life and substance. Various guarantees create zones of privacy. The right of association contained in the penumbra of the First Amendment is one, as we have seen. The Third Amendment in its prohibition against the quartering of soldiers "in any house" in time of peace without the consent of the owner is another facet of that privacy. The Fourth Amendment explicitly affirms the "right of the people to be secure in their persons, houses, papers, and effects, against unreasonable searches and seizures." The Fifth Amendment in its Self-Incrimination Clause enables the citizen to create a zone of privacy which government may not force him to surrender to his detriment. The Ninth Amendment provides: "The enumeration in the Constitution, of certain rights, shall not be construed to deny or disparage others retained by the people."

The present case concerns a relationship lying within the zone of privacy created by several fundamental constitutional guarantees. And it concerns a law which, in forbidding the use of contraceptives rather than regulating their manufacture or sale, seeks to achieve its goals by means having a maximum destructive impact upon that relationship. Would we allow the police to search the sacred precincts of marital bedrooms for telltale signs of the use of contraceptives? The very idea is repulsive to the notions of privacy surrounding the marriage relationship. . . .

We deal with a right of privacy older than the Bill of Rights—older than our political parties, older than our school system. Marriage is a coming together for better or for worse, hopefully enduring, and intimate to the degree of being sacred. It is an association that promotes a way of life, not causes; a harmony in living, not political faiths; a bilateral loyalty, not commercial or social projects. Yet it is an association for as noble a purpose as any involved in our prior decisions.

Reversed.

ROE V. WADE

20. LEGALIZING ABORTION

Roe v. Wade *was an extension of the right of privacy concept introduced in* Griswold. Roe *has probably caused more political turmoil than any other decision of the Court in the second half of the twentieth century. Presented with a Texas law forbidding abortion except where it was necessary to save the life of the mother, the Supreme Court ruled that state prohibitions on abortion such as this one in Texas violated a woman's right to privacy in deciding what she wanted to do about terminating her own pregnancy. As Justice Harry Blackmun wrote for the majority opinion, "freedom of personal choice in matters of marriage and family life is one of the liberties protected by the due process clause of the Fourteenth Amendment. . . . That right necessarily includes the right of a woman to decide whether or not to terminate her pregnancy."*

Source: U.S. Supreme Court, *Roe v. Wade* (1973).

In his dissent, Justice Rehnquist argued that the fact that a majority of states had for a long time restricted abortion demonstrated that the right to an abortion could not be considered a "fundamental right." In addition, he noted that when the Fourteenth Amendment was ratified in 1868, there "apparently was no question concerning the validity" of restrictive abortion laws in thirty-six states. From this, he concluded that the Fourteenth Amendment does not protect a right of abortion.

In 1992 the Supreme Court in Planned Parenthood v. Casey *reaffirmed* Roe v. Wade's *support for a woman's right of abortion, but at the same time upheld certain restrictions on abortion if they did not constitute an "undue burden" on the fundamental right of abortion. When presented in 1992 with another opportunity to overturn* Roe v. Wade *in an appeal from a court decision invalidating the strong anti-abortion law from Guam, the Supreme Court chose to let the lower court ruling stand.*

In Rust v. Sullivan, *the Supreme Court upheld the Reagan administration's regulations prohibiting federally funded family planning clinics from even discussing abortion as an option. One of President Bill Clinton's first orders was to rescind these regulations.*

Justice BLACKMUN delivered the opinion of the Court.

The Texas statutes that concern us here make it a crime to "procure an abortion," or to attempt one, except with respect to "an abortion procured or attempted by medical advice for the purpose of saving the life of the mother." Similar statutes are in existence in a majority of the States. . . .

The principal thrust of appellant's attack on the Texas statutes is that they improperly invade a right, said to be possessed by the pregnant woman, to choose to terminate her pregnancy. Appellant would discover this right in the concept of personal "liberty" embodied in the Fourteenth Amendment's Due Process Clause; or in personal, marital, familial, and sexual privacy said to be protected by the Bill of Rights or its penumbras; or among those rights reserved to the people by the Ninth Amendment. . . .

The Constitution does not explicitly mention any right of privacy. In a line of decisions, however, the Court has recognized that a right of personal privacy, or a guarantee of certain areas or zones of privacy, does exist under the Constitution. In varying contexts, the Court or individual Justices have, indeed, found at least the roots of that right in the First Amendment, *Stanley v. Georgia,* 394 U.S. 557 (1969); in the Fourth and Fifth Amendments, *Terry v. Ohio,* 392 U.S. 1 (1968); in the penumbras of the Bill of Rights, *Griswold v. Connecticut;* in the Ninth Amendment, id., at 486 (Goldberg, J., concurring); or in the concept of liberty guaranteed by the first section of the Fourteenth Amendment. These decisions make it clear that only personal rights that can be deemed "fundamental" or "implicit in the concept of ordered liberty," *Palko v. Connecticut,* 302 U.S. 319 (1937), are included in this guarantee of personal privacy. They also make it clear that the right has some extension to activities relating to marriage, procreation, contraception, family relationships, child rearing and education.

This right of privacy, whether it be founded in the Fourteenth Amendment's concept of personal liberty and restrictions upon state action, as we feel it is, or, as the District Court determined, in the Ninth Amendment's reservation of rights to the people, is broad enough to encompass a woman's decision whether or not to terminate her pregnancy. The detriment that the State would impose upon the pregnant woman by denying this choice altogether is apparent. Specific and direct harm medically diagnosable even in early pregnancy may be involved. Maternity, or additional offspring, may force upon the woman a distressful life and future. Psychological harm may be imminent. Mental and physical health may be taxed by child care. There is also the distress, for all concerned, associated with the unwanted child, and there is the problem of bringing a child into a family already unable, psychologically and otherwise, to care for it. In other cases, as in this one, the additional difficulties and continuing stigma of unwed motherhood may be involved. All these are factors the woman and her responsible physician necessarily will consider in consultation.

On the basis of elements such as these, appellant and some amici argue that the woman's right is absolute and that she is entitled to terminate her pregnancy at whatever time, in whatever way, and for whatever reason she alone chooses. With this we do not agree. Appellant's arguments that Texas either has no valid interest at all in regulating the abortion decision, or no interest strong enough to support any limitation upon the woman's sole determination, is unpersuasive. The Court's decisions recognizing a right of privacy also acknowledge that some state regulation in areas protected by that right is appropriate. . . . A state may properly assert important interests in safeguarding health, in maintaining medical standards, and in protecting potential life. At some point in pregnancy, these respective interests become sufficiently compelling to sustain regulation of the factors that govern the abortion decision. The privacy right involved, therefore, cannot be said to be absolute. In fact, it is not clear to us that the claim asserted by some amici that one has an unlimited right to do with one's body as one pleases bears a close relationship to the right of privacy previously articulated in the Court's decisions. The Court has refused to recognize an unlimited right of this kind in the past.

We, therefore, conclude that the right of personal privacy includes the abortion decision, but that this right is not unqualified and must be considered against important state interests in regulation. . . .

Where certain "fundamental rights" are involved, the Court has held that regulation limiting these rights may be justified only by a "compelling state interest," and that legislative enactments must be narrowly drawn to express only the legitimate state interests at stake. . . .

Texas urges that . . . life begins at conception and is present throughout pregnancy, and that, therefore, the State has a compelling interest in protecting that life from and after conception. We need not resolve the difficult question of when life begins. When those trained in the respective disciplines of medicine, philosophy, and theology are unable to arrive at any consensus, the judiciary, at this point in the development of man's knowledge, is not in a position to speculate as to the answer.

[The Court concludes that the point where the state's interest in the life of the unborn fetus may supersede the woman's right to privacy is at viability—the point where the fetus is potentially able to live outside the mother's womb, albeit with aid. This occurs at approximately 7 months, but can occur as early as 24 weeks.]

. . . . [W]e do not agree that, by adopting one theory of life, Texas may override the rights of the pregnant woman that are at stake. We repeat, however, that the State does have an important and legitimate interest in preserving and protecting the health of the pregnant woman, whether she be a resident of the State or a non-resident who seeks medical consultation and treatment there, and that it has still another important and legitimate interest in protecting the potentiality of human life. These interests are separate and distinct. Each grows in substantiality as the woman approaches term and, at a point during pregnancy, each becomes "compelling."

With respect to the State's important and legitimate interest in the health of the mother, the "compelling" point, in the light of present medical knowledge, is at approximately the end of the first trimester. This is so because of the now-established medical fact, that until the end of the first trimester mortality in abortion may be less than mortality in normal childbirth. It follows that, from and after this point, a State may regulate the abortion procedure to the extent that the regulation reasonably relates to the preservation and protection of maternal health. Examples of permissible state regulation in this area are requirements as to the qualifications of the person who is to perform the abortion; as to the licensure of that person; as to the facility in which the procedure is to be performed, that is, whether it must be a hospital or may be a clinic or some other place of less-than-hospital status; as to the licensing of the facility; and the like.

This means, on the other hand, that, for the period of pregnancy prior to this "compelling" point, the attending physician, in consultation with his patient, is free to determine, without regulation by the State, that, in his medical judgment, the patient's pregnancy should be terminated. If that decision is reached, the judgment may be effectuated by an abortion free of interference by the State.

With respect to the State's important and legitimate interest in potential life, the "compelling" point is at viability. This is so because the fetus then presumably has the capability of meaningful life outside the mother's womb. State regulation protective of fetal life after viability thus has both logical and biological justifications. If the State is interested in protecting fetal life after viability, it may go so far as to proscribe abortion during that period, except when it is necessary to preserve the life or health of the mother.

WEBSTER V. REPRODUCTIVE HEALTH SERVICES

21. STATE REGULATION OF ABORTION

In the wake of Roe v. Wade *many states tested its meaning by enacting various laws that regulated abortion but fell short of banning the procedure. Missouri passed a law that prohibited abortions in all facilities owned or leased by the state, and required that physicians conduct medical tests to determine the viability of all fetuses believed to be at least 20 weeks. In* Webster, *the Supreme Court upheld both of these provisions. As to the latter, it ruled that the provision was "reasonably designed to ensure that abortions are not performed where the fetus is viable." While stopping short of reversing* Roe v. Wade, *the decision in* Webster *recognized the powers of states to seriously limit a woman's right to an abortion. Justice Harry Blackmun, who wrote the Court's opinion in* Roe v. Wade, *dissented in* Webster, *lamenting that the decision "casts into darkness the hopes and visions of every woman in this country who had come to believe that the Constitution guaranteed her the right to exercise some control over her unique ability to bear children."*

The Webster *decision suddenly made abortion* the *issue of state politics. Now many candidates for a governorship or state legislature must take a stand. This is vexing for politicians of both parties because abortion is not clearly an issue of the left or the right.*

Section 188.029 of the Missouri Act provides:

"Before a physician performs an abortion on a woman he has reason to believe is carrying an unborn child of twenty or more weeks gestational age, the

---

Source: U.S. Supreme Court, *Webster v. Reproductive Health Services* (1989).

> physician shall first determine if the unborn child is viable by using and exercising that degree of care, skill, and proficiency commonly exercised by the ordinarily skillful, careful, and prudent physician engaged in similar practice under the same or similar conditions. In making this determination of viability, the physician shall perform or cause to be performed such medical examinations and tests as are necessary to make a finding of the gestational age, weight, and lung maturity of the unborn child and shall enter such findings and determination of viability in the medical record of the mother."

We think the viability-testing provision makes sense only if the second sentence is read to require only those tests that are useful to making subsidiary findings as to viability. If we construe this provision to require a physician to perform those tests needed to make the three specified findings in all circumstances, including when the physician's reasonable professional judgment indicates that the tests would be irrelevant to determining viability or even dangerous to the mother and the fetus, the second sentence of 188.029 would conflict with the first sentence's requirement that a physician apply his reasonable professional skill and judgment. It would also be incongruous to the provision, especially the word "necessary," to require the performance of tests irrelevant to the expressed statutory purpose of determining viability. It thus seems clear to us that the Court of Appeals' construction of 188.029 violates well-accepted canons of statutory interpretation used in the Missouri courts. . . .

The viability-testing provision of the Missouri Act is concerned with promoting the State's interest in potential human life rather than in maternal health. Section 188.029 creates what is essentially a presumption of viability at 20 weeks, which the physician must rebut with tests indicating that the fetus is not viable prior to performing an abortion. It also directs the physician's determination as to viability by specifying consideration, if feasible, of gestational age, fetal weight, and lung capacity. The District Court found that "the medical evidence is uncontradicted that a 20-week fetus is not viable," and that "23½ to 24 weeks gestation is the earliest point in pregnancy where a reasonable possibility of viability exists." But it also found that there may be a 4-week error in estimating gestational age, which supports testing at 20 weeks.

In *Roe v. Wade,* the Court recognized that the State has "important and legitimate" interests in protecting maternal health and in the potentiality of human life. During the second trimester, the State "may, if it chooses, regulate the abortion procedure in ways that are reasonably related to maternal health." After viability, when the State's interest in potential human life was held to become compelling, the State "may, if it chooses, regulate, and even proscribe, abortion except where it is necessary, in appropriate medical judgment, for the preservation of the life or health of the mother. . . . "

Stare decisis is a cornerstone of our legal system, but it has less power in constitutional cases, where, save for constitutional amendments, this Court is the only body able to make needed changes. We have not refrained from reconsideration of a prior construction of the Constitution that has proved "unsound in principle and unworkable in practice." We think the *Roe* trimester framework falls into that category.

In the first place, the rigid *Roe* framework is hardly consistent with the notion of a Constitution cast in general terms, as ours is, and usually speaking in general principles, as ours does. The key elements of the *Roe* framework—trimesters and viability—are not found in the text of the Constitution or in any place else one would expect to find a constitutional principle. Since the bounds of the inquiry are essentially indeterminate, the result has been a web of legal rules that have become increasingly intricate, resembling a code of regulations rather than a body of constitutional doctrine. As JUSTICE WHITE has put it, the trimester framework has left this Court to serve as the country's "ex officio medical board with powers to approve or disapprove medical and operative practices and standards throughout the United States."

In the second place, we do not see why the State's interest in protecting potential human life should come into existence only at the point of viability, and that there should therefore be a rigid line allowing state regulation after viability but prohibiting it before viability. The dissenters in *Thornburgh,* writing in the context of the *Roe* trimester analysis, would have recognized this fact by positing against the "fundamental right" recognized in *Roe* the State's "compelling interest" in protecting potential human life throughout pregnancy. . . . "

The tests that 188.029 requires the physician to perform are designed to determine viability. The State here has chosen viability as the point at which its interest in potential human life must be safeguarded. See Mo. Rev. Stat. 188.030 (1986) ("No abortion of a viable unborn child shall be performed unless necessary to preserve the life or health of the woman"). It is true that the test in question increase the expense of abortion, and regulate the discretion of the physician in determining the viability of the fetus. Since the tests will undoubtedly show in many cases that the fetus is not viable, the test will have been performed for what were in fact second-trimester abortions. But we are satisfied that the requirement of these tests permissibly furthers the State's interest in protecting potential human life, and we therefore believe 188.029 to be constitutional.

JUSTICE BLACKMUN takes us to task for our failure to join in a "great issues" debate as to whether the Constitution includes an "unenumerated" general right to privacy as recognized in cases such as *Griswold v. Connecticut,* and *Roe.* But *Griswold v. Connecticut,* unlike *Roe,* did not purport to adopt a whole framework, complete with detailed rules and distinctions, to govern the cases in which the asserted liberty interest would apply. As such, it was far different from the opinion, if not the holding, of *Roe v. Wade,* which sought to establish a constitutional framework for judging state regulation of abortion during the entire term of pregnancy. That framework sought to deal with areas of medical practice traditionally subject to state regulation, and it sought to balance once and for all by reference only to the calendar the claims of the State to protect the fetus as a form of human life against the claims of a woman to decide for herself whether or not to abort a fetus she was carrying. . . . The Missouri testing requirement here is reasonably designed to ensure that abortions are not performed where the fetus is viable—an end which all concede is legitimate—and that is sufficient to sustain its constitutionality.

JUSTICE BLACKMUN also accuses us, inter alia, of cowardice and illegitimacy in dealing with "the most politically divisive domestic legal issue of our time." There is no doubt that our holding today will allow some governmental regulation of abortion that would have been prohibited under the language of cases such as *Colautti v. Franklin,* and *Akron v. Akron Center for Reproductive Health, Inc.* But the goal of constitutional adjudication is surely not to remove inexorably "politically divisive" issues from the ambit of the legislative process, whereby the people through their elected representatives deal with matters of concern to them. The goal of constitutional adjudication is to hold true the balance between that which the Constitution puts beyond the reach of the democratic process and that which it does not. We think we have done that today. JUSTICE BLACKMUN'S suggestion, that legislative bodies, in a Nation where more than half of our population is women, will treat our decision today as an invitation to enact abortion regulation reminiscent of the Dark Ages not only misreads our views but does scant justice to those who serve in such bodies and the people who elect them. . . .

Because none of the challenged provisions of the Missouri Act properly before us conflict with the Constitution, the judgment of the Court of Appeals is

Reversed.

TEXAS V. JOHNSON

22. BURNING THE AMERICAN FLAG

Gregory Lee Johnson was convicted under a Texas statute punishing the desecrating of a venerated object when he burned an American flag at the site of the 1984 Republican National Convention while chanting "America, the red, white, and blue, we spit on you." Although the state of Texas tried to convince the Court that the law was a legitimate attempt to avoid breaches of the peace and that flag burning constituted "fighting words," which states may prohibit, the Supreme Court ruled that Johnson was engaged in "expressive

Source: U.S. Supreme Court, *Texas v. Johnson* (1989).

> *conduct," a protected form of free speech under the First Amendment. Justice William J. Brennan, in the majority opinion, said, "If there is a bedrock principle underlying the First Amendment, it is that the Government may not prohibit the expression of an idea simply because society finds the idea itself offensive or disagreeable. We have not recognized an exception to this principle even where our flag has been involved. . . . We can imagine no more appropriate response to burning a flag than waving one's own, no better way to counter a flag-burner's message than by saluting the flag that burns, no surer means of preserving the dignity of the flag that burned than by—as one witness here did—according its remains a respectful burial."*
>
> *In response to this ruling Congress enacted the Flag Protection Act of 1989, which made it a crime to desecrate the flag of the United States. The Court then held in* United States v. Eichman *(1990) that the act was an unconstitutional violation of free speech. This created an immediate and emotional debate over the desirability of a constitutional amendment to ban flag burning. With unintentional humor, President George Bush on June 12, 1990, warned that [flag burning] "endangers the fabric of our country."*

After publicly burning an American flag as a means of political protest, Gregory Lee Johnson was convicted of desecrating a flag in violation of Texas law. This case presents the question whether his conviction is consistent with the First Amendment. We hold that is it not.

While the Republican National Convention was taking place in Dallas in 1984, respondent Johnson participated in a political demonstration dubbed the "Republican War Chest Tour." As explained in literature distributed by the demonstrators and in speeches made by them, the purpose of this event was to protest the policies of the Reagan administration and of certain Dallas-based corporations. The demonstrators marched through Dallas streets, changing political slogans and stopping at several corporate locations to stage "die-ins" intended to dramatize the consequences of nuclear war. On several occasions they spray-painted the walls of buildings and overturned potted plants, but Johnson himself took no part in such activities. He did, however, accept an American flag handed to him by a fellow protestor who had taken it from a flagpole outside one of the targeted buildings.

The demonstration ended in front of Dallas City Hall, where Johnson unfurled the American flag, doused it with kerosene, and set it on fire. While the flag burned, the protestors chanted: "America, the red, white, and blue, we spit on you." After the demonstrators dispersed, a witness to the flag burning collected the flag's remains and buried them in his backyard. No one was physically injured or threatened with injury, though several witnesses testified that they had been seriously offended by the flag burning.

Of the approximately 100 demonstrators, Johnson alone was charged with a crime. The only criminal offense with which he was charged was the desecration of a venerated object in violation of Tex. Penal Code Ann. 42.09(a)(3) (1989). After a trial, he was convicted, sentenced to one year in prison, and fined $2,000. The Court of Appeals for the Fifth District of Texas at Dallas affirmed Johnson's conviction, 706 S. W. 2d 120 (1986), but the Texas Court of Criminal Appeals reversed, 755 S. W. 2d 92 (1988), holding that the State could not, consistent with the First Amendment, punish Johnson for burning the flag in these circumstances.

The Court of Criminal Appeals began by recognizing that Johnson's conduct was symbolic speech protected by the First Amendment: "Given the context of an organized demonstration, speeches, slogans, and the distribution of literature, anyone who observed appellant's act would have understood the message that appellant intended to convey. The act for which appellant was convicted was clearly 'speech' contemplated by the First Amendment." To justify Johnson's conviction for engaging in symbolic speech, the State asserted two interests: preserving the flag as a symbol of national unity and preventing breaches of the peace. The Court of Criminal Appeals held that neither interest supported his conviction. . . .

As to the State's goal of preventing breaches of the peace, the court concluded that the flag-desecration statute was not drawn narrowly enough to encompass only those flag burnings that were likely to result in a serious disturbance of the peace. And in fact, the court emphasized, the flag burning in this particular case did not threaten such a reaction. "'Serious offense' occurred," the court admitted, "but there was no breach of peace nor does the record reflect that the situation was potentially explosive. One cannot equate 'serious offense' with incitement to breach the peace." The court also stressed that another Texas statute, Tex. Penal Code Ann. 42.01 (1989), prohibited breaches of the peace. Citing *Boos v. Barry,* the court decided that 42.01 demonstrated Texas' ability to prevent disturbances of the peace without punishing this flag desecration.

Because it reversed Johnson's conviction on the ground that 42.09 was unconstitutional as applied to him, the state court did not address Johnson's argument that the statute was, on its face, unconstitutionally vague and overbroad. We granted certiorari, and now affirm.

The First Amendment literally forbids the abridgment only of "speech," but we have long recognized that its protection does not end at the spoken or written word. While we have rejected "the view that an apparently limitless variety of conduct can be labeled 'speech' whenever the person engaging in the conduct intends thereby to express an idea," we have acknowledged that conduct may be "sufficiently imbued with elements of communication to fall within the scope of the First and Fourteenth Amendments."

In deciding whether particular conduct possesses sufficient communicative elements to bring the First Amendment into play, we have asked whether "[a]n intent to convey a particularized message was present, and [whether] the likelihood was great that the message would be understood by those who viewed it." Hence, we have recognized the expressive nature of students' wearing of black armbands to protest American military involvement in Vietnam, *Tinker v. Des Moines Independent Community School Dist.,* of a sit-in by blacks in a "whites only" area to protest *Brown v. Louisiana,* of the wearing of American military uniforms in a dramatic presentation criticizing American involvement in Vietnam, and of picketing about a wide variety of causes, see, e.g., *Food Employees v. Logan Valley Plaza, Inc., United States v. Grace.*

Especially pertinent to this case are our decisions recognizing the communicative nature of conduct relating to flags. Attaching a peace sign to the flag, *Spence,* refusing to salute the flag, *Barnette,* and displaying a red flag, *Stromberg v. California,* we have held, all may find shelter under the First Amendment. . . . That we have had little difficulty identifying an expressive element in conduct relating to flags should not be surprising. The very purpose of a national flag is to serve as a symbol of our country; it is, one might say, "the one visible manifestation of two hundred years of nationhood . . . "

Pregnant with expressive content, the flag as readily signifies this Nation as does the combination of letters found in "America."

We have not automatically concluded, however, that any action taken with respect to our flag is expressive. Instead, in characterizing such action for First Amendment purposes, we have considered the context in which it occurred. In *Spence,* for example, we emphasized that Spence's taping of a peace sign to his flag was "roughly simultaneous with and concededly triggered by the Cambodian incursion and the Kent State tragedy." The State of Washington had conceded, in fact, that Spence's conduct was a form of communication, and we stated that "the State's concession is inevitable on this record."

The State of Texas conceded for purposes of its oral argument in this case that Johnson's conduct was expressive conduct, and this concession seems to us as prudent as was Washington's in Spence. Johnson burned an American flag as part—indeed, as the culmination—of a political demonstration that coincided with the convening of the Republican Party and its renomination of Ronald Reagan for President. The expressive, overtly political nature of this conduct was both intentional and overwhelmingly apparent. At his trial Johnson explained his reasons for burning the flag as follows: "The American Flag was burned as Ronald Reagan was being renominated as President. And a more powerful statement of symbolic speech, whether you agree with it or not, couldn't have been made at that time. It's quite a just position [juxtaposition]. We had new patriotism and no patriotism." In these circumstances, Johnson's burning of the flag was conduct "sufficiently imbued with elements of communication," to implicate the First Amendment. . . .

Texas claims that its interest in preventing breaches of the peace justifies Johnson's conviction for flag desecration. However, no disturbance of the peace actually occurred or threatened to occur because of Johnson's burning of the flag. Although the State stresses the disruptive behavior of the protestors during their march toward City Hall, it admits that "no actual breach of the peace occurred at the time of the flag-burning or in response to the flag-burning." The State's emphasis on the protestors' disorderly actions prior to arriving at City Hall is not only somewhat surprising given that no charges were brought on the basis of this conduct, but it also fails to show that a disturbance of the peace was a likely reaction to Johnson's conduct. The only evidence offered by the State at trial to show the reaction to Johnson's actions was the testimony of several persons who had been seriously offended by the flag-burning.

The State's position, therefore, amounts to a claim that an audience that takes serious offense at particular expression is necessarily likely to disturb the peace and that the expression may be prohibited on this basis. Our precedents do not countenance such a presumption. On the contrary, they recognize that a principal "function of free speech under our system of government is to invite dispute. It may indeed best serve its high purpose when it induces a condition of unrest, creates dissatisfaction with conditions as they are, or even stirs people to anger. . . . "

Nor does Johnson's expressive conduct fall within that small class of "fighting words" that are "likely to provoke the average person to retaliation, and thereby cause a breach of the peace." *Chaplinsky v. New Hampshire.* No reasonable onlooker would have regarded Johnson's generalized expression of dissatisfaction with the politics of the Federal Government as a direct personal insult or an invitation to exchange fisticuffs.

We thus conclude that the State's interest in maintaining order is not implicated on these facts. The State need not worry that our holding will disable it from preserving the peace. We do not suggest that the First Amendment forbids a State to prevent "imminent lawless action." And, in fact, Texas already has a statute specifically prohibiting breaches of the peace, Tex. Penal Code Ann. 42.01 (1989), which tends to confirm that Texas need not punish this flag desecration in order to keep the peace. . . .

If there is a bedrock principle underlying the First Amendment, it is that the government may not prohibit the expression of an idea simply because society finds the idea itself offensive or disagreeable. . . .

We have not recognized an exception to this principle even where our flag has been involved. In *Street v. New York,* we held that a State may not criminally punish a person for uttering words critical of the flag. . . .

In holding in *Barnette* that the Constitution did not leave this course open to the government, Justice Jackson described one of our society's defining principles in words deserving of their frequent repetition: "If there is any fixed star in our constitutional constellation, it is that no official, high or petty, can prescribe what shall be orthodox in politics, nationalism, religion, or other matters of opinion or force citizens to confess by work or act their faith therein. . . . "

We are fortified in today's conclusion by our conviction that forbidding criminal punishment for conduct such as Johnson's will not endanger the special role played by our flag or the feelings it inspires. To paraphrase Justice Holmes, we submit that nobody can suppose that this one gesture of an unknown man will change our Nation's attitude towards its flag. Indeed, Texas' argument that the burning of an American flag "is an act having a high likelihood to cause a breach of the peace," and its statute's implicit assumption that physical mistreatment of the flag will lead to "serious offense," tend to confirm that the flag's special role is not in danger; if it were, no one would riot or take offense because a flag had been burned.

We are tempted to say, in fact, that the flag's deservedly cherished place in our community will be strengthened, not weakened, by our holding today. Our decision is a reaffirmation of the principles of freedom and inclusiveness that the flag best reflects, and of the conviction that our toleration of criticism such as Johnson's is a sign and source of our strength. Indeed, one of the proudest images of our flag, the one immortalized in our own national anthem, is of the bombardment it survived at Fort McHenry. It is the Nation's resilience, not its rigidity, that Texas sees reflected in the flag—and it is that resilience that we reassert today.

The way to preserve the flag's special role is not to punish those who feel differently about these matters. It is to persuade them that they are wrong. "To courageous, self-reliant men, with confidence in the power of free and fearless reasoning applied through the processes of popular government, no danger flowing from speech can be deemed clear and present, unless the incidence of the evil apprehended is so imminent that it may befall before there is opportunity for full discussion. If there be time to expose through discussion the falsehood and fallacies, to avert the evil by the processes of education, the remedy to be applied is more speech, not enforced silence." And, precisely because it is our flag that is involved, one's response to the flag burner may exploit the uniquely persuasive power of the flag itself. We can imagine no more appropriate response to burning a flag than waving one's own, no better way to counter a flag burner's message than by saluting the flag that burns, no surer means of preserving the dignity even of the flag that burned than by—as one witness here did—according its remains a respectful burial. We do not consecrate the flag by punishing its desecration, for in doing so we dilute the freedom that this cherished emblem represents.

Johnson was convicted for engaging in expressive conduct. The State's interest in preventing breaches of the peace does not support his conviction because Johnson's conduct did not threaten to disturb the peace. Nor does the State's interest in preserving the flag as a symbol of nationhood and national unity justify his criminal conviction for engaging in political expression. The judgment of the Texas Court of Criminal Appeals is therefore

Affirmed.

Section III
Review Questions

1. *Gitlow* began the process of "incorporation." Should the entire Bill of Rights be made applicable to the states through the due process clause? Would it be better to permit states more flexibility in interpreting the concept of free speech?

2. The *Gideon* decision guaranteed the right to counsel in state criminal prosecutions. But are all lawyers equal? Do you think that poor defendants get the same type or quality of defense as wealthy defendants who hire top criminal lawyers?

3. *Miranda* required that police inform suspects in custody of their rights before interrogating them. Why would a lawyer ever permit his client to tell the police anything that might be incriminating?

4. Do you think that informing suspects of their right to "lawyer up" hinders the police? Can you think of any ways in which the police still are legally able to interrogate suspects without a lawyer being present?

5. Why should reliable evidence be excluded from a criminal trial simply because a police officer has made a mistake?

6. How does the exclusionary rule deter police misconduct? Doesn't the rule punish the public more than the police? Can you think of any other ways to control police misconduct or error that would be better than the exclusionary rule?

7. The *Sheppard* decision permits the admission of illegally obtained evidence so long as the police error was a "good faith" mistake. Is it likely that the definition of "good faith" will be expanded in subsequent court rulings? Should it be?

8. How can the "right to privacy" be called a fundamental right if it does not appear in the Bill of Rights? Would it be fair to say that if the founders had considered it to be fundamental, it would have been included?

9. How does *Roe v. Wade* conclude that state legislatures cannot prevent a woman from terminating an early pregnancy, but can prevent and regulate abortions to be performed later in the pregnancy? If the constitutional language is ambiguous—and it usually is—how should the Supreme Court decide if a statute is unconstitutional?

10. Inasmuch as the *Webster* decision holds that states may regulate abortions on viable fetuses, what will happen when medical technology makes it possible for younger and younger fetuses to survive?

11. What makes certain kinds of conduct—such as burning an American flag—"expressive conduct" deserving of protection as free speech? If most Americans want flag burning to be considered a crime, why should the Supreme Court refuse to permit it?

IV

Civil Rights

FREDERICK DOUGLASS

23. CHALLENGING THE STATUS QUO

Frederick Douglass (1817–1895), co-editor of The Liberator, *a major abolitionist publication, passionately fought against slavery and believed that electoral politics could ultimately be the tool of liberation for American blacks. His Fourth of July speech stands out among his many famous speeches as the most inspiring. In it he vividly explains the different meaning of that day to white and black Americans: "This Fourth of July is* yours, *not* mine. You *may* rejoice, *I must mourn." To the American slave, he said, this day "reveals to him, more than all other days in the year, the gross injustice and cruelty to which he is the constant victim."*

Mr. President, Friends and Fellow Citizens: . . . This, for the purpose of this celebration, is the Fourth of July. It is the birthday of your National Independence, and of your political freedom. This, to you, is what the Passover was to the emancipated people of God. It carries your minds back to the day, and to the act of your great deliverance; and to the signs, and to the wonders, associated with that act, and that day. This celebration also marks the beginning of another year of your national life; and reminds you that the Republic of America is now 76 years old. I am glad, fellow-citizens, that your nation is so young. Seventy-six years, although a good old age for a man, is but a mere speck in the life of a nation. Three score years and ten is the alloted time for individual men; but nations number their years by thousands. According to this fact, you are, even now, only in the beginning of your national career, still lingering in the period of childhood. I repeat, I am glad this is so. There is hope in the thought, and hope is much needed, under the dark clouds which lower above the horizon. The eye of the reformer is met with angry flashes, portending disastrous times; but his heart may well beat lighter at the thought that America is young, and that she is still in the impressible stage of her existence. May he not hope that high lessons of wisdom, of justice and of truth, will yet give direction to her destiny? Were the nation older, the patriot's heart might be sadder, and the reformer's brow heavier. Its future might be shrouded in gloom, and the hope of its prophets go out in sorrow. There is consolation in the thought that

Source: From Frederick Douglass, "Fourth of July Oration" (1852).

America is young—Great streams are not easily turned from channels, worn deep in the course of ages. They may sometimes rise in quiet and stately majesty, and inundate the land, refreshing and fertilizing the earth with their mysterious properties. They may also rise in wrath and fury, and bear away, on their angry waves, the accumulated wealth of years of toil and hardship. They, however, gradually flow back to the same old channel, and flow on as serenely as ever. But, while the river may not be turned aside, it may dry up, and leave nothing behind but the withered branch, and the unsightly rock, to howl in the abyss-sweeping wind, the sad tale of departed glory. As with rivers so with nations. . . .

Fellow-citizens, above your national, tumultuous joy, I hear the mournful wail of millions! whose chains, heavy and grievous yesterday, are, to-day, rendered more intolerable by the jubilee shouts that reach them. If I do forget, if I do not faithfully remember those bleeding children of sorrow this day, "may my right hand forget her cunning, and may my tongue cleave to the roof of my mouth!" To forget them, to pass lightly over their wrongs, and to chime in with the popular theme, would be treason most scandalous and shocking, and would make me a reproach before God and the world. My subject, then, fellow-citizens, is American slavery. I shall see this day and its popular characteristics from the slave's point of view. Standing there identified with the American bondman, making his wrongs mine, I do not hesitate to declare, with all my soul, that the character and conduct of this nation never looked blacker to me than on this 4th of July! Whether we turn to the declarations of the past, or to the professions of the present, the conduct of the nation seems equally hideous and revolting. America is false to the past, false to the present, and solemnly binds herself to be false to the future. Standing with God and the crushed and bleeding slave on this occasion, I will, in the name of humanity which is outraged, in the name of liberty which is fettered, in the name of the constitution and the Bible which are disregarded and trampled upon, dare to call in question and to denounce, with all the emphasis I can command, everything that serves to perpetuate slavery—the great sin and shame of America! "I will not equivocate; I will not excuse"; I will use the severest language I can command; and yet not one word shall escape me that any man, whose judgment is not blinded by prejudice, or who is not at heart a slave-holder, shall not confess to be right and just. . . .

For the present, it is enough to affirm the equal manhood of the Negro race. It is not astonishing that, while we are ploughing, planting, and reaping, using all kinds of mechanical tools, erecting houses, constructing bridges, building ships, working in metals of brass, iron, copper, silver and gold; that, while we are reading, writing and ciphering, acting as clerks, merchants and secretaries, having among us lawyers, doctors, ministers, poets, authors, editors, orators and teachers; that, while we are engaged in all manner of enterprises common to other men, digging gold in California, capturing the whale in the Pacific, feeding sheep and cattle on the hillside, living, moving, acting, thinking, planning, living in families as husbands, wives and children, and, above all, confessing and worshipping the Christian's God, and looking hopefully for life and immortality beyond the grave, we are called upon to prove that we are men!

Would you have me argue that man is entitled to liberty? that he is the rightful owner of his own body? You have already declared it. Must I argue the wrongfulness of slavery? Is that a question for Republicans? Is it to be settled by the rules of logic and argumentation, as a matter beset with great difficulty, involving a doubtful application of the principle of justice, hard to be understood? How should I look to-day, in the presence of Americans, dividing, and subdividing a discourse, to show that men have a natural right to freedom? speaking of it relatively and positively, negatively and affirmatively. To do so, would be to make myself ridiculous, and to offer an insult to your understanding.—There is not a man beneath the canopy of heaven that does not know that slavery is wrong *for him.*

What, am I to argue that it is wrong to make men brutes, to rob them of their liberty, to work them without wages, to keep them ignorant of their relations to their fellow men, to beat them with sticks, to flay their flesh with the lash, to load their limbs with irons, to hunt them with dogs, to sell them at auction, to sunder their families, to knock out their teeth, to burn their flesh, to starve them into obedience and submission to their masters? Must I argue that a system thus marked with blood, and stained with pollution is *wrong?* . . .

What, to the American slave, is your 4th of July? I answer; a day that reveals to him, more than all other days in the year, the gross injustice and cruelty to which he is the constant victim. To him, your celebration is a sham; your boasted liberty, an unholy license; your national greatness, swelling vanity; your sounds of rejoicing are empty and heartless; your denunciation of tyrants, brass fronted impudence; your shouts of liberty and equality, hollow mockery; your prayers and hymns, your sermons and thanksgivings, with all your religious parade and solemnity, are, to him, mere bombast, fraud, deception, impiety, and hypocrisy—a thin veil to cover up crimes which would disgrace a nation of savages. There is not a nation on the earth guilty of practices more shocking and bloody than are the people of the United States, at this very hour. . . .

Fellow-citizens, I will not enlarge further on your national inconsistencies. The existence of slavery in this country brands your republicanism as a sham, your humanity as a base pretense, and your Christianity as a lie. It destroys your moral power abroad: it corrupts your politicians at home. It saps the foundations of religion; it makes your name a hissing and a bye-word to a mocking earth. It is the antagonistic force in your government, the only thing that seriously disturbs and endangers your *Union.* It fetters your progress; it is the enemy of improvement; the deadly foe of education; it fosters pride; it breeds insolence; it promotes vice; it shelters crime; it is a curse to the earth that supports it; and yet you cling to it as if it were the sheet anchor of all your hopes.

Oh! be warned! be warned! a horrible reptile is coiled up in your nation's bosom; the venomous creature is nursing at the tender breast of your youthful republic; *for the love of God, tear away,* and fling from you the hideous monster, and *let the weight of twenty millions crush and destroy it forever!*

But it is answered in reply to all this, that precisely what I have now denounced is, in fact, guaranteed and sanctioned by the Constitution of the United States; that, the right to hold, and to hunt slaves is a part of that Constitution framed by the illustrious Fathers of this Republic. . . .

Now, take the Constitution according to its plain reading, and I defy the presentation of a single pro-slavery clause in it. On the other hand, it will be found to contain principles and purposes, entirely hostile to the existence of slavery.

I have detained my audience entirely too long already. At some future period I will gladly avail myself of an opportunity to give this subject a full and fair discussion.

Allow me to say, in conclusion, notwithstanding the dark picture I have this day presented, of the state of the nation, I do not despair of this country. There are forces in operation which must inevitably work the downfall of slavery. "The arm of the Lord is not shortened," and the doom of slavery is certain. I, therefore, leave off where I began, with hope. While drawing encouragement from "the Declaration of Independence," the great principles it contains, and the genius of American Institutions, my spirit is also cheered by the obvious tendencies of the age. Nations do not now stand in the same relation to each other that they did ages ago. No nation can now shut itself up from the surrounding world and trot round in the same old path of its fathers without interference. The time was when such could be done. Long established customs of hurtful character could formerly fence themselves in, and do their evil work with social impunity. Knowledge was then confined and enjoyed by the privileged few, and the multitude walked on in mental darkness. But a change has now come over the affairs of mankind. Walled cities and empires have become unfashionable. The arm of commerce has borne away the gates of the strong city. Intelligence is penetrating the darkest corners of the globe. It makes its pathway over and under the sea, as well as on earth. Wind, steam, and lightning are its chartered agents. Oceans no longer divide, but link nations together. From Boston to London is now a holiday excursion. Space is comparatively annihilated.—Thoughts expressed on one side of the Atlantic are distinctly heard on the other.

The far off and almost fabulous Pacific rolls in grandeur at our feet. The Celestial Empire, the mystery of ages, is being solved. The fiat of the Almighty, "Let there be Light," has not yet spent its force. No abuse, no outrage whether in taste, sport or avarice, can now hide itself from the all-pervading light. . . .

PLESSY V. FERGUSON

24. SEPARATE BUT EQUAL FACILITIES

This was the case in which the Supreme Court accepted racially segregated facilities so long as they were "equal." The Court did this by upholding a Louisiana law requiring that "colored" and white people travel in separate, but equal, railway cars. Although the Fourteenth Amendment required that no state deprive any person of equal protection of the laws, Court interpretations like this one continued to permit states to discriminate on the basis of race. While the Plessy *court accepted racial inequality so long as "equal" facilities were provided, in reality the courts tolerated profoundly* unequal *facilities in many contexts.*

Justice John Marshall Harlan was the lone dissenter in Plessy *and his classic ringing dissent was quoted by Thurgood Marshall in the battle to desegregate the schools in the 1950s. Harlan insisted that the U.S. Constitution was color-blind, a view that remains at the heart of the 1990s debate over affirmative action policies. As Harlan put it, "The law regards man as man, and takes no account of his surroundings or of his color when his civil rights as guaranteed by the supreme law of the land are involved."*

Justice HARLAN dissenting.

In respect of civil rights, common to all citizens, the constitution of the United States does not, I think, permit any public authority to know the race of those entitled to be protected in the enjoyment of such rights. Every true man has pride of race, and under appropriate circumstances, when the rights of others, his equals before the law, are not to be affected, it is his privilege to express such pride and to take such action based upon it as to him seems proper. But I deny that any legislative body or judicial tribunal may have regard to the race of citizens when the civil rights of those citizens are involved. Indeed, such legislation as that here in question is inconsistent not only with that equality of rights which pertains to citizenship, national and state, but with the personal liberty enjoyed by every one within the United States. . . .

Source: U.S. Supreme Court, *Plessy v. Ferguson* (1896).

It was said in argument that the statute of Louisiana does not discriminate against either race, but prescribes a rule applicable alike to white and colored citizens. But this argument does not meet the difficulty. Every one knows that the statute in question had its origin in the purpose, not so much to exclude white persons from railroad cars occupied by blacks, as to exclude colored people from coaches occupied or assigned to white persons. . . .

It is one thing for railroad carriers to furnish, or to be required by law to furnish, equal accommodations for all whom they are under a legal duty to carry. It is quite another thing for government to forbid citizens of the white and black races from traveling in the same public conveyance, and to punish officers of railroad companies for permitting persons of the two races to occupy the same passenger coach. If a state can prescribe, as a rule of civil conduct, that whites and blacks shall not travel as passengers in the same railroad coach, why may it not so regulate the use of the streets of its cities and towns as to compel white citizens to keep on one side of a street, and black citizens to keep on the other? Why may it not, upon like grounds, punish whites and blacks who ride together in street cars or in open vehicles on a public road or street? Why may it not require sheriffs to assign whites to one side of a court room, and blacks to the other? And why may it not also prohibit the commingling of the two races in the galleries of legislative halls or in public assemblages convened for the consideration of the political questions of the day? Further, if this statute of Louisiana is consistent with the personal liberty of citizens, why may not the state require the separation in railroad coaches of native and naturalized citizens of the United States, or of Protestants and Roman Catholics?

The answer given at the argument to these questions was that regulations of the kind they suggest would be unreasonable, and could not, therefore, stand before the law. Is it meant that the determination of questions of legislative power depends upon the inquiry whether the statute whose validity is questioned is, in the judgment of the courts, a reasonable one, taking all the circumstances into consideration? A statute may be unreasonable merely because a sound public policy forbade its enactment. But I do not understand that the courts have anything to do with the policy or expediency of legislation. . . .

The white race deems itself to be the dominant race in this country. And so it is, in prestige, in achievements, in education, in wealth, and in power. So, I doubt not, it will continue to be for all time, if it remains true to its great heritage, and holds fast to the principles of constitutional liberty. But in view of the constitution, in the eye of the law, there is in this country no superior, dominant, ruling class of citizens. There is no caste here. Our constitution is colorblind, and neither knows nor tolerates classes among citizens. In respect of civil fights, all citizens are equal before the law. The humblest is the peer of the most powerful. The law regards man as man, and takes no account of his surroundings or of his color when his civil rights as guarantied by the supreme law of the land are involved. It is therefore to be regretted that this high tribunal, the final expositor of the fundamental law of the land, has reached the conclusion that it is competent for a state to regulate the enjoyment by citizens of their civil rights solely upon the basis of race.

In my opinion, the judgment this day rendered will, in time, prove to be quite as pernicious as the decision made by this tribunal in the *Dred Scott Case*. . . .

The present decision, it may well be apprehended, will not only stimulate aggressions, more or less brutal and irritating, upon the admitted rights of colored citizens, but will encourage the belief that it is possible, by means of state enactments, to defeat the beneficient purposes which the people of the United States had in view when they adopted the recent amendments of the constitution, by one of which the blacks of this country were made citizens of the United States and of the states in which they respectively reside, and whose privileges and immunities, as citizens, the states are forbidden to abridge. Sixty millions of whites are in no danger from the presence here of eight millions of blacks. The destinies of the two races, in this country, are indissolubly linked together, and the interests of both require that the common government of all shall not permit the seeds of race hate to be planted under the sanction of law. What can more certainly arouse race hate, what more certainly create and perpetuate a feeling of distrust between these races, than state enactments which, in fact, proceed on the ground that colored citizens are so inferior and degraded that they cannot be allowed to sit in public coaches occupied by white citizens? That, as all will admit, is the real meaning of such legislation as was enacted in Louisiana. . . .

I am of opinion that the statute of Louisiana is inconsistent with the personal liberty of citizens, white and black, in that state, and hostile to both the spirit and letter of the constitution of the United States. If laws of like character should be enacted in the several states of the Union, the effect would be in the highest degree mischievous. Slavery, as an institution tolerated by law, would, it is true, have disappeared from our country; but there would remain a power in the states, by sinister legislation, to interfere with the full enjoyment of the blessings of freedom, to regulate civil rights, common to all citizens, upon the basis of race, and to place in a condition of legal inferiority a large body of American citizens, now constituting a part of the political community, called the "People of the United States," for whom, and by whom through representatives, our government is administered. Such a system is inconsistent with the guaranty given by the constitution to each state of a republican form of government, and may be stricken down by congressional action, or by the courts in the discharge of their solemn duty to maintain the supreme law of the land, anything in the constitution or laws of any state to the contrary notwithstanding.

For the reason stated, I am constrained to withhold my assent from the opinion.

BROWN V. BOARD OF EDUCATION

25. DESEGREGATING THE SCHOOLS

In a landmark reversal of the Plessy *case,* Brown v. Board of Education *held that the doctrine of "separate but equal" was unconstitutional. This case challenged the application of the "separate but equal" rule to public schools and the Court agreed, ruling that "separate educational facilities are inherently unequal." Relying heavily on social scientific evidence, the Court concluded that African American students suffered educational and psychological harm when forced by law to attend racially segregated schools.*

The decision in Brown *triggered social and political forces that produced major changes in the legal status of African Americans. Ironically, in the 1990s many educators have rejected as simplistic or insulting the view that African Americans cannot have success in segregated schools and some educators have even argued in favor of special schools for African American males.*

Mr. Chief Justice WARREN, delivering the opinion of the Court in the Brown case, said in part:

These cases come to us from the States of Kansas, South Carolina, Virginia, and Delaware. They are premised on different facts and different local conditions, but a common legal question justifies their consideration together in this consolidated opinion.

In each of the cases, minors of the Negro race, through their legal representatives, seek the aid of the courts in obtaining admission to the public schools of their community on a nonsegregated basis. In each instance, they had been denied admission to schools attended by white children under laws requiring or permitting segregation according to race. This segregation was alleged to deprive plaintiffs of the equal protection of the laws under the Fourteenth Amendment. . . .

The plaintiffs contend that segregated public schools are not "equal" and cannot be made "equal," and that hence they are deprived of the equal protection of the laws. Because of the obvious importance of the question presented,

---

Source: U.S. Supreme Court, *Brown v. Board of Education of Topeka* (1954).

the Court took jurisdiction. Argument was heard in the 1952 Term, and reargument was heard this Term on certain questions propounded by the Court.

Reargument was largely devoted to the circumstances surrounding the adoption of the Fourteenth Amendment in 1868. It covered exhaustively consideration of the Amendment in Congress, ratification by the states, then existing practices in racial segregation, and the views of proponents and opponents of the Amendment. This discussion and our own investigation convince us that, although these sources cast some light, it is not enough to resolve the problem with which we are faced. At best, they are inconclusive. The most avid proponents of the post-War Amendments undoubtedly intended them to remove all legal distinctions among "all persons born or naturalized in the United States." Their opponents, just as certainly, were antagonistic to both the letter and the spirit of the Amendments and wished them to have the most limited effect. What others in Congress and the state legislatures had in mind cannot be determined with any degree of certainty.

An additional reason for the inconclusive nature of the Amendment's history, with respect to segregated schools, is the status of public education at that time. In the South, the movement toward free common schools, supported by general taxation, had not yet taken hold. Education of white children was largely in the hands of private groups. Education of Negroes was almost nonexistent, and practically all of the race were illiterate. In fact, any education of Negroes was forbidden by law in some states. Today, in contrast, many Negroes have achieved outstanding success in the arts and sciences as well as in the business and professional world. It is true that public school education at the time of the Amendment had advanced further in the North, but the effect of the Amendment on Northern States was generally ignored in the congressional debates. Even in the North, the conditions of public education did not approximate those existing today. The curriculum was usually rudimentary; ungraded schools were common in rural areas; the school term was but three months a year in many states; and compulsory school attendance was virtually unknown. As a consequence, it is not surprising that there should be so little in the history of the Fourteenth Amendment relating to its intended effect on public education.

In the first cases in this Court construing the Fourteenth Amendment, decided shortly after its adoption the Court interpreted it as proscribing all state-imposed discriminations against the Negro race. The doctrine of "separate but equal" did not make its appearance in this Court until 1896 in the case of *Plessy v. Ferguson,* involving not education but transportation. American courts have since labored with the doctrine for over half a century. In this Court, there have been six cases involving the "separate but equal" doctrine in the field of public education. In *Cumming v. Board of Education of Richmond County* [1899] and *Gong Lum v. Rice* [1927] the validity of the doctrine itself was not challenged. In more recent cases, all on the graduate school level, inequality was found in that specific benefits enjoyed by white students were denied to Negro students of the same educational qualifications. *State of Missouri ex rel.*

Gaines v. Canada [1938], *Sipuel v. Board of Regents of University of Oklahoma* [1948], *Sweatt v. Painter* [1950], *McLaurin v. Oklahoma State Regents* [1950]. In none of these cases was it necessary to reexamine the doctrine to grant relief to the Negro plaintiff. And in *Sweatt v. Painter* the Court expressly reserved decision on the question whether *Plessy v. Ferguson* should be held inapplicable to public education.

In the instant cases, that question is directly presented. Here, unlike *Sweatt v. Painter,* there are findings below that the Negro and white schools involved have been equalized, or are being equalized, with respect to buildings, curricula, qualifications and salaries of teachers, and other "tangible" factors. Our decision, therefore, cannot turn on merely a comparison of these tangible factors in the Negro and white schools involved in each of the cases. We must look instead to the effect of segregation itself on public education.

In approaching this problem, we cannot turn the clock back to 1868 when the Amendment was adopted, or even to 1896 when *Plessy v. Ferguson* was written. We must consider public education in the light of its full development and its present place in American life throughout the Nation. Only in this way can it be determined if segregation in public schools deprives these plaintiffs of the equal protection of the laws.

Today, education is perhaps the most important function of state and local governments. Compulsory school attendance laws and the great expenditures for education both demonstrate our recognition of the importance of education to our democratic society. It is required in the performance of our most basic public responsibilities, even service in the armed forces. It is the very foundation of good citizenship. Today it is a principal instrument in awakening the child to cultural values, in preparing him to adjust normally to his environment. In these days, it is doubtful that any child may reasonably be expected to succeed in life if he is denied the opportunity of an education. Such an opportunity, where the state has undertaken to provide it, is a right which must be made available to all on equal terms.

We come then to the question presented: Does segregation of children in public schools, solely on the basis of race, even though the facilities and other "tangible" factors may be equal, deprive the children of the minority group of equal educational opportunities? We believe that it does.

In *Sweatt v. Painter,* in finding that a segregated law school for Negroes could not provide them equal educational opportunities, this Court relied in large part on "those qualities which are incapable of objective measurement but which make for greatness in a law school." In *McLaurin v. Oklahoma State Regents,* the Court, in requiring that a Negro admitted to a white graduate school be treated like all other students, again resorted to intangible considerations: ". . . his ability to study, to engage in discussions and exchange views with other students, and, in general, to learn his profession." Such considerations apply with added force to children in grade and high schools. To separate them from others of similar age and qualifications solely because of their race generates a feeling of inferiority as to their status in the community that may affect their hearts and minds in a way unlikely ever to be undone. The effect of this separation on their educational opportunities was well stated by a finding in the Kansas case by a court which nevertheless felt compelled to rule against the Negro plaintiffs:

"Segregation of white and colored children in public schools has a detrimental effect upon the colored children. The impact is greater when it has the sanction of the law; for the policy of separating the races is usually interpreted as denoting the inferiority of the Negro group. A sense of inferiority affects the motivation of a child to learn. Segregation with the sanction of law, therefore, has a tendency to [retard] the educational and mental development of Negro children and to deprive them of some of the benefits they would receive in a racial[ly] integrated school system." Whatever may have been the extent of psychological knowledge at the time of *Plessy v. Ferguson,* this finding is amply supported by modern authority. Any language in *Plessy v. Ferguson* contrary to this finding is rejected.

We conclude that in the field of public education the doctrine of "separate but equal" has no place. Separate educational facilities are inherently unequal. Therefore, we hold that the plaintiffs and others similarly situated for whom the actions have been brought are, by reason of the segregation complained of, deprived of the equal protection of the laws guaranteed by the Fourteenth Amendment. This disposition makes unnecessary any discussion whether such segregation also violates the Due Process Clause of the Fourteenth Amendment.

Because these are class actions, because of the wide applicability of this decision, and because of the great variety of local conditions, the formulation of decrees in these cases presents problems of considerable complexity. On reargument, the consideration of appropriate relief was necessarily subordinated to the primary question—the constitutionality of segregation in public education. We have now announced that such segregation is a denial of the equal protection of the laws. In order that we may have the full assistance of the parties in formulating decrees, the cases will be restored to the docket, and the parties are requested to present further argument on Questions 4 and 5 previously propounded by the Court for the reargument this Term. The Attorney General of the United States is again invited to participate. The Attorneys General of the states requiring or permitting segregation in public education will also be permitted to appear as amici curiae upon request to do so by September 15, 1954, and submission of briefs by October 1, 1954.

It is so ordered.

BAKER V. CARR

26. REAPPORTIONMENT AND EQUAL REPRESENTATION

This was the case in which the Supreme Court decided that the problem of inequality of representation between urban and rural legislative districts was a "justiciable" issue—that is, one that a court may properly hear. Previously, reapportionment had been held to be a "political question"—one that was beyond the authority of the Court to decide.

In Baker v. Carr, *the Court decided that the equal protection clause of the Fourteenth Amendment authorized the Court to consider claims of "malapportionment" where population shifts had produced legislative districts as much as 100 times bigger than other districts. Such differences meant that the people living in rapidly growing urban areas were significantly underrepresented in their state legislatures. The decision opened the federal courts to the problems of malapportionment and established the basis for the "one man, one vote" standard that was later applied to both congressional and state legislative election districts.*

Mr. Justice BRENNAN:

This civil action was brought to redress the alleged deprivation of federal constitutional rights. The complaint, alleging that by means of a 1901 statute of Tennessee apportioning the members of the General Assembly among the state's 95 counties, "these plaintiffs and others similarly situated, are denied the equal protection of the laws accorded them by the Fourteenth Amendment to the Constitution of the United States by virtue of the debasement of their votes," was dismissed by a three-judge court in the Middle District of Tennessee. The court held that it lacked jurisdiction of the subject matter and also that no claim was stated upon which relief could be granted. We hold that the dismissal was in error, and remand the cause to the District Court for trial and further proceedings consistent with this opinion. . . .

The Tennessee Constitution provides in Article II as follows:

> Sec. 4. *Census.*—An enumeration of the qualified voters, and an apportionment of the Representatives in the General Assembly, shall be made in the year

---

Source: U.S. Supreme Court, *Baker v. Carr* (1962).

> one thousand eight hundred and seventy-one, and within every subsequent term of ten years.
>
> Sec. 5. *Apportionment of representatives.*—The number of Representatives shall, at the several periods of making the enumeration, be apportioned among the several counties or districts, according to the number of qualified voters in each. . . .
>
> Sec. 6. *Apportionment of senators.*—The number of Senators shall, at the several periods of making the enumeration, be apportioned among the several counties or districts according to the number of qualified electors in each, and shall not exceed one-third in the number of representatives. . . .

Thus, Tennessee's standard for allocating legislative representation among her counties is the total number of qualified voters resident in the respective counties, subject only to minor qualifications. Decennial reapportionment in compliance with the constitutional scheme was effected by the General Assembly each decade from 1871 to 1901. . . .

In the more than 60 years since that action, all proposals in both Houses of the General Assembly for reapportionment have failed to pass.

Between 1901 and 1961, Tennessee has experienced substantial growth and redistribution of her population. In 1901, the population was 2,020, 616, of whom 487,380 were eligible to vote. The 1960 federal census reports the State's population at 3,567,089, of whom 2,092,891 are eligible to vote. The relative standings of the counties in terms of qualified voters have changed significantly. It is primarily the continued application of the 1901 Apportionment Act to this shifted and enlarged voting population which gives rise to the present controversy.

Indeed, the complaint alleges that the 1901 statute, even as of the time of its passage, "made no apportionment of Representatives and Senators in accordance with the constitutional formula . . . , but instead arbitrarily and capriciously apportioned representatives in the Senate and House without re- ference . . . to any logical or reasonable formula whatever." It is further alleged that "because of the population changes since 1900, and the failure of the legislature to reapportion itself since 1901," the 1901 statute became "unconstitutional and obsolete." Appellants also argue that, because of the composition of the legislature effected by the 1901 apportionment act, redress in the form of a state constitutional amendment to change the entire mechanism for reapportioning, or any other change short of that, is difficult or impossible. The complaint concludes that "these plaintiffs and others similarly situated, are denied the equal protection of the laws accorded them by the Fourteenth Amendment to the Constitution of the United States by virtue of the debasement of their votes." They seek a declaration that the 1901 statute is unconstitutional and an injunction restraining the appellees from acting to conduct any further elections under it. They also pray that unless and until the General Assembly enacts a valid reapportionment, the District Court should either decree a reapportionment by mathematical application of the Tennessee constitutional formulae to the most recent federal census figures, or direct the appellees to conduct legislative elections, primary and general, at large. They also pray for such other and further relief as may be appropriate. . . .

In light of the District Court's treatment of the case, we hold today only (a) that the court possessed jurisdiction of the subject matter; (b) that a justiciable cause of action is stated upon which appellants would be entitled to appropriate relief; and (c) because appellees raise the issue before this Court, that the appellants have standing to challenge the Tennessee apportionment statutes. Beyond noting that we have no cause at this stage to doubt the District Court will be able to fashion relief if violations of constitutional rights are found, it is improper now to consider what remedy would be most appropriate if appellants prevail at the trial. . . .

We hold that the appellants do have standing to maintain this suit. Our decisions plainly support this conclusion. Many of the cases have assumed rather than articulated the premise in deciding the merits of similar claims. And *Colegrove v. Green* squarely held that voters who allege facts showing disadvantage to themselves as individuals have standing to sue. A number of cases decided after *Colegrove* recognized the standing of the voters there involved to bring those actions. . . .

In . . . *Colegrove v. Green,* the court stated: "From a review of these decisions there can be no doubt that the federal rule . . . is that the federal courts . . . will not intervene in cases of this type to compel legislative reapportionment." 179 F. Supp. at 826. We understand the District Court to have read the cited cases as compelling the conclusion that since the appellants sought to have a legislative apportionment held unconstitutional, their suit presented a "political question" and was therefore nonjusticiable. We hold that this challenge to an apportionment presents no nonjusticiable "political question." The cited cases do not hold the contrary.

Of course the mere fact that the suit seeks protection of a political right does not mean it presents a political question. . . .

But it is argued that this case shares the characteristics of decisions that constitute a category not yet considered, cases concerning the Constitution's guaranty, in Art. IV, Sect. 4, of a republican form of government. A conclusion as to whether the case at bar does present a political question cannot be confidently reached until we have considered those cases with special care. We shall discover that Guaranty Clause claims involve elements which define a "political question," and for that reason and no other, they are nonjusticiable. In particular, we shall discover that the nonjusticiability of such claims has nothing to do with their touching upon matters of state governmental organization. . . .

We come, finally, to the ultimate inquiry whether our precedents as to what constitutes a nonjusticiable "political question" bring the case before us under the umbrella of that doctrine. A natural beginning is to note whether any of the common characteristics which we have been able to identify and label descriptively are present. We find none: The question here is the consistency of state action with the federal Constitution. We have no question decided, or to be decided, by a political branch of government coequal with this Court. Nor do we risk embarrassment of our government abroad, or grave disturbance at home if we take issue with Tennessee as to the constitutionality of her action here challenged. Nor need the appellants, in order to succeed in this action, ask the Court to enter upon policy determinations for which judicially manageable standards are lacking. Judicial standards under the Equal Protection Clause are well developed and familiar, and it has been open to courts since the enactment of the Fourteenth Amendment to determine, if on the particular facts they must, that a discrimination reflects *no* policy, but simply arbitrary and capricious action.

This case does, in one sense, involve the allocation of political power within a state, and the appellants might conceivably have added a claim under the Guaranty Clause. Of course, as we have seen, any reliance on that clause would be futile. Both because any reliance on the Guaranty Clause could not have succeeded it does not follow that appellants may not be heard on the Equal Protection claim which in fact they tender. True, it must be clear that the Fourteenth Amendment claim is not so enmeshed with those political question elements which render Guaranty Clause claims nonjusticiable as actually to present a political question itself. But we have found that not to be the case here. . . .

We conclude that the complaint's allegations of a denial of equal protection present a justiciable constitutional cause of action upon which appellants are entitled to a trial and a decision. The right asserted is within the reach of judicial protection under the Fourteenth Amendment.

The judgment of the District Court is reversed. . . .

Justices Douglas, Clark, and Stewart, filed concurring opinions. Frankfurter and Harlan dissented.

Section IV
Review Questions

1. Why did Frederick Douglass urge his audience in 1852 to understand that the Fourth of July is a day of mourning, not celebration, for African Americans? How do you think this holiday is viewed by contemporary African Americans?

2. What is the essence of Justice Harlan's objection to the "separate but equal" standard upheld by the Supreme Court in *Plessy v. Ferguson?*

3. The ruling in *Brown v. Board of Education* applied only to schools that were segregated by law (de jure segregation). Do you think that children in schools that are segregated by housing patterns (de facto segregation) suffer the same consequences as those the Court was concerned about in *Brown?* Do children even know the difference?

4. How much progress do you think has been made since the National Advisory Commission on Civil Disorders concluded that the United States was moving toward two societies: one black, one white—separate and unequal?

5. Why does the Court in *Baker v. Carr* believe that legislative districts with substantially different populations violate the Fourteenth Amendment?

V

Public Opinion

WALTER LIPPMANN

27. THE PSEUDO-ENVIRONMENT OF PUBLIC OPINION

Public opinion plays a special role in the politics of democratic governments because the starting point for all forms of democracy is that the decisions of elected political leaders should reflect the "will of the people." This apparently simple idea, however, turns out to be extremely complicated. How, for example, should U.S. leaders discover what the "people" want them to do on particular issues? Walter Lippmann (1889–1974), a journalist and political philosopher, often wrestled with the nature of public opinion and its influence on the relationship between leaders and followers in the United States.

Lippmann feared that the American public's superficial and easily manipulated opinions about important questions of public policy would ultimately undermine the democratic system. For Lippmann, the proper role of American political leaders is not to follow blindly the whims of the public, but rather to educate and lead the public.

In this excerpt from Public Opinion, *Lippmann explains why public opinion cannot be trusted. He argues that "men respond as powerfully to fictions as they do to realities." We rely too much on "pseudo-environments," mental pictures that rarely correspond to the "real" environments in which we live.*

There is an island in the ocean where in 1914 a few Englishmen, Frenchmen, and Germans lived. No cable reaches that island, and the British mail steamer comes but once in sixty days. In September it had not yet come, and the islanders were still talking about the latest newspaper which told about the approaching trial of Madame Caillaux for the shooting of Gaston Calmette. It was, therefore, with more than usual eagerness that the whole colony assembled at the quay on a day in mid-September to hear from the captain what the

---

Source: Reprinted with the permission of Scribner, an imprint of Simon & Schuster Adult Publishing Group, from *Public Opinion* by Walter Lippmann. Copyright © 1922 Walter Lippmann; copyright renewed © 1950 by Walter Lippmann.

verdict had been. They learned that for over six weeks now those of them who were English and those of them who were French had been fighting in behalf of the sanctity of treaties against those of them who were Germans. For six strange weeks, they had acted as if they were friends, when in fact they were enemies.

But their plight was not so different from that of most of the population of Europe. They had been mistaken for six weeks, on the continent the interval may have been only six days or six hours. There was an interval. There was a moment when the picture of Europe on which men were conducting their business as usual, did not in any way correspond to the Europe which was about to make a jumble of their lives. There was a time for each man when he was still adjusted to an environment that no longer existed. All over the world as late as July 25th men were making goods that they would not be able to ship, buying goods they would not be able to import, careers were being planned, enterprises contemplated, hopes and expectations entertained, all in the belief that the world as known was the world as it was. Men were writing books describing that world. They trusted the picture in their heads. And then over four years later, on a Thursday morning, came the news of an armistice, and people gave vent to their unutterable relief that the slaughter was over. Yet in the five days before the real armistice came, though the end of the war had been celebrated, several thousand young men died on the battlefields.

Looking back we can see how indirectly we know the environment in which nevertheless we live. We can see that the news of it comes to us now fast, now slowly; but that whatever we believe to be a true picture, we treat as if it were the environment itself. It is harder to remember that about the beliefs upon which we are now acting, but in respect to other peoples and other ages we flatter ourselves that it is easy to see when they were in deadly earnest about ludicrous pictures of the world. We insist, because of our superior hindsight, that the world as they needed to know it, and the world as they did know it, were often two quite contradictory things. We can see, too, that while they governed and fought, traded and reformed in the world as they imagined it to be, they produced results, or failed to produce any, in the world as it was. They started for the Indies and found America. They diagnosed evil and hanged old women. They thought they could grow rich by always selling and never buying. A caliph, obeying what he conceived to be the Will of Allah, burned the library at Alexandria. . . .

The only feeling that anyone can have about an event he does not experience is the feeling aroused by his mental image of that event. That is why until we know what others think they know, we cannot truly understand their acts. . . .

It is the insertion between man and his environment of the pseudo-environment. To that pseudo-environment his behavior is a response. But because it *is* behavior, the consequences, if they are acts, operate not in the pseudo-environment where the behavior is stimulated, but in the real environment where action eventuates. If the behavior is not a practical act, but what we call roughly thought and emotion, it may be a long time before there is any noticeable break in the texture of the fictitious world. But when the stimulus of the pseudo-fact results in action on things or other people, contradiction soon develops. Then comes the sensation of butting one's head against a stone wall, of learning by experience, and witnessing Herbert Spencer's tragedy of the murder of a Beautiful Theory by a Gang of Brutal Facts, the discomfort in short of a maladjustment. For certainly, at the level of social life, what is called the adjustment of man to his environment takes place through the medium of fictions.

By fictions I do not mean lies. I mean a representation of the environment which is in lesser or greater degree made by man himself. The range of fiction extends all the way from complete hallucination to the scientists' perfectly self-conscious use of a schematic model, or his decision that for his particular problem accuracy beyond a certain number of decimal places is not important. A work of fiction may have almost any degree of fidelity, and so long as the degree of fidelity can be taken into account, fiction is not misleading. In fact, human culture is very largely the selection, the rearrangement, the tracing of patterns upon, and the stylizing of, what William James called "the random irradiations and resettlements of our ideas."[1] The alternative to the use of fictions is direct exposure to the ebb and flow of sensation. That is not a real alternative, for however refreshing it is to see at times with a perfectly innocent eye, innocence itself is not wisdom, though a source and corrective of wisdom.

For the real environment is altogether too big, too complex, and too fleeting for direct acquaintance. We are not equipped to deal with so much subtlety, so much variety, so many permutations and combinations. And although we have to act in that environment, we have to reconstruct it on a simpler model before we can manage with it. To traverse the world men must have maps of the world. Their persistent difficulty is to secure maps on which their own need, or someone else's need, has not sketched in the coast of Bohemia. . . .

I should like to think only about the world-wide spectacle of men acting upon their environment, moved by stimuli from their pseudo-environments. For when full allowance has been made for deliberate fraud, political science has still to account for such facts as two nations attacking one another, each convinced that it is acting in self-defense, or two classes at war each certain that it speaks for the common interest. They live, we are likely to say, in different worlds. More accurately, they live in the same world, but they think and feel in different ones.

It is to these special worlds, it is to these private or group, or class, or provincial, or occupational, or national, or sectarian artifacts, that the political adjustment of mankind in the Great Society takes place. Their variety and complication are impossible to describe. Yet these fictions determine a very great part of men's political behavior. We must think of perhaps fifty sovereign parliaments consisting of at least a hundred legislative bodies. With them belong at least fifty hierarchies of provincial and municipal assemblies, which with their executive, administrative and legislative organs, constitute formal authority on earth. But that does not begin to reveal the complexity of political life. For in each of these innumerable centers of authority there are parties, and these parties are themselves hierarchies with their roots in classes, sections, cliques and clans; and within these are the individual politicians, each the personal center of a web of connection and memory and fear and hope.

Somehow or other, for reasons often necessarily obscure, as the result of domination or compromise or a logroll, there emerge from these political bodies commands, which set armies in motion or make peace, conscript life, tax, exile, imprison, protect property or confiscate it, encourage one kind of enterprise and discourage another, facilitate immigration or obstruct it, improve communication or censor it, establish schools, build navies, proclaim "policies," and "destiny," raise economic barriers, make property or unmake it, bring one people under the rule of another, or favor one class as against another. For each of these decisions some view of the facts is taken to be conclusive, some view of the circumstances is accepted as the basis of inference and as the stimulus of feeling. What view of the facts, and why that one?

And yet even this does not begin to exhaust the real complexity. The formal political structure exists in a social environment, where there are innumerable large and small corporations and institutions, voluntary and semi-voluntary associations, national, provincial, urban and neighborhood groupings, which often as not make the decision that the political body registers. On what are these decisions based? . . .

This, then, will be the clue to our inquiry. We shall assume that what each man does is based not on direct and certain knowledge, but on pictures made by himself or given to him. If his atlas tells him that the world is flat he will not sail near what he believes to be the edge of our planet for fear of falling off. If his maps include a fountain of eternal youth, a Ponce de Leon will go in quest of it. If someone digs up yellow dirt that looks like gold, he will for a time act exactly as if he had found gold. The way in which the world is imagined determines at any particular moment what men will do. It does not determine what they will achieve. It determines their effort, their feelings, their hopes, not their accomplishments and results.

NOTE

1. James, *Principles of Psychology,* Vol. II, p. 638.

GEORGE GALLUP

28. POLLING THE PUBLIC

Even if one believes that political leaders ought to follow public opinion, the problem of measuring public opinion poses a major obstacle. George Gallup (1901–1984) is the best known of American pollsters. His Gallup Poll has become synonymous with the measurement of public opinion.

Gallup was one of the first to use systematic scientific methods to measure public opinion. Following up on the use of probability sampling used in early efforts at market research, Gallup developed sophisticated techniques for discovering what the public thought. Since the 1930s, the Gallup Poll has regularly asked Americans their opinions on all types of subjects, from their preferences on political parties to their views about topless bathing suits. The information collected by Gallup and his associates provides an interesting basis for comparisons of American public opinion through most of the twentieth century.

George Gallup defended his new techniques of measuring public opinion as a great contribution to democratic life. Contrary to Walter Lippmann who feared procedures that might magnify the influence of public opinion, Gallup expressed great faith in the masses and argued for finding out as much as possible about their views. He wrote before World War II, "The American people have a remarkably high degree of common sense. These people may not be brilliant or intellectual or particularly well read, but they possess a quality of good sense which is manifested time and again in their expressions of opinion on present-day issues."

We have a national election every two years only. In a world which moves as rapidly as the modern world does, it is often desirable to know the people's will on basic policies at more frequent intervals. We cannot put issues off and

---

Source: From George Gallup, "Polling the Public" from *Public Opinion in a Democracy.* Copyright © 1944, 1948 by George Gallup, renewed 1976 by Princeton University Press. Reprinted by permission of Princeton University Press.

say "let them be decided at the next election." World events do not wait on elections. We need to know the will of the people at all times.

If we know the collective will of the people at all times the efficiency of democracy can be increased, because we can substitute specific knowledge of public opinion for blind groping and guesswork. Statesmen who know the true state of public opinion can then formulate plans with a sure knowledge of what the voting public is thinking. They can know what degree of opposition to any proposed plan exists, and what efforts are necessary to gain public acceptance for it. The responsibility for initiating action should, as always, rest with the political leaders of the country. But the collective will or attitude of the people needs to be learned without delay.

THE WILL OF THE PEOPLE

How is the will of the people to be known at all times?

Before I offer an answer to this question, I would like to examine some of the principal channels by which, at the present time, public opinion is expressed.

The most important is of course a national election. An election is the only official and binding expression of the people's judgment. But, as viewed from a strictly objective point of view, elections are a confusing and imperfect way of registering national opinion. In the first place, they come only at infrequent intervals. In the second place, as Bryce pointed out in *The American Commonwealth,* it is virtually impossible to separate issues from candidates. How can we tell whether the public is voting for the man or for his platform? How can we tell whether all the candidate's views are endorsed, or whether some are favored and others opposed by the voters? Because society grows more and more complex, the tendency is to have more and more issues in an election. Some may be discussed; others not. Suppose a candidate for office takes a position on a great many public issues during the campaign. If elected, he inevitably assumes that the public has endorsed all his planks, whereas this may actually not be the case. . . .

THE ROLE OF THE ELECTED REPRESENTATIVE

A second method by which public opinion now expresses itself is through elected representatives. The legislator is, technically speaking, supposed to represent the interests of all voters in his constituency. But under the two-party system there is a strong temptation for him to represent, and be influenced by, only the voters of his own party. He is subject to the pressure of party discipline and of wishes of party leaders back home. His very continuance in office may depend on giving way to such pressure. Under these circumstances his behavior in Congress is likely to be governed not by what he thinks the voters of his State want, but by what he thinks the leaders of his own party in that State want. . . .

Even in the event that an elected representative does try to perform his duty of representing the whole people, he is confronted with the problem: What is the will of the people? Shall he judge their views by the letters they write him or the telegrams they send him? Too often such expressions of opinion come only from an articulate minority. Shall the congressman judge their views by the visitors or delegations that come to him from his home district?

PRESSURE GROUPS AND THE WHOLE NATION

Legislators are constantly subject to the influence of organized lobbies and pressure groups. Senator Tydings, in a lecture here in Princeton, pointed out recently that the United States is the most fertile soil on earth for the activity of pressure groups. The American people represent a conglomeration of races, all with different cultural backgrounds. Sections and groups struggle with one another to fix national and international policy. And frequently in such struggles, as Senator Tydings pointed out, "self-interest and sectionalism, rather than the promotion of national welfare, dominate the contest." Senator Tydings mentions some twenty important group interests. These include labor, agriculture, veterans, pension plan advocates, chambers of commerce, racial organizations, isolationists and internationalists, high-tariff and low-tariff groups, preparedness and disarmament groups, budget balancers and spending advocates, soft-money associations and hard-money associations, transportation groups and states fighters and centralizationists.

The legislator obviously owes a duty to his home district to legislate in its best interests. But he also owes a duty to legislate in the best interests of the whole nation. In order, however, to carry out this second duty he must *know* what the nation thinks. Since he doesn't always know what the voters in his own district think, it is just that much more difficult for him to learn the views of the nation. Yet if he could know those views at all times he could legislate more often in the interest of the whole country. . . .

THE CROSS-SECTION SURVEY

This effort to discover public opinion has been largely responsible for the introduction of a new instrument for determining public opinion—the cross-section or sampling survey. By means of nationwide studies taken at frequent intervals, research workers are today attempting to measure and give voice to the sentiments of the whole people on vital issues of the day.

Where does this new technique fit into the scheme of things under our form of government? Is it a useful instrument of democracy? Will it prove to be vicious and harmful, or will it contribute to the efficiency of the democratic process?

The sampling referendum is simply a procedure for sounding the opinions of a relatively small number of persons, selected in such manner as to reflect with a high degree of accuracy the views of the whole voting population. In effect such surveys canvass the opinions of a miniature electorate.

Cross-section surveys do not place their chief reliance upon numbers. The technique is based on the fact that a few thousand voters correctly selected will faithfully reflect the views of an electorate of millions of voters. The key to success in this work is the cross section—the proper selection of voters included in the sample. Elaborate precautions must be taken to secure the views of members of all political parties—of rich and poor, old and young, of men and women, farmers and city dwellers, persons of all religious faiths—in short, voters of all types living in every State in the land. And all must be included in correct proportion. . . .

RELIABILITY OF OPINION SURVEYS

Whether opinion surveys will prove to be a useful contribution to democracy depends largely on their reliability in measuring opinion. During the last four years the sampling procedure, as used in measuring public opinion, has been subjected to many tests. In general these tests indicate that present techniques can attain a high degree of accuracy, and it seems reasonable to assume that with the development of this infant science, the accuracy of its measurements will be constantly improved.

The most practical way at present to measure the accuracy of the sampling referendum is to compare forecasts of elections with election results. Such a test is by no means perfect, because a preelection survey must not only measure opinion in respect to candidates but must also predict just what groups of people will actually take the trouble to cast their ballots. Add to this the problem of measuring the effect of weather on turnout, also the activities of corrupt political machines, and it can easily be seen that election results are by no means a perfect test of the accuracy of this new technique. . . .

Many thoughtful students of government have asked: Why shouldn't the Government itself, rather than private organizations, conduct these sampling surveys? A few political scientists have even suggested the establishment of a permanent federal bureau for sounding public opinion, arguing that if this new technique is a contribution to democracy, the government has a duty to take it over.

The danger in this proposal, as I see it, lies in the temptation it would place in the way of the party in power to conduct surveys to prove itself right and to suppress those which proved it to be wrong. A private organization, on the other hand, must stand or fall not so much on what it reports or fails to report as on the accuracy of its results, and the impartiality of its interpretations. An important requirement in a democracy is complete and reliable news reports of the activities of all branches of the government and of the views of all leaders and parties. But few persons would argue that, for this reason, the government should take over the press, and all its news gathering associations. . . .

CLOTURE ON DEBATE?

It is sometimes argued that public opinion surveys impose a cloture on debate. When the advocates of one side of an issue are shown to be in the majority, so the argument runs, the other side will lose hope and abandon their cause believing that further efforts are futile.

Again let me say that there is little evidence to support this view. Every election necessarily produces a minority. In 1936 the Republicans polled less than 40 percent of the vote. Yet the fact that the Republicans were defeated badly wasn't enough to lead them to quit the battle. They continued to fight against the New Deal with as much vigor as before. An even better example is afforded by the Socialist Party. For years the Socialist candidate for President has received but a small fraction of the total popular vote, and could count on sure defeat. Yet the Socialist Party continues as a party, and continues to poll about the same number of votes.

Sampling surveys will never impose a cloture on debate so long as it is the nature of public opinion to change. The will of the people is dynamic; opinions are constantly changing. A year ago an overwhelming majority of voters were skeptical of the prospects of the Republican Party in 1940. Today, half the voters think the G.O.P. will win. If elections themselves do not impose cloture on debate, is it likely that opinion surveys will?

POSSIBLE EFFECT ON REPRESENTATIVE GOVERNMENT

The form of government we live under is a representative form of government. What will be the effect on representative government if the will of the people is known at all times? Will legislators become mere rubber stamps, mere puppets, and the function of representation be lost?

Under a system of frequent opinion measurement, the function of representation is not lost, for two reasons. First, it is well understood that the people have not the time or the inclination to pass on all the problems that confront their leaders. They cannot be expected to express judgment on technical questions of administration and government. They can pass judgment only on basic general policies. As society grows more complex there is a greater and greater need for experts. Once the voters have indicated their approval of a general policy or plan of action, experts are required to carry it out.

Second, it is not the province of the people to initiate legislation, but to decide which of the programs offered they like best. National policies do not spring full-blown from the common people. Leaders, knowing the general will of the people, must take the initiative in forming policies that will carry out the general will and must put them into effect.

Before the advent of the sampling referendum, legislators were not isolated from their constituencies. They read the local newspapers; they toured their districts and talked with voters; they received letters from their home State; they entertained delegations who claimed to speak for large and important blocs of voters. The change that is brought about by sampling referenda is merely one which provides these legislators with a truer measure of opinion in their districts and in the nation. . . .

HOW WISE ARE THE COMMON PEOPLE?

The sampling surveys of recent years have provided much evidence concerning the wisdom of the common people. Anyone is free to examine this evidence. And I think that the person who does examine it will come away believing as I do that, collectively, the American people have a remarkably high degree of common sense. These people may not be brilliant or intellectual or particularly well read, but they possess a quality of good sense which is manifested time and again in their expressions of opinion on present-day issues. . . .

It is not difficult to understand why the conception of the stupidity of the masses has so many adherents. Talk to the first hundred persons whom you happen to meet in the street about many important issues of the day, and the chances are great that you will be struck by their lack of accurate or complete knowledge on these issues. Few of them will likely have sufficient information in this particular field to express a well founded judgment.

But fortunately a democracy does not require that every voter be well informed on every issue. In fact a democracy does not depend so much on the enlightenment of each individual, as upon the quality of the collective judgment or intelligence of thousands of individuals. . . .

It would of course be foolish to argue that the collective views of the common people always represent the most intelligent and most accurate answer to any question. But results of sampling referenda on hundreds of issues do indicate, in my opinion, that we can place great faith in the collective judgment or intelligence of the people.

THE NEW ENGLAND TOWN MEETING RESTORED

One of the earliest and purest forms of democracy in this country was the New England town meeting. The people gathered in one room to discuss and to vote on the questions of the community. There was a free exchange of opinions in the presence of all the members. The town meeting was a simple and effective way of articulating public opinion, and the decisions made by the meeting kept close to the public will. When a democracy thus operates on a small scale it is able to express itself swiftly and with certainty.

But as communities grew, the town meeting became unwieldy. As a result the common people became less articulate, less able to debate the vital issues in the manner of their New England forefathers. Interest in politics lagged. Opinion had to express itself by the slow and cumbersome method of election, no longer facilitated by the town meeting with its frequent give and take of ideas. The indifference and apathy of voters made it possible for vicious and corrupt political machines to take over the administration of government in many states and cities.

The New England town meeting was valuable because it provided a forum for the exchange of views among all citizens of the community and for a vote on these views. Today, the New England town meeting idea has, in a sense, been restored. The wide distribution of daily newspapers reporting the views of statesmen on issues of the day, the almost universal ownership of radios which bring the whole nation within the hearing of any voice, and now the advent of the sampling referendum which provides a means of determining quickly the response of the public to debate on issues of the day, have in effect created a town meeting on a national scale.

How nearly the goal has been achieved is indicated in the following data recently gathered by the American Institute of Public Opinion. Of the 45,000,000 persons who voted in the last presidential election, approximately 40,000,000 read a daily newspaper, 40,000,000 have radios, and only 2,250,000 of the entire group of voters in the nation neither have a radio nor take a daily newspaper.

This means that the nation is literally in one great room. The newspapers and the radio conduct the debate on national issues, presenting both information and argument on both sides, just as the townsfolk did in person in the old town meeting. And finally, through the process of the sampling referendum, the people, having heard the debate on both sides of every issue, can express their will. After one hundred and fifty years we return to the town meeting. This time the whole nation is within the doors.

JAMES W. PROTHRO AND
CHARLES M. GRIGG

29. WHAT DO AMERICANS REALLY BELIEVE?

The political beliefs of Americans include a widely shared commitment to abstract statements of basic democratic principles, but far less agreement on these same principles when applied to fellow citizens whose views or lifestyles are offensive or threatening. In this classic study of American public opinion, Prothro and Grigg discovered, for example, that nearly 95 percent of all Americans agreed with the statement "The minority should be free to criticize the majority." However, when asked to apply the same principle to the statement "If a person wanted to make a speech in this city against churches and religion, he should be allowed to speak," the degree of agreement dropped dramatically.

The bitter debate in 1990 about the right of political protesters to desecrate the United States flag as an expression of their opposition to government policy is a good recent example of this same phenomenon—the difference between beliefs in freedom in the abstract and beliefs in freedom when distasteful concrete situations arise.

The idea that consensus on fundamental principles is essential to democracy is a recurrent proposition in political theory. Perhaps because of its general acceptance, the proposition has never been formulated in very precise terms. When authoritative sources state, for example, that "a successful democracy requires the existence of a large measure of consensus in society," exactly what is meant? We assume that the term "successful democracy," although far from precise, carries a widely shared meaning among political scientists. But we are not told in this typical assertion on what *issues* or *problems* consensus must exist. Presumably they are the basic issues about how political power should be won. Nor are we told what degree of agreement democracy requires.

Source: From "Fundamental Principles of Democracy: Bases of Agreement and Disagreement," by James W. Prothro and Charles M. Grigg in *Journal of Politics*, Vol. 22 (1960). Reprinted by permission of Blackwell Publishing.

Since the word "consensus" is used to refer to "general agreement or concord," however, a "large measure of consensus" presumably falls somewhere close to 100 per cent. For the purpose of examining the proposition as it is generally formulated, then, we interpret it as asserting: a necessary condition for the existence of a democratic government is widespread agreement (approaching 100 per cent) among the adult members of society on at least the basic questions about how political power is won. Specifically, we propose to submit this proposition to empirical examination in an effort to give it more precise meaning and to discover bases of agreement and/or disagreement on fundamental principles. . . .

The discovery that consensus on democratic principles is restricted to a few general and vague formulations might come as a surprise to a person whose only acquaintance with democracy was through the literature of political theory; it will hardly surprise those who have lived in a democracy. Every village cynic knows that the local church-goer who sings the creed with greatest fervor often abandons the same ideas when they are put in less lyrical form. Political scientists are certainly not so naive as to expect much greater consistency in the secular sphere. The theorists who argue the necessity of consensus on such matters as the existence or absence of multi-faceted truth, true equality in the right of free speech, and dedication to an equal vote for every citizen are no doubt as aware of these human frailties as the village cynic. But we tend to regard that which seems a *logically necessary* belief in the light of democratic processes as being *empirically necessary* to the existence of those processes. We assume, in a two-step translation, that what people *should* (logically) believe is what they *must* believe (this being a democracy), and that what they *must* believe is what they *do* believe.

In undertaking to discover what kind of consensus actually exists, we assumed that we would find the anticipated agreement on the basic principles of democracy when they were put in a highly abstract form, but that consensus would not be found on more concrete questions involving the application of these principles. We further assumed that regional and class-related variations would be found on the specific formulation of democratic principles. In pinning down these assumptions, we are no doubt demonstrating the obvious—but such a demonstration appears necessary if the obvious is to be incorporated into the logic of political theory. With empirical support for these two assumptions, we can put the proposition about consensus in more precise form and test the following hypothesis: *consensus in a meaningful sense (at both the abstract and specific levels) exists among some segment(s) of the population (which can be called the "carriers of the creed").* Should our findings support this hypothesis, we could reformulate the proposition about democratic consensus with reference to a smaller group than the total population, whereupon it could be tested more fully, both in the United States and in other democracies, for further refinement.

PROCEDURE

Our research design was based upon the major assumption that the United States is a democracy. Taking this point for granted, we prepared an interviewing schedule around the presumably basic principles of democracy and interviewed samples of voters in two American cities to elicit their attitudes toward these principles.

While the general research design was thus quite simple, the preparation of a questionnaire including the basic points on which agreement is thought to be necessary was a difficult and critical step. From the literature on consensus cited above and from general literature on democracy, however, we conclude that the principles regarded as most essential to democracy are majority rule and minority rights (or freedom to dissent). At the abstract level, then, our interviewers asked for expressions of agreement or disagreement on the following statements:

Principle of Democracy Itself
Democracy is the best form of government.

Principle of Majority Rule
Public officials should be chosen by majority vote.
Every citizen should have an equal chance to influence government policy.

Principle of Minority Rights
The minority should be free to criticize majority decisions.
People in the minority should be free to try to win majority support for their opinions.

From these general statements, specific embodiments of the principles of democracy were derived.

Principle of Majority Rule in Specific Terms

1. In a city referendum, only people who are well informed about the problem being voted on should be allowed to vote.
2. In a city referendum deciding on tax-supported undertakings, only taxpayers should be allowed to vote.
3. If a Negro were legally elected mayor of this city, the white people should not allow him to take office.
4. If a Communist were legally elected mayor of this city, the people should not allow him to take office.
5. A professional organization like the AMA (the American Medical Association) has a right to try to increase the influence of doctors by getting them to vote as a bloc in elections.

PRINCIPLE OF MINORITY RULE IN SPECIFIC TERMS

6. If a person wanted to make a speech in this city against churches and religion, he should be allowed to speak.
7. If a person wanted to make a speech in this city favoring government ownership of all the railroads and big industries, he should be allowed to speak.
8. If an admitted Communist wanted to make a speech in this city favoring Communism, he should be allowed to speak.
9. A Negro should not be allowed to run for mayor of this city.
10. A Communist should not be allowed to run for mayor of this city.

These specific propositions are designed to embody the principles of majority rule and minority rights in such a clear fashion that a "correct" or "democratic" response can be deduced from endorsement of the general principles. The democratic responses to statements 1 and 2 are negative, for example, since a restriction of the franchise to the well-informed or to tax-payers would violate the principle that "Every citizen should have an equal chance to influence government policy." The same general principle requires an affirmative answer to the fifth statement, which applies the right of people to "influence government policy" to the election efforts of a specific professional group. The correct responses to statements 3 and 4 are negative because denial of an office to any person "legally elected" would violate the principle that "public officials should be chosen by majority vote."

Of the five statements derived from the broad principle of minority rights, 6, 7, and 8 put the right of "the minority . . . to criticize majority decisions" and "to try to win majority support for their opinions" in terms of specific minority spokesmen; agreement is therefore the correct or democratic answer. Disagreement is the correct response to statements 9 and 10, since denial of the right to seek office to members of minority ethnic or ideological groups directly violates their right "to try to win majority support for their opinions."

Since the proposition being tested asserts the existence of consensus, the interviewing sample could logically have been drawn from any group of Americans. Because we assume regional and class differences, however, we could not rely on the most available respondents, our own college students. The registered voters of two academic communities, Ann Arbor, Michigan, and Tallahassee, Florida, were selected as the sampling population, primarily because they fitted the needs of the hypothesis, and partly because of their accessibility. Although a nation-wide survey was ruled out simply on the ground of costs, these atypical communities offer certain advantages for our problem. First, they do permit at least a limited regional comparison of attitudes on democratic fundamentals. Second, they skew the sample by over-representing the more highly educated, thus permitting detailed comparison of the highly educated with the poorly educated, a comparison that could hardly be made with samples from more typical communities.

The over-representation of the highly educated also served to "stack the cards" in favor of the proposition on consensus. Since our hypothesis holds that consensus is limited, we further stacked the cards against the hypothesis by choosing the sample from registered voters rather than from all residents of the two communities. Although the necessity of consensus is stated in terms of the society as a whole, a line of regression is available in the argument that it need exist only among those who take part in politics. Hence our restriction of the sample to a population of registered voters.

In each city the sample was drawn by the system of random numbers from the official lists of registered voters. The sample represents one per cent of the registered voters from the current registration list in each of the two communities. In a few cases the addresses given were incorrect, but if the person selected could be located in the community, he was included in the sample. A few questions on a limited number of individuals were not recorded in usable form, which accounts for a slight variation in the totals in the tables presented in the paper.

FINDINGS: THE CONSENSUS PROBLEM

In the two communities from which our samples were drawn, consensus can be said to exist among the voters on the basic principles of democracy when they are put in abstract terms. The degree of agreement on these principles ranges from 94.7 to 98.0 per cent, which appears to represent consensus in a truly meaningful sense and to support the first of our preliminary assumptions. On the generalized principles, then, we need not look for "bases of disagreement"—the agreement transcends community, educational, economic, age, sex, party, and other common bases of differences in opinion. We may stop with the conclusion that opinions on these abstract principles have a cultural base.

When these broad principles are translated into more specific propositions, however, consensus breaks down completely. . . . Agreement does not reach 90 per cent on any of the ten propositions, either from the two samples combined or from the communities considered separately. Indeed, respondents in both communities are closer to perfect discord than to perfect consensus on over half the statements. If we keep in mind that a 50–50 division represents a total absence of consensus, then degrees of agreement ranging from 25 to 75 per cent can be understood as closer to the total absence of consensus (50 per cent agreement) than to its perfect realization (100 per cent agreement). Responses from voters in both communities fall in this "discord" range on six of the statements (1, 4, 5, 6, 8, and 10); voters in the Southern community approach maximum discord on two additional statements (3 and 9), both of which put democratic principles in terms of Negro participation in public office. These findings strongly support the second of our preliminary assumptions, that consensus does not exist on more concrete questions involving the application of democratic principles.

Three of the statements that evoke more discord than consensus deal with the extension of democratic principles to Communists, a highly unpopular group in the United States. But it should be noted that these statements are put in terms of generally approved behaviors (speaking and seeking public office), not conspiratorial or other reprehensible activities. And the other statements on which discord exceeds consensus refer to groups (as well as activities) that are not in opposition to the American form of government: the right of all citizens to vote, the right of a professional group to maximize its voting strength, and the right to criticize churches and religion.

The extent to which consensus breaks down on the specific formulation of democratic principles is even greater than suggested by our discussion of the range of discord. To this point we have ignored the content of the opinions on these principles, which would permit an overwhelming *rejection* of the democratic principle to be accepted as consensus. Specifically, responses to statement 2 were not counted as falling in the "discord" category, but the approach to consensus in this case lies in rejection of the democratic principle of the "majority vote" with an "equal chance" for "every citizen." But the proposition about consensus holds, of course, that the consensus is in favor of democratic principles. On four statements (2, 4, 5, and 10) a majority of the voters in Ann Arbor express "undemocratic" opinions; and on six statements (1, 2, 4, 5, 8, and 10) a majority of the voters in Tallahassee express "undemocratic" opinions.

However the reactions to our specific statements are approached, they run counter to the idea of extended consensus. On none of them is there the real consensus that we found on the abstract form of the principles; responses to over half of the statements are closer to perfect discord than perfect consensus; and the responses to about half of the statements express the "wrong" answers. Unlike the general statements, then, the specific propositions call for an appraisal of bases of agreement and disagreement.

FINDINGS: BASES OF AGREEMENT AND DISAGREEMENT

The report of findings on the consensus problem has already suggested that regional subcultures are one basis of differences in opinions on democratic principles. . . .

Community, education and income all have an effect on opinions about democratic principles. More "correct" responses came from the Midwestern than from the Southern community, from those with high education than from those with less education, and from those with high income than from those with low income. The systematic nature of these differences supports the assumption that regional and class-related factors affect attitudes toward democratic principles when they are put in specific terms.

Which of these variables has the greatest effect on attitudes toward basic principles of democracy? [Data] suggests that education is most important on two counts: (1) for every statement, the greatest difference in opinions is found in the high education-low education dichotomy; (2) for every statement, the grouping with the most "correct" or "democratic" responses is the high education category. Before education can be accepted as the independent variable in relation to democratic attitudes, however, the relationship must be examined for true independence. Since more Ann Arbor than Tallahassee respondents fall in the high education category, and since more high income than low income respondents have high education, the education variable might prove to be spurious—with the concealed community and income factors accounting for its apparent effect. . . . When we control for community and income, differences between the high and low education respondents remain. When we control for education, on the other hand, the smaller differences reported . . . by community and income tend to disappear.

Since educational differences hold up consistently when other factors are "partialled out," education may be accepted as the most consequential basis of opinions on basic democratic principles. Regardless of their other group identifications, people with high education accept democratic principles more than any other grouping. While the highly educated thus come closest to qualifying as the carriers of the democratic creed, the data do not support our hypothesis; consensus in a meaningful sense (on both the abstract and the specific principles) is not found even among those with high education. On only three of the ten specific statements (3, 7, and 9) does agreement among those with high education reach 90 per cent in Ann Arbor, and in Tallahassee it fails to reach 90 per cent on any of the statements. On the proposition that the vote should be restricted to tax-payers in referenda deciding on tax-supported undertakings, 75.8 per cent of the highly educated in Ann Arbor and 81.5 per cent in Tallahassee reject the democratic principle of an equal vote for every citizen. And on five statements (1, 4, 5, 8, and 10) the highly educated in both communities are closer to perfect discord than to perfect harmony. Even when the necessity of consensus is reformulated in terms of the group most in accord with democratic principles, then, consensus cannot be said to exist.

SUMMARY AND CONCLUSIONS

The attitudes of voters in selected Midwestern and Southern communities offer no support for the hypothesis that democracy requires a large measure of consensus among the carriers of the creed, *i.e.*, those most consistently in accord with democratic principles. As expected, general consensus was found on the idea of democracy itself and on the broad principles of majority rule and minority rights, but it disappeared when these principles were put in more specific form. Indeed, the voters in both communities were closer to complete discord than to complete consensus; they did not reach consensus on any of the ten specific statements incorporating the principles of majority rule and minority rights; and majorities expressed the "undemocratic" attitude on about half of the statements.

In trying to identify the carriers of the creed, the expected regional and class-related variations were found in attitudes toward democratic principles in specific form, with education having the most marked effect. While attitudes on democratic fundamentals were not found to vary appreciably according to age, sex or party affiliation, they did vary according to education, community, and income. The greatest difference on every statement was between the high-education group and the low-education group, and the high-education group gave the most democratic response to every question, whether compared with other educational, community or income groupings. Education, but not community or income, held up consistently as a basis of disagreement when other factors were controlled. We accordingly conclude that endorsement of democratic principles is not a function of class as such (of which income is also a criterion), but of greater acquaintance with the logical implications of the broad democratic principles. Note, for example, that the highly educated renounce in much greater degree than any other group the restriction of the vote to the well-informed, a restriction that would presumably affect them least of all.

Although high education was the primary basis of agreement on democratic principles, actual consensus was not found even among this segment of the voting population. The approach to consensus is closer among the highly educated in Ann Arbor, where greater agreement exists on the extension of democratic rights to Negroes, but in both communities the highly educated are closer to discord than consensus on half of the statements. On the basis of these findings, our hypothesis appears to be invalid.

Our failure to find a more extended consensus may, of course, be attributed to the possibility that the statements we formulated do not incorporate the particular "fundamentals" that are actually necessary to democracy. When the approach to consensus is in the "undemocratic" direction—as in the question about restricting the vote to tax-payers—two possible objections to our interviewing schedule are suggested. First, perhaps the question is not a logical derivation from the basic principles with which we began. Second, perhaps the respondents are not interpreting the questions in any uniform way.

On the first point, the logical connection of the specific proposition with the general proposition is virtually self-evident. In syllogistic terms, we have: major premise—every citizen should have an equal chance to influence government policy; minor premise—non-tax-payers are citizens; conclusion—non-tax-payers should be allowed to vote in a city referendum deciding on tax-supported undertakings. Since decisions on tax-supported undertakings are clearly matters of government policy, rejection of the conclusion is inconsistent with acceptance of the major premise. As a matter of policy, perhaps the vote should be restricted—as it often is—under the circumstances indicated. We simply note that such a position is inconsistent with the unqualified major premise.

As to the second apparent difficulty, varying interpretations of the questions undoubtedly influenced the results. As our pre-test of the questionnaire indicated, the wordings finally chosen conveyed common meanings but tapped different attitudes embedded in different frames of reference. In surveys, as in real political situations, citizens are confronted with the need for making decisions about questions to which they attribute varying implications. We can infer, for example, that the respondents who repudiate free speech for Communists are responding in terms of anti-Communist rather than anti–free speech sentiments, especially since they endorse the idea of free speech in general. Conversely, those who endorse free speech for Communists are presumably reflecting a more consistent dedication to free speech rather than pro-Communist sentiments. But our concern in this study is with the opinions themselves rather than with the varying functions that a given opinion may perform for different individuals. The significant fact is that the opinions (and presumably the frames of reference that produce them) vary systematically from group to group, not randomly or on a meaninglessly idiosyncratic basis.

Assuming that the United States is a democracy, we cannot say without qualification that consensus on fundamental principles is a necessary condition for the existence of democracy. Nor does it appear valid to say that, although consensus need not pervade the entire voting population, it must exist at least among the highly educated, who are the carriers of the creed. Our data are not inconsistent, of course, with the qualified proposition that consensus on fundamental principles in a highly abstract form is a necessary condition for the existence of democracy. But the implication of political theory that consensus includes more specific principles is empirically invalid. Our findings accordingly suggest that the intuitive insights and logical inferences of political theorists need to be subjected more consistently to empirical validation.

Discussions of consensus tend to overlook the functional nature of apathy for the democratic system. No one is surprised to hear that what people *say* they *believe* and what they *actually do* are not necessarily the same. We usually assume that verbal positions represent a higher level—a more "democratic" stance—than non-verbal behavior. But something close to the opposite may also be true: many people express undemocratic principles in response to questioning but are too apathetic to act on their undemocratic opinions in concrete situations. And in most cases, fortunately for the democratic system, those with the most undemocratic principles are also those who are least likely to act. A sizeable number (42.0 per cent) of our Southern respondents said, for example, that "a Negro should not be allowed to run for mayor of this city," but a few months before the survey a Negro actually did conduct an active campaign for that office without any efforts being made by the "white" people to obstruct his candidacy.

In this case, the behavior was more democratic than the verbal expressions. If the leadership elements—the carriers of the creed—had encouraged undemocratic action, it might have materialized (as it did in Little Rock in the school desegregation crisis). But, in fact, people with basically undemocratic opinions either abstained from acting or acted in a perfectly democratic fashion. "The successful working of the system is not deliberately aimed at by those who work it," John Plamenatz says, "but is the result of their behaving as they do." As J. Roland Pennock puts it, democracy can tolerate less conscious agreement on principles if people are willing to compromise and to follow set rules and procedures. Loose talk of consensus as a self-evident requirement of democracy should have no place beside such insightful observations as these. Carl J. Friedrich appears to have been correct in asserting, eighteen years ago, that democracy depends on habitual patterns of behavior rather than on conscious agreement on democratic "principles." His argument has been largely ignored because, like the position from which he dissented, it was advanced without the support of directly relevant research findings. Our results are offered as a step toward settling the question on empirical grounds.

V. O. KEY JR.

30. LEADERS MOLD AND INFLUENCE PUBLIC OPINION

V. O. Key (1908–1963), the political scientist who did pioneering work in empirical studies of political behavior, picked up the debate and reinforced the position articulated by Lippmann that government officials in a democracy must not rely exclusively on public opinion: Leaders should lead, not simply follow the masses. The corollary to this proposition, however, is that responsibility for the success or failure of the American political system rests squarely on the shoulders of its leaders, not on the public at large.

In Key's view, public opinion on an issue at any particular time is largely the product of the "preachings of the influentials, of this generation and of several past generations." Key believed, as did Lippmann before him, that the public simply does not have well-formed opinions on specific issues. Whatever views are held by the public result from the definitions and interpretations placed on

---

Source: From V. O. Key Jr., *Public Opinion and American Democracy* (New York: Alfred A. Knopf, 1961). Reprinted by permission of Sandra Gettys.

events by the influentials and opinion leaders of the nation. As Key put it, "The masses do not corrupt themselves; if they are corrupt, they have been corrupted."

A WORKING VIEW OF PUBLIC OPINION

For purposes of political analysis one need not strain painfully toward the formation of a theoretical representation of an eerie entity called "public opinion." One need not seek to find "the" public embodied in some kind of amorphous social structure that goes through recurring patterns of action as it reaches a decision. "Public opinion" in this discussion may simply be taken to mean those opinions held by private persons which governments find it prudent to heed. Governments may be compelled toward action or inaction by such opinion; in other instances they may ignore it, perhaps at their peril; they may attempt to alter it; or they may divert or pacify it. So defined, opinion may be shared by many or by few people. It may be the veriest whim, or it may be a settled conviction. The opinion may represent a general agreement formed after the widest discussion; it may be far less firmly founded. It may even be contingent opinion—that is, estimates by decision makers of probable responses to actions they consider taking. Whatever the character or distribution of opinion, governments may need to estimate its nature as an incident to many of their actions.[1] Probably any regime needs to heed at least some opinions outside the government; yet the range of opinions that enter into the calculations of governors obviously varies among societies with their political norms and customs.

This view of public opinion resembles the conceptions of several other commentators. Speier defines, for the purposes of historical analysis, "public opinion" as "opinions on matters of concern to the nation freely and publicly expressed by men outside the government who claim a right that their opinions should influence or determine the actions, personnel, or structure of their government."[2] Wirth observed that the "decisive part of public opinion, then, is the organization of views on issues that exercise an impact upon those who are in a position to make decisions."[3] In the context of a criticism of those pollsters who regard all the responses obtained by their interviewers as public opinion, Blumer remarks that "the character of public opinion in terms of meaningful operation must be sought in the array of views and positions which enter into the consideration of those who have to take action on public opinion."[4]

Virtues and Consequences of a Broad View of Opinion

The adoption of a broad, and somewhat vague, conception of public opinion has consequences for a general survey of the field. While it permits an avoidance of some analytical problems, it also brings within the range of the discussion an extremely wide variety of phenomena. When public opinion is regarded as those opinions that may influence government, it is unnecessary to assume that "the public" exists as any particular sort of loosely structured association or other ghostly sociological entity. On a given question the operative public may consist of a highly structured association, while on another matter opinions may be diffused through a wide public that lacks any special organization. The form of the public concerned about subsidies to maritime shipping could plausibly be expected to differ radically from that of the public concerned about honesty in public office. On one issue the public may consist of one sector of the population; on another, of a quite different sector. Not much overlap would be expected between those deeply interested in policy toward upland game and those concerned about practices in the licensing of plumbers. Or publics may be differentiated by the nature of their involvement in public questions. Almond speaks of the "mass public" and the "attentive public." The mass public, informed by the mass media, pays heed to the tone of discussion of issues and responds by moods of apprehension or complacency. The attentive public, a far smaller group, follows public issues in an analytical manner, is relatively well informed, and constitutes a critical audience for the discussion of public affairs.[5]

To emphasize, in the definition of opinion, relevance for government is to bring opinions with widely varying properties or qualities within our range of concern. Lowell limited opinion to "the acceptance of one among two or more inconsistent views which are capable of being accepted by a rational mind as true."[6] By "opinion" Young means "a belief or conviction more verifiable and stronger in intensity than a mere hunch or impression but less strong than truly verifiable or positive knowledge."[7] Under the present conception no such restricted view of opinion is necessary. Lightly held views and transient anxieties, prejudices, preferences, demands, and convictions all have their relevance for governmental action. Nor need the common distinction between opinion and the mores exclude a set of attitudes from our range of interest. Some students of public opinion conclude that they need to concern themselves only with those contentious issues about which opinion is in process of formation and that settled matters—the mores, the enduring attitudes, the customs—are beyond their purview. Although these distinctions between types of citizen outlook are analytically useful, governments must take both kinds of views into account. The prescriptions of custom may control particular actions; particular actions may aim to modify custom, an objective best undertaken after reflection about the probable public response.

These comments on the qualities of "opinion" bring within the limits of that term a considerable range of views—from whim to conviction to custom—but the term acquires an even broader connotation by mention of the objects about which opinion may be considered "public." The most common assumption is that public opinion concerns issues of substantive policy; yet our emphasis on opinions to which governments need to pay heed requires attention to opinions about many objects other than issues. Indeed, a contented—or discontented—people may have opinions that are most relevant politically but in the main about matters other than concrete issues. They may be exercised about economic conditions; they may have anxieties about the threat of war. In either case their views may not be, at least for most people, centered sharply on well-defined policy issues. Or people may have images of institutions or expectations about institutional performance or evaluations of public personnel—all questions of the most direct relevance for governmental actions though not formulated as policy issues.

Although all regimes must pay heed to the opinions of their peoples, obviously in democratic orders opinion plays a different role than in dictatorial states. When the doctrine prevails that citizens have a right to be heard and governments have a duty to hear, private opinion may have an impact on most major public actions. For the maximum participation of the public (or the publics) a practice of disclosure or notice of prospective actions and of announcement of the considerations underlying actions must be followed. Freedom of association and freedom of expression of opinion on public matters need also to exist. For these reasons, public opinion is sometimes regarded as that opinion communicated to the government. Yet, in practice, governments may (and often do) give weight to latent opinion; in advance of action, they need to estimate the kinds of opinions that may be expressed if a given course is followed or proposed. Hence, communication of views to the government is not essential to transform opinion into public opinion, although communication may be the general rule.

NOTES

1. The conception of public opinion advanced here, it is cheerfully conceded, is difficult to apply in research. If one is to know what opinions governments heed, one must know the inner thoughts of presidents, congressmen, and other officials. It is even more difficult to know what opinions prudent governments should heed for the sake of the success of their policies or even for their survival.
2. Hans Speier: "Historical Development of Public Opinion," *American Journal of Sociology,* LV (1949–50), 376.
3. Louis Wirth: "Consensus and Mass Communication," *American Sociological Review,* XIII (1948), 1–15.
4. Herbert Blumer: "Public Opinion and Public Opinion Polling," *American Sociological Review,* XIII (1948), 545.
5. Gabriel Almond: "Public Opinion and National Security Policy," *Public Opinion Quarterly,* XX (1956), 371–8.
6. A. Lawrence Lowell: *Public Opinion in War and Peace* (Cambridge: Harvard University Press, 1923), 12.
7. Kimball Young, "Comments on the Nature of 'Public' and 'Public Opinion,'" *International Journal of Opinion and Attitude Research,* II (1948), 387.

RICHARD HOFSTADTER

31. THE PARANOID STYLE IN AMERICAN POLITICS

The recurrent belief by a wide range of American political groups that there is a national conspiracy against them is referred to as the paranoid style of American politics. Examples include gay groups that maintain that AIDS was "invented" by the government to destroy them; black groups that believe that illicit and dangerous drug use is encouraged by the government; and right wing militia groups that believe that the U.S. government is conspiring with the United Nations to destroy them.

Historian Richard Hofstadter coined the phrase "paranoid style" to describe this belief in a conspiracy to destroy one or another of the fundamental values of American life. He writes that only the term paranoid *"adequately evokes the sense of heated exaggeration, suspiciousness, and conspiratorial fantasy that I have in mind." Americans who kill physicians who perform abortions, bomb abortion clinics, or blow up federal buildings all believe that they must engage in violence in order to save the country from hostile, destructive, and evil forces that are destroying the fabric of American life. The same style could be seen among those politicians during the Cold War era who believed that a worldwide communist conspiracy was always on the verge of destroying the American way of life. Hofstadter's work represents a classic statement of the recurring tendency in American politics to see this paranoid style emerge under conditions of social or political stress.*

American politics has often been an arena for angry minds. In recent years we have seen angry minds at work mainly among extreme right-wingers, who have now demonstrated in the Goldwater movement how much political leverage can be got out of the animosities and passions of a small minority. But behind this I believe there is a style of mind that is far from new and that is not necessarily right-wing. I call it the paranoid style simply because no other word adequately evokes the sense of heated exaggeration, suspiciousness, and conspiratorial fantasy that I have in mind. In using the expression "paranoid

---

Source: From "The Paranoid Style in American Politics" by Richard Hofstadter, p. 77–82, 85–86 in the November 1964 Issue of *Harper's*. Copyright © 1964.

style" I am not speaking in a clinical sense, but borrowing a clinical term for other purposes. I have neither the competence nor the desire to classify any figures of the past or present as certifiable lunatics. In fact, the idea of the paranoid style as a force in politics would have little contemporary relevance or historical value if it were applied only to men with profoundly disturbed minds. It is the use of paranoid modes of expression by more or less normal people that makes the phenomenon significant.

Of course this term is pejorative, and it is meant to be; the paranoid style has a greater affinity for bad causes than good. But nothing really prevents a sound program or demand from being advocated in the paranoid style. Style has more to do with the way in which ideas are believed and advocated than with the truth or falsity of their content. I am interested here in getting at our political psychology through our political rhetoric. The paranoid style is an old and recurrent phenomenon in our public life which has been frequently linked with movements of suspicious discontent.

Here is Senator McCarthy, speaking in June 1951 about the parlous situation of the United States:

> How can we account for our present situation unless we believe that men high in this government are concerting to deliver us to disaster? This must be the product of a great conspiracy on a scale so immense as to dwarf any previous such venture in the history of man. A conspiracy of infamy so black that, when it is finally exposed, its principals shall be forever deserving of the maledictions of all honest men. . . . What can be made of this unbroken series of decisions and acts contributing to the strategy of defeat? They cannot be attributed to incompetence. . . . The laws of probability would dictate that part of . . . [the] decisions would serve the country's interest.

Now turn back fifty years to a manifesto signed in 1895 by a number of leaders of the Populist party:

> As early as 1865–66 a conspiracy was entered into between the gold gamblers of Europe and America. . . . For nearly thirty years these conspirators have kept the people quarreling over less important matters while they have pursued with unrelenting zeal their one central purpose. . . . Every device of treachery, every resource of statecraft, and every artifice known to the secret cabals of the international gold ring are being used to deal a blow to the prosperity of the people and the financial and commercial independence of the country.

Next, a Texas newspaper article of 1855:

> . . . It is a notorious fact that the Monarchs of Europe and the Pope of Rome are at this very moment plotting our destruction and threatening the extinction of our political, civil, and religious institutions. We have the best reasons for believing that corruption has found its way into our Executive Chamber, and that our Executive head is tainted with the infectious venom of Catholicism. . . . The Pope has recently sent his ambassador of state to this country on a secret commission, the effect of which is an extraordinary boldness of the Catholic Church throughout the United States. . . . These minions of the Pope are boldly insulting our Senators; reprimanding our Statesmen; propagating

> the adulterous union of Church and State; abusing with foul calumny all governments but Catholic; and spewing out the bitterest execrations on all Protestantism. The Catholics in the United States receive from abroad more than $200,000 annually for the propagation of their creed. Add to this the vast revenue collected here. . . .

These quotations give the keynote of the style. In the history of the United States one finds it, for example, in the anti-Masonic movement, the nativist and anti-Catholic movement, in certain spokesmen of abolitionism who regarded the United States as being in the grip of a slaveholders' conspiracy, in many alarmists about the Mormons, in some Greenback and Populist writers who constructed a great conspiracy of international bankers, in the exposure of a Munitions-makers' Conspiracy of World War I, in the popular left-wing press, in the contemporary American right wing, and on both sides of the race controversy today, among White Citizens' Councils and Black Muslims. I do not propose to try to trace the variations of the paranoid style that can be found in all these movements, but will confine myself to a few leading episodes in our past history in which the style emerged in full and archetypal splendor.

ILLUMINISM AND MASONRY

I begin with a particularly revealing episode—the panic that broke out in some quarters at the end of the eighteenth century over the allegedly subversive activities of the Bavarian Illuminati. This panic was a part of the general reaction to the French Revolution. In the United States it was heightened by the response of certain men, mostly in New England and among the established clergy, to the rise of Jeffersonian democracy. Illuminism had been started in 1776 by Adam Weishaupt, a professor of law at the University of Ingolstadt. Its teachings today seem to be no more than another version of Enlightenment rationalism, spiced with the anticlerical atmosphere of eighteenth-century Bavaria. It was a somewhat naive and utopian movement which aspired ultimately to bring the human race under the rules of reason. Its humanitarian rationalism appears to have acquired a fairly wide influence in Masonic lodges.

Americans first learned of Illuminism in 1797, from a volume published in Edinburgh (later reprinted in New York) under the title, *Proofs of a Conspiracy Against All the Religions and Governments of Europe, Carried on in the Secret Meetings of Free Masons, Illuminati, and Reading Societies*. Its author was a well-known Scottish scientist, John Robison, who had himself been a somewhat casual adherent of Masonry in Britain, but whose imagination had been inflamed by what he considered to be the far less innocent Masonic movement on the Continent. Robison seems to have made his work as factual as he could, but when he came to estimating the moral character and the political influence of Illuminism, he made the characteristic paranoid leap into fantasy. The association, he thought, was formed "for the express purpose of ROOTING OUT ALL RELIGIOUS ESTABLISHMENTS AND OVERTURNING ALL THE EXISTING GOVERNMENTS OF EUROPE." It had become "one great and wicked project fermenting and working all over Europe," and to it he attributed a central role in bringing about the French Revolution. He saw it as a libertine, anti-Christian movement, given to the corruption of women, the cultivation of sensual pleasures, and the violation of property rights. Its members had plans for making a tea that caused abortion—a secret substance that "blinds or kills when spurted in the face," and a device that sounds like a stench bomb—a "method for filling a bedchamber with pestilential vapours."

These notions were quick to make themselves felt in America. In May 1798, a minister of the Massachusetts Congregational establishment in Boston, Jedidiah Morse, delivered a timely sermon to the young country, which was then sharply divided between Jeffersonians and Federalists, Francophiles and Anglomen. Having read Robison, Morse was convinced that the United States too was the victim of a Jacobinical plot touched off by Illuminism, and that the country should be rallied to defend itself. His warnings were heeded throughout New England wherever Federalists brooded about the rising tide of religious infidelity or Jeffersonian democracy. Timothy Dwight, the president of Yale, followed Morse's sermon with a Fourth-of-July discourse on *The Duty of Americans in the Present Crisis,* in which he held forth against the Antichrist in his own glowing rhetoric. Soon the pulpits of New England were ringing with denunciations of the Illuminati, as though the country were swarming with them.

The anti-Masonic movement of the late 1820s and the 1830s took up and extended the obsession with conspiracy. At first, this movement may seem to be no more than an extension or repetition of the anti-Masonic theme sounded in the outcry against the Bavarian Illuminati. But whereas the panic of the 1790s was confined mainly to New England and linked to an ultraconservative point of view, the later anti-Masonic movement affected many parts of the northern United States, and was intimately linked with popular democracy and rural egalitarianism. Although anti-Masonry happened to be anti-Jacksonian (Jackson was a Mason), it manifested the same animus against the closure of opportunity for the common man and against aristocratic institutions that one finds in the Jacksonian crusade against the Bank of the United States.

The anti-Masonic movement was a product not merely of natural enthusiasm but also of the vicissitudes of party politics. It was joined and used by a great many men who did not fully share its original anti-Masonic feelings. It attracted the support of several reputable statesmen who had only mild sympathy with its fundamental bias, but who as politicians could not afford to ignore it. Still, it was a folk movement of considerable power, and the rural enthusiasts who provided its real impetus believed in it wholeheartedly.

As a secret society, Masonry was considered to be a standing conspiracy against republican government. It was held to be particularly liable to treason—for example, Aaron Burr's famous conspiracy was alleged to have been conducted by Masons. Masonry was accused of constituting a separate system of loyalty, a separate imperium within the framework of federal and state governments, which was inconsistent with loyalty to them. Quite plausibly it was argued that the Masons had set up a jurisdiction of their own, with their own obligations and punishments, liable to enforcement even by the penalty of death. So basic was the conflict felt to be between secrecy and democracy that other, more innocent societies such as Phi Beta Kappa came under attack.

Since Masons were pledged to come to each other's aid under circumstances of distress, and to extend fraternal indulgence at all times, it was held that the order nullified the enforcement of regular law. Masonic constables, sheriffs, juries, and judges must all be in league with Masonic criminals and fugitives. The press was believed to have been so "muzzled" by Masonic editors and proprietors that news of Masonic malfeasance could be suppressed. At a moment when almost every alleged citadel of privilege in America was under democratic assault, Masonry was attacked as a fraternity of the privileged, closing business opportunities and nearly monopolizing political offices.

Certain elements of truth and reality there may have been in these views of Masonry. What must be emphasized here, however, is the apocalyptic and absolutistic framework in which this hostility was commonly expressed. Anti-Masons were not content simply to say that secret societies were rather a bad idea. The author of the standard exposition of anti-Masonry declared that Freemasonry was "not only the most abominable but also the most dangerous institution that ever was imposed on man. . . . It may truly be said to be HELL'S MASTER PIECE."

THE JESUIT THREAT

Fear of a Masonic plot had hardly been quieted when the rumors arose of a Catholic plot against American values. One meets here again the same frame of mind, but a different villain. The anti-Catholic movement converged with a growing nativism, and while they were not identical, together they cut such a wide swath in American life that they were bound to embrace many moderates to whom the paranoid style, in its full glory, did not appeal. Moreover, we need not dismiss out of hand as totally parochial or mean-spirited the desire of Yankee Americans to maintain an ethnically and religiously homogeneous society nor the particular Protestant commitments to individualism and freedom that were brought into play. But the movement had a large paranoid infusion, and the most influential anti-Catholic militants certainly had a strong affinity for the paranoid style.

Two books which appeared in 1835 described the new danger to the American way of life and may be taken as expressions of the anti-Catholic mentality. One, *Foreign Conspiracies against the Liberties of the United States,* was from the hand of the celebrated painter and inventor of the telegraph, S. F. B. Morse. "A conspiracy exists," Morse proclaimed, and "its plans are already in operation . . . we are attacked in a vulnerable quarter which cannot be defended by our ships, our forts, or our armies." The main source of the conspiracy Morse found in Metternich's government: "*Austria is now acting in this country.* She has devised a grand scheme. She has organized a great plan for doing something here. . . . She has her Jesuit missionaries traveling through the land; she has supplied them with money, and has furnished a fountain for a regular supply." Were the plot successful, Morse said, some scion of the House of Hapsburg would soon be installed as Emperor of the United States.

"It is an ascertained fact," wrote another Protestant militant,

> that Jesuits are prowling about all parts of the United States in every possible disguise, expressly to ascertain the advantageous situations and modes to disseminate Popery. A minister of the Gospel from Ohio has informed us that he discovered one carrying on his devices in his congregation; and he says that the western country swarms with them under the name of puppet show men, dancing masters, music teachers, peddlers of images and ornaments, barrel organ players, and similar practitioners.

Lyman Beecher, the elder of a famous family and the father of Harriet Beecher Stowe, wrote in the same year his *Plea for the West,* in which he considered the possibility that the Christian millennium might come in the American states. Everything depended, in his judgment, upon what influences dominated the great West, where the future of the country lay. There Protestantism was engaged in a life-or-death struggle with Catholicism. "Whatever we do, it must be done quickly. . . . " A great tide of immigration, hostile to free institutions, was sweeping in upon the country, subsidized and sent by "the potentates of Europe," multiplying tumult and violence, filling jails, crowding poorhouses, quadrupling taxation, and sending increasing thousands of voters to "lay their inexperienced hand upon the helm of our power."

Anti-Catholicism has always been the pornography of the Puritan. Whereas the anti-Masons had envisaged drinking bouts and had entertained themselves with sado-masochistic fantasies about the actual enforcement of grisly Masonic oaths,* the anti-Catholics invented an immense lore about libertine priests, the confessional as an opportunity for seduction, licentious convents and monasteries. Probably the most widely read contemporary book in the United States before *Uncle Tom's Cabin* was a work supposedly written by one Maria Monk, entitled *Awful Disclosures,* which appeared in 1836. The author, who purported to have escaped from the Hotel Dieu nunnery in Montreal after five years there as novice and nun, reported her convent life in elaborate and circumstantial detail. She reported having been told by the Mother Superior that she must "obey the priests in all things"; to her "utter astonishment and horror," she soon found what the nature of such obedience was. Infants born of convent liaisons were baptized and then killed, she said, so that they might ascend at once to heaven. Her book, hotly attacked and defended, continued to be read and believed even after her mother gave testimony that Maria had been somewhat addled ever since childhood after she had rammed

---

* Many anti-Masons had been fascinated by the penalties invoked if Masons failed to live up to their obligations. My own favorite is the oath attributed to a royal archmason who invited "having my skull smote off, and my brains exposed to the scorching rays of the sun."

a pencil into her head. Maria died in prison in 1849, after having been arrested in a brothel as a pickpocket.

Anti-Catholicism, like anti-Masonry, mixed its fortunes with American party politics, and it became an enduring factor in American politics. The American Protective Association of the 1890s revived it with ideological variations more suitable to the times—the depression of 1893, for example, was alleged to be an intentional creation of the Catholics who began it by starting a run on the banks. Some spokesmen of the movement circulated a bogus encyclical attributed to Leo XIII instructing American Catholics on a certain date in 1893 to exterminate all heretics, and a great many anti-Catholics daily expected a nationwide uprising. The myth of an impending Catholic war of mutilation and extermination of heretics persisted into the twentieth century.

WHY THEY FEEL DISPOSSESSED

If, after our historically discontinuous examples of the paranoid style, we now take the long jump to the contemporary right wing, we find some rather important differences from the nineteenth-century movements. The spokesmen of those earlier movements felt that they stood for causes and personal types that were still in possession of their country—that they were fending off threats to a still established way of life. But the modern right wing, as Daniel Bell has put it, feels dispossessed: America has been largely taken away from them and their kind, though they are determined to try to repossess it and to prevent the final destructive act of subversion. The old American virtues have already been eaten away by cosmopolitans and intellectuals; the old competitive capitalism has been gradually undermined by socialist and communist schemers; the old national security and independence have been destroyed by treasonous plots, having as their most powerful agents not merely outsiders and foreigners as of old but major statesmen who are at the very centers of American power. Their predecessors had discovered conspiracies; the modern radical right finds conspiracy to be betrayal from on high.

Important changes may also be traced to the effects of the mass media. The villains of the modern right are much more vivid than those of their paranoid predecessors, much better known to the public; the literature of the paranoid style is by the same token richer and more circumstantial in personal description and personal invective. For the vaguely delineated villains of the anti-Masons, for the obscure and disguised Jesuit agents, the little-known papal delegates of the anti-Catholics, for the shadowy international bankers of the monetary conspiracies, we may now substitute eminent public figures like Presidents Roosevelt, Truman, and Eisenhower, Secretaries of State like Marshall, Acheson, and Dulles, Justices of the Supreme Court like Frankfurter and Warren, and the whole battery of lesser but still famous and vivid alleged conspirators headed by Alger Hiss.

Events since 1939 have given the contemporary right-wing paranoid a vast theatre for his imagination, full of rich and proliferating detail, replete with realistic cues and undeniable proofs of the validity of his suspicions. The theatre of action is now the entire world, and he can draw not only on the events of World War II, but also on those of the Korean War and the Cold War. Any historian of warfare knows it is in good part a comedy of errors and a museum of incompetence; but if for every error and every act of incompetence one can substitute an act of treason, many points of fascinating interpretation are open to the paranoid imagination. In the end, the real mystery, for one who reads the primary works of paranoid scholarship, is not how the United States has been brought to its present dangerous position but how it has managed to survive at all.

The basic elements of contemporary right-wing thought can be reduced to three: First, there has been the now-familiar sustained conspiracy, running over more than a generation, and reaching its climax in Roosevelt's New Deal, to undermine free capitalism, to bring the economy under the direction of the federal government, and to pave the way for socialism or communism. A great many right-wingers would agree with Frank Chodorov, the author of *The Income Tax: The Root of All Evil,* that this campaign began with the passage of the income-tax amendment to the Constitution in 1913.

The second contention is that top government officialdom has been so infiltrated by Communists that American policy, at least since the days leading up to Pearl Harbor, has been dominated by men who were shrewdly and consistently selling out American national interests.

Finally, the country is infused with a network of Communist agents, just as in the old days it was infiltrated by Jesuit agents, so that the whole apparatus of education, religion, the press, and the mass media is engaged in a common effort to paralyze the resistance of loyal Americans.

Perhaps the most representative document of the McCarthyist phase was a long indictment of Secretary of State George C. Marshall, delivered in 1951 in the Senate by Senator McCarthy, and later published in a somewhat different form. McCarthy pictured Marshall as the focal figure in a betrayal of American interests stretching in time from the strategic plans for World War II to the formulation of the Marshall Plan. Marshall was associated with practically every American failure or defeat, McCarthy insisted, and none of this was either accident or incompetence. There was a "baffling pattern" of Marshall's interventions in the war, which always conduced to the well-being of the Kremlin. The sharp decline in America's relative strength from 1945 to 1951 did not "just happen"; it was "brought about, step by step, by will and intention," the consequence not of mistakes but of a treasonous conspiracy, "a conspiracy on a scale so immense as to dwarf any previous such venture in the history of man."

Today, the mantle of McCarthy has fallen on a retired candy manufacturer, Robert H. Welch, Jr., who is less strategically placed and has a much smaller but better organized following than the Senator. A few years ago Welch proclaimed that "Communist influences are now in almost complete control of our government"—note the care and scrupulousness of that "almost." He has offered a full scale interpretation of our recent history in which

Communists figure at every turn: They started a run on American banks in 1933 that forced their closure; they contrived the recognition of the Soviet Union by the United States in the same year, just in time to save the Soviets from economic collapse; they have stirred up the fuss over segregation in the South; they have taken over the Supreme Court and made it "one of the most important agencies of Communism."

Close attention to history wins for Mr. Welch an insight into affairs that is given to few of us. "For many reasons and after a lot of study," he wrote some years ago, "I personally believe [John Foster] Dulles to be a Communist agent." The job of Professor Arthur F. Burns as head of Eisenhower's Council of Economic Advisers was "merely a coverup for Burns's liaison work between Eisenhower and some of his Communist bosses." Eisenhower's brother Milton was "actually [his] superior and boss within the Communist party." As for Eisenhower himself, Welch characterized him, in words that have made the candy manufacturer famous, as "a dedicated, conscious agent of the Communist conspiracy"—a conclusion, he added, "based on an accumulation of detailed evidence so extensive and so palpable that it seems to put this conviction beyond any reasonable doubt."

EMULATING THE ENEMY

The paranoid spokesman sees the fate of conspiracy in apocalyptic terms—he traffics in the birth and death of whole worlds, whole political orders, whole systems of human values. He is always manning the barricades of civilization. He constantly lives at a turning point. Like religious millennialists he expresses the anxiety of those who are living through the last days and he is sometimes disposed to set a date for the apocalypse. ("Time is running out," said Welch in 1951. "Evidence is piling up on many sides and from many sources that October 1952 is the fatal month when Stalin will attack.")

As a member of the avant-garde who is capable of perceiving the conspiracy before it is fully obvious to an as yet unaroused public, the paranoid is a militant leader. He does not see social conflict as something to be mediated and compromised, in the manner of the working politician. Since what is at stake is always a conflict between absolute good and absolute evil, what is necessary is not compromise but the will to fight things out to a finish. Since the enemy is thought of as being totally evil and totally unappeasable, he must be totally eliminated—if not from the world, at least from the theatre of operations to which the paranoid directs his attention. This demand for total triumph leads to the formulation of hopelessly unrealistic goals, and since these goals are not even remotely attainable, failure constantly heightens the paranoid's sense of frustration. Even partial success leaves him with the same feeling of powerlessness with which he began, and this in turn only strengthens his awareness of the vast and terrifying quality of the enemy he opposes.

This enemy is clearly delineated: he is a perfect model of malice, a kind of amoral superman—sinister, ubiquitous, powerful, cruel, sensual, luxury-loving.

Unlike the rest of us, the enemy is not caught in the toils of the vast mechanism of history, himself a victim of his past, his desires, his limitations. He wills, indeed he manufactures, the mechanism of history, or tries to deflect the normal course of history in an evil way. He makes crises, starts runs on banks, causes depressions, manufactures disasters, and then enjoys and profits from the misery he has produced. The paranoid's interpretation of history is distinctly personal: decisive events are not taken as part of the stream of history, but as the consequences of someone's will. Very often the enemy is held to possess some especially effective source of power: he controls the press; he has unlimited funds; he has a new secret for influencing the mind (brainwashing); he has a special technique for seduction (the Catholic confessional).

It is hard to resist the conclusion that this enemy is on many counts a projection of the self; both the ideal and the unacceptable aspects of the self are attributed to him. The enemy may be the cosmopolitan intellectual, but the paranoid will outdo him in the apparatus of scholarship, even of pedantry. Secret organizations set up to combat secret organizations give the same flattery. The Ku Klux Klan imitated Catholicism to the point of donning priestly vestments, developing an elaborate ritual and an equally elaborate hierarchy. The John Birch Society emulates Communist cells and quasi-secret operation through "front" groups, and preaches a ruthless prosecution of the ideological war along lines very similar to those it finds in the Communist enemy.* Spokesmen of the various fundamentalist anti-Communist "crusades" openly express their admiration for the dedication and discipline the Communist cause calls forth.

On the other hand, the sexual freedom often attributed to the enemy, his lack of moral inhibition, his possession of especially effective techniques for fulfilling his desires, give exponents of the paranoid style an opportunity to project and express unacknowledgeable aspects of their own psychological concerns. Catholics and Mormons—later, Negroes and Jews—have lent themselves to a preoccupation with illicit sex. Very often the fantasies of true believers reveal strong sadomasochistic outlets, vividly expressed, for example, in the delight of anti-Masons with the cruelty of Masonic punishments.

RENEGADES AND PEDANTS

A special significance attaches to the figure of the renegade from the enemy cause. The anti-Masonic movement seemed at times to be the creation of ex-Masons; certainly the highest significance was attributed to their revelations, and every word they said was believed. Anti-Catholicism used the runaway

---

* In his recent book, *How to Win an Election,* Stephen C. Shadegg cites a statement attributed to Mao Tse-tung: "Give me just two or three men in a village and I will take the village." Shadegg comments: "In the Goldwater campaigns of 1952 and 1958 and in all other campaigns where I have served as a consultant I have followed the advice of Mao Tse-tung." "I would suggest," writes Senator Goldwater in *Why Not Victory?* "that we analyze and copy the strategy of the enemy; theirs has worked and ours has not."

nun and the apostate priest; the place of ex-Communists in the avant-garde anti-Communist movements of our time is well known. In some part, the special authority accorded the renegade derives from the obsession with secrecy so characteristic of such movements: the renegade is the man or woman who has been in the arcanum, and brings forth with him or her the final verification of suspicions which might otherwise have been doubted by a skeptical world. But I think there is a deeper eschatological significance that attaches to the person of the renegade: in the spiritual wrestling match between good and evil which is the paranoid's archetypal model of the world, the renegade is living proof that all the conversions are not made by the wrong side. He brings with him the promise of redemption and victory.

A final characteristic of the paranoid style is related to the quality of its pedantry. One of the impressive things about paranoid literature is the contrast between its fantasied conclusions and the almost touching concern with factuality it invariably shows. It produces heroic strivings for evidence to prove that the unbelievable is the only thing that can be believed. Of course, there are highbrow, lowbrow, and middlebrow paranoids, as there are likely to be in any political tendency. But respectable paranoid literature not only starts from certain moral commitments that can indeed be justified but also carefully and all but obsessively accumulates "evidence." The difference between this "evidence" and that commonly employed by others is that it seems less a means of entering into normal political controversy than a means of warding off the profane intrusions of the secular political world. The paranoid seems to have little expectation of actually convincing a hostile world, but he can accumulate evidence in order to protect his cherished convictions from it.

Paranoid writing begins with certain broad defensible judgments. There *was* something to be said for the anti-Masons. After all, a secret society composed of influential men bound by special obligations could conceivably pose some kind of threat to the civil order in which they were suspended. There was also something to be said for the Protestant principles of individuality and freedom, as well as for the nativist desire to develop in North America a homogeneous civilization. Again, in our time an actual laxity in security allowed some Communists to find a place in governmental circles, and innumerable decisions of World War II and the Cold War could be faulted.

The higher paranoid scholarship is nothing if not coherent—in fact the paranoid mind is far more coherent than the real world. It is nothing if not scholarly in technique. McCarthy's 96-page pamphlet, *McCarthyism,* contains no less than 313 footnote references, and Mr. Welch's incredible assault on Eisenhower, *The Politician,* has one hundred pages of bibliography and notes. The entire right-wing movement of our time is a parade of experts, study groups, monographs, footnotes, and bibliographies. Sometimes the right-wing striving for scholarly depth and an inclusive world view has startling consequences: Mr. Welch, for example, has charged that the popularity of Arnold Toynbee's historical work is the consequence of a plot on the part of Fabians, "Labour party bosses in England," and various members of the Anglo-American "liberal establishment" to overshadow the much more truthful and illuminating work of Oswald Spengler.

THE DOUBLE SUFFERER

The paranoid style is not confined to our own country and time; it is an international phenomenon. Studying the millennial sects of Europe from the eleventh to the sixteenth century, Norman Cohn believed he found a persistent psychic complex that corresponds broadly with what I have been considering—a style made up of certain preoccupations and fantasies: "the megalomaniac view of oneself as the Elect, wholly good, abominably persecuted, yet assured of ultimate triumph; the attribution of gigantic and demonic powers to the adversary; the refusal to accept the ineluctable limitations and imperfections of human existence, such as transience, dissention, conflict, fallibility whether intellectual or moral; the obsession with inerrable prophecies . . . systematized misinterpretations, always gross and often grotesque."

This glimpse across a long span of time emboldens me to make the conjecture—it is no more than that—that a mentality disposed to see the world in this way may be a persistent psychic phenomenon, more or less constantly affecting a modest minority of the population. But certain religious traditions, certain social structures and national inheritances, certain historical catastrophes or frustrations may be conducive to the release of such psychic energies, and to situations in which they can more readily be built into mass movements or political parties. In American experience ethnic and religious conflict have plainly been a major focus for militant and suspicious minds of this sort, but class conflicts also can mobilize such energies. Perhaps the central situation conducive to the diffusion of the paranoid tendency is a confrontation of opposed interests which are (or are felt to be) totally irreconcilable, and thus by nature not susceptible to the normal political processes of bargain and compromise. The situation becomes worse when the representatives of a particular social interest—perhaps because of the very unrealistic and unrealizable nature of its demands—are shut out of the political process. Having no access to political bargaining or the making of decisions, they find their original conception that the world of power is sinister and malicious fully confirmed. They see only the consequences of power—and this through distorting lenses—and have no chance to observe its actual machinery. A distinguished historian has said that one of the most valuable things about history is that it teaches us how things do *not* happen. It is precisely this kind of awareness that the paranoid fails to develop. He has a special resistance of his own, of course, to developing such awareness, but circumstances often deprive him of exposure to events that might enlighten him—and in any case he resists enlightenment.

We are all sufferers from history, but the paranoid is a double sufferer, since he is afflicted not only by the real world, with the rest of us, but by his fantasies as well.

SECTION V
REVIEW QUESTIONS

1. What did Walter Lippman believe to be the dangers posed by measuring public opinion and relying on the results to guide public policy?

2. George Gallup believed that "We need to know the will of the people at all times." Are you convinced that this is either possible or desirable?

3. Do people who answer pollsters' questions necessarily know anything about the issues they are expressing opinions on? How does this affect the value of poll results?

4. Presidents are often criticized for doing and saying only what the polls suggest will be popular. Do you think a president should try to lead the people rather than follow the polls?

5. What is the primary lesson to be learned from James Prothro and Charles Grigg's classic study of the attitudes of Americans toward democratic principles?

6. To what extent is public opinion more the *result* of government actions than the *cause* of government actions? What does V. O. Key believe to be the relationship between political elites and mass public opinion? Do you agree?

7. Identify recent examples of what Richard Hofstadter called the "paranoid style in American politics." Do you think that this style is more common than when Hofstadter first identified it more than forty years ago? Why or why not?

VI

Political Parties

HAROLD GOSNELL

32. URBAN POLITICAL MACHINES

Gosnell captures the advantages and disadvantages of the old style machine politics in his classic description of Chicago politics in the 1930s. Many of the functions performed by governmental agencies since the days of the New Deal were handled quite efficiently by the old political machines. The precinct captain could usually be depended on for jobs, housing, welfare, and food during bad economic times. In the heyday of urban political machines in the first half of the twentieth century, a single political party boss—sometimes not even holding an elective office—dominated the formal processes of government by controlling jobs and building personal loyalty by doing favors for voters and business leaders alike. Although the pure political-machine organizational style has virtually disappeared in urban America, its significance in American political party history is well preserved in Gosnell's work.

THE ROLE OF URBAN POLITICS

What is the balance sheet of machine politics in an urban center such as Chicago during a period of economic crisis? On the credit side of the ledger should be placed the success of the bosses in softening class conflicts. By granting petty favors to various nationalistic and local groups, by taking advantage of the subsidies offered by the national government, by keeping the attention of the voters distracted by factional quarrels and sham disputes, the party machines have kept minor party movements from gaining any headway. From the standpoint of the business leaders, this function of parties has been very useful. Some of the submerged groups may not be so appreciative; but the fact remains that during the years 1930–36 the city was comparatively free from violent labor disputes, hunger riots, and class warfare. The decentralized, chaotic, and inadequate character of the governmental organization of the city has discouraged far-reaching demands upon local authorities.

Source: From Harold F. Gosnell, *Machine Politics: Chicago Model,* Chapter 9, pp. 183–93 (Chicago: The University of Chicago Press, 1937). Copyright © 1938 The University of Chicago Press. All rights reserved. Reprinted by permission.

During the depression the machine has also acted as a kind of buffer for the various governmental agencies which have had to deal with the distressed. Eviction cases, emergency hunger cases, and emergency clothing shortages were sometimes cared for in the first instance by the ward and precinct committeemen. The relief activities of the party workers were not systematic and, of course, were not disinterested, but they were devoid of red tape. Ward heelers asked no embarrassing questions, and they supplied at once any material aid they could. The demands of the period were such that the party organizations could not hope to meet more than a minute fraction of them, but they did leave the impression that they knew the ropes of the relief game.

The stability of the machine was reassuring to various groups that no upsetting innovations would be tried in local government. Ward leaders in particular showed an amazingly low turnover, considering the stresses and strains that accompanied the economic crisis. Business men, journalists, underworld leaders, bankers, and labor chiefs knew that they could count upon the local machine to do business in the old way in spite of changes that had taken place in the role of the national government. Inefficiency in local government could be tolerated if it meant resistance to the extension of the local public services. The largest industrialists, newspaper proprietors, bankers, and gambling kings did not want a state income tax, a modern tax-collection system, or an expansion of municipal services and budgets. Party bosses were a bulwark against such changes. Those citizens who might have benefited from such modifications of the role of local government were indifferent, deficient in promotional skills, misled by the press, and disillusioned by the failure of reform waves to leave many permanent traces.

While the depression has not eliminated the influence of the spoils tradition in city hall, it has drastically purged one of the major party organizations. The economic crisis greatly reduced national and local incomes and made the burden of taxation relatively much greater than it had been in the prosperous twenties. A city can support more than one political machine when real estate values are rising and incomes are going up. During such times the taxpayers are not so tax conscious as in lean times, and the general public is more indifferent to graft exposures and wasteful expenditure of public funds. In a period of economic depression there is graft enough for only one machine. The law of the pendulum in democratic countries operates against the party which is in power when the economic deprivations are first being felt. Those major party factions which were in power at the time of the stock market crash were swept from the public offices. There has undoubtedly been a decrease in the total amount of political grafting in the city during the past eight years. Relative to the opportunities available, there may not be any great decrease; but there are fewer political mouths to feed out of the public crib, since local political power has been concentrated in a single organization.

Under pressure from the financial interests the political bosses have been compelled, in the last few years, to make drastic economies. Tax collections have been insufficient to meet the local governmental expenses, and the unpaid public employee is not a great asset to the political machine. The banks have been unwilling to lend money unless total public expenditures were reduced. While many of the economies have not improved governmental efficiency, and there are still many strongholds of patronage and spoils, there have been some improvements, which have left the political bosses with less patronage. Greater publicity regarding tax assessments and collections has loosened the strangle hold which the corrupt politicians once had over a lucrative source of campaign funds. The demand for economy has aided the movement for the consolidation of overlapping authorities and the concentration of official responsibility for fiscal affairs.

In the field of public administration there have been a number of developments in recent years which have tended to lessen the influence of spoils. There has been a trend toward stricter supervision of the local tax authorities, and the newer forms of taxation are less open to political abuses. The Illinois sales tax, objectionable as it is from the theoretical point of view, is a tax which can be administered with comparatively little leakage. The advances which have been made in the field of public welfare administration have made the social service activities of the precinct committeemen more and more unnecessary. There have been fewer occasions when the party officials can step in and mitigate the harshness of the law. The growth of such services as parole, probation, community case work, rehabilitation and public employment bureaus has reduced the importance of the precinct captain as a community agent. These gains have been achieved for the most part through the efforts of the state and national governments. The most that can be said for the local machine is that it has furnished no effective opposition to these innovations.

The depression has also brought greater recognition for the merit system in the municipal service. In Chicago the civil service rules were extended to certain park districts by the new Park District Law, to the Sanitary District by legislation in 1935, to the employees of the county assessor by the new taxation legislation, and to some of the other county employees by administrative action. While the Illinois civil service legislation has been reasonably sound, the practical application of the rules has left much to be desired. The spirit of the merit system has been violated by an excessive number of temporary employees, by a vicious system of waivers which nullifies the function of promotional examinations, by the old-fashioned practice of "framing" efficient employees, by the retention of inefficient political employees by means of legal chicanery, and from time to time by outright bribery and corruption. Leaders of both of the major parties have sinned against the civil service commandments. A pre-depression mayor of one party was frankly hostile to the merit system. Post-depression mayors of another party have given lip service to the system but have administered it as politicians.

One might expect that, when hard times brought a great relative increase in the size of the tax burden, the taxpayers would demand greater service and revolt against the perversion of government by spoilsmen. The defeat of established machines in New York and Philadelphia since 1929 might be interpreted

between alternatives of action. In order to keep the parties apart, one must consider the relations between each and public policy. The reasons for the growing emphasis on public policy in party politics are to be found, above all, in the very operations of modern government.

2. The New Importance of Program

The crux of public affairs lies in the necessity for more effective formulation of general policies and programs and for better integration of all of the far-flung activities of modern government. It is in terms of party programs that political leaders can attempt to consolidate public attitudes toward the work plans of government.

3. The Potentialities of the Party System

The potentialities of the two-party system are suggested, on the one hand, by the fact that for all practical purposes the major parties monopolize elections; and, on the other, by the fact that both parties have in the past managed to adapt themselves to the demands made upon them by external necessities. It is good practical politics to reconsider party organization in the light of the changing conditions of politics. Happily such an effort entails an application of ideas about the party system that are no longer unfamiliar.

2. WHAT KIND OF PARTY SYSTEM IS NEEDED?

The party system that is needed must be democratic, responsible and effective.

I. A Stronger Two-Party System

1. The Need for an Effective Party System An effective party system requires, first, that the parties are able to bring forth programs to which they commit themselves and, second, that the parties possess sufficient internal cohesion to carry out these programs. Such a degree of unity within the parties cannot be brought about without party procedures that give a large body of people an opportunity to share in the development of the party program.

2. The Need for an Effective Opposition Party The fundamental requirement of accountability is a two-party system in which the opposition party acts as the critic of the party in power, developing, defining and presenting the policy alternatives which are necessary for a true choice in reaching public decisions. The opposition most conducive to responsible government is an organized party opposition.

II. Better Integrated Parties

1. The Need for a Party System with Greater Resistance to Pressure There is little to suggest that the phenomenal growth of interest organizations in recent decades has come to its end. The whole development makes necessary a reinforced party system that can cope with the multiplied organized pressures. Compromise among interests is compatible with the aims of a free society only when the terms of reference reflect an openly acknowledged concept of the public interest.

2. The Need for a Party System with Sufficient Party Loyalty Needed clarification of party policy will not cause the parties to differ more fundamentally or more sharply than they have in the past. Nor is it to be assumed that increasing concern with their programs will cause the parties to erect between themselves an ideological wall. Parties have the right and duty to announce the terms to govern participation in the common enterprise. The emphasis in all consideration of party discipline must be on positive measures to create a strong and general agreement on policies. A basis for party cohesion in Congress will be established as soon as the parties interest themselves sufficiently in their congressional candidates to set up strong and active campaign organizations in the constituencies.

III. More Responsible Parties

1. The Need for Parties Responsible to the Public Party responsibility means the responsibility of both parties to the general public, as enforced in elections. Party responsibility to the public, enforced in elections, implies that there be more than one party, for the public can hold a party responsible only if it has a choice. As a means of achieving responsibility, the clarification of party policy also tends to keep public debate on a more realistic level, restraining the inclination of party spokesmen to make unsubstantiated statements and charges.

2. The Need for Parties Responsible to Their Members Party responsibility includes also the responsibility of party leaders to the party membership, as enforced in primaries, caucuses and conventions. The external and the internal kinds of party responsibility need not conflict. Intraparty conflict will be minimized if it is generally recognized that national, state and local party leaders have a common responsibility to the party membership. National party leaders have a legitimate interest in the nomination of congressional candidates.

3. THE INADEQUACY OF THE EXISTING PARTY SYSTEM

I. Beginning Transition

1. *Change and Self-Examination* Marked changes in the structure and processes of American society have necessarily affected the party system. The prevailing climate of self-examination as well as the current tendencies toward change in the party system give point to inquiries like that represented by our report.

2. *Burden of the Past* Formal party organization in its main features is still substantially what it was before the Civil War. Under these circumstances the main trends of American politics have tended to outflank the party system.

II. Some Basic Problems

1. *The Federal Basis* The two parties are organized on a federal basis. The national and state party organizations are largely independent of one another, without appreciable common approach to problems of party policy and strategy. The real issue is not over the federal form of organization but over the right balance of forces within this type of organization. A corollary of the kind of federalism now expressed in the party system is an excessive measure of internal separatism.

2. *The Location of Leadership* Party organization does not vest leadership of the party as a whole in either a single person or a committee. There is at present no central figure or organ which could claim authority to take up party problems, policies and strategy.

3. *The Ambiguity of Membership* No understandings or rules or criteria exist with respect to membership in a party. Those who suggest that elections should deal with personalities but not with programs suggest at the same time that party membership should mean nothing at all.

III. Specific Deficiencies

1. *National Party Organs* The National Convention, as at present constituted and operated, is an unwieldy, unrepresentative and less than responsible body. The National Committee is seldom a generally influential body and much less a working body. House and Senate campaign committees do not always have a good working relationship with the National Committee. Although interest in

questions of party policy has grown, the national party organs are not so constituted nor so coordinated as to make it simple for them to pay enough attention to these questions.

2. Party Platforms Alternatives between the parties are defined so badly that it is often difficult to determine what the election has decided even in broadest terms. The prevailing procedure for the writing and adoption of national party platforms is too hurried and too remote from the process by which actual decisions are made to command the respect of the whole party and the electorate. The platform should be the end product of a long search for a working agreement within the party.

3. Intraparty Democracy Too little consideration has been given to ways and means of bringing about a constructive relationship between the party and its members. In making the most of popular participation, the performance of American parties is very unsatisfactory.

4. Party Research A party stands as much in need of research as does business enterprise or the government itself.

4. NEW DEMANDS UPON PARTY LEADERSHIP

I. The Nature of Modern Public Policy

1. Broad Range of Policy The expanding responsibilities of modern government have brought about so extensive an interlacing of governmental action with the country's economic and social life that the need for coordinated and coherent programs, legislative as well as administrative, has become paramount. In a democracy no general program can be adopted and carried out without wide public support.

2. Impact on the Public In a predominantly industrial society, public policy tends to be widely inclusive, involving in its objectives and effects very large segments of the public or even the whole country.

3. Governmental Program Machinery On the side of government, in the administrative and the legislative spheres, the twin needs for program formulation and for program machinery have long been recognized. The governmental advance toward program formulation needs now to be paralleled in the political sphere proper—above all, in the party system.

II. Rise of Nation-Wide Policy Issues

1. *An Historic Trend* The changes in the nature and scope of public policy are the result of changes in the social structure and in the economy of the United States.

2. *Past and Present Factors* There has been in recent decades a continuing decline of sectionalism. Party organization designed to deal with the increasing volume of national issues must give wide range to the national party leadership.

3. *New Interest Groups in Politics* The economic and social factors that have reduced the weight of sectionalism have also resulted in the development of a new type of interest groups, built upon large membership. To a much greater extent than in the past, they operate as if they were auxiliary organizations of one or the other party.

5. The Question of Constitutional Amendment

1. *A Cabinet System?* A responsible cabinet system makes the leaders of the majority collectively accountable for the conduct of the government.

2. *Strong Parties as a Condition* To amend the Constitution in order to create a responsible cabinet system is not a practicable way of getting more effective parties.

3. *Adaption within the Constitution* The parties can do much to adapt the usages under the Constitution to their purposes.

MORRIS FIORINA

34. THE DECLINE OF RESPONSIBLE PARTY GOVERNMENT

Political scientist Morris P. Fiorina laments the decline of "responsible party" government, arguing that strong parties offer the best or only way for voters to participate meaningfully in the governing process. Echoing the American Political Science Association's statement on responsible party government issued 30 years earlier, Fiorina maintains that the consequences for American politics of our seriously weakened political parties include a decline in the ability of political leaders to act decisively, an increase in the importance of single-issue politics, and a growing alienation of Americans from their political system.

Fiorina's plea for more disciplined political parties offering coherent programs to the voters was heeded by the Republicans in 1994. The midterm congressional elections that year resulted in major gains for the Republicans. In fact, not since 1954 had the Republicans gained control of both the House and Senate. During the campaign, Republican Representatives Newt Gingrich and Dick Armey persuaded hundreds of Republican congressional candidates to sign what they called a "Contract With America," in which the signers promised to vote for ten major policy initiatives during the first hundred days of the 104th Congress. The commitment of so many congressional candidates of one party to an explicit party platform was an unusual expression of the classic "responsible party" model articulated by the American Political Science Association and supported by many political scientists such as Morris Fiorina. Speaking with one voice, the Republicans were telling the voters: Elect us and we will carry out our part of the contract by enacting the measures we have pledged to enact. In the "responsible party" model, the voters could then reward or punish the Republicans two years later.

Source: "The Decline of Collective Responsibility in American Politics" from *Daedalus*, Vol. 109, No. 3 (Summer 1980), p. 25–46. © 1980 by the American Academy of Arts and Sciences. Reprinted by permission of MIT Press Journals. Footnotes have been renumbered.

> *Included in the "contract" were pledges to cut taxes, amend the Constitution to require a balanced budget and to impose term limits on members of Congress, reform the federal criminal law in order to "take back our streets," and restore "common sense" to the civil justice system by limiting punitive damages and making the losing party in a civil suit pay the costs of litigation.*
>
> *Although Speaker Gingrich did place nearly all of these proposals before the House of Representatives and most were passed by the Republican majority, the Senate was much less responsive and few were enacted into law.*

Though the founding fathers believed in the necessity of establishing a genuinely national government, they took great pains to design one that could not lightly do things *to* its citizens; what government might do *for* its citizens was to be limited to the functions of what we know now as the "watchman state." Thus the Founders composed the constitutional litany familiar to every schoolchild: they created a federal system, they distributed and blended powers within and across the federal levels, and they encouraged the occupants of the various positions to check and balance each other by structuring incentives so that one officeholder's ambitions would be likely to conflict with others'. The resulting system of institutional arrangements predictably hampers efforts to undertake major initiatives and favors maintenance of the status quo.

Given the historical record faced by the Founders, their emphasis on constraining government is understandable. But we face a later historical record, one that shows two hundred years of increasing demands for government to act positively. Moreover, developments unforeseen by the Founders increasingly raise the likelihood that the uncoordinated actions of individuals and groups will inflict serious damage on the nation as a whole. The by-products of the industrial and technological revolutions impose physical risks not only on us, but on future generations as well. Resource shortages and international cartels raise the spectre of economic ruin. And the simple proliferation of special interests with their intense, particularistic demands threatens to render us politically incapable of taking actions that might either advance the state of society or prevent foreseeable deteriorations in that state. None of this is to suggest that we should forget about what government can do *to* us—the contemporary concern with the proper scope and methods of government intervention in the social and economic orders is long overdue. But the modern age demands as well that we worry about our ability to make government work *for* us. The problem is that we are gradually losing that ability, and a principal reason for this loss is the steady erosion of *responsibility* in American politics.

What do I mean by this important quality, responsibility? To say that some person or group is responsible for a state of affairs is to assert that he or they have the ability to take legitimate actions that have a major impact on that state of affairs. More colloquially, when someone is responsible, we know whom to blame. . . .

Unfortunately, the importance of responsibility in a democracy is matched by the difficulty of attaining it. In an autocracy, individual responsibility suffices; the location of power in a single individual locates responsibility in that individual as well. But individual responsibility is insufficient whenever more than one person shares governmental authority. We can hold a particular congressman individually responsible for a personal transgression such as bribe-taking. We can even hold a president individually responsible for military moves where he presents Congress and the citizenry with a *fait accompli*. But on most national issues individual responsibility is difficult to assess. If one were to go to Washington, randomly accost a Democratic congressman, and berate him about a 20-percent rate of inflation, imagine the response. More than likely it would run, "Don't blame me. If 'they' had done what I've advocated for *x* years, things would be fine today. . . ."

American institutional structure makes this kind of game-playing all too easy. In order to overcome it we must lay the credit or blame for national conditions on all those who had any hand in bringing them about: some form of *collective responsibility* is essential.

The only way collective responsibility has ever existed, and can exist given our institutions, is through the agency of the political party; in American politics, responsibility requires cohesive parties. This is an old claim to be sure, but its age does not detract from its present relevance.[1] In fact, the continuing decline in public esteem for the parties and continuing efforts to "reform" them out of the political process suggest that old arguments for party responsibility have not been made often enough, or, at least, convincingly enough, so I will make these arguments once again in this essay.

A strong political party can generate collective responsibility by creating incentive for leaders, followers, and popular supporters to think and act in collective terms. First, by providing party leaders with the capability (e.g., control of institutional patronage, nominations, and so on) to discipline party members, genuine leadership becomes possible. Legislative output is less likely to be a least common denominator—a residue of myriad conflicting proposals—and more likely to consist of a program actually intended to solve a problem or move the nation in a particular direction. Second, the subordination of individual officeholders to the party lessens their ability to separate themselves from party actions. Like it or not, their performance becomes identified with the performance of the collectivity to which they belong. Third, with individual candidate variation greatly reduced, voters have less incentive to support individuals and more incentive to support or oppose the party as a whole. And fourth, the circle closes as party-line voting in the electorate provides party leaders with the incentive to propose policies that will earn the support of a national majority, and party back-benchers with the personal incentive to cooperate with leaders in the attempt to compile a good record for the party as a whole.

In the American context, strong parties have traditionally clarified politics in two ways. First, they allow citizens to assess responsibility easily, at least when the government is unified, which it more often was in earlier eras when party meant more than it does today.[2] Citizens need only evaluate the social, economic, and international conditions they observe and make a simple decision for or against change. They do not need to decide whether the energy, inflation, urban, and defense policies advocated by their congressman would be superior to those advocated by Carter—were any of them to be enacted!

The second way in which strong parties clarify American politics follows from the first. When citizens assess responsibility on the party as a whole, party members have personal incentives to see the party evaluated favorably. They have little to gain from gutting their president's program one day and attacking him for lack of leadership the next, since they share in the president's fate when voters do not differentiate within the party. Put simply, party responsibility provides party members with a personal stake in their collective performance.

Admittedly, party responsibility is a blunt instrument. The objection immediately arises that party responsibility condemns junior Democratic representatives to suffer electorally for an inflation they could do little to affect. An unhappy situation, true, but unless we accept it, Congress as a whole escapes electoral retribution for an inflation they *could* have done something to affect. Responsibility requires acceptance of both conditions. The choice is between a blunt instrument or none at all.

Of course, the United States is not Great Britain. We have neither the institutions nor the traditions to support a British brand of responsible party government, and I do not see either the possibility or the necessity for such a system in America. In the past the United States has enjoyed eras in which party was a much stronger force than today. And until recently—a generation, roughly—parties have provided an "adequate" degree of collective responsibility. They have done so by connecting the electoral fates of party members, via presidential coattails, for example, and by transforming elections into referenda on party performance, as with congressional off-year elections.

In earlier times, when citizens voted for the party, not the person, parties had incentives to nominate good candidates, because poor ones could have harmful fallout on the ticket as a whole.[3] In particular, the existence of presidential coattails (positive and negative) provided an inducement to avoid the nomination of narrowly based candidates, no matter how committed their supporters. And, once in office, the existence of party voting in the electorate provided party members with the incentive to compile a good *party* record. In particular, the tendency of national midterm elections to serve as referenda on the performance of the president provided a clear inducement for congressmen to do what they could to see that their president was perceived as a solid performer. By stimulating electoral phenomena such as coattail effects and midterm referenda, party transformed some degree of personal ambition into concern with collective performance. . . .

THE CONTINUING DECLINE OF PARTY IN THE UNITED STATES

Party is a simple term that covers a multitude of complicated organizations and processes. It manifests itself most concretely as the set of party organizations that exist principally at the state and local levels. It manifests itself most elusively as a psychological presence in the mind of the citizen. Somewhere in between, and partly a function of the first two, is the manifestation of party as a force in government. The discussion in this section will hold to this traditional schema, though it is clear that the three aspects of party have important interconnections.

Party Organizations

In the United States, party organization had traditionally meant state and local party organization. The national party generally has been a loose confederacy of subnational units that swings into action for a brief period every four years. This characterization remains true today, despite the somewhat greater influence and augmented functions of the national organizations.[4] Though such things are difficult to measure precisely, there is general agreement that the formal party organizations have undergone a secular decline since their peak at the end of the nineteenth century. The prototype of the old-style organization was the urban machine, a form approximated today only in Chicago.

Several long-term trends have served to undercut old-style party organizations. The patronage system has been steadily chopped back since passage of the Civil Service Act of 1883. The social welfare functions of the parties have passed to the government as the modern welfare state developed. And, less concretely, the entire ethos of the old-style party organization is increasingly at odds with modern ideas of government based on rational expertise. These long-term trends spawned specific attacks on the old party organizations. In the late nineteenth and early twentieth centuries the Populists, Progressives, and asserted other reformers fought electoral corruption with the Australian Ballot and personal registration systems. They attempted to break the hold of the party bosses over nominations by mandating the direct primary. They attacked the urban machines with drives for nonpartisan at-large elections and nonpartisan city managers. None of these reforms destroyed the parties; they managed to live with the reforms better than most reformers had hoped. But the reforms reflected changing popular attitudes toward the parties and accelerated the secular decline in the influence of the party organizations.

The New Deal period temporarily arrested the deterioration of the party organizations, at least on the Democratic side. Unified party control under a "political" president provided favorable conditions for the state and local organizations.[5] But following the heyday of the New Deal (and ironically, in part, because of government assumption of subnational parties' functions) the decline continued.

In the 1970s two series of reforms further weakened the influence of organized parties in American national politics. The first was a series of legal changes deliberately intended to lessen organized party influence in the presidential nominating process. In the Democratic party, "New Politics" activists captured the national party apparatus and imposed a series of rules changes designed to "open up" the politics of presidential nominations. The Republican party—long more amateur and open than the Democratic party—adopted weaker versions of the Democratic rules changes. In addition, modifications of state electoral laws to conform to the Democratic rules changes (enforced by the federal courts) stimulated Republican rules changes as well. . . .

A second series of 1970s reforms lessened the role of formal party organizations in the conduct of political campaigns. These are financing regulations growing out of the Federal Election Campaign Act of 1971 as amended in 1974 and 1976. In this case the reforms were aimed at cleaning up corruption in the financing of campaigns; their effects on the parties were a by-product, though many individuals accurately predicted its nature. Serious presidential candidates are now publicly financed. Though the law permits the national party to spend two cents per eligible voter on behalf of the nominee, it also obliges the candidate to set up a finance committee separate from the national party. Between this legally mandated separation and fear of violating spending limits or accounting regulations, for example, the law has the effect of encouraging the candidate to keep his party at arm's length. . . .

The ultimate results of such reforms are easy to predict. A lesser party role in the nominating and financing of candidates encourages candidates to organize and conduct independent campaigns, which further weakens the role of parties. Of course, party is not the entire story in this regard. Other modern day changes contribute to the diminished party role in campaign politics. For one thing, party foot soldiers are no longer so important, given the existence of a large leisured middle class that participates out of duty or enjoyment, but that participates on behalf of particular candidates and issues rather than parties. Similarly, contemporary campaigns rely heavily on survey research, the mass media, and modern advertising methods—all provided by independent consultants outside the formal party apparatus. Although these developments are not directly related to the contemporary reforms, their effect is the same: the diminution of the role of parties in conducting political campaigns. And if parties do not grant nominations, fund their choices, and work for them, why should those choices feel any commitment to their party?

PARTY IN THE ELECTORATE

In the citizenry at large, party takes the form of a psychological attachment. The typical American traditionally has been likely to identify with one or the other of the two major parties. Such identifications are transmitted across generations to some degree, and within the individual they tend to be fairly stable.[6] But there is mounting evidence that the basis of identification lies in the individual's experiences (direct and vicarious, through family and social groups) with the parties in the past.[7] Our current party system, of course, is based on the dislocations of the Depression period and the New Deal attempts to alleviate them. Though only a small proportion of those who experienced the Depression directly are active voters today, the general outlines of citizen party identifications much resemble those established at that time.

Again, there is reason to believe that the extent of citizen attachments to parties has undergone a long-term decline from a late nineteenth century high.[8] And again, the New Deal appears to have been a period during which the decline was arrested, even temporarily reversed. But again, the decline of party has reasserted itself in the 1970s. . . .

As the 1960s wore on, the heretofore stable distribution of citizen party identifications began to change in the general direction of weakened attachments to the parties. Between 1960 and 1976, independents, broadly defined, increased from less than a quarter to more than a third of the voting-age population. Strong identifiers declined from slightly more than a third to about a quarter of the population. . . .

Indisputably, party in the electorate has declined in recent years. Why? To some extent the electoral decline results from the organizational decline. Few party organizations any longer have the tangible incentives to turn out the faithful and assure their loyalty. Candidates run independent campaigns and deemphasize their partisan ties whenever they see any short-term electoral gain in doing so. If party is increasingly less important in the nomination and election of candidates, it is not surprising that such diminished importance is reflected in the attitudes and behavior of the voter.

Certain long-term sociological and technological trends also appear to work against party in the electorate. The population is younger, and younger citizens traditionally are less attached to the parties than their elders. The population is more highly educated; fewer voters need some means of simplifying the choices they face in the political arena, and party, of course, has been the principal means of simplification. And the media revolution has vastly expanded the amount of information easily available to the citizenry. Candidates would have little incentive to operate campaigns independent of the parties if there were no means to apprise the citizenry of their independence. The media provide the means.

Finally, our present party system is an old one. For increasing numbers of citizens, party attachments based on the Great Depression seem lacking in relevance to the problems of the late twentieth century. Beginning with the racial issue in the 1960s, proceeding to the social issue of the 1970s, and to the energy, environment, and inflation issues of today, the parties have been rent by internal dissension. Sometimes they failed to take stands, at other times they took the wrong ones from the standpoint of the rank and file, and at most times they have failed to solve the new problems in any genuine sense. Since 1965 the parties have done little or nothing to earn the loyalties of modern Americans.

PARTY IN GOVERNMENT

If the organizational capabilities of the parties have weakened, and their psychological ties to the voters have loosened, one would expect predictable consequences for the party in government. In particular, one would expect to see an increasing degree of split party control within and across the levels of American government. The evidence on this point is overwhelming.

At the state level, twenty-seven of the fifty governments were under divided party control after the 1978 election. In seventeen states a governor of one party opposed a legislature controlled by the other, and in ten others a bicameral legislature was split between the parties. By way of contrast, twenty years ago the number of states with divided party control was sixteen.

At the federal level the trend is similar. In 1953 only twelve states sent a senator of each party to Washington. The number increased to sixteen by 1961, to twenty-one by 1972, and stands at twenty-seven today. Of course, the senators in each state are elected at different times. But the same patterns emerge when we examine simultaneous elections. There is an increasing tendency for congressional districts to support a congressman of one party and the presidential candidate of the other. At the turn of the century it was extremely rare for a congressional district to report a split result. But since that time the trend has been steadily upward. We may well be heading for a record in 1980 as a vulnerable Democratic president runs with 250-odd not-so-vulnerable Democratic congressmen. . . .

The increased fragmentation of the party in government makes it more difficult for government officeholders to work together than in times past (not that it has ever been terribly easy). Voters meanwhile have a more difficult time attributing responsibility for government performance, and this only further fragments party control. The result is lessened collective responsibility in the system. . . .

SOME CONSEQUENCE OF THE DECLINE OF COLLECTIVE RESPONSIBILITY

The weakening of party has contributed directly to the severity of several of the important problems the nation faces. For some of these, such as the government's inability to deal with inflation and energy, the connections are obvious. But for other problems, such as the growing importance of single-issue politics and the growing alienation of the American citizenry, the connections are more subtle.

IMMOBILISM

As the electoral interdependence of the party in government declines, its ability to act also declines. If responsibility can be shifted to another level or to another officeholder, there is less incentive to stick one's own neck out in an attempt to solve a given problem. Leadership becomes more difficult, the ever-present bias toward the short-term solution becomes more pronounced, and the possibility of solving any given problem lessens. . . .

No one seriously believes that the American constitutional order is in danger of collapse (and certainly we have no de Gaulle waiting in the wings). But political inability to take actions that entail short-run costs ordinarily will result in much higher costs in the long run—we cannot continually depend on the technological fix. So the present American immobilism cannot be dismissed lightly. The sad thing is that the American people appear to understand the depth of our present problems and, at least in principle, appear prepared to sacrifice in furtherance of the long-run good. But they will not have an opportunity to choose between two or more such long-term plans. Although both parties promise tough, equitable policies, in the present state of our politics, neither can deliver.

Single-Issue Politics

In recent years both political analysts and politicians have decried the increased importance of single-issue groups in American politics. Some in fact would claim that the present immobilism in our politics owes more to the rise of single-issue groups than to the decline of party. A little thought, however, should reveal that the two trends are connected. Is single-issue politics a recent phenomenon? The contention is doubtful; such groups have always been active participants in American politics. The gun lobby already was a classic example at the time of President Kennedy's assassination. And however impressive the antiabortionists appear today, remember the temperance movement, which succeeded in getting its constitutional amendment. American history contains numerous forerunners of today's groups, from anti-Masons to abolitionists to the Klan—singularity of purpose is by no means a modern phenomenon. Why, then, do we hear all the contemporary hoopla about single-issue groups? Probably because politicians fear them now more than before and thus allow them to play a larger role in our politics. Why should this be so? Simply because the parties are too weak to protect their members and thus to contain single-issue politics.

In earlier times single-issue groups were under greater pressures to reach accommodations with the parties. After all, the parties nominated candidates, financed candidates, worked for candidates, and, perhaps most important, party voting protected candidates. When a contemporary single-issue group threatens to "get" an officeholder, the threat must be taken seriously. The group can go into his district, recruit a primary or general election challenger, or both, and bankroll that candidate. Even if the sentiment espoused by the group is not the majority sentiment of the district, few officeholders relish the thought of a strong, well-financed opponent. Things were different when strong parties existed. Party leaders controlled the nomination process and would fight to maintain that control. An outside challenge would merely serve to galvanize the party into action to protect its prerogatives. Only if a single-issue group represented the dominant sentiment in a given area could it count on controlling the party organization itself, and thereby electoral politics in that area.

Not only did the party organization have greater ability to resist single-issue pressures at the electoral level, but the party in government had greater ability to control the agenda, and thereby contain single-issue pressures at the policy-making level. Today we seem condemned to go through an annual agony over federal abortion funding. There is little doubt that politicians on both sides would prefer to reach some reasonable compromise at the committee level and settle the issue. But in today's decentralized Congress there is no way to put the lid on. In contrast, historians tell us that in the late nineteenth century a large portion of the Republican constituency was far less interested in the tariff and other questions of national economic development than in whether German immigrants should be permitted to teach their native language in their local schools, and whether Catholics and "liturgical Protestants" should be permitted to consume alcohol.[9] Interestingly, however, the national agenda of the period is devoid of such issues. And when they do show up on the state level, the exceptions prove the rule; they produce party splits and striking defeats for the party that allowed them to surface. . . .

In sum, a strong party that is held accountable for the government of a nation-state has both the ability and the incentive to contain particularistic pressures. It controls nominations, elections, and the agenda, and it collectively realizes that small minorities are small minorities no matter how intense they are. But as the parties decline they lose control over nominations and campaigns, they lose the loyalty of the voters, and they lose control of the agenda. Party officeholders cease to be held collectively accountable for party performance, but they become individually exposed to the political pressure of myriad interest groups. The decline of party permits interest groups to wield greater influence, their success encourages the formation of still more interest groups, politics becomes increasingly fragmented, and collective responsibility becomes still more elusive.

Popular Alienation from Government

For at least a decade political analysts have pondered the significance of survey data indicative of a steady increase in the alienation of the American public from the political process. . . . The American public is in a nasty mood, a cynical, distrusting, and resentful mood. The question is, Why? . . .

If the same national problems not only persist but worsen while ever-greater amounts of revenue are directed at them, why shouldn't the typical citizen conclude that most of the money must be wasted by incompetent officials? If narrowly based interest groups increasingly affect our politics, why shouldn't citizens increasingly conclude that the interests run the government?

For fifteen years the citizenry has listened to a steady stream of promises but has seen very little in the way of follow-through. An increasing proportion of the electorate does not believe that elections make a difference, a fact that largely explains the much-discussed post-1960 decline in voting turnout.

Continued public disillusionment with the political process poses several real dangers. For one thing, disillusionment begets further disillusionment. Leadership becomes more difficult if citizens do not trust their leaders and will not give them the benefit of a doubt. Policy failure becomes more likely if citizens expect the policy to fail. Waste increases and government competence decreases as citizen disrespect for politics encourages a lesser breed of person to make careers in government. And "government by a few big interests" becomes more than a cliché if citizens increasingly decide the cliché is true and cease participating for that reason.

Finally, there is the real danger that continued disappointment with particular government officials ultimately metamorphoses into disillusionment with government per se. Increasing numbers of citizens believe that government is not simply overextended but perhaps incapable of any further bettering of the world. Yes, government is overextended, inefficiency is pervasive, and ineffectiveness is all too common. But government is one of the few instruments of collective action we have, and even those committed to selective pruning of government programs cannot blithely allow the concept of an activist government to fall into disrepute.

The concept of democracy does not submit to precise definition, a claim supported by the existence of numerous nonidentical definitions. To most people democracy embodies a number of valued qualities. Unfortunately, there is no reason to believe that all such valued qualities are mutually compatible. At the least, maximizing the attainment of one quality may require accepting middling levels of another.

Recent American political thought has emphasized government *of* the people and *by* the people. Attempts have been made to insure that all preferences receive a hearing, especially through direct expression of those preferences, but if not, at least through faithful representation. Citizen *participation* is the reigning value, and arrangements that foster widespread participation are much in favor.

Of late, however, some political commentators have begun to wonder whether contemporary thought places sufficient emphasis on government *for* the people. In stressing participation have we lost sight of *accountability?* Surely, we should be as concerned with what government produces as with how many participate. What good is participation if the citizenry is unable to determine who merits their support.

Participation and responsiblitiy are not logically incompatible, but there is a degree of tension between the two, and the quest for either may be carried to extremes. Participation maximizers find themselves involved with quotas and virtual representation schemes, while responsibility maximizers can find themselves with a closed shop under boss rule.[10] Moreover, both qualities can weaken the democracy they supposedly underpin. Unfettered participation produces Hyde Amendments and immobilism. Responsible parties can use agenda power to thwart democratic decision—for more than a century the Democratic party used what control it had to suppress the racial issue. Neither participation nor responsibility should be pursued at the expense of all other values, but that is what has happened with participation over the course of the past two decades, and we now reap the consequences in our politics.

NOTES

1. This argument was expounded at the turn of the century by writers such as Woodrow Wilson and A. Lawrence Lowell. It enjoyed a resurgence at mid-century in the thinking of scholars such as E. E. Schattschneider. For a thorough exegesis of the party responsibility argument, see Austin Ranney, *The Doctrine of Responsible Party Government* (Urbana: University of Illinois Press, 1962).
2. During the postwar period the national government has experienced divided party control about half the time. In the preceding half century there were only six years of divided control.
3. At this point skeptics invariably ask, "What about Warren G. Harding?" The statement in the text is meant to express a tendency. Certainly, in the first sixty years of this century we did not see a string of candidates comparable to the products of the amateur politics of the past fourteen years (Goldwater, MacGovern, Carter, Reagan).
4. See Gerald Pomper, "The Decline of the Party in American Elections," *Political Science Quarterly*, 92(1977): 21–41; John Kessel P*residential Campaign Politics: Coalition strategies and Citizen Responses* (Homewood, Illinois: Dorsey, 1980), ch. 10; Austin Ranney, "The Political Parties: Reform and Decline," in Anthony King (ed.), *The New American Political System* (Washington, D.C.: American Enterprise Institute, 1978), 213–47. Both Kessel and Pomper have discussed the increased importance of the national party organizations in terms of maintenance of continuing operations, imposition of national rules and standards on the local parties, and so on. I believe with Ranney, however, that, considering all levels of the party together, there has been a decline in organizational strength even as the national party apparatuses have grown more influential.
5. Though federal employment increased considerably during the New Deal era, the proportion covered by civil service declined. Thus the erosion of the patronage system was temporarily halted. In addition, scholars have documented the political basis of New Deal spending and program decisions. See Gavin Wright, "The Political Economy of New Deal Spending: An Econometric Analysis," *Review of Economics and Statistics*, 56(1974): 30–38.
6. Angus Campbell, et al., *The American Voter* (New York: Wiley, 1960), chs. 6, 7.
7. See Morris Fiorina, *Retrospective Voting in American National Elections* (New Haven: Yale University Press, forthcoming), ch. 5.
8. For a discussion, see Walter Dean Burnham, *Critical Elections and the Mainsprings of American Politics* (New York: Norton, 1970).
9. Paul Kleppner, *The Cross of Culture: A Social Analysis of Midwestern Politics, 1850–1900* (New York: Free Press, 1970), ch. 2.
10. S. E. Finer, *The Changing British Party System,* 1945–1979 (Washington, D.C.: American Enterprise Institute, 1980).

MAURICE DUVERGER

35. ELECTORAL BASIS OF THE TWO-PARTY SYSTEM

Political party systems vary widely among democratic nations. Some, like the United States, have only two significant large political parties, while others, such as France or Italy, continue to have many smaller parties. French political scientist Maurice Duverger's classic explanation for these differences was based on the different electoral systems found in these countries. Duverger asserted that countries in which legislative officials are elected by a simple plurality, where only one representative is elected in each district, will have only two large parties. This is because there is a great incentive for the various factions to unite behind a single candidate when that is the best way to win more votes than the other side. In a race for Congress, for instance, splinter groups backing their own candidates have almost no chance to win because the candidate who has even one more vote than all the rest wins. By contrast, electoral systems in which parties receive a number of district representatives proportional to their party's vote tend to encourage small parties. Thus, it is clear that any system of proportional representation that might be adopted in the United States would necessarily weaken the two-party system.

It is not perhaps unnecessary to remind readers here that the descriptions given in this work are provisional and hypothetical in character, often being based on documentation too restricted and cursory to permit of definite conclusions. Frequently we have had to draw imaginary lines to link the few shining points scattered in the dark: the resultant patterns can give only a very approximate idea of reality. The development of the science of political parties (it could perhaps be called *stasiology*) will no doubt lead to the revision of many of the patterns we have traced. None the less some general phenomena seem more or less established, and from them some general conclusions can be drawn.

Source: From Maurice Duverger, *Political Parties: Their Organization and Activity in the Modern State* (New York: John Wiley & Sons, Inc 1951). Reprinted by permission of Armand Colin.

The opponents of "party systems" will find much ammunition in this book. The organization of political parties is certainly not in conformity with orthodox notions of democracy. Their internal structure is essentially autocratic and oligarchic: their leaders are not really appointed by the members, in spite of appearances, but co-opted or nominated by the central body; they tend to form a ruling class, isolated from the militants, a caste that is more or less exclusive. In so far as they are elected, the party oligarchy is widened without ever becoming a democracy, for the election is carried out by the members, who are a minority in comparison with those who give their votes to the party in general elections. Parliamentary representatives are increasingly subject to the authority of the party inner circle: this means that the mass of electors is dominated by the small group of members and militants, itself subordinate to the ruling bodies of the party. The argument must be carried further: even supposing that parties were ruled by parliamentary representatives it would be an illusion to think them democratic. For elections themselves ill-interpret the true state of opinion. Parties create opinion as much as they represent it; they form it by propaganda; they impose a prefabricated mould upon it: the party system is not only the reflection of public opinion but also the result of external technical factors (like ballot procedure) which are imposed upon opinion. The party system is less a photograph of opinion than opinion is a projection of the party system.

The general development of parties tends to emphasize their deviation from the democratic regime. Growing centralization is increasingly diminishing the influence of members over leaders, while on the other hand strengthening the influence of leaders upon members. Electoral processes are gradually losing ground in the appointment of leaders: co-option or nomination from above, which used to be modestly veiled, are now partially acknowledged in constitutions and sometimes loudly proclaimed as a sign of progress (in Fascist parties). The development of vertical linking and the watertight compartments which are the result restrict the freedom of action of the base and increase the sphere of influence of the apex; they make possible a close regimentation of party members that can prevent any move towards independence of the centre and can preserve strict orthodoxy. Discipline among members is tightened both by these material means and by an even greater effort of propaganda and persuasion which leads them to venerate the Party and its leaders and to believe in their infallibility: the critical attitude gives way to an attitude of adoration. Parliamentary representatives themselves are compelled to an obedience which transforms them into voting machines controlled by the leaders of the party. Thus there arise closed, disciplined, mechanized bodies, monolithic parties whose organization outwardly resembles that of an army, but whose methods of regimentation are infinitely more adaptable and efficient, being based on a training of minds rather than bodies. Their hold over men is strengthened: parties become totalitarian. They require of their members closer adherence; they provide complete and final philosophies of the universe. Zeal, faith, enthusiasm, and intolerance are the rule in these modern churches: party struggles turn into religious wars.

But would a system without parties be more satisfactory? That is the real question. Would opinion be better represented if candidates were to present themselves individually before the electorate without it being able really to know their attitudes? Would liberty be better preserved if the government found itself faced with only a scattering of individuals not grouped in political formations?

We are living on a completely artificial notion of democracy forged by lawyers on the basis of eighteenth-century philosophical ideas. "Government of the people by the people," "Government of the nation by its representatives," these are fine phrases for arousing enthusiasm and fashioning eloquent perorations. Fine phrases with an empty ring. No people has ever been known to govern itself and none ever will. All government is oligarchic: it necessarily implies the domination of the many by the few. Rousseau, whom his commentators have forgotten to read, was well aware of this: "In the strict sense of the term, no true democracy has ever existed and none will ever exist. It is contrary to the natural order for the majority to rule and the minority to be ruled."[1] The will of the people is profoundly anarchic: it wants to do as it pleases. It vaguely considers government as a necessary evil: its instinctive attitude towards it is hostility. Alain has given a remarkable analysis of the natural conflict between the governors and the governed. All government implies discipline. All discipline is imposed from without: "self-discipline" is itself the result of education, which implies a prior external discipline, and is always very limited. Government and constraint are inseparable, but by definition constraint is external to the constrained. A people does not constrain itself; it is constrained. It does not govern itself; it is governed. To proclaim the identity of governors and governed, of constrainers and constrained is an admirable way of justifying the obedience of the latter to the former. It is pure abstraction and verbal juggling.

True democracy is something different, more modest but more real. It is defined in the first place as liberty "for the people and for all sections of the people," as the 1793 Constituents put it. Not only liberty for those privileged by birth, fortune, position, or education, but real liberty for all, and this implies a certain standard of living, a certain basic education, some kind of social equality, some kind of political equilibrium. The Marxist distinction between nominal liberties and real liberties is only partly correct; it is true that the political liberties recognized by Western regimes remain a formality for a large section of the masses for lack of an adequate standard of living, of adequate education, of social equality or of an adequate political equilibrium. Yet they may become real liberties: there is no point in beginning by suppressing them. Now the study of contemporary political phenomena reveals one obvious fact: in countries which have attained a certain degree of material civilization and a certain standard of living (Europe, North America, Great Britain and the white Dominions), liberty and the party system coincide. In the nineteenth century, when economic and financial powers alone disposed of the Press, of techniques of information and propaganda and of a means of organizing the electorate, democracy did not exist: the rise of parties and especially of working-class parties has alone made possible any real and active cooperation by the whole people in political affairs. Even totalitarian parties, like the Communist party, make a contribution in some countries to the existence of democracy: their suppression in France and Italy would threaten to strengthen (for a time at least) the conservative elements, and so to upset the equilibrium which ensures a minimum of liberty to every "section of the people": the existence of more than one party is both the cause and the reflection of this equilibrium.

In countries where the standard of living and education of the people are still much inferior (Asia, Africa, South America) the coincidence no longer occurs. Here parties are formal in character: rival factions struggle for power, using the voters as a soft dough to be kneaded as they will; corruption develops and the privileged classes take advantage of the situation to prolong their control. Under certain circumstances, the single party may provide a first organization of the masses, enabling them gradually to acquire some political training; the authoritarian regime it produces may suppress feudal systems of all kinds and conditions and create the economic and social conditions required for the future development of political liberty. The structure of the transitional regime must however be such that it will not destroy all hope of later liberal developments.

At the same time the system makes it possible to form a ruling class, sprung from the people, to replace the old. On this question, pluralist and single-party regimes are at one. The deepest significance of political parties is that they tend to the creation of new elites, and this restores to the notion of representation its true meaning, the only real one. All government is by nature oligarchic but the origins and the training of the oligarchs may be very different and these determine their actions. The formula "Government of the people by the people" must be replaced by this formula "Government of the people *by an elite sprung from the people.*" A regime without parties ensures the permanence of ruling elites chosen by birth, wealth, or position: to secure admission to the governing oligarchy a man of the people must accomplish a considerable effort to rise above his initial position; he must also work his way up the ladder of middle-class education and lose contact with the class in which he was born. A regime without parties is of necessity a conservative regime. It corresponds to the property franchise or else to an attempt to cripple universal suffrage by imposing on the people leaders who do not come from their ranks; it is further removed from democracy than the party regime. Historically speaking parties were born when the masses of the people really made their entrance into political life; they provided the necessary framework enabling the masses to recruit from among themselves their own elites. Parties are always more developed on the Left than on the Right because they are always more necessary on the Left than on the Right. To suppress them would be an admirable way for the Right to paralyse the Left. The classic protests against their interference in political life, against the domination exercised by militants over deputies, by Congresses and committees over parliament take no account of the capital developments of the last fifty years which have accentuated the formal character of ministers and parliaments. Whereas they were once exclusively the instruments of private, financial and economic interests, they have today become instruments in the hands of the parties, amongst which the place of mass parties is becoming increasingly important. This transformation represents an advance of democracy, not a retreat. From this point of view the single party itself represents a progress if it is not compared with pluralist systems but considered within the framework proper to it, dictatorship. A dictatorship with a single people's party tending to create a new ruling class is nearer to democracy than party-less dictatorships of the personal or military type which strengthen the feudal powers in their control.

Democracy is not threatened by the party regime but by present-day trends in party internal organization: the danger does not lie in the existence of parties but in the military, religious, and totalitarian form they sometimes assume. Two further facts of importance must be emphasized in this connection. All parties have not adopted the same kind of organization. In Great Britain, Canada, Australia, Northern Europe, the only groups to display this tendency are small and uninfluential. The same is true of the United States, where the development of primaries has had the result of weakening party organization rather than strengthening it. Closed totalitarian parties of the *Bund* type still remain the exception throughout the world: if evolution is to lead towards them, it has scarcely yet begun and many factors may check it or deflect it.

From another point of view certain features in these new party structures ensure an admirable training of the political leading strata as well as closer and more faithful contact between the mass of the people and their ruling elites; isolated from their context, these features might increase the democratic nature of parties instead of destroying it. The real way of protecting democracy against the toxins that it secretes within itself in the course of its development does not lie in cutting it off from modern techniques for organizing the masses and recruiting leaders—such an operation would make of it an empty vessel, a vain show—but in diverting these to its use, for they are in the last resort mere tools, capable no doubt of being used for good as well as for evil. To refuse to use them is to refuse to act. If it were true that democracy is incompatible with them, this would no doubt mean that democracy is incompatible with the conditions of the present day. All the speeches upon the benefits of craftsmanship and the evils of industrialization do not alter the fact that the artisan's day is done and that we live in an age of mass-production; regrets for the individualist and decentralized cadre parties of the nineteenth century and imprecations against the vast centralized and disciplined parties of today do not alter the fact that the latter alone suit the structure of contemporary societies.

NOTE

1. *Social Contract*, Book III, Ch. IV.

E. E. SCHATTSCHNEIDER

36. THE SOCIALIZATION OF CONFLICT

Picking up on the theme of responsible party government is political scientist E. E. Schattschneider's realistic restatement of the role of political parties in democratic theory. He emphasized that democracy is an inherently competitive political system where the contending leaders and organizations—political parties—define the alternatives of public policy. The public participates by choosing among them.

Because he did not think it possible for Americans—or the citizens of any large country—to effectively participate directly in political decision-making, Schattschneider emphasized the importance of the role that political parties have in defining choices for the voters.

If we assume that the people "govern," it follows that the governing majority ought to know more than any majority has ever known or ever could know. This is the *reductio ad absurdum* of democratic theory. We cannot get out of the dilemma by (1) making a great effort to educate everyone to the point where they know enough to make these decisions nor (2) by restricting participation to the people who do know all about these matters. The first is impossible. The second is absurd because *no one* knows enough to govern by this standard. The trouble is that we have defined democracy in such a way that we are in danger of putting ourselves out of business.

There is no escape from the problem of ignorance, because *nobody knows enough to run the government*. Presidents, senators, governors, judges, professors, doctors of philosophy, editors and the like are only a little less ignorant than the rest of us. Even an expert is a person who chooses to be ignorant about many things so that he may know all about one.

The whole theory of knowledge underlying these concepts of democracy is false—it proves too much. It proves not only that democracy is impossible; it proves equally that life itself is impossible. Everybody has to accommodate himself

---

Source: From E. E. Schattschneider, "The Socialization of Conflict" from *The Semisovereign People*. Copyright © 1960 by E. E. Schattschneider and renewed 1988 by Frank W. Schattschneider. Reprinted by permission of Harcourt Brace & Company.

to the fact that he deals with an incredible number of matters about which he knows very little. This is true of all aspects of life, not merely of politics.

The compulsion to know everything is the road to insanity.

People are able to survive in the modern world by learning to distinguish between what they must know and what they do not need to know. We get a clue to the solution of the problem when we begin to realize that it is not necessary to be an automotive engineer to buy an automobile or to be an obstetrician in order to have a baby. Our survival depends on our ability to judge things by their results and our ability to establish relations of confidence and responsibility so that we can take advantage of what other people know. We could not live in modern society if we did not place confidence daily in a thousand ways in pharmacists, surgeons, pilots, bank clerks, engineers, plumbers, technicians, lawyers, civil servants, accountants, courts, telephone operators, craftsmen and a host of others. We pass judgment on the most complex mechanisms on the basis of the *results* they produce. Economists, trying to explain the operation of the economy, use a political expression when they speak of the "sovereignty of the consumer," precisely because they realize that it is not necessary to know how to *make* a television set in order to buy one intelligently. Democracy is like nearly everything else we do; it is a form of collaboration of ignorant people and experts.

Primitive democratic theorists never tire of telling us that democracy was designed to work in New England town meetings, not in a modern national state. The analysis is fatuous. We might as well attempt to return to a handicraft economy. The crisis is a purely theoretical one because operating democratic political systems have in fact already accomplished what is theoretically impossible and are doing it every day. It is only the theory that has broken down. The problem of modern democracy is the problem of learning to live in the modern world.

We can find our way through the maze if we learn to distinguish between different kinds of knowledge, between what amateurs know and what professionals know, between what generalists know and what specialists know. The problem is not how 180 million Aristotles can run a democracy, but how we can organize a political community of 180 million ordinary people so that it remains sensitive to their needs. This is a problem of *leadership, organization, alternatives and systems of responsibility and confidence.* The emphasis is on the role of leadership and organization in a democracy, not on the spontaneous generation of something at the grass roots. If we approach the problem from this side, it does not look impossible. The achievements of the American regime are tremendous, but they have been brought about in spite of the theoretical illusions under which we have labored.

The people are involved in public affairs by the conflict system. Conflicts open up questions for public intervention. Out of conflict the alternatives of public policy arise. Conflict is the occasion for political organization and leadership. In a free political system it is difficult to avoid public involvement in conflict; the ordinary, regular operations of the government give rise to controversy, and controversy is catching.

The beginning of wisdom in democratic theory is to distinguish between the things the people can do and the things the people cannot do. The worst possible disservice that can be done to the democratic cause is to attribute to the people a mystical, magical omnipotence which takes no cognizance of what very large numbers of people cannot do by the sheer weight of numbers. At this point the common definition of democracy has invited us to make fools of ourselves.

What 180 million people can do spontaneously, on their own initiative, is not much more than a locomotive can do without rails. The public is like a very rich man who is unable to supervise closely all of his enterprise. His problem is to learn how to compel his agents to define his options.

What we are saying is that conflict, competition, leadership, and organization are the essence of democratic politics. Inherent in the operations of a democracy are special conditions which permit large numbers of people to function.

The problem is how to organize the political system so as to make the best possible use of the power of the public in view of its limitations. A popular decision bringing into focus the force of public support requires a tremendous effort to define the alternatives, to organize the discussion and mobilize opinion. The government and the political organizations are in the business of manufacturing this kind of alternatives.

What has been said here has not been said to belittle the power of the people but to shed some light on what it is. The power of the people is not made less by the fact that it cannot be used for trivial matters. The whole world can be run on the basis of a remarkably small number of decisions. The power of the people in a democracy depends on the *importance* of the decisions made by the electorate, not on the *number* of decisions they make. Since the adoption of the Constitution the party in power has been turned out by the opposition party fourteen times, and in about six of these instances the consequences have been so great that we could not understand American history without taking account of them.

The most important thing about any democratic regime is the *way* in which it *uses* and exploits popular sovereignty, what questions it refers to the public for decision or guidance, how it refers them to the public, how the alternatives are defined and how it respects the limitations of the public. A good democratic system protects the public against the demand that it do impossible things. The unforgivable sin of democratic politics is to dissipate the power of the public by putting it to trivial uses. What we need is a movement for the conservation of the political resources of the American people.

Above everything, *the people are powerless if the political enterprise is not competitive.* It is the competition of political organizations that provides the people with the opportunity to make a choice. Without this opportunity popular sovereignty amounts to nothing.

The common definition of democracy may be harmless if it is properly understood, but the fact is that it is very commonly misunderstood. It would be more imaginative to say that some things we now are actually doing are democratic even though they do not fit the traditional definition. Definitions of democracy since the time of Aristotle have been made on the assumption that the "many" in a democracy do the same things that the "one" does in a monarchy and the "few" do in an aristocracy. But obviously the shift from the "one" to the "many" is not merely a change in the number of people participating in power but *a change in the way the power is exercised.* The 180 million cannot do what a single ruler can do. This is not because the 180 million are stupid or ignorant but because it is physically impossible for 180 million to act the way one acts. In the interests of clarity and the survival of the political system we need a definition of democracy that recognizes the limitations that nature imposes on large numbers.

A working definition must capitalize on the limitations of the people as well as their powers. We do this when we say that liberty and leadership are the greatest of democratic concepts. *Democracy is a competitive political system in which competing leaders and organizations define the alternatives of public policy in such a way that the public can participate in the decision-making process.* The initiative in this political system is to be found largely in the government or in the opposition. The people profit by this system, but they cannot, by themselves, do the work of the system. We have already had a great deal of experience with this kind of system. Is it not about time that we begin to recognize its democratic implications?

Conflict, competition, organization, leadership and responsibility are the ingredients of a working definition of democracy. Democracy is a political system in which the people have a choice among the alternatives created by competing political organizations and leaders. The advantage of this definition over the traditional definition is that it is *operational,* it describes something that actually happens. It describes something feasible. It does not make impossible demands on the public. Moreover, it describes a going democratic concern whose achievements are tremendous.

The involvement of the public in politics is a natural outgrowth of the kind of conflict that almost inevitably arises in a free society. The exploitation of this situation by responsible political leaders and organizations is the essence of democracy; the socialization of conflict is the essential democratic process.

KEVIN P. PHILLIPS

37. The Emerging Republican Majority

Democratic Party dominance growing out of the 1930s New Deal liberalism of President Franklin Roosevelt began to show serious signs of strain as early as the mid-1960s as social issues such as drugs, crime, race, abortion, and women's rights came to dominate the political agenda.

In what now seems like a visionary book, Kevin Phillips predicted in 1969 that the Republican Party would soon emerge as the majority party because it more closely resembled the views of the vast majority of Americans on these social issues. The success of the Republicans under the leadership of Ronald Reagan and George Bush in the 1980s and 1990s suggests that Phillips recognized ahead of many others the forces that would alter the party loyalties of Americans.

The devastating failures of candidates Jimmy Carter, Walter Mondale, and Michael Dukakis in the 1980, 1984, and 1988 presidential races support Phillips's idea that the Democratic Party of the 1970's and 1980's was in considerable trouble. This was reinforced when the Republicans took control of the Congress in 1994. Nonetheless, the traditional support enjoyed by the Democratic Party during times of economic stress coupled with the increasing public concern about domestic issues such as health care and education resulted in a significant electoral college victory in 1992 for Bill Clinton. But his victory signifies only a brief change in Democratic presidential fortunes as the Republicans won the presidency in 2000 and 2004.

The long-range meaning of the political upheaval of 1968 rests on the Republican opportunity to fashion a majority among the 57 per cent of the American electorate which voted to eject the Democratic Party from national power. To begin with, more than half of this protesting 57 per cent were firm Republicans from areas—Southern California to Long Island's Suffolk County—or

---

Source: From *The Emerging Republican Majority* by Kevin Phillips, copyright © 1969 by Arlington House, Inc. Used by permission of Arlington House, a division of Random House, Inc.

sociocultural backgrounds with a growing GOP bias. Some voted for George Wallace, but most backed Richard Nixon, providing the bulk of his Election Day support. Only a small minority of 1968 Nixon backers—perhaps several million liberal Republicans and independents from Maine and Oregon to Fifth Avenue—cast what may be their last Republican presidential ballots because of the partisan re-alignment taking place. The third major anti-Democratic voting stream of 1968—and the most decisive—was that of the fifteen million or so conservative Democrats who shunned Hubert Humphrey to divide about evenly between Richard Nixon and George Wallace. Such elements stretched from the "Okie" Great Central Valley of California to the mountain towns of Idaho, Florida's space centers, rural South Carolina, Bavarian Minnesota, the Irish sidewalks of New York and the Levittowns of Megalopolis.

Although most of George Wallace's votes came from Democrats rather than Republicans, they were conservatives—Southerners, Borderers, German and Irish Catholics—who had been trending Republican prior to 1968. . . . The Wallace vote followed the cultural geography of obsolescent conservative (often Southern) Democratic tradition. There was no reliable Wallace backing among blue-collar workers and poor whites as a class; industrial centers in the Yankee sphere of influence from Duluth to Scranton, Fall River and Biddeford shunned the Alabama ex-governor with a mere 2 per cent to 3 per cent of the vote. Areas of eroding Democratic tradition were the great breeding grounds of Wallace voters.

In the South, Wallace drew principally on conservative Democrats quitting the party they had long succored and controlled. Generally speaking, Wallace's Southern strength was greatest in the Democratic Party's historic (pre-1964) lowland strongholds, while the Alabaman's worst Southern percentages came in the Republican highlands. White voters throughout most sections of the Deep South went two-to-one for Wallace. In the more Republican Outer South, only one white voter out of three supported the third-party candidate. In the South as a whole, 85 to 90 per cent of the white electorate cast Nixon or Wallace votes against the re-aligning national Democratic Party in 1968, an unprecedented magnitude of disaffection which indicates the availability of the Wallace vote to the future GOP.

Four of the five Wallace states had gone Republican in 1964, and although the Alabaman greatly enlarged the scope of Southern revolt by attracting most of the (poor white or Outer South Black Belt) Southerners who had hitherto resisted Republican or States Rights candidacies, much of his tide had already been flowing for Goldwater. Nor does the Nixon Administration have to bid much ideologically for this electorate. Despite his success in enlarging the scope of white Southern revolt, George Wallace failed to reach far enough or strongly enough beyond the Deep South to give his American Independent Party the national base required for a viable future. Republican Nixon won most of the Outer South, establishing the GOP as the ascending party of the local white majority. Having achieved statewide success only in the Deep South, and facing competition from a Southern Republicanism mindful of its opportunity, the Wallace movement cannot maintain an adequate political base and is bound to serve, like past American third parties, as a way station for groups abandoning one party for another. Some Wallace voters were long-time Republicans, but the great majority were conservative Democrats who have been moving—and should continue to do so—towards the GOP. . . .

Successful moderate conservatism is also likely to attract to the Republican side some of the Northern blue-collar workers who flirted with George Wallace but ultimately backed Hubert Humphrey. Fears that a Republican administration would undermine Social Security, Medicare, collective bargaining and aid to education played a major part in keeping socially conservative blue-collar workers and senior citizens loyal to the 1968 Democratic candidate. Assuming that a Nixon administration can dispel these apprehensions, it ought to be able to repeat—with much more permanence—Eisenhower's great blue-collar success of 1956. Sociologically, the Republican Party is becoming much more lower-middle class and much less establishmentarian than it was during the Nineteen-Fifties, and pursuit of an increasing portion of the Northern blue-collar electorate—an expansion of its 1968 Catholic triumph in greater New York City—would be a logical extension of this trend. . . .

The upcoming cycle of American politics is likely to match a dominant Republican Party based in the Heartland, South and California against a minority Democratic Party based in the Northeast and the Pacific Northwest (and encompassing Southern as well as Northern Negroes). With such support behind it, the GOP can easily afford to lose the states of Massachusetts, New York, and Michigan—and is likely to do so except in landslide years. Together with the District of Columbia, the top ten Humphrey states—Hawaii, Washington, Minnesota, Michigan, West Virginia, New York, Connecticut, Rhode Island, Massachusetts and Maine—should prove to be the core of national Democratic strength. . . . The new battlegrounds of quadrennial presidential politics are likely to be California, Ohio and Pennsylvania.

Unluckily for the Democrats, their major impetus is centered in stagnant Northern industrial states—and within those states, in old decaying cities, in a Yankee countryside that has fewer people than in 1900, and in the most expensive suburbs. Beyond this, in the South and West, the Democrats dominate only two expanding voting blocs—Latins and Negroes. From space-center Florida across the booming Texas plains to the Los Angeles–San Diego suburban corridor, the nation's fastest-growing areas are strongly Republican and conservative. Even in the Northeast, the few rapidly growing suburbs are conservative-trending areas. Because of this demographic pattern, the South and West are gaining electoral votes and national political power at the expense of the Northeast. . . . The conservative Sun Belt cities are undergoing a population boom—and getting more conservative—while the old liberal cities of the Northeast decline. And the Northeast is steadily losing relative political importance to the Sun Belt.

One of the greatest political myths of the decade—a product of liberal self-interest—is that the Republican Party cannot attain national dominance without mobilizing liberal support in the big cities, appealing to "liberal" youth, empathizing with "liberal" urbanization, gaining substantial Negro support and courting the affluent young professional classes of "suburbia." The actual demographic and political facts convey a very different message.

. . . The big city political era is over in the United States. . . . With Negroes moving into the cities, whites have moved out. Moreover, white urban populations are getting increasingly conservative. Richard Nixon and George Wallace together won 40 per cent of the vote in liberal New York City. Perhaps more to the point, leading big city states like New York, Michigan and Massachusetts are no longer necessary for national Republican victory.

Youth is important, but voters under 25 cast only 7.4 per cent of the nation's ballots in 1968. And while many Northeastern young people are more liberal and Democratic than their parents—especially the affluent and anarchic progeny of the Establishment—the reverse seems to be true in Southern, Border, Rocky Mountain, Catholic, lower middle-class and working-class areas. In these locales, the young electorate's trend against local political tradition helps the GOP, as does resentment of the blithe nihilism of the children of the affluent society.

While urbanization *is* changing the face of America, and the GOP must take political note of this fact, it presents the opposite of a problem. A generation ago, the coming of age of the working-class central cities condemned the Republican Party to minority status, but the new "urbanization"—suburbanization is often a better description—is a middle-class impetus shaping the same ignominy for the Democrats. All across the nation, the fastest-growing urban areas are steadily increasing their *Republican* pluralities, while the old central cities—seat of the New Deal era—are casting steadily fewer votes for Democratic liberalism. No major American city is losing population so rapidly as arch-Democratic and establishmentarian Boston, while the fastest-growing urban area in the nation is Southern California's staunchly conservative Orange County, and the fastest growing cities are conservative strongholds like Phoenix, Dallas, Houston, Anaheim, San Diego and Fort Lauderdale.

Centered in the Sun Belt, the nation's heaviest suburban growth is solidly middle-class and conservative. Contemporary suburban expansion in the Northeast pales next to the spread of the Florida, Texas, Arizona and Southern California suburbs. Rapid, although less spectacular, suburban growth is occurring in the areas around Camden (New Jersey), Washington, D.C., Richmond, Atlanta, Memphis, St. Louis, Chicago, Oklahoma City, Tulsa and Denver. These suburbs are also conservative, often highly so. And even the few fast-growing Northeastern suburban counties—Suffolk, New York; Burlington, New Jersey; Prince Georges, Maryland—are conservative-trending, middle-class sections. The principal exception is Maryland's rich but fast-expanding Montgomery County, liberal seat of the upper echelons of Washington's federal bureaucracy.

From a national perspective, the silk-stocking liberal suburbs of Boston, New York, Philadelphia, San Francisco and (to a lesser extent) Chicago and

Washington cast only a minute fraction of the ballots wielded by the preponderance of unfashionable lower-middle- and middle-income suburbs. And because more and more new suburbanites come from lower-middle-income back-grounds, the gap should widen. . . .

The emerging Republican majority spoke clearly in 1968 for a shift away from the sociological jurisprudence, moral permissiveness, experimental residential, welfare and educational programming and massive federal spending by which the Liberal (mostly Democratic) Establishment sought to propagate liberal institutions and ideology—and all the while reap growing economic benefits. The dominion of this impetus is inherent in the list of Republican-trending groups and potentially Republican Wallace electorates of 1968: Southerners, Borderers, Germans, Scotch-Irish, Pennsylvania Dutch, Irish, Italians, Eastern Europeans and other urban Catholics, middle-class suburbanites, Sun Belt residents, Rocky Mountain and Pacific Interior populists. Democrats among these groups were principally alienated from their party by its social programs and increasing identification with the Northeastern Establishment and ghetto alike. Except among isolationist Germans, resentment of the Vietnamese war, far from helping to forge the GOP majority, actually produced *Democratic* gains among the groups most affected: silk-stocking Megalopolitans, the San Francisco-Berkeley-Madison-Ann Arbor electorate, Scandinavian progressives and Jews. As for the Republican trend groups, nothing characterizes their outlook so much as a desire to dispel the Liberal Establishment's philosophy of taxation and redistribution (partly to itself) and reverse the encroachment of government in the social life of the nation.

Shorn of power, stripped of vested interests in misleading and unsuccessful programs, the Liberal Establishment may narrow its gap between words and deeds which helped to drive racial and youthful minorities into open revolt. So changed, Democratic liberalism will once again become a vital and creative force in national politics, usually too innovative to win a presidential race, but injecting a needed leavening of humanism into the middle-class *realpolitik* of the new Republican coalition.

SECTION VI
REVIEW QUESTIONS

1. Harold Gosnell's "balance sheet of machine politics" concludes in 1938 that the "power of money" should be better regulated. How much progress has been made in reducing dependence on wealthy campaign contributors since the heyday of the political machine?

2. Why have "responsible parties" never emerged in American politics? Why does the American Political Science Association believe that stronger political parties are better than decentralized political parties?

3. What does E. E. Schattschneider see as the main obstacle to democracy and what is his solution to that problem?

4. Kevin Phillips predicted in 1969 that the "upcoming cycle of American politics is likely to match a dominant Republican Party based in the Heartland, South and California against a minority Democratic Party based in the Northeast and the Pacific Northwest (and encompassing Southern as well as Northern Negroes)." How accurate was his prediction? How do you think the parties will evolve over the next twenty-five years?

VII

Elections and Voters

SUSAN B. ANTHONY

38. Women and the Right to Vote

Susan B. Anthony (1820–1906) was one of the first American feminists and the leading women's rights advocate of the nineteenth century. She was a founder in 1869 of the National American Women's Suffrage Association, the precursor organization to the present-day League of Women Voters. In this speech she forcefully argues against all laws that discriminate against women. Whereas Charles Beard believed that the Constitution reflects the interests of an economic elite, Susan B. Anthony's argument suggests that because the founding fathers were all males, the Constitution was written to further exclusively the interests of men.

Friends and fellow-citizens: I stand before you tonight under indictment for the alleged crime of having voted at the last Presidential election, without having a lawful right to vote. It shall be my work this evening to prove to you that in thus voting, I not only committed no crime, but, instead, simply exercised my citizen's rights, guaranteed to me and all United States citizens by the National Constitution, beyond the power of any State to deny. . . .

The preamble of the Federal Constitution says:

> We, the people of the United States, in order to form a more perfect union, establish justice, insure domestic tranquillity, provide for the common defense, promote the general welfare, and secure the blessings of liberty to ourselves and our posterity, do ordain and establish this Constitution for the United States of America.

It was we, the people; not we, the white male citizens; nor yet we, the male citizens; but we, the whole people, who formed the Union. And we formed it, not to give the blessings of liberty, but to secure them; not to the half of ourselves and the half of our posterity, but to the whole people—women as well as men. And it is a downright mockery to talk to women of their enjoyment of the blessings of liberty while they are denied the use of the only means of securing them provided by this democratic-republican government—the ballot. . . .

For any State to make sex a qualification that must ever result in the disenfranchisement of one entire half of the people is to pass a bill of attainder, or an

---

Source: From Susan B. Anthony, "Speech in Defense of Equal Suffrage" (1873).

ex post facto law, and is therefore a violation of the supreme law of the land. By it the blessings of liberty are forever withheld from women and their female posterity. To them this government has no just powers derived from the consent of the governed. To them this government is not a democracy. It is not a republic. It is an odious aristocracy; a hateful oligarchy of sex; the most hateful aristocracy ever established on the face of the globe; an oligarchy of wealth, where the rich govern the poor. An oligarchy of learning, where the educated govern the ignorant, or even an oligarchy of race, where the Saxon rules the African, might be endured; but this oligarchy of sex, which makes fathers, brothers, husband, sons, the oligarchs over the mother and sisters, the wife and daughters of every household—which ordains all men sovereigns, all women subjects, carries dissension, discord and rebellion into every home of the nation. . . .

Webster, Worcester and Bouvier all define a citizen to be a person in the United States, entitled to vote and hold office.

The only question left to be settled now is: Are women persons? And I hardly believe any of our opponents will have the hardihood to say they are not. Being persons, then, women are citizens; and no State has a right to make any law, or to enforce any old law, that shall abridge their privileges or immunities. Hence, every discrimination against women in the constitutions and laws of the several States is today null and void, precisely as is every one against Negroes.

GEORGE WASHINGTON PLUNKITT

39. HOLDING YOUR DISTRICT

Politicians today are scrutinized under a microscope and any suggestion of unethical conduct—whether personal or public—makes front page news and the lead story on television news broadcasts. The most obvious practices of the old-time political machine—buying votes and stuffing ballot boxes—have become uncommon. But more sophisticated means of getting and keeping voters in your camp continue unabated. The practices of bringing federal installations into a congressional district, providing access to large campaign contributors, and using influence to protect constituents certainly have not disappeared.

Source: From William L. Riordan, *Plunkitt of Tammany Hall* (New York: McClure Phillips, 1905).

In this classic account of machine politics in New York's Tammany Hall, George Washington Plunkitt describes how he "holds his district." Plunkitt's basic principle is as true today as it was then: "There's only one way to hold your district: you must study human nature and act accordin'." If voters in his district needed work, Plunkitt found them a job. If they liked to sing, Plunkitt invited them to join the neighborhood glee club. While the strategies and practices have changed, the truth of this underlying insight is evident today in every congressional office in Washington where professional staff people now work long hours "study[ing] human nature and act[ing] accordin'."

TO HOLD YOUR DISTRICT: STUDY HUMAN NATURE AND ACT ACCORDIN'

There's only one way to hold a district: you must study human nature and act accordin'. You can't study human nature in books. Books is a hindrance more than anything else. If you have been to college, so much the worse for you. You'll have to unlearn all you learned before you can get right down to human nature, and unlearnin' takes a lot of time. Some men can never forget what they learned at college. Such men may get to be district leaders by a fluke, but they never last.

To learn real human nature you have to go among the people, see them and be seen. I know every man, woman, and child in the Fifteenth District, except them that's been born this summer—and I know some of them, too. I know what they like and what they don't like, what they are strong at and what they are weak in, and I reach them by approachin' at the right side.

For instance, here's how I gather in the young men. I hear of a young feller that's proud of his voice, thinks that he can sing fine. I ask him to come around to Washington Hall and join our Glee Club. He comes and sings, and he's a follower of Plunkitt for life. Another young feller gains a reputation as a baseball player in a vacant lot. I bring him into our baseball club. That fixes him. You'll find him workin' for my ticket at the polls next election day. Then there's the feller that likes rowin' on the river, the young feller that makes a name as a waltzer on his block, the young feller that's handy with his dukes—I rope them all in by givin' them opportunities to show themselves off. I don't trouble them with political arguments. I just study human nature and act accordin'.

But you may say this game won't work with the high-toned fellers, the fellers that go through college and then join the Citizens' Union. Of course it wouldn't work. I have a special treatment for them. I ain't like the patent medicine man that gives the same medicine for all diseases. The Citizens' Union kind of young man! I love him! He's the daintiest morsel of the lot, and he don't often escape me.

Before telling you how I catch him, let me mention that before the election last year, the Citizens' Union said they had four hundred or five hundred enrolled voters in my district. They had a lovely headquarters, too, beautiful roll-top desks and the cutest rugs in the world. If I was accused of havin' contributed to fix up the nest for them, I wouldn't deny it under oath. What do I mean by that? Never mind. You can guess from the sequel, if you're sharp.

Well, election day came. The Citizens' Union's candidate for Senator, who ran against me, just polled five votes in the district, while I polled something more than 14,000 votes. What became of the 400 or 500 Citizens' Union enrolled voters in my district? Some people guessed that many of them were good Plunkitt men all along and worked with the Cits just to bring them into the Plunkitt camp by election day. You can guess that way, too, if you want to. I never contradict stories about me, especially in hot weather. I just call your attention to the fact that on last election day 395 Citizens' Union enrolled voters in my district were missin' and unaccounted for.

I tell you frankly, though, how I have captured some of the Citizens' Union's young men. I have a plan that never fails. I watch the City Record to see when there's civil service examinations for good things. Then I take my young Cit in hand, tell him all about the good thing and get him worked up till he goes and takes an examination. I don't bother about him any more. It's a cinch that he comes back to me in a few days and asks to join Tammany Hall. Come over to Washington Hall some night and I'll show you a list of names on our rolls marked "C.S." which means, "bucked up against civil service."

As to the older voters, I reach them, too. No, I don't send them campaign literature. That's rot. People can get all the political stuff they want to read—and a good deal more, too—in the papers. Who reads speeches, nowadays, anyhow? It's bad enough to listen to them. You ain't goin' to gain any votes by stuffin' the letter boxes with campaign documents. Like as not you'll lose votes, for there's nothin' a man hates more than to hear the letter carrier ring his bell and go to the letter box expectin' to find a letter he was lookin' for, and find only a lot of printed politics. I met a man this very mornin' who told me he voted the Democratic State ticket last year just because the Republicans kept crammin' his letter box with campaign documents.

What tells in holdin' your grip on your district is to go right down among the poor families and help them in the different ways they need help. I've got a regular system for this. If there's a fire in Ninth, Tenth, or Eleventh Avenue, for example, any hour of the day or night, I'm usually there with some of my election district captains as soon as the fire engines. If a family is burned out I don't ask whether they are Republicans or Democrats, and I don't refer them to the Charity Organization Society, which would investigate their case in a month or two and decide they were worthy of help about the time they are dead from starvation. I just get quarters for them, buy clothes for them if their clothes were burned up, and fix them up till they get things runnin' again. It's philanthropy, but it's politics, too—mighty good politics. Who can tell how many votes one of these fires bring me? The poor are the most grateful people in the world, and, let me tell you, they have more friends in their neighborhoods than the rich have in theirs.

If there's a family in my district in want I know it before the charitable societies do, and me and my men are first on the ground. I have a special corps to look up such cases. The consequence is that the poor look up to George W. Plunkitt as a father, come to him in trouble—and don't forget him on election day.

Another thing, I can always get a job for a deservin' man. I make it a point to keep on the track of jobs, and it seldom happens that I don't have a few up my sleeve ready for use. I know every big employer in the district and in the whole city, for that matter, and they ain't in the habit of sayin' no to me when I ask them for a job.

And the children—the little roses of the district! Do I forget them? Oh, no! They know me, every one of them, and they know that a sight of Uncle George and candy means the same thing. Some of them are the best kind of vote-getters. I'll tell you a case. Last year a little Eleventh Avenue rosebud, whose father is a Republican, caught hold of his whiskers on election day and said she wouldn't let go till he'd promise to vote for me. And she didn't.

JOE MCGINNISS

40. SELLING CANDIDATES AS PRODUCTS

V. O. Key's argument that elections are meaningful because voters are rational has not been universally accepted. An alternative view of voters imagines them to be easily manipulated by advertising techniques, particularly on television. In the modern era of "spin doctors," media specialists who work to depict their candidate and political events in a favorable light, it is hard to remember how shocking it was for many Americans to read Joe McGinniss's conclusion that elections were nothing more

Source: Joe McGinniss, *The Selling of the President*. Copyright © 1969 by JoeMac, Inc. Reprinted by permission of Janklow & Nesbit Associates.

than advertising campaigns selling politicians instead of consumer products. As McGinniss put it, citizens do "not so much vote for a candidate as make a psychological purchase of him." In the excerpt that follows, McGinniss describes the way in which Richard Nixon's "handlers" worked in 1968 to manipulate public perceptions of their candidate so as to change his negative image that remained from his campaign against John F. Kennedy in the 1960 race for the White House.

Politics, in a sense, has always been a con game.

The American voter, insisting upon his belief in a higher order, clings to his religion, which promises another, better life; and defends passionately the illusion that the men he chooses to lead him are of finer nature than he.

It has been traditional that the successful politician honor this illusion. To succeed today, he must embellish it. Particularly if he wants to be President.

"Potential presidents are measured against an ideal that's a combination of leading man, God, father, hero, pope, king, with maybe just a touch of the avenging Furies thrown in," an adviser to Richard Nixon wrote in a memorandum late in 1967. Then, perhaps aware that Nixon qualified only as father, he discussed improvements that would have to be made—not upon Nixon himself, but upon the image of him that was received by the voter.

That there is a difference between the individual and his image is human nature. Or American nature, at least. That the difference is exaggerated and exploited electronically is the reason for this book.

Advertising, in many ways, is a con game, too. Human beings do not need new automobiles every third year; a color television set brings little enrichment of the human experience; a higher or lower hemline no expansion of consciousness, no increase in the capacity to love.

It is not surprising, then, that politicians and advertising men should have discovered one another. And, once they recognized that the citizen did not so much vote for a candidate as make a psychological purchase of him, not surprising that they began to work together.

The voter, as reluctant to face political reality as any other kind, was hardly an unwilling victim. "The deeper problems connected with advertising," Daniel Boorstin has written in *The Image,* "come less from the unscrupulousness of our 'deceivers' than from our pleasure in being deceived, less from the desire to seduce than from the desire to be seduced. . . .

"In the last half-century we have misled ourselves . . . about men . . . and how much greatness can be found among them. . . . We have become so accustomed to our illusions that we mistake them for reality. We demand them. And we demand that there be always more of them, bigger and better and more vivid."

The Presidency seems the ultimate extension of our error.

Advertising agencies have tried openly to sell Presidents since 1952. When Dwight Eisenhower ran for re-election in 1956, the agency of Batton, Barton, Durstine and Osborn, which had been on a retainer throughout his first four years, accepted his campaign as a regular account. Leonard Hall, national Republican chairman, said: "You sell your candidates and your programs the way a business sells its products."

The only change over the past twelve years has been that, as technical sophistication has increased, so has circumspection. The ad men were removed from the parlor but were given a suite upstairs. . . .

Nixon gathered about himself a group of young men attuned to the political uses of television. They arrived at his side by different routes. One, William Gavin, was a thirty-one-year-old English teacher in a suburban high school outside Philadelphia in 1967, when he wrote Richard Nixon urging him to run for President and base his campaign on TV. Gavin wrote on stationery borrowed from the University of Pennsylvania because he thought Nixon would pay more attention if the letter seemed to be from a college professor.

> Dear Mr. Nixon:
>
> May I offer two suggestions concerning your plans for 1968?
>
> 1. Run. You can win. Nothing can happen to you, politically speaking, that is worse than what has happened to you. Ortega y Gasset in his *The Revolt of the Masses* says: "These ideas are the only genuine ideas; the ideas of the shipwrecked. All the rest is rhetoric, posturing, farce. He who does not really feel himself lost, is lost without remission . . ." You, in effect, are "lost"; that is why you are the only political figure with the vision to see things the way they are and not as Leftist or Rightist kooks would have them be. Run. You will win.
>
> 2. A tip for television: instead of those wooden performances beloved by politicians, instead of a glamorboy technique, instead of safety, be bold. Why not have live press conferences as your campaign on television? People will see you daring all, asking and answering questions from reporters, and not simply answering phony "questions" made up by your staff. This would be dynamic; it would be daring. Instead of the medium using you, you would be using the medium. Go on "live" and risk all. It is the only way to convince people of the truth: that you are beyond rhetoric, that you can face reality, unlike your opponents, who will rely on public relations. Television hurt you because you were not yourself; it didn't hurt the "real" Nixon. The real Nixon can revolutionize the use of television by dynamically going "live" and answering everything, the loaded and the unloaded question. Invite your opponents to this kind of a debate.
>
> Good luck, and I know you can win if you see yourself for what you are; a man who had been beaten, humiliated, hated, but who can still see the truth.

A Nixon staff member had lunch with Gavin a couple of times after the letter was received and hired him.

William Gavin was brought to the White House as a speech writer in January of 1969.

Harry Treleaven, hired as creative director of advertising in the fall of 1967, immediately went to work on the more serious of Nixon's personality problems. One was his lack of humor.

"Can be corrected to a degree," Treleaven wrote, "but let's not be too obvious about it. Romney's cornball attempts have hurt him. If we're going to be witty, let a pro write the words."

Treleaven also worried about Nixon's lack of warmth, but decided that "he can be helped greatly in this respect by how he is handled. . . . Give him words to say that will show his *emotional* involvement in the issues. . . . Buchanan wrote about RFK talking about the starving children in Recife. *That's* what we have to inject. . . .

"He should be presented in some kind of 'situation' rather than cold in a studio. The situation should look unstaged even if it's not."

Some of the most effective ideas belonged to Raymond K. Price, a former editorial writer for the *New York Herald Tribune,* who became Nixon's best and most prominent speech writer in the campaign. Price later composed much of the inaugural address.

In 1967, he began with the assumption that, "The natural human use of reason is to support prejudice, not to arrive at opinions." Which led to the conclusion that rational arguments would "only be effective if we can get the people to make the *emotional* leap, or what theologians call [the] 'leap of faith.'"

Price suggested attacking the "personal factors" rather than the "historical factors" which were the basis of the low opinion so many people had of Richard Nixon.

"These tend to be more a gut reaction," Price wrote, "unarticulated, non-analytical, a product of the particular chemistry between the voter and the *image* of the candidate. *We have to be very clear on this point: that the response is to the image, not to the man.* . . . It's not what's *there* that counts, it's what's projected—and carrying it one step further, it's not what *he* projects but rather what the voter receives. It's not the man we have to change, but rather the *received impression.* And this impression often depends more on the medium and its use than it does on the candidate himself."

So there would not have to be a "new Nixon." Simply a new approach to television.

"What, then, does this mean in terms of our uses of time and of media?" Price wrote.

"For one thing, it means investing whatever time RN needs in order to work out firmly in his own mind that vision of the nation's future that he wants to be identified with. This is crucial. . . . "

So, at the age of fifty-four, after twenty years in public life, Richard Nixon was still felt *by his own staff* to be in need of time to "work out firmly in his own mind that vision of the nation's future that he wants to be identified with."

"Secondly," Price wrote, "it suggests that we take the time and the money to experiment, in a controlled manner, with film and television techniques, with particular emphasis on pinpointing those *controlled* uses of the television medium that can *best* convey the *image* we want to get across . . .

"The TV medium itself introduces an element of distortion, in terms of its effect on the candidate and of the often subliminal ways in which the image is received. And it inevitably is going to convey a partial image—thus ours is the task of finding how to control its use so the part that gets across is the part we want to have gotten across. . . .

"Voters are basically lazy, basically uninterested in making an *effort* to understand what we're talking about . . . ," Price wrote. "Reason requires a high degree of discipline, of concentration; impression is easier. Reason pushes the viewer back, it assaults him, it demands that he agree or disagree; impression can envelop him, invite him in, without making an intellectual demand. . . . When we argue with him we demand that he make the effort of replying. We seek to engage his intellect, and for most people this is the most difficult work of all. The emotions are more easily roused, closer to the surface, more malleable. . . . "

So, for the New Hampshire primary, Price recommended "saturation with a film, in which the candidate can be shown better than he can be shown in person because it can be edited, so only the best moments are shown; then a quick parading of the candidate in the flesh so that the guy they've gotten intimately acquainted with on the screen takes on a living presence—not saying anything, just being seen. . . .

"[Nixon] has to come across as a person larger than life, the stuff of legend. People are stirred by the legend, including the living legend, not by the man himself. It's the aura that surrounds the charismatic figure more than it is the figure itself, that draws the followers. Our task is to build that aura. . . .

"So let's not be afraid of television gimmicks . . . get the voters to like the guy and the battle's two-thirds won."

So this was how they went into it. Trying, with one hand, to build the illusion that Richard Nixon, in addition to his attributes of mind and heart, considered, in the words of Patrick K. Buchanan, a speech writer, "communicating with the people . . . one of the great joys of seeking the Presidency"; while with the other they shielded him, controlled him, and controlled the atmosphere around him. It was as if they were building not a President but an Astrodome, where the wind would never blow, the temperature would never rise or fall, and the ball never bounce erratically on the artificial grass.

They could do this, and succeed, because of the special nature of the man. There was, apparently, something in Richard Nixon's character which sought this shelter. Something which craved regulation, which flourished best in the darkness, behind clichés, behind phalanxes of antiseptic advisers. Some part of him that could breathe freely only inside a hotel suite that cost a hundred dollars a day.

And it worked. As he moved serenely through his primary campaign, there was new cadence to Richard Nixon's speech and motion; new confidence in his heart. And, a new image of him on the television screen.

TV both reflected and contributed to his strength. Because he was winning he looked like a winner on the screen. Because he was suddenly projecting well on the medium he had feared, he went about his other tasks with assurance. The one fed upon the other, building to an astonishing peak in August as the Republican convention began and he emerged from his regal isolation, traveling to Miami not so much to be nominated as coronated. On live, but controlled, TV.

WALTER DEAN BURNHAM

41. CRITICAL REALIGNING ELECTIONS

American presidential elections have been classified according to which party wins and what coalitions of Americans identify themselves with those parties. Using these measures, elections may be "maintaining" (party loyalties remain stable and the majority party wins), "deviating" (basic party loyalties remain stable but the majority party loses), "converting" (the majority party wins but major shifts can be seen in who supports the party), and "critical" or "realigning" (the majority party not only loses the election but also loses its standing as the majority party). Walter Dean Burnham's analysis of critical realigning elections suggests that major upheavals occur cyclically in the history of American politics and that each is associated with a significant increase in intensity in which large numbers of voters change their party identifications. It seems that the Democratic victory for Bill Clinton in 1992 did not represent the beginning of a cycle of realignment in sources of support for the parties, but rather a

---

Source: From *Critical Elections and the Mainstream of American Politics* by Walter Dean Burnham. Copyright © 1970 by W. W. Norton & Company, Inc. Used by permission of W. W. Norton & Company, Inc.

mere deviation in the recent Republican domination of the White House.

For many decades it has been generally recognized that American electoral politics is not quite "all of a piece" despite its apparent diverse uniformity. Some elections have more important long-range consequences for the political system as a whole than others, and seem to "decide" substantive issues in a more clear-cut way. There has been long agreement among historians that the elections of 1800, 1828, 1860, 1896, and 1932, for example, were fundamental turning points in the course of American electoral politics.

Since the appearance in 1955 of V. O. Key's seminal article, "A Theory of Critical Elections," political scientists have moved to give this concept quantitative depth and meaning. . . . It now seems time to attempt at least an interim assessment of the structure, function, and implications of critical realignment for the American political process. Such an effort is motivated in particular by the author's view that critical realignments are of fundamental importance not only to the system of political action called "the American political process" but also to the clarifications of some aspects of its operation. It seems particularly important in a period of obvious political upheaval not only to identify these phenomena and place them in time, but to integrate them into a larger (if still very modest) theory of movement in American politics.

Such a theory must inevitably emphasize the elements of stress and abrupt transformation in our political life at the expense of the consensual, gradualist perspectives which have until recently dominated the scholar's vision of American political processes and behavior. For the realignment phenomenon focuses our attention on "the dark side of the moon." It reminds us that politics as usual in the United States is not politics as always; that there are discrete types of voting behavior and quite different levels of voter response to political stimuli, depending on what those stimuli are and at what point in time they occur; and that American political institutions and leadership, once defined (or redefined) in a "normal phase" of our politics, seem to become part of the very conditions that threaten to overthrow them. . . .

In its "ideal-typical" form, the critical realignment differs from stable alignment eras, secular realignments, and deviating elections in the following basic ways.

1. The critical realignment is characteristically associated with short-lived but very intense disruptions of traditional patterns of voting behavior. Majority parties become minorities; politics which was once competitive becomes non-competitive or, alternatively, hitherto one-party areas now become arenas of intense partisan competition; and large blocks of the active electorate—minorities, to be sure, but perhaps involving as much as a fifth to a third of the voters—shift their partisan allegiance.

2. Critical elections are characterized by abnormally high intensity as well.

a. This intensity typically spills over into the party nominating and platform-writing machinery during the upheaval and results in major shifts in convention behavior from the integrative "norm" as well as in transformations in the internal loci of power in the major party most heavily affected by the pressures of realignment. Ordinarily accepted "rules of the game" are flouted; the party's processes, instead of performing their usual integrative functions, themselves contribute to polarization.

b. The rise in intensity is associated with a considerable increase in ideological polarizations, at first within one or more of the major parties and then between them. Issue distances between the parties are markedly increased, and elections tend to involve highly salient issue-clusters, often with strongly emotional and symbolic overtones, far more than is customary in American electoral politics. One curious property of established leadership as it drifts into the stress of realignment seems to be a tendency to become more rigid and dogmatic, which itself contributes greatly to the explosive "bursting stress" of realignment. . . .

c. The rise in intensity is also normally to be found in abnormally heavy voter participation for the time. This significant increase in political mobilization is not always or uniformly present, to be sure. It is particularly true of realigning cycles with a strong sectional thrust that the areas which are propelled most strongly to one party or the other tend to be those in which turnout does not increase much, or even declines. Similarly, while increases in participation during the 1928–36 period were very heavy in most of the country, they were slight or nonexistent in the South, because the restrictive structure of local politics which had been created at the turn of the century was not disturbed until long after World War II. Moreover, the net effect of the New Deal realignment was to make the South even more lopsidedly Democratic than it had been before. With such exceptions, however, there has still been a general tendency toward markedly increased participation during realigning eras.

3. Historically speaking, at least, national critical realignments have not occurred at random. Instead, there has been a remarkably uniform periodicity in their appearance. . . .

4. It has been argued, with much truth, that American political parties are essentially constituent parties. That is to say, the political-party subsystem is sited in a socioeconomic system of very great heterogeneity and diversity. For a variety of reasons (to be discussed in greater detail later) this party system has tended to be preoccupied with performing the functions of integration and "automatic" aggregation of highly diverse and often antagonistic subgroupings in the population to the near exclusion of concern for development of "modern" mass organization in the European sense.

Critical realignments emerge directly from the dynamics of this constituent-function supremacy in American politics in ways and with implications which will be analyzed subsequently. Here we will only note that since they involve constitutional readjustments in the broadest sense of the term, they are intimately associated with and followed by transformations in large clusters of policy. This produces correspondingly profound alternations in policy and influences the grand institutional structures of American government. In other words, realignments are themselves constituent acts: they arise from emergent tensions in society which, not adequately controlled by the organization or outputs of party politics as usual, escalate to a flash point; they are issue-oriented phenomena, centrally associated with these tensions and more or less leading to resolution adjustments; they result in significant transformations in the general shape of policy; and they have relatively profound aftereffects on the roles played by institutional elites. They are involved with redefinitions of the universe of voters, political parties, and the broad boundaries of the politically possible.

To recapitulate, then, eras of critical realignment are marked by short, sharp reorganizations of the mass coalitional bases of the major parties which occur at periodic intervals on the national level; are often preceded by major third-party revolts which reveal the incapacity of "politics as usual" to integrate, much less aggregate, emergent political demand; are closely associated with abnormal stress in the socioeconomic system; are marked by ideological polarizations and issue-distances between the major parties which are exceptionally large by normal standards; and have durable consequences as constituent acts which determine the outer boundaries of policy in general, though not necessarily of policies in detail.

KATHLEEN HALL JAMIESON

42. DIRTY POLITICS

Although it may always have been an accurate description of political life, Kathleen Hall Jamieson's concise statement that "what is known is not necessarily what is believed, what is shown is not necessarily what is seen, and what is said is not necessarily what is heard" had by the 1980s and 1990s become the guiding principles for American political campaigns.

Jamieson recounts how the Republicans used dramatic and questionable political spots to blame the Democratic presidential candidate, Massachusetts Governor

---

Source: From *Dirty Politics: Deception, Distraction, and Democracy* by Kathleen Hall Jamieson. Copyright © 1993 by Kathleen Hall Jamieson. Reprinted by permission of Oxford University Press.

Michael Dukakis, for allowing a convicted murderer, Willie Horton, to receive a weekend pass during which he committed kidnap and rape. In a now famous 30-second television spot the announcer says over a photo of Bush that Bush believes in the death penalty. Next, over a photo of Dukakis, he says that not only does Dukakis oppose the death penalty, but as governor he "allowed first-degree murderers to have weekend passes from prison." Then, over a mugshot of Willie Horton, a black man, the announcer says, "One man was Willie Horton, who murdered a boy in a robbery, stabbing him 19 times. Despite a life sentence, Horton received 10 weekend passes from prison. Horton fled, kidnapped a young couple, stabbing the man and repeatedly raping his girlfriend."

The pictures and script of the ad campaign clearly were designed to create the perception that Governor Dukakis was personally responsible for furloughing 268 convicts who committed acts of violence, even murder, while out of prison. In contrast, of course, Republican candidate George Bush was to be seen as tough on crime and compassionate toward victims. Because the spot was produced and run by Americans for Bush, an independent group that was not formally part of the Bush campaign, he could and did technically disavow it while at the same time benefiting from its subtle racism. Both Horton and the television spot became dominant issues throughout the 1988 presidential campaign. As for Horton, he went back to prison, where he told reporters that Bush "may just be a cheap political opportunist. I can't help but question his moral judgment."

Jamieson's analysis of this successful Republican campaign spot raises serious ethical issues and troubling political questions regarding the increasingly sophisticated art of manipulating public perceptions of political candidates.

William Horton and Michael Dukakis are now twinned in our memory. The fact that the memories are factually inaccurate does not diminish their power. Dukakis did not pardon Horton nor did the furloughed convict kill.

Although it does recount the facts of the Horton case, this chapter is not one more rehash of who did what to whom in the 1988 campaign. Instead, it sets a context for the book by examining how voters and reporters came to know what they know of politics. It argues that, in politics as in life, what is known is not necessarily what is believed, what is shown is not necessarily what is seen, and what is said is not necessarily what is heard. It then examines how in the Horton case consultants exploited the psychological quirks that characterize humans.

These quirks include a pack-ratlike tendency to gather up and interrelate information from various places, a disposition to weigh accessible, dramatic data more heavily than abstract statistical information, and a predilection for letting fears shape perception of what constitutes "fact."

At the same time, we have conventionalized journalistic norms that reward messages that are dramatic, personal, concise, visual, and take the form of narrative. In 1988, the psychological dispositions of the public coupled with the news norms to produce an environment in which an atypical but dramatic personification of deep-seated fears would displace other issues and dominate the discourse of the campaign. That dramatic, visual, personalized narrative told the "story" of William Horton.

VOTERS ARE PACK RATS

The role that ads, Bush rhetoric, news, and audience psychology played in transforming William Horton's name for some into a symbol of the terrors of crime and for others of the exploitation of racist fears shows the powerful ways in which messages interact and the varying responses they evoke in individuals. Like pack rats, voters gather bits and pieces of political information and store them in a single place. Lost in the storage is a clear recall of where this or that "fact" came from. Information obtained from news mixes with that from ads, for example.

Although Bush had been telling the tale on the stump since June, in the second week in September 1988, the Horton story broke into prime time in the form of a National Security Political Action Committee (NSPAC) ad. The ad tied Michael Dukakis to a convicted murderer who had jumped furlough and gone on to rape a Maryland woman and assault her fiancé. The convict was black, the couple white.

The ad opens with side-by-side pictures of Dukakis and Bush. Dukakis's hair is unkempt, the photo dark. Bush, by contrast, is smiling and bathed in light. As the pictures appear, an announcer says "Bush and Dukakis on crime." A picture of Bush flashes on the screen. "Bush supports the death penalty for first-degree murderers." A picture of Dukakis. "Dukakis not only opposes the death penalty, he allowed first-degree murderers to have weekend passes from prison." A close-up mug shot of Horton flashes onto the screen. "One was Willie Horton, who murdered a boy in a robbery, stabbing him nineteen times." A blurry black-and-white photo of Horton apparently being arrested appears. "Despite a life sentence, Horton received ten weekend passes from prison." The words "kidnapping," "stabbing," and "raping" appear on the screen with Horton's picture as the announcer adds, "Horton fled, kidnapping a young couple, stabbing the man and repeatedly raping his girlfriend." The final photo again shows Michael Dukakis. The announcer notes "Weekend prison passes. Dukakis on crime."

When the Bush campaign's "revolving door" ad began to air on October 5, viewers read Horton from the PAC ad into the furlough ad. This stark black-and-white Bush ad opened with bleak prison scenes. It then cut to a procession of convicts circling through a revolving gate and marching toward the nation's living rooms. By carefully juxtaposing words and pictures, the ad invited the false inference that 268 first-degree murderers were furloughed by Dukakis to rape and kidnap. As the bleak visuals appeared, the announcer said that Dukakis had vetoed the death penalty and given furloughs to "first-degree murderers not eligible for parole. While out, many committed other crimes like kidnapping and rape."

The furlough ad contains three false statements and invites one illegitimate inference. The structure of the ad prompts listeners to hear "first-degree murderers not eligible for parole" as the antecedent referent for "many." Many of whom committed crimes? First-degree murderers not eligible for parole. Many of whom went on to commit crimes like kidnapping and rape? First-degree murderers not eligible for parole.

But many unparoleable first-degree murderers did not escape. Of the 268 furloughed convicts who jumped furlough during Dukakis's first two terms, only four had ever been convicted first-degree murderers not eligible for parole. Of those four not "many" but one went on to kidnap and rape. That one was William Horton. By flashing "268 escaped" on the screen as the announcer speaks of "many first-degree murderers," the ad invites the false inference that 268 murderers jumped furlough to rape and kidnap. Again, the single individual who fits this description is Horton. Finally, the actual number who were more than four hours late in returning from furlough during Dukakis's two and a half terms was not 268 but 275. In Dukakis's first two terms, 268 escapes were made by the 11,497 individuals who were given a total of 67,378 furloughs. In the ten-year period encompassing his two completed terms and the first two years of his third term (1987–88), 275 of 76,455 furloughs resulted in escape.

This figure of 275 in ten years compares with 269 who escaped in the three years in which the program was run by Dukakis's Republican predecessor, who created the furlough program.[1]

Still the battle of drama against data continued. After the Bush campaign's furlough ad had been on the air for two and a half weeks, in the third week of October, PAC ads featuring the victims of Horton began airing. One showed the man whose fiancée had been raped by the furloughed Horton. "Mike Dukakis and Willie Horton changed our lives forever," said Cliff Barnes, speaking in tight close-up. "He was serving a life term, without the possibility of a parole, when Governor Dukakis gave him a few days off. Horton broke into our home. For twelve hours, I was beaten, slashed, and terrorized. My wife, Angie, was brutally raped. When his liberal experiment failed, Dukakis simply looked away. He also vetoed the death penalty bill. Regardless of the election, we are worried people don't know enough about Mike Dukakis."

The second ad was narrated by the sister of the teenager killed by Horton. "Governor Dukakis's liberal furlough experiments failed. We are all victims. First, Dukakis let killers out of prison. He also vetoed the death penalty. Willie Horton stabbed my teenage brother nineteen times. Joey died. Horton was sentenced to life without parole, but Dukakis gave him a furlough. He never returned. Horton went on to rape and torture others. I worry that people here don't know enough about Dukakis's record." The words that recur in the two ads are: "liberal," "experiment," "rape," worry that "people don't know enough about Dukakis," "vetoed the death penalty."

Taken together the ads created a coherent narrative. Dukakis furloughed Horton (PAC ads), just as he had furloughed 267 other escapees (Bush revolving door ad). Horton raped a woman and stabbed her fiancé (crime-quiz and victim PAC ads). Viewers could infer what must have happened to the victims of the other 267 escapees.[2]

The narrative was reinforced by print and radio. The "get out of jail free courtesy of Dukakis" card reappeared in 400,000 fliers mailed by the Bush campaign to Texans. "He let convicted rapists, murderers and drug dealers out of prison on weekend passes," said the flier. "And even after—while out on furlough—they raped and tried to kill again."[3]

ALAMO PAC, a political action committee based in San Antonio, Texas, produced one ad that paralleled the claims of the furlough ad but focused on drugs. While showing a drug dealer at a high school, the ad noted that Dukakis had vetoed mandatory prison terms for convicted drug dealers, had fought the death penalty for drug "murderers," and supported weekend furloughs for drug convicts. A second ALAMO PAC ad showed a burglar, presumably freed under a furlough program, creeping into a darkened bedroom.

Clips from Bush's speeches that appeared in the news reinforced the Horton–Dukakis link. In Xenia, Ohio, in early October, Bush talked in what the *New York Times* described as "vivid detail . . . about the notorious case of Willie Horton." Press accounts vivified the case by supplying details and occasional pictures of Horton. The *New York Times* described Horton as "the murderer who left the Massachusetts prison system on a weekend furlough, only to be caught a year later after he raped a Maryland woman and brutally beat her fiancé."[4] At a rally in Medina, Ohio, Bush referred to the Massachusetts governor as "the furlough king." In Trenton, New Jersey, Bush noted that "the victims of crime are given no furlough from their pain and suffering."[5]

The sister of one of Horton's victims and the man Horton had assaulted while on furlough began holding press conferences just as PAC ads featuring them were beginning to air. In Texas, newspapers devoted front-page space to Donna Fournier Cuomo, whose seventeen-year-old brother Horton supposedly killed, and Cliff Barnes, then the fiancé of the woman the escapee had raped. The press tours were underwritten by a two-million dollar fund raised by the

Committee for the Presidency, the pro-Bush Political Action Committee[6] that sponsored the "victim" ads.

In 1988, broadcast news stories allied segments from three ads to create new congeries of images. The ads included clips from the furlough ad, still photos of furloughed convict William Horton, close-ups of the sister of a man Horton "murdered," and the husband of a woman Horton raped. Horton's victims and the murdered teenager's sister recounted their stories. Since Robert McClure and Thomas Patterson's pioneering study of the relationship of ads and news, we have known that viewers import segments of one story into another,[7] a phenomenon McClure and Patterson call "meltdown."

This phenomenon is well explained by former NBC president Robert Mulholland. "I think during the campaign the average viewer starts to get a little confused. I'm expecting any day now to see Willie Horton endorse a line of jeans. . . . Some of the ads start to look like news stories, they're the same length, 30 seconds. . . . Television is not just separated in the minds of the viewer between this is news, this is commercial, and this is entertainment. Sometimes it all gets fuzzed up because it all comes into the home through the same little piece of glass."[8]

The "melting down" of these images explains the controversy surrounding the Bush campaign's use of William Horton. In late fall 1988 a rising chorus of Democrats condemned George Bush and his Republican handlers for the "Willie Horton" ad. Feigning cherubic innocence, Bush's surrogates pointed out that no picture of the black murderer and rapist Horton had ever appeared in a Bush-sponsored ad.

From Bush strategist Lee Atwater to Bush media advisor Roger Ailes, Bush's aides were telling the literal truth. The scowling convict's mug shot appeared only in the ads of presumably independent political action committees. But the psychological impact was similar. In his stump speeches, Bush routinely raised the case of the furloughed convict without mentioning his race. But once a viewer had seen the PAC ad or a news clip about it, the images of Horton, his victims, and the circling convicts were likely to meld into a coherent narrative reinforced almost daily by Bush's recounting of it in his campaign speeches.

NOT ALL INFORMATION IS CREATED EQUAL

Democratic nominee Michael Dukakis both opposed the death penalty and favored furloughs. It is no accident that the image chosen by the Republicans to symbolize the Massachusetts furlough system was a black male. By explaining that they used Horton not because he was black but because he "slashed" a Maryland man and raped his fiancée, the Republicans tacitly acknowledged the atypicality of the case. No other furloughed first-degree murderer—white or black—either murdered or raped while out. During the primaries a double murderer did jump furlough but was caught and returned. As one of the authors of the Lawrence, Massachusetts *Eagle-Tribune's* series notes, the Bush campaign could have selected a white criminal had it wanted. "We did a page 1 story on a white murderer," recalls Sue Forrest. "He was a former cop who was furloughed. My colleagues wrote a story on five furlough cases. Four were white. The fifth was Horton." Former trooper Armand Therrein killed his business partner and a policeman. On December 11, 1987, he jumped work detail. A month later, he was recaptured. The Republicans opted for a street crime involving strangers and a black villain over the story of a white cop-gone-bad who killed a friend for insurance money. Since the Bush campaign relied on the *Eagle-Tribune* for its information on the furlough program, it presumably knew of these cases.

Horton was not a representative instance of the furlough program. Nor were his crimes typical of crime in the United States, where murder, assault, and nearly nine out of ten rapes are intraracial, not interracial.

Yet by late October, Bush was observing that the Horton case had "come to symbolize, and represent—accurately, I believe—the misguided outlook of my opponent when it comes to crime."[9] In my judgment, a single aberrational incident was taken by the Republicans, the press, and the public to be typical of crime, and Dukakis's handling of it seen as symptomatic of the failures of liberalism because dramatic, personalized evidence carries more weight psychologically than do statistics. Moreover, the Horton case played both into the widely held presupposition that Democrats are "soft on crime" and into the conventions of network news.

NEWS NORMS FOCUS ON DRAMA, STRATEGIC INTENT, AND EFFECT

The Horton narrative fit the requirements of news. Unlike the "soft" news found in feature stories of the sort pioneered by Charles Kuralt on television, hard news is about an event that treats an issue of ongoing concern. Because violent crime is dramatic, conflict ridden, evokes intense emotions, disrupts the social order, threatens the community, and can be verified by such official sources as police, it is "newsworthy."[10] If one believed Bush's version of the facts, a convicted murderer who should have been executed had been furloughed to rape, torture, and murder again. In newscasts, the villain Horton appeared incarnated in a menacing mug shot. To personalize and dramatize, the news camera showed him in close-up; the less inflammatory visuals in the controversial PAC ad were shot mid-screen. Appearing in tight close-ups both in news and in the ads, the sister of the teenager Horton allegedly killed and the fiancé and now husband of the woman he raped told of their torment and urged a vote against the second villain in the story, Michael Dukakis.

The story structure of news lends itself to reporting that personalizes. A violent crime is committed by one individual against others. A good story has a protagonist and an antagonist, in this case a villain and a victim, the forces of disorder against the force of law. The "typical news story is organized dramatically to identify a problem, to describe it in a narrative of rising action, to locate the protagonists and set them against each other (usually in short interviews), and to create some sort of resolution. This format gives coherence to data, and it makes an item a story in the most literal sense, a story that is likely to gain and hold an audience."[11] The Horton story offered to the news media by the Republicans met these criteria.

The first network story to air on the Horton case (CBS, December 2, 1987) uses interviews to set out the contours of what could have been a prime-time crime show. "The man who murdered my seventeen-year-old brother in 1974 was given a furlough," reports Donna Cuomo. "To think that these people deserve a second chance to get out there and we just have to hope that they're not going to do something to somebody else is—it's crazy." Cuomo is trying to get Massachusetts to ban such furloughs, notes the reporter. What prompts her activity? Horton, whom she assumes was her brother's killer, was given a furlough. "He enjoyed, he enjoyed torturing people," says the husband of the woman raped by Horton. "There, there, all the begging and pleading really egged this guy on." Dukakis is quoted saying that after the Horton case, the state tightened its guidelines. But that's not good enough for the woman raped by the furloughed convict. Commenting on the claim that the Massachusetts furlough system has a 99.9 percent success rate, she says, "If 99.9 percent are proven good and there's 1% that's bad, then that tells me the system does not work. I'm a human being and my life has almost been destroyed, and I almost lost my life, not only my husband's life." There is someone who shares her view. "For the Maryland judge who sentenced Horton," says the correspondent, "a furlough or even a return to Massachusetts was unthinkable." "The man should never breathe a breath of free air again," says the circuit court judge. "He is devoid of conscience and he should die in prison."

As the news reports unfold the story, personal details give texture to the identities of the victim while Horton remains a menacing mug shot. "I don't think any of you can understand what it's like to be tied up in a basement and listen to your wife being violated and beaten," says Cliff Barnes (CBS, July 20, 1988). "He's a big guy," says the rape victim (NBC, January 21, 1988); "He overpowered me and slugged me in the face with a gun and he knocked me to the ground and he tied me behind my back." "It was like a nightmare, you know, seeing this man after what he did to Joey is out on furlough and he is just free to go to a mall or whatever he pleases," says Donna Cuomo. And in the backdrop of the narrative is the law-and-order judge who finally locked Horton up for life. "I just don't know anything about their [Massachusetts'] system. I have no assurance that he won't be on furlough or parole or whatever the devil it is in the matter of two or three years" (NBC, January 21, 1988).

After April when Dukakis signs the bill outlawing furloughs for cases like Horton's, the narrative runs into problems. The victims revive the storyline and hence news interest by asking for an apology from Dukakis. A Republican-sponsored national tour ensures that their request would attract coverage. "My wife and I have never heard from the Dukakis administration," says Barnes. "There's never been even an apology to us for what happened to us." "In Ohio," adds the correspondent, "Bush called on Dukakis to apologize to the victims for a program he called a tragic mistake" (ABC, November 7, 1988). "There has never been even an apology to what happened to us," says Barnes. "Whenever it's been brought up it's been accused of being an aberration or one failure in a successful system, which is a blatant lie." Note that when Barnes asserts without evidence that theirs is not an isolated case, his claim goes unchallenged. Then Bush too joins the chorus faulting Dukakis for not apologizing. "As far as I know the Governor never acknowledged that his furlough program was a tragic mistake" (NBC, October 7, 1988). In the campaign's final weeks, Barnes reappears in news decrying the Dukakis record in a synoptic ad. "For twelve hours I was beaten, slashed, and terrorized, and my wife Angie was brutally raped," he says (NBC, October 28, 1988).

Into this narrative context, Bush fits one soundbite after another. "Willie Horton was in jail, found guilty by a jury of his peers for murdering a seventeen-year-old kid after torturing him." (There is no direct evidence that Horton killed Fournier. Nor was there evidence of torture. But neither of those facts will be brought out in network news.) "What did the Democratic governor of Massachusetts think he was doing when he let convicted first-degree murderers out on weekend passes?" asked Bush. "In no other state would a cold-blooded murderer like Willie Horton have been set free to terrorize innocent people" (CBS, June 26, 1988).

Whenever a soundbite about Horton made its way into news, the requirement that reporters create a context evoked the whole Horton story. As a result, it was told and retold. "Dukakis accused the Bush campaign of exploiting the case of Willie Horton," noted Chris Wallace, adding "the Massachusetts prisoner who brutalized a couple while on furlough" (NBC, October 19, 1988). "The literature," which Dukakis is dismissing as "garbage," says, "quote: 'All the murderers and rapists and drug pushers and child molesters in Massachusetts vote for Michael Dukakis,'" notes ABC's Sam Donaldson (October 19, 1988). "And it refers to Willie Horton, the Massachusetts prisoner who brutalized a Maryland couple while out on furlough. . . . " "The Bush campaign has scored big with TV ads on crime," says CBS's Bruce Morton, "especially on a Massachusetts furlough program under which murderer Willie Horton on furlough committed rape and assault" (October 21, 1988).

The vivid language in which reporters recounted the "Horton story" magnified its recall; by framing his rebuttal in statistics about the effectiveness of the furlough program, Dukakis used abstractions against tangible, visual, personalized threat. Because they prompt visualization and create conceptual hooks on which information can be hung, evocative words are more readily remembered than more abstract ones. The vivid, concrete nature of the words used to capsulize Bush's charges coupled with memories of ads add visual points of reference to reporters' words.

This is the case, for example, when Brokaw says "The Vice President repeatedly has attacked Dukakis on the issue of the Massachusetts prison furlough program, specifically a convicted killer on furlough who brutally attacked a man and a woman. Some new perspective on that issue tonight. A study out today says that more than two hundred thousand furloughs were granted last year to fifty-three thousand prisoners in this country and that there were few problems. The study says that Massachusetts reported a furlough success rate of ninety-nine point nine percent" (NBC, October 12, 1988). Concrete language is more evocative than statistical abstractions. Exposed to Horton's face for weeks by the saturation-level PAC campaign, viewers now saw the convicts through the story of Horton.

In news and ads, the Dukakis campaign did as Brokaw had done—responded to evocative narrative with lifeless statistics. "The Dukakis campaign accused Bush of exploiting a tragedy," notes Lisa Myers. "A spokesman claimed the Governor has a tough anti-crime record, with more cops on the beat, five times as many drug offenders behind bars, and overall crime in Massachusetts down 13 percent" (NBC, October 7, 1988).

But the overall thrust of the coverage was uncovering strategic intent and effect. "If Willie Horton is a central issue in October of 1988," comments syndicated columnist Mark Shields, "then Michael Dukakis's chances of a mandate for 1989 are pretty limited" (CBS, July 20, 1988). "What if the big word at the end of October is not Willie Horton but drugs," asks Lesley Stahl of a Democratic consultant. "We win," he responds. "And so," she adds, "the Republicans will keep pushing the Horton line. Bush intends to keep up the pressure, which might even include a campaign commercial starring Willie Horton's victims." The power of the underlying story of violence and victimization is intensified as the piece closes. It is the victim who seems to be summarizing the story.

Angela Barnes: "I'm so mad at this justice. There's none. There's no justice."

Lesley Stahl: "Lesley Stahl. CBS. Atlanta."

In the final weeks of the campaign, Dukakis gained some control over the Horton narrative when his campaign offered reporters a "strategy" peg explaining the Republicans' motivation. On the David Brinkley show, Dukakis's running mate alleged that the Republican use of Horton was racist. But here too the charge elicited recitations of the narrative. "Yesterday on ABC, Dukakis running mate Lloyd Bentsen said he thinks there is an element of racist appeal in Bush's continued citation of Willie Horton, now the star of television ads. Horton, a black man, who raped a white woman while on furlough from a Massachusetts prison" (ABC, October 24, 1988). The Republicans "also denied any racial intent in TV spots about black murder convict

Willie Horton, who raped a Maryland woman and stabbed her husband, both white, while on prison furlough from Massachusetts" (ABC, October 25, 1988).

The personal, dramatic, conflict-ridden nature of the Horton case eased it into network news in 1988. The process was abetted by the fact that it spoke to an ongoing news theme—crime—and could be communicated in telegraphic sound and sightbites. As NBC's Ken Bode explained, "Bush's tough talk on crime works because it fits what most Californians see on their news each day" (NBC, October 28, 1988).

Once Horton's case began to resonate with voters, its place in the news lineup was secure. The fact of Horton explained the perception that Bush was tough on crime, reasoned reporters. So, for example, after indicating that "Bush's aides say they would have used the Horton case even if he weren't black," Lisa Myers closes a story late in the campaign by observing, "A key part of Bush's strategy has been to drive up negative opinions of Dukakis, to cast him as a liberal. That strategy clearly has worked and senior Bush aides say that no matter how much Dukakis whines about it they aren't going to change now" (NBC, October 24, 1988). . . .

THE PSYCHOLOGY OF THE BUSH USE OF HORTON

Did the Horton case, while atypical and inflammatory, tell a larger psychological truth? Is it possible to lie—by claiming that Horton murdered on furlough when he did not, inviting false inferences about the number of Horton-like instances that had occurred in Massachusetts, and encouraging unwarranted fears about blacks raping and murdering whites—and still tell a psychological truth? No. Had he been a federal prisoner, the death penalty that Bush favored for drug kingpins would not have executed Horton. Under the terms in effect under the Reagan–Bush administration, Horton would have been eligible for furlough.

To reporters who called him in his Maryland prison during the campaign, Horton claimed, as he had at his trial, that he did not stab the youth he and two others were convicted of killing. Indeed, one court official indicated that another of the threesome had confessed to being the killer; the confession was disallowed because the suspect had not been read his Miranda rights. Under Massachusetts' felony rule, the prosecution did not have to ascertain which of the three committed the murder, only that all three were in some way involved. Horton claimed to have been in the getaway car. The prosecutors didn't know if Horton had held the knife; there was "reasonable doubt"; but, by virtue of his presence at the scene, they did know he was an accomplice. As parties to the robbery that occasioned the murder, all would be convicted.

Had a death penalty state handled the evidence on the robbery and murder that led to Horton's conviction in Massachusetts, Horton would not have been executed. The reason is simple. In 1982 in *Enmund v. Florida* [458 U.S. 782, 797 (1982)], the U.S. Supreme Court had invalidated a death sentence in a case that paralleled the one in Massachusetts. Like Horton, the convict in question had been an accessory to a robbery. Under the doctrine that said that a person party to a felony that results in a murder is guilty of the murder even if it cannot be proven that he committed it, Enmund had been convicted of capital murder. Invoking the Eighth Amendment's ban on disproportionate punishment, the Supreme Court set aside the death sentence.

Those who see relevance in the Horton case argue that a liberal Democrat would appoint to the high court justices more disposed to protect the rights of criminals than of the accused. And in that argument resides the final irony of the Horton case. The rollback of the rights of the accused under the conservative Supreme Court could ultimately mean that the original confession obtained from Horton's colleague might have been deemed acceptable. Under the rules of a Bush but not a Dukakis court, Horton might not have been convicted of first-degree murder at all. And hence he would have been on the streets permanently, sooner than he was under the "liberal" court's requirements.

All narrative capitalizes on the human capacity and disposition to construct stories. A compelling narrative such as the Horton saga controls our interpretation of data by offering a plausible, internally coherent story that resonates with the audience while accounting causally for otherwise discordant or fragmentary information.[12]

When news and ads trace the trauma and drama of a kidnapping and rape by a convicted murderer on furlough, the repetition and the story structure give it added power in memory. Visceral, visual identifications and appositions are better able to be retrieved than statistical abstractions.

Repeatedly aired oppositional material carries an additional power. Material aired again and again is more likely to stay fresh in our minds. The same is true for attacks.

Cognitive accessibility is upped by those message traits that characterize the Republicans' use of Horton: the dramatic, the personally relevant, the frequently repeated topic or claim[13]—the menacing mug shot, circling convicts, empathic victims—and seemingly uncaring perpetrator—the Massachusetts governor.

When it came to William Horton, our quirks as consumers of political information worked for the Republicans and against the Democrats. In our psychic equations, something nasty has greater power and influence than something nice. When evaluating "social stimuli," negative information carries more weight than positive information.[14] Additionally, negative information seems better able than positive to alter existing impressions[15] and is easier to recall.[16] Televised images that elicit negative emotion result in better recall than those that evoke positive ones.[17] As a result, attacks are better remembered than positive reasons for voting for a candidate.[18] And dissatisfied, disapproving voters are more likely to appear at their polling place than their more satisfied neighbors.[19]

Messages that induce fear dampen our disposition to scrutinize them for gaps in logic. When the message is fear arousing, personal involvement and interest in it minimize systematic evaluation.[20] In the language of cognitive psychology, "[L]arge levels of negative affect such as fear may override cognitive processing."[21]

The Horton story magnifies fear of crime, identifies that fear with Dukakis, and offers a surefire way of alleviating the anxiety—vote for Bush. What successful use of fear appeal and narrative share is a capacity to focus audiences on one interpretation of reality while rendering others implausible. When fear is aroused, attention narrows,[22] simple autonomic behaviors are facilitated, complex, effort-filled ones inhibited,[23] and creative thought dampened.[24]

The mood induced by exposure to communication can affect our probability judgments as well. Johnson and Tversky[25] asked college students to read descriptions that were assembled as if they were newspaper stories. After reading the material, the students were asked to estimate how frequently those within a group of 50,000 people would experience specific dangers (e.g., fire, leukemia, traffic accidents) within a one-year period. When the "newspaper" described the violent death of a male undergraduate, the estimates these college students offered increased for all of the risks, including those that were fundamentally dissimilar to the type described in the article. When the story concerned a happy event that occurred to a young man, the frequency estimates decreased.

Here is the answer to the question Peter Jennings put to Michael Dukakis near the end of the campaign. Why, wondered Jennings, for those we talk to across America, is "Willie Horton" so powerful an image (ABC, November 4, 1988)? The answer is that the fear the story inspired minimized the likelihood that it would be evaluated analytically and its atypicality noted; repetition of its riveting details in ads and news invited us to generalize from it. So, when the Bush furlough ad stated "many first-degree murderers" as the phrase "268 escaped" appeared on the screen, the inference that 268 "Willie Hortons" had been released to kidnap and rape was all but inevitable.

The power of the Horton mini-series was magnified as it unfolded soap-opera-like in news and ads; broadcasts that focused on the tale's strategic intent and effect couldn't effectively challenge its typicality. And since statistics don't displace stories nor data, drama, the native language of Dukakis didn't summon persuasive visions of the cops he had put on the street or the murders and rapes that hadn't been committed in a state whose crime rate was down. Abetted by news reports, amplified by Republican ads, assimilated through the cognitive quirks of audiences, William Horton came to incarnate liberalism's failures and voters' fears.

NOTES

1. I have compiled these figures from Table 4, p. 15, of "1989 Annual Statistical Report of the Furlough Program," Massachusetts Department of Correction, January 1991.

2. Those who read newspaper accounts of the furlough program learned that Horton was the only furloughed Massachusetts first-degree murderer who committed a violent crime. Most furloughed escapees committed auto theft. A quarter of the reported escapees hadn't escaped at all and had returned voluntarily but more than two hours late from the furlough. See Kathleen Hall Jamieson, "For Televised Mendacity, This Year Is the Worst Ever," *Washington Post,* October 30, 1988, C1, C2.

3. Dave McNeely, "Bush, Dukakis Commercials Becoming Hottest Campaign Issue," *Austin American-Statesman,* October 25, 1988, B3.

4. Maureen Dowd, "Bush Portrays His Opponent as Sympathetic to Criminals," *New York Times,* October 8, 1988, 9.

5. Gerald M. Boyd, "Bush's Attack on Crime Appeals to the Emotions," *New York Times,* October 11, 1988, 12.

6. Mike Hailey, "Crime Victims Condemn Dukakis," *Austin American-Statesman,* October 11, 1988, B3.

7. See also: J. P. Robinson, D. Davis, H. Sahin, and T. O'Toole, "Comprehension of Television News: How Alert Is the Audience?" Paper presented to the Association for Education in Journalism, Boston, 1980.

8. "MacNeil/Lehrer NewsHour," November 8, 1988.

9. "Top Democrats Accuse Bush Campaign of Inflaming Racial Fears," *New York Times,* October 24, 1988, 10.

10. One study found that crime was the third largest category of news covered by newspapers. Sanford Sherizen, "Social Creation of Crime News: All the News Fitted to Print," in *Deviance and Mass Media,* ed. Charles Winick (Beverly Hills: Sage, 1978), 208, 215.

11. Kathleen Hall Jamieson and Karlyn Kohrs Campbell, *Interplay of Influence: News, Advertising, Politics and the Mass Media,* 3rd ed. (Belmont, Calif.: Wadsworth, 1992), 33.

12. Cf. Hayden White, "The Value of Narrativity in the Representation of Reality," in *On Narrative,* ed. W. J. T. Mitchell (Chicago: University of Chicago Press, 1981), 23; Paul Ricoeur, *Time and Narrative,* trans. Kathleen McLaughlin and David Pellauer (Chicago: University of Chicago Press, 1984–86), Vol. 1, 74ff.; Jerome Bruner, *Actual Minds, Possible Worlds* (Cambridge, Mass.: Harvard University Press, 1986). I do not wish to imply that narrative is an illegitimate way of knowing or that narrative necessarily works in service of our predispositions and fears. As Bennett and Edelman note, "If stories can be constructed to wall off the senses to the dilemmas and contradictions of social life, perhaps they also can be presented in ways that open up the mind to creative possibilities developed in ways that provoke intellectual struggle, the resolution of contradiction, and the creation of a more workable human order" (W. L. Bennett and M. Edelman, "Toward a New Political Narrative," *Journal of Communication* 35 [1985], 161–62).

For a discussion of rhetorical functions of narrative, see W. R. Fisher, *Human Communication as Narrative* (Columbia: University of South Carolina Press, 1987); C. M. Condit, "Crafting Virtue: The Rhetorical Construction of Public Morality," *Quarterly Journal of Speech* 73 (1987), 79–97; W. G. Kirkwood, "Storytelling and Self Confrontation: Parables as Communication Strategies," *Quarterly Journal of Speech* 69 (1983), 58–74; W. F. Lewis, "Telling America's Story: Narrative Form and the Reagan Presidency," *Quarterly Journal of Speech* 73 (1987), 280–302; M. C. McGee and J. S. Nelson, "Narrative Reason in Public Argument," *Journal of Communication* 35,

(1985), 139–55; R. C. Rowland, "On Limiting the Narrative Paradigm: Three Case Studies," *Communication Monographs* 56 (1989), 39–54; V. W. Turner, "Social Dramas and Stories about Them," *Critical Inquiry* 7 (1980), 141–68; B. Warnick, "The Narrative Paradigm: Another Story," *Quarterly Journal of Speech* 73 (1987), 172–82.
13. See E. T. Higgins, J. A. Bargh, and W. Lombardi, "Nature of Priming Effects on Categorization," *Journal of Experimental Psychology: Learning, Memory, and Cognition* 11 (1985), 59–69. This heuristic is also well explored in S. Popkin, *The Reasoning Voter* (Chicago: University of Chicago Press, 1991).
14. R. Lau, "Negativity in Political Perception," *Political Behavior* 4 (1982), 353–77; R. Lau, "Two Explanations for Negativity Effects in Political Behavior," *American Journal of Political Science* 29 (1985), 119–38.
15. K. Kellermann, "The Negativity Effect and Its Implications for Initial Interaction," *Communication Monographs* 51 (1984), 37–55.
16. B. Reeves, E. Thorson, and J. Schleuder, "Attention to Television: Psychological Theories and Chronometric Measures," in *Perspectives on Media Effects,* eds. J. Bryant and D. Zillmann (Hillside, N.J.: Lawrence Erlbaum, 1986), 251–79.
17. J. Newhagen and B. Reeves, "Emotion and Memory Response for Negative Political Advertising: A Study of the 1988 Presidential Campaign." Paper presented to the Association for Education in Journalism and Mass Communication, Washington, D.C., 1989.
18. M. A. Shapiro and R. H. J. Reiger, "Comparing Positive and Negative Political Advertising." Paper presented to the International Communication Association, San Francisco, 1989. See also J. Schleuder, M. McCombs, and W. Wanta, "Inside the Agenda Setting Process: How Political Advertising and TV News Prime Viewers to Think About Issues and Candidates." Paper presented to the Association for Education in Journalism and Mass Communication, Washington, D.C., 1989.
19. S. Kernell, "Presidential Popularity and Negative Voting: An Alternative Explanation of the Midterm Congressional Decline of the President's Party," *American Political Science Review* 71 (1977), 44–66.
20. Christopher Jepson and Shelly Chaiken, "Chronic Issue-Specific Fear Inhibits Systematic Processing of Persuasive Communications," in *Communication, Cognition, and Anxiety,* ed. Melanie Booth-Butterfield (Newbury Park, Calif.: Sage, 1990), 61–84.
21. A. Lang, "Involuntary Attention and Physiological Arousal Evoked by Structural Features and Emotional Content of TV Commercials," *Communication Research* 17 (1990), 275–99.

In processing messages we rely not on statistically warranted inferences but on rules of thumb, or heuristics, that have certain predictable biases. These rules of thumb carry nonprobablistic presuppositions about how things work. Even after explanations show the operation and unreliability of a heuristic, we continue to apply it. Understanding their form and mode of operation has become an important concern of scholars of communication.

Computers, by contrast, rely on algorithms. An algorithm is a solution procedure which, if followed correctly, yields a correct answer.

The rule of thumb most relevant to my concerns here is the availability heuristic. Ease of retrieval increases the likelihood that we will misjudge the probability of the event occurring. Because airplane crashes are presented in vivid detail and kill a large group at one time, for example, a single plane crash is likely to be better remembered than reports of hundreds of passenger car accidents. From this, some mistakenly conclude that it is safer to ride in a car than to fly. In the words of Tversky and Kahneman, the availability heuristic evaluates "the frequency of classes or the probability of events . . . by the ease with which relevant issues come to mind" ("Availability: A Heuristic for Judging Frequency and Probability," *Cognitive Psychology* 5 [1973], 207–232, at 207.).

22. J. A. Easterbrook, "The Effect of Emotion on the Utilization and the Organization of Behavior," *Psychological Review* 66 (1959), 183–201.
23. R. B. Zajonc, "Social Facilitation," *Science* 149 (1965), 269–74.
24. C. J. Neweth, "Differential Contributions of Majority and Minority Influence," *Psychological Review* 93 (1986), 23–32.
25. E. J. Johnson and A. Tversky, "Affect, Generalization, and the Perception of Risk," *Journal of Personality and Social Psychology* 45 (1983), 20–31.

SECTION VII
REVIEW QUESTIONS

1. Does Susan B. Anthony's argument—that because the founders were all men, they found it rational to deny women the right to vote—suggest that even today it might be true that elected officials cannot or do not adequately represent groups to which they do not belong? Would this be a good argument for some type of group-based representation system? For affirmative action in various sectors of American life?

2. From his description of how "to hold your district," can you identify George Washington Plunkitt's view of "human nature"? Is he right? Does he overstate the case? Are people capable of acting in the broader public interest if it conflicts with their private interests? Are you?

3. Joe McGinniss's explicit recognition that political campaigns are basically like advertising campaigns to sell soap or cereal shocked many Americans when it appeared in 1969. Were political campaigns ever anything else? Have politicians simply become more sophisticated? What is so offensive about McGinniss's thesis anyhow? Don't you learn a great deal about candidates from political advertising?

4. What are the four types of elections in Walter Dean Burnham's classification scheme? Did the 1992 election of Bill Clinton mark a cycle of realignment? Did the ensuing series of scandals have an impact on that cycle?

5. After reading Kathleen Hall Jamieson's account of the use of the Willie Horton case in the 1988 presidential campaign, do you think that the Republicans acted unethically? Was the Willie Horton campaign nothing but a way of "selling" a candidate? How fair or unfair was the Horton campaign? If a cereal company attacked a competing cereal company's product as accurately/inaccurately as the Republicans depicted Governor Dukakis' role in the Horton case, would you find that to be "acceptable" advertising?

VIII

Lobbyists and Interest Groups

JAMES MADISON

43. CONTROLLING FACTIONS

James Madison's discussion of "factions" in The Federalist, *No. 10, remains the classic defense of a pluralistic democratic society. Madison argued that since the sources of division among groups of people could not be eliminated, the government should be structured so as to control the effects of these divisions. In this eloquent discussion of the new government to be created by the Constitution, Madison explained that minority factions could do little harm, but the majority factions had to be controlled. Because the new country was in the form of a republic, rather than a pure democracy, Madison was convinced that tyrannical majorities would not be able to gain power. The fact that the republic was to encompass a large number of people over a wide geographic area would protect against the emergence of a tyrannical majority faction.*

Among the numerous advantages promised by a well-constructed Union, none deserves to be more accurately developed than its tendency to break and control the violence of faction. The friend of popular governments never finds himself so much alarmed for their character and fate as when he contemplates their propensity to this dangerous vice. He will not fail, therefore, to set a due value on any plan, which, without violating the principles to which he is attached, provides a proper cure for it. The instability, injustice, and confusion introduced into the public councils have, in truth, been the mortal diseases under which popular governments have everywhere perished, as they continue to be the favorite and fruitful topics from which the adversaries to liberty derive their most specious declamations. The valuable improvements made by the American constitutions on the popular models, both ancient and modern, cannot certainly be too much admired; but it would be an unwarrantable partiality to contend that they have as effectually obviated the danger on this side, as was wished and expected. Complaints are everywhere heard from our most considerate and virtuous citizens, equally the friends of public and private faith and of public and personal liberty, that our governments are too unstable, that the public good is disregarded in the conflicts of rival parties, and that

---

Source: The Federalist, No. 10 (1787).

measures are too often decided, not according to the rules of justice and the rights of the minor party, but by the superior force of an interested and overbearing majority. However anxiously we may wish that these complaints had no foundation, the evidence of known facts will not permit us to deny that they are in some degree true. It will be found, indeed, on a candid review of our situation, that some of the distresses under which we labor have been erroneously charged on the operation of our governments; but it will be found, at the same time, that other causes will not alone account for many of our heaviest misfortunes; and, particularly, for that prevailing and increasing distrust of public engagements and alarm for private rights which are echoed from one end of the continent to the other. These must be chiefly, if not wholly, effects of the unsteadiness and injustice with which a factious spirit has tainted our public administration.

By a faction I understand a number of citizens, whether amounting to a majority or minority of the whole, who are united and actuated by some common impulse of passion, or of interest, adverse to the rights of other citizens, or to the permanent and aggregate interests of the community.

There are two methods of curing the mischiefs of faction: the one, by removing its causes; the other, by controlling its effects.

There are again two methods of removing the causes of faction: the one, by destroying the liberty which is essential to its existence; the other, by giving to every citizen the same opinions, the same passions, and the same interests.

It could never be more truly said than of the first remedy that it was worse than the disease. Liberty is to faction what air is to fire, an aliment without which it instantly expires. But it could not be a less folly to abolish liberty, which is essential to political life, because it nourishes faction than it would be to wish the annihilation of air, which is essential to animal life, because it imparts to fire its destructive tendency.

The second expedient is as impracticable as the first would be unwise. As long as the reason of man continues fallible, and he is at liberty to exercise it, different opinions will be formed. As long as the connection subsists between his reason and his self-love, his opinions and his passions will have a reciprocal influence on each other; and the former will be objects to which the latter will attach themselves. The diversity in the faculties of men, from which the rights of property originate, is not less an insuperable obstacle to a uniformity of interests. The protection of these faculties is the first object of government. From the protection of different and unequal faculties of acquiring property, the possession of different degrees and kinds of property immediately results; and from the influence of these on the sentiments and views of the respective proprietors ensues a division of the society into different interests and parties.

The latent causes of faction are thus sown in the nature of man; and we see them everywhere brought into different degrees of activity, according to the different circumstances of civil society. A zeal for different opinions concerning religion, concerning government, and many other points, as well of speculation as of practice; an attachment to different leaders ambitiously contending for pre-eminence and power: or to persons of other descriptions whose fortunes have been interesting to the human passions, have, in turn, divided mankind into parties, inflamed them with mutual animosity, and rendered them much more disposed to vex and oppress each other than to co-operate for their common good. So strong is this propensity of mankind to fall into mutual animosities that where no substantial occasion presents itself the most frivolous and fanciful distinctions have been sufficient to kindle their unfriendly passions and excite their most violent conflicts. But the most common and durable source of factions has been the various and unequal distribution of property. Those who hold and those who are without property have ever formed distinct interests in society. Those who are creditors, and those who are debtors, fall under a like discrimination. A landed interest, a manufacturing interest, a mercantile interest, a moneyed interest, with many lesser interests, grow up of necessity in civilized nations, and divide them into different classes, actuated by different sentiments and views. The regulation of these various and interfering interests forms the principal task of modern legislation and involves the spirit of party and faction in the necessary and ordinary operations of government.

No man is allowed to be a judge in his own cause because his interest would certainly bias his judgment, and, not improbably, corrupt his integrity. With equal, nay with greater reason, a body of men are unfit to be both judges and parties at the same time; yet what are many of the most important acts of legislation but so many judicial determinations, not indeed concerning the rights of single persons, but concerning the rights of large bodies of citizens? And what are the different classes of legislators but advocates and parties to the causes which they determine? Is a law proposed concerning private debts? It is a question to which the creditors are parties on one side and the debtors on the other. Justice ought to hold the balance between them. Yet the parties are, and must be, themselves the judges; and the most numerous party, or in other words, the most powerful faction must be expected to prevail. Shall domestic manufacturers be encouraged, and in what degree, by restrictions on foreign manufacturers? are questions which would be differently decided by the landed and the manufacturing classes, and probably by neither with a sole regard to justice and the public good. The apportionment of taxes on the various descriptions of property is an act which seems to require the most exact impartiality; yet there is, perhaps, no legislative act in which greater opportunity and temptation are given to a predominant party to trample on the rules of justice. Every shilling with which they overburden the inferior number is a shilling saved to their own pockets.

It is in vain to say that enlightened statesmen will be able to adjust these clashing interests and render them all subservient to the public good. Enlightened statesmen will not always be at the helm. Nor, in many cases, can such an adjustment be made at all without taking into view indirect and remote considerations, which will rarely prevail over the immediate interest which one party may find in disregarding the rights of another or the good of the whole.

The inference to which we are brought is that the *causes* of faction cannot be removed and that relief is only to be sought in the means of controlling its *effects*.

If a faction consists of less than a majority, relief is supplied by the republican principle, which enables the majority to defeat its sinister views by regular vote. It may clog the administration, it may convulse the society; but it will be unable to execute and mask its violence under the forms of the Constitution. When a majority is included in a faction, the form of popular government, on the other hand, enables it to sacrifice to its ruling passion or interest both the public good and the rights of other citizens. To secure the public good and private rights against the danger of such a faction, and at the same time to preserve the spirit and the form of popular government, is then the great object to which our inquiries are directed. Let me add that it is the great desideratum by which alone this form of government can be rescued from the opprobrium under which it has so long labored and be recommended to the esteem and adoption of mankind.

By what means is this object attainable? Evidently by one of two only. Either the existence of the same passion or interest in a majority at the same time must be prevented, or the majority, having such coexistent passion or interest, must be rendered, by their number and local situation, unable to concert and carry into effect schemes of oppression. If the impulse and the opportunity be suffered to coincide, we well know that neither moral nor religious motives can be relied on as an adequate control. They are not found to be such on the injustice and violence of individuals, and lose their efficacy in proportion to the number combined together, that is, in proportion as their efficacy becomes needful.

From this view of the subject it may be concluded that a pure democracy, by which I mean a society consisting of a small number of citizens, who assemble and administer the government in person, can admit of no cure for the mischiefs of faction. A common passion or interest will, in almost every case, be felt by a majority of the whole; a communication and concert results from the form of government itself; and there is nothing to check the inducements to sacrifice the weaker party or an obnoxious individual. Hence it is that such democracies have ever been spectacles of turbulence and contention; have ever been found incompatible with personal security or the rights of property; and have in general been as short in their lives as they have been violent in their deaths. Theoretic politicians, who have patronized this species of government, have erroneously supposed that by reducing mankind to a perfect equality in their political rights, they would at the same time be perfectly equalized and assimilated in their possessions, their opinions, and their passions.

A republic, by which I mean a government in which the scheme of representation takes place, opens a different prospect and promises the cure for which we are seeking. Let us examine the points in which it varies from pure democracy, and we shall comprehend both the nature of the cure and the efficacy which it must derive from the Union.

The two great points of difference between a democracy and a republic are: first, the delegation of the government, in the latter, to a small number of citizens elected by the rest: secondly, the greater number of citizens and greater sphere of country over which the latter may be extended.

The effect of the first difference is, on the one hand, to refine and enlarge the public views by passing them through the medium of a chosen body of citizens, whose wisdom may best discern the true interest of their country and whose patriotism and love of justice will be least likely to sacrifice it to temporary or partial considerations. Under such a regulation it may well happen that the public voice, pronounced by the representatives of the people, will be more consonant to the public good than if pronounced by the people themselves, convened for the purpose. On the other hand, the effect may be inverted. Men of factious tempers, of local prejudices, or of sinister designs, may, by intrigue, by corruption, or by other means, first obtain the suffrages, and then betray the interests of the people. The question resulting is, whether small or extensive republics are most favorable to the election of proper guardians of the public weal; and it is clearly decided in favor of the latter by two obvious considerations.

In the first place it is to be remarked that however small the republic may be the representatives must be raised to a certain number in order to guard against the cabals of a few; and that however large it may be they must be limited to a certain number in order to guard against the confusion of a multitude. Hence, the number of representatives in the two cases not being in proportion to that of the constituents, and being proportionally greatest in the small republic, it follows that if the proportion of fit characters be not less in the large than in the small republic, the former will present a greater opinion, and consequently a greater probability of a fit choice.

In the next place, as each representative will be chosen by a greater number of citizens in the large than in the small republic, it will be more difficult for unworthy candidates to practise with success the vicious arts by which elections are too often carried; and the suffrages of people being more free, will be more likely to center on men who possess the most attractive merit and the most diffusive and established characters.

It must be confessed that in this, as in most other cases, there is a mean, on both sides of which inconveniencies will be found to lie. By enlarging too much the number of electors, you render the representative too little acquainted with all their local circumstances and lesser interests; as by reducing it too much, you render him unduly attached to these, and too little fit to comprehend and pursue great and national objects. The federal Constitution forms a happy combination in this respect; the great and aggregate interests being referred to the national, the local and particular to the State legislatures.

The other point of difference is the greater number of citizens and extent of territory which may be brought within the compass of republican than of democratic government; and it is this circumstance principally which renders factious combinations less to be dreaded in the former than in the latter. The smaller the society, the fewer probably will be the distinct parties and interests composing it; the fewer the distinct parties and interests, the more frequently will a majority be found of the same party; and the smaller the number of individuals composing a majority, and the smaller the compass within which they are placed, the more easily will they concert and execute their plans of oppression. Extend the sphere and you take in a greater variety of parties and interests; you make it less probable that a majority of the whole will have a common motive to invade the rights of other citizens; or if such a common motive exists, it will be more difficult for all who feel it to discover their own strength and to act in unison with each other. Besides other impediments, it may be remarked that, where there is a consciousness of unjust or dishonorable purposes, communication is always checked by distrust in proportion to the number whose concurrence is necessary.

Hence, it clearly appears that the same advantage which a republic has over a democracy in controlling the effects of faction is enjoyed by a large over a small republic—is enjoyed by the Union over the States composing it. Does this advantage consist in the substitution of representatives whose enlightened views and virtuous sentiments render them superior to local prejudices and to schemes of injustice? It will not be denied that the representation of the Union will be most likely to possess these requisite endowments. Does it consist in the greater security afforded by a greater variety of parties, against the event of any one party being able to outnumber and oppress the rest? In an equal degree does the increased variety of parties comprised within the Union increase this security. Does it, in fine, consist in the greater obstacles opposed to the concert accomplishment of the secret wishes of an unjust and interested majority? Here again the extent of the Union gives it the most palpable advantage.

The influence of factious leaders may kindle a flame within their particular States but will be unable to spread a general conflagration through the other States. A religious sect may degenerate into a political faction in a part of the Confederacy; but the variety of sects dispersed over the entire face of it must secure the national councils against any danger from that source. A rage for paper money, for an abolition of debts, for an equal division of property, or for any other improper or wicked project, will be less apt to pervade the whole body of the Union than a particular member of it, in the same proportion as such a malady is more likely to taint a particular county or district than an entire State.

In the extent and proper structure of the Union, therefore, we behold a republican remedy for the diseases most incident to republican government. And according to the degree of pleasure and pride we feel in being republicans ought to be our zeal in cherishing the spirit and supporting the character of federalists.

JOHN C. CALHOUN

44. THE CONCURRENT MAJORITY

The leading political voice of the South in the first half of the nineteenth century, John C. Calhoun (1782–1850) argued that binding political decisions could be made only by "concurrent" not "simple" majorities. Concurrent majorities would represent all major elements of society rather than a simple numerical majority that might go against the significant and legitimate interests of members of the numerical minority. The doctrine of concurrent majority in Calhoun's theory "excludes the possibility of oppression by giving each interest the means of protecting itself . . . against all measures calculated to advance the peculiar interest of others at its expense." Although his motive was to protect the proslavery policies of the Southern states, his position in favor of consensus government represents a major argument for the protection of minorities in a democratic society.

THE NUMERICAL VERSUS THE CONCURRENT MAJORITY

It results, from what has been said, that there are two different modes in which the sense of the community may be taken: one, simply by the right of suffrage, unaided; the other, by the right through a proper organism. Each collects the sense of the majority. But one regards numbers only and considers the whole community as a unit having but one common interest throughout, and collects the sense of the greater number of the whole as that of the community. The other, on the contrary, regards interests as well as numbers—considering the community as made up of different and conflicting interests, as far as the action of the government is concerned—and takes the sense of each through its majority or appropriate organ, and the united sense of all as the sense of the entire community. The former of these I shall call the numerical or absolute majority. I call it the constitutional majority because it is an essential element in every constitutional government, be its form what it may. So great is the difference, politically speaking, between the two majorities that they cannot

Source: From John C. Calhoun, *A Disquisition on Government* (1851).

be confounded without leading to great and fatal errors; and yet the distinction between them has been so entirely overlooked that when the term "majority" is used in political discussions, it is applied exclusively to designate the numerical—as if there were no other. Until this distinction is recognized and better understood, there will continue to be great liability to error in properly constructing constitutional governments, especially of the popular form, and of preserving them when properly constructed. Until then, the latter will have a strong tendency to slide, first, into the government of the numerical majority, and, finally, into absolute government of some other form. To show that such must be the case, and the same time to mark more strongly the difference between the two in order to guard against the danger of overlooking it, I propose to consider the subject more at length.

THE NUMERICAL MAJORITY NOT THE PEOPLE

The first and leading error which naturally arises from overlooking the distinction referred to is to confound the numerical majority with the people, and this so completely as to regard them as identical. This is a consequence that necessarily results from considering the numerical as the only majority. All admit that a popular government, or democracy, is the government of the people, for the terms imply this. A perfect government of the kind would be one which would embrace the consent of every citizen or member of the community; but as this is impracticable in the opinion of those who regard the numerical as the only majority and who can perceive no other way by which the sense of the people can be taken, they are compelled to adopt this as the only true basis of popular government, in contradistinction to governments of the aristocratical or monarchical form. Being thus constrained, they are, in the next place, forced to regard the numerical majority as in effect the entire people; that is, the greater part as the whole, and the government of the greater part as the government of the whole. It is thus the two come to be confounded and a part made identical with the whole. And it is thus also that all the rights, powers, and immunities of the whole people come to be attributed to the numerical majority—and, among others, the supreme, sovereign authority of establishing and abolishing governments at pleasure.

This radical error, the consequence of confounding the two and of regarding the numerical as the only majority, has contributed more than any other cause to prevent the formation of popular constitutional governments and to destroy them even when they have been formed. It leads to the conclusion that in their formation and establishment nothing more is necessary than the right of suffrage and the allotment to each division of the community a representation in the government in proportion to numbers. If the numerical majority were really the people, and if to take its sense truly were to take the sense of the people truly, a government so constituted would be a true and perfect model of a popular constitutional government; and every departure from it would detract from its excellence. But as such is not the case, as the numerical majority, instead of being the people, is only a portion of them, such a government, instead of being a true and perfect model of the people's government, that is, a people self-governed, is but the government of a part over a part—the major over the minor portion.

But this misconception of the true elements of constitutional government does not stop here. It leads to others equally false and fatal, in reference to the best means of preserving and perpetuating them, when, from some fortunate combination of circumstances, they are correctly formed. For they who fall into these errors regard the restrictions which organism imposes on the will of the numerical majority as restrictions on the will of the people and, therefore, as not only useless but wrongful and mischievous. And hence they endeavor to destroy organism under the delusive hope of making government more democratic.

Such are some of the consequences of confounding the two and of regarding the numerical as the only majority. And in this may be found the reason why so few popular governments have been properly constructed and why, of these few, so small a number have proved durable. Such must continue to be the result so long as these errors continue to be prevalent. . . .

CONCURRENT MAJORITY ESSENTIAL TO CONSTITUTIONAL GOVERNMENT

Having now explained the reasons why it is so difficult to form and preserve popular constitutional government so long as the distinction between the two majorities is overlooked and the opinion prevails that a written constitution, with suitable restrictions and a proper division of its powers, is sufficient to counteract the tendency of the numerical majority to the abuse of power—I shall next proceed to explain, more fully, why the concurrent majority is an indispensable element in forming constitutional governments and why the numerical majority, of itself, must, in all cases, make governments absolute.

The necessary consequence of taking the sense of the community by the concurrent majority is, as has been explained, to give to each interest or portion of the community a negative on the others. It is this mutual negative among its various conflicting interests which invests each with the power of protecting itself, and places the rights and safety of each where only they can be securely placed, under its own guardianship. Without this there can be no systematic, peaceful, or effective resistance to the natural tendency of each to come into conflict with the others; and without this there can be no constitution. It is this negative power—the power of preventing or arresting the action of the government, be it called by what term it may, veto, interposition, nullification, check, or balance of power—which in fact forms the constitution. They are all but different names for the negative power. In all its forms, and under all its names, it results from the concurrent majority. Without this there can be no negative, and without a negative, no constitution. The assertion is true in reference to all constitutional governments, be their forms what they may. It is, indeed, the *negative* power which makes the constitution, and the *positive* which makes the government. The one is the power of acting, and the other the power of preventing or arresting action. The two, combined, make constitutional governments.

But, as there can be no constitution without the negative power, and no negative power without the concurrent majority, it follows necessarily that, where the numerical majority has the sole control of the government, there can be no constitution, as constitution implies limitation or restriction—and, of course, is inconsistent with the idea of sole or exclusive power. And hence the numerical, unmixed with the concurrent, majority necessarily forms, in all cases, absolute government.

It is, indeed, the single or *one power* which excludes the negative and constitutes absolute government, and not the *number* in whom the power is vested. The numerical majority is as truly a *single power*—and excludes the negative as completely as the absolute government of one or of the few. The former is as much the absolute government of the democratic or popular form as the latter of the monarchical or aristocratical. It has, accordingly, in common with them the same tendency to oppression and abuse of power.

Constitutional governments, of whatever form, are, indeed, much more similar to each other in their structure and character than they are, respectively, to the absolute governments, even of their own class. All constitutional governments, of whatever class they may be, take the sense of community, by its parts—each through its appropriate organ—and regard the sense of all its parts as the sense of the whole. They all rest on the right of suffrage and the responsibility of rulers, directly or indirectly. On the contrary, all absolute governments, of whatever form, concentrate power in one uncontrolled and irresponsible individual or body whose will is regarded as the sense of the community. And hence the great and broad distinction between governments is not that of the one, the few, or the many, but of the constitutional and the absolute.

From this there results another distinction which, although secondary in its character, very strongly marks the difference between these forms of government. I refer to their respective conservative principle—that is, the principle by which they are upheld and preserved. This principle in constitutional governments is *compromise;* and in absolute governments is *force,* as will be next explained.

It has been already shown that the same constitution of man which leads those who govern to oppress the governed, if not prevented, will, with equal force and certainty, lead the latter to resist oppression when possessed of the means of doing so peaceably and successfully. But absolute governments, of all forms, exclude all other means of resistance to their authority than that of force, and, of course, leave no other alternative to the governed but to acquiesce in oppression, however great it may be, or to resort to force to put down the government. But the dread of such a resort must necessarily lead the government to prepare to meet force in order to protect itself, and hence, of necessity, force becomes the conservative principle of all such governments.

On the contrary, the government of the concurrent majority, where the organism is perfect, excludes the possibility of oppression by giving to each interest, or portion, or order—where there are established classes—the means of protecting itself by its negative against all measures calculated to advance the peculiar interests of others at its expense. Its effect, then, is to cause the different interests, portions, or orders, as the case may be, to desist from attempting to adopt any measure calculated to promote the prosperity of one, or more, by sacrificing that of others: and thus to force them to unite in such measures only as would promote the prosperity of all, as the only means to prevent the suspension of the action of the government, and, thereby, to avoid anarchy, the greatest of all evils. It is by means of such authorized and effectual resistance that oppression is prevented and the necessity of resorting to force superseded in governments of the concurrent majority; and hence compromise, instead of force, becomes their conservative principle.

It would, perhaps, be more strictly correct to trace the conservative principle of constitutional governments to the necessity which compels the different interests, or portions, or orders to compromise—as the only way to promote their respective prosperity and to avoid anarchy—rather than to the compromise itself. No necessity can be more urgent and imperious than that of avoiding anarchy. It is the same as that which makes government indispensable to preserve society, and is not less imperative than that which compels obedience to superior force. Traced to this source, the voice of a people—uttered under the necessity of avoiding the greatest of calamities through the organs of a government so constructed as to suppress the expression of all partial and selfish interests, and to give a full and faithful utterance to the sense of the whole community, in reference to its common welfare—may, without impiety, be called *the voice of God*. To call any other so would be impious.

DAVID B. TRUMAN

45. Defending Pluralist Politics

David Truman, the best known of the modern interest group theorists, defends the legitimacy of organized interest groups in democratic politics and describes public policy decisions as the outcome of competition among these groups. Truman believes that in the United States all

Source: From David B. Truman, *The Governmental Process* (New York: Alfred A. Knopf, 1951). Reprinted by permission of the author.

> *organized interests have the opportunity to influence the government because of what he termed a "multiplicity of points of access." By this he meant that a weak political party system combined with separated powers and a federal structure assure that persistent groups will almost inevitably find some way to influence public policy. Group conflict, he went on to argue, would be moderated by the fact that individuals belong to many different groups that have conflicting interests among them. This "overlapping membership" would tend to prevent "the possibility of irreconcilable conflict."*

Men, wherever they are observed, are creatures participating in those established patterns of interaction that we call groups. Excepting perhaps the most casual and transitory, these continuing interactions, like all such interpersonal relationships, involve power. This power is exhibited in two closely interdependent ways. In the first place, the group exerts power over its members; an individual's group affiliations largely determine his attitudes, values, and the frames of reference in terms of which he interprets his experiences. For a measure of conformity to the norms of the group is the price of acceptance within it. Such power is exerted not only by an individual's present group relationships; it also may derive from past affiliations such as the childhood family as well as from groups to which the individual aspires to belong and whose characteristic shared attitudes he also holds. In the second place, the group, if it is or becomes an interest group, which any group in a society may be, exerts power over other groups in the society when it successfully imposes claims upon them.

Many interest groups, probably an increasing proportion in the United States, are politicized. That is, either from the outset or from time to time in the course of their development they make their claims through or upon the institutions of government. Both the forms and functions of government in turn are a reflection of the activities and claims of such groups. The constitution-writing proclivities of Americans clearly reveal the influence of demands from such sources, and the statutory creation of new functions reflects their continuing operation. Many of these forms and functions have received such widespread acceptance from the start or in the course of time that they appear to be independent of the overt activities of organized interest groups. The judiciary is such a form. The building of city streets and the control of vehicular traffic are examples of such a function. However, if the judiciary or a segment of it operates in a fashion sharply contrary to the expectations of an appreciable portion of the community or if its role is strongly attacked, the group basis of its structure and powers is likely to become apparent. Similarly, if street construction greatly increases tax rates or if the control of traffic unnecessarily inconveniences either pedestrians or motorists, the exposure of these functions to the demands of competing interests will not be obscure. Interests that are widely held in the society may be reflected in government without their being organized in groups.

They are what we have called potential groups. If the claims implied by the interests of these potential groups are quickly and adequately represented, interaction among those people who share the underlying interests or attitudes is unnecessary. But the interest base of accepted governmental forms and functions and their potential involvement in overt group activities are ever present even when not patently operative.

The institutions of government are centers of interest-based power; their connections with interest groups may be latent or overt and their activities range in political character from the routinized and widely accepted to the unstable and highly controversial. In order to make claims, political interest groups will seek access to the key points of decision within these institutions. Such points are scattered throughout the structure, including not only the formally established branches of government but also the political parties in their various forms and the relationships between governmental units and other interest groups.

The extent to which a group achieves effective access to the institutions of government is the resultant of a complex of interdependent factors. For the sake of simplicity these may be classified in three somewhat overlapping categories: (1) factors relating to a group's strategic position in the society; (2) factors associated with the internal characteristics of the group; and (3) factors peculiar to the governmental institutions themselves. In the first category are: the group's status or prestige in the society, affecting the ease with which it commands deference from those outside its bounds; the standing it and its activities have when measured against the widely held but largely unorganized interests or "rules of the game"; the extent to which government officials are formally or informally "members" of the group; and the usefulness of the group as a source of technical and political knowledge. The second category includes: the degree and appropriateness of the group's organization; the degree of cohesion it can achieve in a given situation, especially in the light of competing group demands upon its membership; the skills of the leadership; and the group's resources in numbers and money. In the third category, are: the operating structure of the government institutions, since such established features involve relatively fixed advantages and handicaps; and the effects of the group life of particular units or branches of the government. . . .

There are two elements in this conception of the political process in the United States that are of crucial significance and that require special emphasis. These are, first, the notion of multiple or overlapping membership and, second, the function of unorganized interests, or potential interest groups.

The idea of overlapping membership stems from the conception of a group as a standardized pattern of interactions rather than as a collection of human units. Although the former may appear to be a rather misty abstraction, it is actually far closer to complex reality than the latter notion. The view of a group as an aggregation of individuals abstracts from the observable fact that in any society, and especially a complex one, no single group affiliation accounts for all of the attitudes or interests of any individual except a fanatic or a compulsive neurotic. No tolerably normal person is totally absorbed in any group in which he participates. The diversity of an individual's activities and his attendant interests involve him in a variety of actual and potential groups. Moreover, the fact that the genetic experiences of no two individuals are identical and the consequent fact that the spectra of their attitudes are in varying degrees dissimilar means that the members of a single group will perceive the group's claims in terms of a diversity of frames of reference. Such heterogeneity may be of little significance until such time as these multiple memberships conflict. Then the cohesion and influence of the affected group depend upon the incorporation or accommodation of the conflicting loyalties of any significant segment of the group, an accommodation that may result in altering the original claims. Thus the leaders of a Parent–Teacher Association must take some account of the fact that their proposals must be acceptable to members who also belong to the local taxpayers' league, to the local chamber of commerce, and to the Catholic Church.

The notion of overlapping membership bears directly upon the problems allegedly created by the appearance of a multiplicity of interest groups. Yet the fact of such overlapping is frequently overlooked or neglected in discussions of the political role of groups. James Madison, whose brilliant analysis in the tenth essay in *The Federalist* we have frequently quoted, relied primarily upon diversity of groups and difficulty of communication to protect the new government from the tyranny of a factious majority. He barely touched on the notion of multiple membership when he observed, almost parenthetically: "Besides other impediments, it may be remarked that, where there is a consciousness of unjust or dishonorable purposes, communication is always checked by distrust in proportion to the number whose concurrence is necessary." John C. Calhoun's idea of the concurrent majority, developed in his posthumously published work, *A Disquisition on Government* (1851), assumed the unified, monolithic character of the groups whose liberties he was so anxious to protect. When his present-day followers unearth his doctrines, moreover, they usually make the same assumption, although implicitly.[1] Others, seeking a satisfactory means of accounting for the continued existence of the political system, sometimes assume that it is the nonparticipant citizens, aroused to unwonted activity, who act as a kind of counterbalance to the solid masses that constitute organized interest groups.[2] Although this phenomenon may occur in times of crisis, reliance upon it reckons insufficiently with the established observation that citizens who are nonparticipant in one aspect of the governmental process, such as voting, rarely show much concern for any phase of political activity. Multiple membership is more important as a restraint upon the activities of organized groups than the rarely aroused protests of chronic nonparticipants. . . .

Any mutual interest, however, any shared attitude, is a potential group. A disturbance in established relationships and expectations anywhere in the society may produce new patterns of interaction aimed at restricting or eliminating the disturbance. Sometimes it may be this possibility of organization that alone gives the potential group a minimum of influence in the political process. Thus Key notes that the Delta planters in Mississippi "must speak for their Negroes in such programs as health and education," although the latter are virtually unorganized and are denied the means of active political participation.[3] It is in this sense that Bentley speaks of a difference in degree between the politics of despotism and that of other "forms" of government. He notes that there is "a process of representation in despotisms which is inevitable in all democracies, and which may be distinguished by quantities and by elaboration of technique, but not in any deeper 'qualitative' way." He speaks of the despot as "representative of his own class, and to a smaller, but none the less real, extent of the ruled class as well."[4] Obstacles to the development of organized groups from potential ones may be presented by inertia or by the activities of opposed groups, but the possibility that severe disturbances will be created if these submerged, potential interests should organize necessitates some recognition of the existence of these interests and gives them at least a minimum of influence.

More important for present purposes than the potential groups representing separate minority elements are those interests or expectations that are so widely held in the society and are so reflected in the behavior of almost all citizens that they are, so to speak, taken for granted. Such "majority" interests are significant not only because they may become the basis for organized interest groups but also because the "membership" of such potential groups overlaps extensively the memberships of the various organized interest groups.[5] The resolution of conflicts between the claims of such organized interests and those of organized interest groups must grant recognition to the former not only because affected individuals may feel strongly attached to them but even more certainly because these interests are widely shared and are a part of many established patterns of behavior the disturbance of which would be difficult and painful. They are likely to be highly valued.

These widely held but unrecognized interests are what we have previously called the "rules of the game." Others have described these attitudes in such terms as "systems of belief," as a "general ideological consensus," and as "a broad body of attitudes and understandings regarding the nature and limits of authority."[6] Each of these interests (attitudes) may be wide or narrow, general or detailed. For the mass of the population they may be loose and ambiguous, though more precise and articulated at the leadership level. In any case the "rules of the game" are interests the serious disturbance of which will result in organized interaction and the assertion of fairly explicit claims for conformity. In the American system the "rules" would include the value generally attached to the dignity of the individual human being, loosely expressed in terms of "fair dealing" or more explicitly verbalized in formulations such as the Bill of Rights. They would embrace what we called "the democratic mold," that is, the approval of forms for broad mass participation in the designation of leaders and in the selection of policies in all social groups and institutions. They would also comprehend certain semi-egalitarian notions of material welfare. This is an illustrative, not an exclusive, list of such interests.

W'18 Schedule

118 (3)	TR	2:30-3:50
118 (4)	MW	8:30-9:50
345	MW	11:30-12:50

NOTES

1. Cf. John Fischer: "Unwritten Rules of American Politics," *Harper's Magazine* (November, 1948), pp. 27–36.
2. Cf. Herring: The *Politics of Democracy,* p. 32.
3. Key: *Southern Politics,* pp. 235 and *passim.*
4. Bentley: *The Process of Government,* pp. 314–5. Copyright 1908 by and used with the permission of Arthur F. Bentley.
5. See the suggestive discussion of this general subject in Robert Bierstedt: "The Sociology of Majorities," *American Sociological Review,* Vol. 13, no. 6 (December, 1948), pp. 700–10.
6. Kluckhohn: *Mirror for Man,* pp. 248 and *passim;* Sebastian de Grazia: *The Political Community: A Study of Anomie* (Chicago: University of Chicago Press, 1948), pp. ix, 80, and *passim;* Almond: *The American People and Foreign Policy,* p. 158; Charles E. Merriam: *Systematic Politics* (Chicago: University of Chicago Press, 1945), p. 213.

THEODORE J. LOWI

46. ATTACKING PLURALIST POLITICS

In The End of Liberalism, *Theodore J. Lowi, the leading critic of interest group pluralism, offered a provocative critique of the American political system and the paralyzing effects on the policymaking process he calls "interest group liberalism." Lowi argues that in this system public authority has been parceled out to private groups, thereby making government unable to act in the public interest. The system of "interest group liberalism" that has emerged permits powerful private interests to promote their private objectives through their control of legislative committees and governmental regulatory agencies. Where earlier observers saw interest group activities as providing balanced policies that benefit all participants in the group process, Lowi condemns the group system and calls for a return to what he calls "juridical democracy." Lowi's scathing critique continues to dominate debate over the future of the American political system.*

Source: From *The End of Liberalism.* First edition by Theodore J. Lowi. Copyright © 1969 by W. W. Norton & Company, Inc. Used by permission of W. W. Norton & Company, Inc.

The corruption of modem democratic government began with the emergence of interest-group liberalism as the public philosophy. Its corrupting influence takes at least four important forms, four counts, therefore, of an indictment for which most of the foregoing chapters are mere documentation. Also to be indicted, on at least three counts, is the philosophic component of the ideology, pluralism.

SUMMATION I: FOUR COUNTS AGAINST THE IDEOLOGY

1. Interest-group liberalism as public philosophy corrupts democratic government because it deranges and confuses expectations about democratic institutions. Liberalism promotes popular decision-making but derogates from the decisions so made by misapplying the notion to the implementation as well as the formulation of policy. It derogates from the processes by treating all values in the process as equivalent interests. It derogates from democratic rights by allowing their exercise in foreign policy, and by assuming they are being exercised when access is provided. Liberal practices reveal a basic disrespect for democracy. Liberal leaders do not wield the authority of democratic government with the resoluteness of men certain of the legitimacy of their positions, the integrity of their institutions, or the justness of the programs they serve.

2. Interest-group liberalism renders government impotent. Liberal governments cannot plan. Liberals are copious in plan but irresolute in planning. Nineteenth-century liberalism was standards without plans. This was an anachronism in the modern state. But twentieth-century liberalism turned out to be plans without standards. As an anachronism it, too, ought to pass. But doctrines are not organisms. They die only in combat over the minds of men, and no doctrine yet exists capable of doing the job. All the popular alternatives are so very irrelevant, helping to explain the longevity of interest-group liberalism. Barry Goldwater most recently proved the irrelevance of one. The *embourgeoisement* of American unions suggests the irrelevance of others.

The Departments of Agriculture, Commerce, and Labor provide illustrations, but hardly exhaust illustrations, of such impotence. Here clearly one sees how liberalism has become a doctrine whose means are its ends, whose combatants are its clientele, whose standards are not even those of the mob but worse, are those the bargainers can fashion to fit the bargain. Delegation of power has become alienation of public domain—the gift of sovereignty to private satrapies. The political barriers to withdrawal of delegation are high enough. But liberalism reinforces these through the rhetoric of justification and often even permanent legal reinforcement: Public corporations—justified, oddly, as efficient planning instruments—permanently alienate rights of central coordination to the directors and to those who own the corporation bonds. Or, as Walter Adams finds, the "most pervasive method . . . for alienating public domain is the certificate of convenience and necessity, or some variation thereof in the form of an exclusive franchise, license or permit. . . . [G]overnment has become increasingly careless and subservient in issuing them. The net result is a general legalization of private monopoly."[1] While the best examples still are probably the 10 self-governing systems of agriculture policy, these are obviously only a small proportion of all the barriers the interest-group liberal ideology has erected to democratic use of government.

3. Interest-group liberalism demoralizes government, because liberal governments cannot achieve justice. The question of justice has engaged the best minds for almost as long as there have been notions of state and politics, certainly ever since Plato defined the ideal as one in which republic and justice were synonymous. And since that time philosophers have been unable to agree on what justice is. But outside the ideal, in the realms of actual government and citizenship, the problem is much simpler. We do not have to define justice at all in order to weight and assess justice in government, because in the case of liberal policies we are prevented by what the law would call a "jurisdictional fact." In the famous jurisdictional case of *Marbury v. Madison* Chief Justice Marshall held that even if all the Justices hated President Jefferson for refusing to accept Marbury and the other "midnight judges" appointed by Adams, there was nothing they could do. They had no authority to judge President Jefferson's action one way or another because the Supreme Court did not possess such jurisdiction over the President. In much the same way, there is something about liberalism that prevents us from raising the question of justice at all, no matter what definition of justice is used.

Liberal governments cannot achieve justice because their policies lack the *sine qua non* of justice—that quality without which a consideration of justice cannot even be initiated. Considerations of the justice in or achieved by an action cannot be made unless a deliberate and conscious attempt was made by the actor to derive his action from a general rule or moral principle governing such a class of acts. One can speak personally of good rules and bad rules, but a homily or a sentiment like liberal legislation, is not a rule at all. The best rule is one which is relevant to the decision or action in question and is general in the sense that those involved with it have no direct control over its operation. A general rule is, hence *a priori.* Any governing regime that makes a virtue out of avoiding such rules puts itself totally outside the context of justice.

Take the homely example of the bull and the china shop. Suppose it was an op art shop and that we consider op worthy only of the junk pile. That being the case, the bull did us a great service, the more so because it was something we always dreamed of doing but were prevented by law from entering and breaking. But however much we may be pleased, we cannot judge the act. We can only like or dislike the consequences. The consequences are haphazard; the bull cannot have intended them. The act was a thoughtless, animal act which bears absolutely no relation to any aesthetic principle. We don't judge the bull. We only celebrate our good fortune. Without the general rule, the bull can reenact his scenes of creative destruction daily and still not be capable of achieving, in this case, aesthetic justice. The whole idea of justice is absurd.

The general rule ought to be a legislative rule because the United States espouses the ideal of representative democracy. However, that is merely an extrinsic feature of the rule. All that counts is the character of the rule itself. Without the rule we can only like or dislike the consequences of the governmental action. In the question of whether justice is achieved, a government without good rules, and without acts carefully derived therefrom, is merely a big bull in an immense china shop.

4. Finally, interest-group liberalism corrupts democratic government in the degree to which it weakens the capacity of governments to live by democratic formalisms. Liberalism weakens democratic institutions by opposing formal procedure with informal bargaining. Liberalism derogates from democracy by derogating from all formality in favor of informality. Formalism is constraining; playing it "by the book" is a role often unpopular in American war films and sports films precisely because it can dramatize personal rigidity and the plight of the individual in collective situations. Because of the impersonality of formal procedures, there is inevitably a separation of the real world between the forms and the realities, and this kind of separation gives rise to cynicism, for informality means that some will escape their collective fate better than others. There has as a consequence always been a certain amount of cynicism toward public objects in the United States, and this may be to the good, since a little cynicism is the father of healthy sophistication. However, when the information is elevated to a positive virtue, and hard-won access becomes a share of official authority, cynicism becomes distrust. It ends in reluctance to submit one's fate to the governmental process under any condition, as is the case in the United States in the mid-1960's.

Public officials more and more frequently find their fates paradoxical and their treatment at the hands of the public fickle and unjust when in fact they are only reaping the results of their own behavior, including their direct and informal treatment of the public and the institutions through which they serve the public. The more government operates by the spreading of access, the more public order seems to suffer. The more public men pursue their constituencies, the more they seem to find their constituencies alienated. Liberalism has promoted concentration of democratic authority but deconcentration of democratic power. Liberalism has opposed privilege in policy formulation only to foster it, quite systematically, in the implementation of policy. Liberalism has consistently failed to recognize, in short, that in a democracy forms are important. In a medieval monarchy all formalisms were at court. Democracy proves, for better or worse, that the masses like that sort of thing too.

Another homely parable may help. In the good old days, everyone in the big city knew that traffic tickets could be fixed. Not everyone could get his ticket fixed, but nonetheless a man who honestly paid his ticket suffered in some degree a dual loss: his money, and his self-esteem for having so little access. Cynicism was widespread, violations were many, but perhaps it did not matter, for there were so few automobiles. Suppose, however, that as the automobile population increased a certain city faced a traffic crisis and the system of ticket fixing came into ill repute. Suppose a mayor, victorious on the Traffic Ticket, decided that, rather than eliminate fixing by universalizing enforcement, he would instead reform the system by universalizing the privileges of ticket fixing. One can imagine how the system would work. One can imagine that some sense of equality would prevail, because everyone could be made almost equally free to bargain with the ticket administrators. But one would find it difficult to imagine how this would make the total city government more legitimate. Meanwhile, the purpose of the ticket would soon have been destroyed.

Traffic regulation, fortunately, was not so reformed. But many other government activities were. The operative principles of interest-group liberalism possess the mentality of a world of universalized ticket fixing: Destroy privilege by universalizing it. Reduce conflict by yielding to it. Redistribute power by the maxim of each according to his claim. Reserve an official place for every major structure of power. Achieve order by worshipping the processes (as distinguished from the forms and the procedures) by which order is presumed to be established.

If these operative principles will achieve equilibrium—and such is far from proven—that is all they will achieve. Democracy will have disappeared, because all of these maxims are founded upon profound lack of confidence in democracy. Democracy fails when it lacks confidence in its own authority.

Democratic forms were supposed to precede and accompany the formulation of policies so that policies could be implemented authoritatively and firmly. Democracy is indeed a form of absolutism, but ours was fairly well contrived to be an absolutist government under the strong control of consent-building prior to taking authoritative action in law. Interest-group liberalism fights the absolutism of democracy but succeeds only in taking away its authoritativeness. Whether it is called "creative federalism" by President Johnson, "cooperation" by the farmers, "local autonomy" by the Republicans, or "participatory democracy" by the New Left, the interest-group liberal effort does not create democratic power but rather negates it.

NOTE

1. Walter S. Adams and Horace Gray, *Monopoly in America* (New York: Macmillan, 1955), pp. 47–48.

SECTION VIII
REVIEW QUESTIONS

1. Why did James Madison in *Federalist* No. 10 express such confidence that a tyrannical majority was unlikely to gain control in the United States? How did Madison believe that the political system would work to control "factions"?

2. What did John Calhoun mean by a "concurrent majority"? Is the type of consensus government advocated by Calhoun a practical goal in a society as diverse as ours? What was Calhoun's political goal in promoting the concept of the "concurrent majority"?

3. In a political environment in which every candidate campaigns as the best choice to fight the "special interests," do you think that David Truman's defense of pluralism sounds quaint and dated? How would Truman reply to this attack on "special interests"?

4. What is the essence of Theodore Lowi's critique of pluralist politics? Is there a policy choice that represents the "public interest"? Is this different from the policy choice that emerges from a struggle among interested groups, assuming that all groups have an opportunity to participate?

IX

Mass Media

GEORGE ORWELL

47. LANGUAGE AND POLITICS

In the modern era of political "spin doctors" who work to manipulate public perceptions of political candidates and political events it is easy to think that such chicanery is of recent origin. In fact, George Orwell's famous essay on politics and language concluded long ago that "Political language . . . is designed to make lies sound truthful and murder respectable." Inasmuch as Americans experience politics almost exclusively through the words of political leaders and the description of political events by reporters and commentators, the use of language continues to play a crucial role in determining who wins and loses elections and how Americans will define political events at home and abroad. Orwell's classic recognition that "The great enemy of clear language is insincerity" remains as significant today as when he wrote it. The public would be well advised to heed Orwell's message that political language always has as its goal persuasion rather than clarity, and that "political chaos is connected with the decay of language."

In our time it is broadly true that political writing is bad writing. Where it is not true, it will generally be found that the writer is some kind of rebel, expressing his private opinions and not a "party line." Orthodoxy, of whatever color, seems to demand a lifeless, imitative style. The political dialects to be found in pamphlets, leading articles, manifestos, White Papers and the speeches of undersecretaries do, of course, vary from party to party, but they are all alike in that one almost never finds in them a fresh, vivid, home-made turn of speech. When one watches some tired hack on the platform mechanically repeating the familiar phrases—*bestial atrocities, iron heel, bloodstained tyranny, free peoples of the world, stand shoulder to shoulder*—one often has a curious feeling that one is not watching a live human being but some kind of dummy: a feeling which suddenly becomes stronger at moments when the light catches the speaker's spectacles and turns them into blank discs which seem to

---

Source: Excerpt from "Politics and the English Language" by George Orwell. Copyright © 1946 by Sonia Brownell Orwell and renewed 1974 by Sonia Orwell. Reprinted from his volume *Shooting an Elephant and Other Essays* by permission of Harcourt Brace & Company.

have no eyes behind them. And this is not altogether fanciful. A speaker who uses that kind of phraseology has gone some distance towards turning himself into a machine. The appropriate noises are coming out of his larynx, but his brain is not involved as it would be if he were choosing his words for himself. If the speech he is making is one that he is accustomed to make over and over again, he may be almost unconscious of what he is saying, as one is when one utters the responses in church. And this reduced state of consciousness, if not indispensable, is at any rate favorable to political conformity.

In our time, political speech and writing are largely the defence of the indefensible. Things like the continuance of British rule in India, the Russian purges and deportations, the dropping of the atom bombs on Japan, can indeed be defended, but only by arguments which are too brutal for most people to face, and which do not square with the professed aims of political parties. Thus political language has to consist largely of euphemism, question-begging and sheer cloudy vagueness. Defenceless villages are bombarded from the air, the inhabitants driven out into the countryside, the cattle machine-gunned, the huts set on fire with incendiary bullets: this is called *pacification*. Millions of peasants are robbed of their farms and sent trudging along the roads with no more than they can carry: this is called *transfer of population* or *rectification of frontiers*. People are imprisoned for years without trial, or shot in the back of the neck or sent to die of scurvy in Arctic lumber camps: this is called *elimination of unreliable elements*. Such phraseology is needed if one wants to name things without calling up mental pictures of them. Consider for instance some comfortable English professor defending Russian totalitarianism. He cannot say outright, "I believe in killing off your opponents when you can get good results by doing so." Probably, therefore, he will say something like this:

"While freely conceding that the Soviet régime exhibits certain features which the humanitarian may be inclined to deplore, we must, I think, agree that a certain curtailment of the right to political opposition is an unavoidable concomitant of transitional periods, and that the rigors which the Russian people have been called upon to undergo have been amply justified in the sphere of concrete achievement."

The inflated style is itself a kind of euphemism. A mass of Latin words falls upon the facts like soft snow, blurring the outlines and covering up all the details. The great enemy of clear language is insincerity. When there is a gap between one's real and one's declared aims, one turns as it were instinctively to long words and exhausted idioms, like a cuttlefish squirting out ink. In our age there is no such thing as "keeping out of politics." All issues are political issues, and politics itself is a mass of lies, evasions, folly, hatred and schizophrenia. When the general atmosphere is bad, language must suffer. I should expect to find—this is a guess which I have not sufficient knowledge to verify—that the German, Russian and Italian languages have all deteriorated in the last ten or fifteen years, as a result of dictatorship.

But if thought corrupts language, language can also corrupt thought. A bad usage can spread by tradition and imitation, even among people who should and do know better. The debased language that I have been discussing is in some ways very convenient. Phrases like *a not unjustifiable assumption, leaves much to be desired, would serve no good purpose, a consideration which we should do well to bear in mind,* are a continuous temptation, a packet of aspirins always at one's elbow. Look back through this essay, and for certain you will find that I have again and again committed the very faults I am protesting against. By this morning's post I have received a pamphlet dealing with conditions in Germany. The author tells me that he "felt impelled" to write it. I open it at random, and here is almost the first sentence that I see: "[The Allies] have an opportunity not only of achieving a radical transformation of Germany's social and political structure in such a way as to avoid a nationalistic reaction in Germany itself, but at the same time of laying the foundations of a co-operative and unified Europe." You see, he "feels impelled" to write—feels, presumably, that he has something new to say—and yet his words, like cavalry horses answering the bugle, group themselves automatically into the familiar dreary pattern. This invasion of one's mind by ready-made phrases *(lay the foundations, achieve a radical transformation)* can only be prevented if one is constantly on guard against them, and every such phrase anaesthetizes a portion of one's brain.

I said earlier that the decadence of our language is probably curable. Those who deny this would argue, if they produced an argument at all, that language merely reflects existing social conditions, and that we cannot influence its development by any direct tinkering with words and constructions. So far as the general tone or spirit of a language goes, this may be true, but it is not true in detail. Silly words and expressions have often disappeared, not through any evolutionary process but owing to the conscious action of a minority. Two recent examples were *explore every avenue* and *leave no stone unturned,* which were killed by the jeers of a few journalists. There is a long list of flyblown metaphors which could similarly be got rid of if enough people would interest themselves in the job; and it should also be possible to laugh the *not un-* formation out of existence, to reduce the amount of Latin and Greek in the average sentence, to drive out foreign phrases and strayed scientific words, and, in general, to make pretentiousness unfashionable. But all these are minor points. The defence of the English language implies more than this, and perhaps it is best to start by saying what it does *not* imply.

To begin with it has nothing to do with archaism, with the salvaging of obsolete words and turns of speech, or with the setting up of a "standard English" which must never be departed from. On the contrary, it is especially concerned with the scrapping of every word or idiom which has outworn its usefulness. It has nothing to do with correct grammar and syntax, which are of no importance so long as one makes one's meaning clear, or with the avoidance of Americanisms, or with having what is called a "good prose style." On the other hand it is not concerned with fake simplicity and the attempt to make written English colloquial. Nor does it even imply in every case preferring the Saxon word to the Latin one, though it does imply using the fewest and shortest words that will cover one's meaning. What is above all needed is to let the meaning choose the word, and not the other way about. In prose, the worst thing one can do with words is to surrender to them. When you think of a concrete object, you think wordlessly, and then, if you want to describe the thing you have been visualizing you probably hunt about till you find the exact words that seem to fit it. When you think of something abstract you are more inclined to use words from the start, and unless you make a conscious effort to prevent it, the existing dialect will come rushing in and do the job for you, at the expense of blurring or even changing your meaning. Probably it is better to put off using words as long as possible and get one's meaning as clear as one can through pictures or sensations. Afterwards one can choose—not simply *accept*—the phrases that will best cover the meaning, and then switch round and decide what impression one's words are likely to make on another person. This last effort of the mind cuts out all stale or mixed images, all prefabricated phrases, needless repetitions, and humbug and vagueness generally. But one can often be in doubt about the effect of a word or a phrase, and one needs rules that one can rely on when instinct fails. I think the following rules will cover most cases:

(i) Never use a metaphor, simile or other figure of speech which you are used to seeing in print.
(ii) Never use a long word where a short one will do.
(iii) If it is possible to cut a word out, always cut it out.
(iv) Never use the passive where you can use the active.
(v) Never use a foreign phrase, a scientific word or a jargon word if you can think of an everyday English equivalent.
(vi) Break any of these rules sooner than say anything outright barbarous.

These rules sound elementary, and so they are, but they demand a deep change of attitude in anyone who has grown used to writing in the style now fashionable. One could keep all of them and still write bad English, but one could not write the kind of stuff that I quoted in those five specimens at the beginning of this article.

I have not here been considering the literary use of language, but merely language as an instrument for expressing and not for concealing or preventing thought. Stuart Chase and others have come near to claiming that all abstract words are meaningless, and have used this as a pretext for advocating a kind of political quietism. Since you don't know what Fascism is, how can you struggle against Fascism? One need not swallow such absurdities as this, but one ought to recognize that the present political chaos is connected with the decay of language, and that one can probably bring about some improvement by starting at the verbal end. If you simplify your English, you are freed from the worst follies of orthodoxy. You cannot speak any of the necessary dialects, and when you make a stupid remark its stupidity will be obvious, even to yourself. Political language—and with variations this is true of all political parties, from Conservatives to Anarchists—is designed to make lies sound truthful and murder respectable, and to give an appearance of solidity to pure wind. One cannot change this all in a moment, but one can at least change one's own habits, and from time to time one can even, if one jeers loudly enough, send some worn-out and useless phrase—some *jackboot, Achilles' heel, hotbed, melting pot, acid test, veritable inferno* or other lump of verbal refuse—into the dustbin where it belongs.

THEODORE H. WHITE

48. THE KENNEDY–NIXON TV DEBATES

Journalist Theodore H. White (1915–1986) wrote a series of bestselling books describing presidential elections from 1960 through 1972. His Making of the President *books set a new standard for political reporting, which had the juiciness of an inside story, the intimacy of a biography, and the perspective of history.*

This excerpt from the first in the series offers an insider's look at the first modern nationally televised presidential debates between Richard M. Nixon and John F. Kennedy. While Vice-President Nixon made the mistake of actually trying to debate, Senator Kennedy concentrated on style and on projecting the correct presidential image. People listening to the debate on radio thought that Nixon had won, but Kennedy's style won him the television audience and the election. The lesson of Nixon's experience in 1960 has been learned by all presidential candidates who have followed: Look good on television or lose!

Both candidates had had representatives in the CBS studio from 8:30 in the morning of the day of the debate.

Mr. Nixon's advisers and representatives, understandably nervous since they could not communicate with their principal, had made the best preparation they could. They had earlier requested that both candidates talk from a lecturn, standing—and Kennedy had agreed. They had asked several days

---

Source: From *The Making of the President: 1960* by Theodore White. Copyright © 1961 by Atheneum Publishers. Reprinted by permission of Atheneum Publishers and the estate of Theodore White.

earlier that the two candidates be seated farther apart from each other than originally planned—and that had been agreed on too. Now, on the day of the debate, they paid meticulous attention to each detail. They were worried about the deep eye shadows in Nixon's face and they requested and adjusted two tiny spotlights ("inkies" in television parlance) to shine directly into his eye wells and illuminate the darkness there; they asked that a table be placed in front of the moderator, and this was agreed to also; they requested that no shots be taken of Nixon's left profile during the debate, and this was also agreed to.

The Kennedy advisers had no requests; they seemed as cocky and confident as their chief.

Nixon entered the studio about an hour before air time and inspected the setting, let himself be televised on an interior camera briefly for the inspection of his advisers, then paced moodily about in the back of the studio. He beckoned the producer to him at one point as he paced and asked as a personal favor that he not be on camera if he happened to be mopping sweat from his face. (That night, contrary to most reports, Nixon was wearing no theatrical make-up. In order to tone down his dark beard stubble on the screen, an adviser had applied only a light coating of "Lazy Shave," a pancake make-up with which a man who has a heavy afternoon beard growth may powder his face to conceal the growth.)

Senator Kennedy arrived fifteen minutes after the Vice-President; he inspected the set; sat for the camera; and his advisers inspected him, then declared they were satisfied. The producer made a remark about the glare of the Senator's white shirt, and Kennedy sent an aide back to his hotel to bring back a blue one, into which he changed just before air time. The men took their seats, the tally lights on the cameras blinked red to show they were live now.

"Good evening," said Howard K. Smith, the gray and handsome moderator. "The television and radio stations of the United States . . . are proud to provide for a discussion of issues in the current political campaign by the two major candidates for the Presidency. The candidates need no introduction. . . . "

And they were on air, before seventy million Americans.

Rereading now the text of the first of the great debates (and of the following three also), one can find only a blurred echo of the emotions that rose from the performance, and the intense, immediate and dramatic impact of the debate on the fortunes of the two candidates.

This, the first of the debates, was committed to a discussion of domestic issues—an area in which the Democrats, by their philosophy and record, make larger promises and offer a more aggressive attitude to the future than the Republicans. Kennedy, opening, declared that the world could not endure half-slave and half-free, and that the posture of America in the world rested fundamentally on its posture at home—how we behaved to each other, what we did to move American society forward at home, this affected not only us, but the world too: "Can freedom be maintained under the most severe attack it has ever known? I think it can be. And I think in the final analysis it depends upon what we do here. I think it's time America started moving again."

Nixon's opening statement, as it reads now in print, was one of good-willed difference: he agreed with Kennedy in all the goals Kennedy had outlined. He differed with Kennedy only in the methods to reach those goals. He lauded the progress made under the seven and a half years of the Eisenhower administration—hospitals, highways, electric power, gross national product, growth rate, were all moving at a rate, he said, never matched before in any administration.

The clue to what was happening can be remembered only in rereading the penultimate passage of Mr. Nixon's opening remarks: "The final point that I would like to make is this: Senator Kennedy has suggested in his speeches that we lack compassion for the poor, for the old, and for others that are unfortunate. . . . I know what it means to be poor . . . I know that Senator Kennedy feels as deeply about these problems as I do, but our disagreement is not about the goals for America but only about the means to reach those goals."

For Mr. Nixon was debating with Mr. Kennedy as if a board of judges were scoring points; he rebutted and refuted, as he went, the inconsistencies or errors of his opponent. Nixon was addressing himself to Kennedy—but Kennedy was addressing himself to the audience that was the nation. In these debates, before this audience, there could be no appeal to the past or to the origins of any ethnic group—there could only be an appeal, across the board, to all Americans and to the future. This across-the-board appeal to all Americans had been Mr. Nixon's strategy from the very beginning—a generalized pressure that would fragment the minorities coalition of the Democrats. Yet here, before the largest audience of Americans in history, Nixon was not addressing himself to his central theme; he was offering no vision of the future that the Republican Party might offer Americans—he was concerned with the cool and undisturbed man who sat across the platform from him, with the personal adversary in the studio, not with the mind of America.

Ten questions followed from the panel of television reporters who sat before the debaters: on the importance of a candidate's age; on the quality of decision in presidential affairs; on farms; on taxes; on schools; on congressional politics; on subversion; and on schools again. In each pair of answers, the same contrast repeated itself: the Senator from Massachusetts, ignoring the direct inquiry when it suited him, used each question as a springboard for an appeal to the mind and the imagination of the audience assembled before the countless sets. But the Vice-President's mind and attention were fixed there in the studio. As one rereads the text, one finds him, over and over again, scoring excellently against the personal adversary in the hall beside him, yet forgetful of the need to score on the mind of the nation he hoped to lead.

The defensive quality of Mr. Nixon's performance (evident from his first enunciation: "The things that Senator Kennedy has said many of us can agree with. . . . I can subscribe completely to the spirit that Senator Kennedy has expressed tonight, the spirit that the United States should move ahead. . . . ") can still be reconstructed from the texts. What cannot be reconstructed is the visual impact of the first debate.

For it was the sight of the two men side by side that carried the punch.

There was, first and above all, the crude, overwhelming impression that side by side the two seemed evenly matched—and this even matching in the popular imagination was for Kennedy a major victory. Until the cameras opened on the Senator and the Vice-President, Kennedy had been the boy under assault and attack by the Vice-President as immature, young, inexperienced. Now, obviously, in flesh and behavior he was the Vice-President's equal.

Not only that, but the contrast of the two faces was astounding. Normally and in private, Kennedy under tension flutters his hands—he adjusts his necktie, slaps his knee, strokes his face. Tonight he was calm and nerveless in appearance. The Vice-President, by contrast, was tense, almost frightened, at turns glowering and, occasionally, haggard-looking to the point of sickness. Probably no picture in American politics tells a better story of crisis and episode than that famous shot of the camera on the Vice-President as he half slouched, his "Lazy Shave" powder faintly streaked with sweat, his eyes exaggerated hollows of blackness, his jaw, jowls, and face drooping with strain.

It is impossible to look again at the still photographs of Nixon in his ordeal and to recollect the circumstances without utmost sympathy. For everything that could have gone wrong that night went wrong. The Vice-President, to begin with, suffers from a handicap that is serious only on television—his is a light, naturally transparent skin. On a visual camera that takes pictures by optical projection this transparent skin photographs cleanly and well. But a television camera projects electronically, by an image-orthicon tube, which is a cousin of the x-ray tube; it seems to go beneath the skin, almost as the x-ray photograph does. On television, the camera on Nixon is usually held away from him, for in close-up his transparent skin shows the tiniest hair growing in the skin follicles beneath the surface, even after he has just shaved. And for the night of the first debate, CBS, understandably zealous, had equipped its camera with brand-new tubes for the most perfect projection possible—a perfection of projection that could only be harmful to the Vice-President. (In the later debates, Nixon was persuaded to wear theatrical make-up to repair the ravage TV's electronic tube makes of his countenance; but for this first debate he wore only "Lazy Shave.")

The scene of the debate, the studio of WBBM, had, further, been tense all day long, as furniture, desks, lecterns, background, had been rearranged and then rearranged again for best effect. Nixon's TV advisers had been told that the background would be gray-scale five, a relatively dark tone; therefore they had urged their principal to dress in a light-gray suit for contrast. Yet the backdrop, when they saw it, was so markedly lighter than they had anticipated that they insisted, rightly, it be repainted. Several times that day it was repainted—but each time the gray tone dried light. (The background indeed was still tacky to the touch when the two candidates went on the air.) Against this light background Nixon, in his light suit, faded into a fuzzed outline, while Kennedy in his dark suit had the crisp picture edge of contrast. The Nixon advisers had, further, adjusted all lighting to a master lighting scheme for their candidate before he went on the air; but in the last few minutes before the debate a horde of still photographers from newspapers and magazines were permitted on the set, and as they milled for their still pictures, they kicked over wires and displaced lights and television cameras from their marked positions.

There was, lastly, the fact that the Vice-President had still not recovered from his illness, and was unrested from the exertions of his first two weeks of intense campaigning. His normal shirt hung loosely about his neck, and his recent weight loss made him appear scrawny. And, most of all, psychologically, his advisers now insist, he lacked the energy to project—for Nixon does best on television when he projects, when he can distract the attention of the viewer from his passive countenance to the theme or the message he wants to give forth, as in his famous "Checkers" appearance on television in 1952.

All this, however, was unknown then to the national audience. Those who heard the debates on radio, according to sample surveys, believed that the two candidates came off almost equal. Yet every survey of those who watched the debates on television indicated that the Vice-President had come off poorly and, in the opinion of many, very poorly. It was the picture image that had done it—and in 1960 television had won the nation away from sound to images, and that was that.

The Vice-President was later to recover from the impression he made in this first debate. But this first debate, the beginning of the contest, was, as in so many human affairs, half the whole. The second debate concerned itself with foreign policy and ranged from Cuba's Castro through the U-2 and espionage to the matter of America's declining prestige, and closed on the first sharp clash of the series—the defense of Quemoy and Matsu.

The third debate resumed, like a needle stuck in a phonograph groove, with the subject of Quemoy and Matsu, hung there almost indefinitely, then broke away with Nixon's stern disapproval of President Truman's bad language, and went on to other matters such as bigotry, labor unions and gold outflow. This, according to all sample surveys, was Nixon's best performance in terms of its impact on the audience. This was the debate in which Nixon spoke from Los Angeles while Kennedy spoke from New York, and it was as if, separated by a continent from the personal presence of his adversary, Nixon were more at ease and could speak directly to the nation that lay between them.

The fourth debate was the dreariest—both candidates had by now almost nothing new left to say, and they repeated themselves on all the matters they had covered in the three previous debates. Curiously enough, the audience which had been highest for the first debate and dropped off slightly for the second and third, returned on the last debate to almost match the total of the first.

No accurate political measurement or reasonable judgment is yet possible on a matter as vast as the TV debates of 1960. When they began, Nixon was generally viewed as being the probable winner of the election contest and Kennedy as fighting an uphill battle; when they were over, the positions of the two contestants were reversed.

No reporter can claim any accuracy in charting the magic and mysterious flow of public opinion between the time a campaign starts and the ultimate tally of feelings at the polls; and so opinion seesawed back and forth for weeks, as it still seesaws back and forth now, long after the debates are over, as to what, specifically, the debates achieved in shaping the campaign and American opinion.

There were fragmentary and episodic achievements that no one could deny.

Any reporter who followed the Kennedy campaign remembers still the quantum jump in the size of crowds that greeted the campaigning Senator from the morrow of the first debate, the morning of Tuesday, September 27th, when he began to campaign in northern Ohio. His crowds had been growing for a full seven days before the debates, but now, overnight, they seethed with enthusiasm and multiplied in numbers, as if the sight of him, in their homes on the video box, had given him a "star quality" reserved only for television and movie idols.

Equally visible was the gloom that descended on Republican leaders around the country; they were angry with their own candidate, angry at his performance, angry most of all at his "me-too" debating style. At Nixon headquarters in Washington, the telephones rang incessantly, demanding that someone get to this "new Nixon" and convince him that only the "old Nixon" could win.

There were other measurable hard political results. On the evening of the first debate, the Democratic governors of the Southern states were gathered for one of their annual conferences at Hot Springs, Arkansas. Except for Governor Luther Hodges of North Carolina, they had until then viewed Kennedy with a range of emotions that ran from resigned apathy to whispered hostility. Watching him on TV that night, they too were suddenly impressed. We do not know whose idea it was to send Kennedy the telegram of congratulations which ten of the eleven signed that evening—but the enthusiasm and excitement of the telegram was not only genuine but a tidemark in the campaign. The Southern governors were with him now; and if they were with him, it meant that the machinery of their political organizations would be with him, too.

It is much more difficult to measure the debates in terms of issues, of education of the American people to the tasks and problems before them. For there certainly were real differences of philosophy and ideas between John F. Kennedy and Richard M. Nixon—yet rarely in American history has there been a political campaign that discussed issues less or clarified them less.

The TV debates, in retrospect, were the greatest opportunity ever for such discussion, but it was an opportunity missed. It is difficult to blame the form of the debates for this entirely; yet the form and the compulsions of the medium must certainly have been contributory. The nature of both TV and radio is that they abhor silence and "dead time." All TV and radio discussion programs are compelled to snap question and answer back and forth as if the contestants were adversaries in an intellectual tennis match. Although every experienced newspaperman and inquirer knows that the most thoughtful and responsive answers to any difficult question come after long pause, and that the longer the pause the more illuminating the thought that follows it, nonetheless the electronic media cannot bear to suffer a pause of more than five seconds; a pause of thirty seconds of dead time on air seems interminable. Thus, snapping their two-and-a-half-minute answers back and forth, both candidates could only react for the cameras and the people, they could not think. And, since two and a half minutes permit only a snatch of naked thought and a spatter of raw facts, both candidates, whenever caught out on a limb with a thought too heavy for two-minute exploration, a thought seemingly too bold or fresh to be accepted by the conditioned American mind, hastily scuttled back toward center as soon as they had enunciated the thought. Thus Kennedy's response to the first question on Quemoy and Matsu was probably one of the sharpest and clearest responses to any question of the debates; in that response, actually, Kennedy was tentatively fingering at one of the supreme problems of American statecraft, our relation with the revolution in Asia. Yet he was out too far with such a thought for a two-minute response and, in succeeding debates, in reply to succeeding questions, he fuzzed the distinction between his position and Nixon's until it was almost impossible to tell them apart.

If there was to be any forum for issues, the TV debates should have provided such a forum. Yet they did not: every conceivable problem was raised by the probing imagination of the veteran correspondents who questioned the candidates. But all problems were answered in two-minute snatches, either with certain facts or with safe convictions. Neither man could pause to indulge in the slow reflection and rumination, the slow questioning of alternatives before decision, that is the inner quality of leadership.

If, then, the TV debates did little to advance the reasonable discussion of issues that is the dream of unblooded political scientists, what did they do?

What they did best was to give the voters of a great democracy a living portrait of two men under stress and let the voters decide, by instinct and emotion, which style and pattern of behavior under stress they preferred in their leader. The political roots of this tribal sense of the whole go as far back as the Roman Senate, or the beer-blown assemblies of the Teutonic tribes that Tacitus describes in his chronicles. This sense of personal choice of leader has been missing for centuries from modern civilization—or else limited to such conclaves of deputized spokesmen of the whole as a meeting of Tammany Hall captains, a gathering of Communist barons in the Kremlin or the dinners of leaders of the English Establishment in the clubs of London. What the TV debates did was to generalize this tribal sense of participation, this emotional judgment of the leader, from the few to the multitude—for the salient fact of the great TV debates is not what the two candidates said, nor how they behaved, but how many of the candidates' fellow Americans gave up their evening hours to ponder the choice between the two.

DANIEL J. BOORSTIN

49. PSEUDO-EVENTS

Historian Daniel Boorstin uses the term pseudo-event *to describe nonspontaneous, planted, or manufactured "news" whose main purpose is to gain publicity for the person or cause that arranged the "event." Modern American politicians have become quite sophisticated in orchestrating pseudo-events. Two common examples are "leaks" of news to the media, a strategy often used by government officials opposed to particular policies, and "trial balloons," the "floating" of an idea to find out how the public and other political leaders will respond before a formal proposal is made. The modern presidential campaign can be analyzed as one "pseudo-event" after another—as one candidate visits a flag factory and another rides in a tank to generate the free, as opposed to paid, TV time that puts them before the public.*

The new kind of synthetic novelty which has flooded our experience I will call "pseudo-events." The common prefix "pseudo" comes from the Greek word meaning false, or intended to deceive. Before I recall the historical forces which have made these pseudo-events possible, have increased the supply of them and the demand for them, I will give a commonplace example.

The owners of a hotel, in an illustration offered by Edward L. Bernays in his pioneer *Crystallizing Public Opinion* (1923), consult a public relations counsel. They ask how to increase their hotel's prestige and so improve their business. In less sophisticated times, the answer might have been to hire a new chef, to improve the plumbing, to paint the rooms, or to install a crystal chandelier in the lobby. The public relations counsel's technique is more indirect. He proposes that the management stage a celebration of the hotel's thirtieth anniversary. A committee is formed, including a prominent banker, a leading society matron, a well-known lawyer, an influential preacher, and an "event" is planned (say a banquet) to call attention to the distinguished service the hotel has been rendering the community. The celebration is held, photographs are taken, the occasion is widely reported, and the object is accomplished. Now this occasion is a pseudo-event, and will illustrate all the essential features of pseudo-events.

Source: Reprinted with the permission of Scribner, an imprint of Simon & Schuster Adult Publishing Group, from *The Image: A Guide to Pseudo-Events in America* by Daniel J. Boorstin. Copyright © 1961 by Daniel J. Boorstin; copyright renewed © 1989.

This celebration, we can see at the outset, is somewhat—but not entirely—misleading. Presumably the public relations counsel would not have been able to form his committee of prominent citizens if the hotel had not actually been rendering service to the community. On the other hand, if the hotel's services had been all that important, instigation by public relations counsel might not have been necessary. Once the celebration has been held, the celebration itself becomes evidence that the hotel really is a distinguished institution. The occasion actually gives the hotel the prestige to which it is pretending.

It is obvious, too, that the value of such a celebration to the owners depends on its being photographed and reported in newspapers, magazines, newsreels, on radio, and over television. It is the report that gives the event its force in the minds of potential customers. The power to make a reportable event is thus the power to make experience. One is reminded of Napoleon's apocryphal reply to his general, who objected that circumstances were unfavorable to a proposed campaign: "Bah, I make circumstances!" The modern public relations counsel—and he is, of course, only one of many twentieth-century creators of pseudo-events—has come close to fulfilling Napoleon's idle boast. "The counsel on public relations," Mr. Bernays explains, "not only knows what news value is, but knowing it, he is in a position to *make news happen*. He is a creator of events."

The intriguing feature of the modern situation, however, comes precisely from the fact that the modern news makers are not God. The news they make happen, the events they create, are somehow not quite real. There remains a tantalizing difference between man-made and God-made events.

A pseudo-event, then, is a happening that possesses the following characteristics:

(1) It is not spontaneous, but comes about because someone has planned, planted, or incited it. Typically, it is not a train wreck or an earthquake, but an interview.

(2) It is planted primarily (not always exclusively) for the immediate purpose of being reported or reproduced. Therefore, its occurrence is arranged for the convenience of the reporting or reproducing media. Its success is measured by how widely it is reported. Time relations in it are commonly fictitious or factitious; the announcement is given out in advance "for future release" and written as if the event had occurred in the past. The question, "Is it real?" is less important than, "Is it newsworthy?"

(3) Its relation to the underlying reality of the situation is ambiguous. Its interest arises largely from this very ambiguity. Concerning a pseudo-event the question, "What does it mean?" has a new dimension. While the news interest in a train wreck is in *what* happened and in the real consequences, the interest in an interview is always, in a sense, in *whether* it really happened and in what might have been the motives. Did the statement really mean what it said?

Without some of this ambiguity a pseudo-event cannot be very interesting.

(4) Usually it is intended to be a self-fulfilling prophecy. The hotel's thirtieth-anniversary celebration, by saying that the hotel is a distinguished institution, actually makes it one. . . .

In the age of pseudo-events it is less the artificial simplification than the artificial complication of experience that confuses us. Whenever in the public mind a pseudo-event competes for attention with a spontaneous event in the same field, the pseudo-event will tend to dominate. What happens on television will overshadow what happens off television. Of course I am concerned here not with our private worlds but with our world of public affairs.

Here are some characteristics of pseudo-events which make them overshadow spontaneous events:

(1) Pseudo-events are more dramatic. A television debate between candidates can be planned to be more suspenseful (for example, by reserving questions which are then popped suddenly) than a casual encounter or consecutive formal speeches planned by each separately.

(2) Pseudo-events, being planned for dissemination, are easier to disseminate and to make vivid. Participants are selected for their newsworthy and dramatic interest.

(3) Pseudo-events can be reported at will, and thus their impression can be reinforced.

(4) Pseudo-events cost money to create; hence somebody has an interest in disseminating, magnifying, advertising, and extolling them as events worth watching or worth believing. They are therefore advertised in advance, and rerun in order to get money's worth.

(5) Pseudo-events, being planned for intelligibility, are more intelligible and hence more reassuring. Even if we cannot discuss intelligently the qualifications of the candidates or the complicated issues, we can at least judge the effectiveness of a television performance. How comforting to have some political matter we can grasp!

(6) Pseudo-events are more sociable, more conversable, and more convenient to witness. Their occurrence is planned for our convenience. The Sunday newspaper appears when we have a lazy morning for it. Television programs appear when we are ready with our glass of beer. In the office the next morning, Jack Paar's (or any other star performer's) regular late-night show at the usual hour will overshadow in conversation a casual event that suddenly came up and had to find its way into the news.

(7) Knowledge of pseudo-events—of what has been reported, or what has been staged, and how—becomes the test of being "informed." News magazines provide us regularly with quiz questions concerning not what has happened but concerning "names in the news"—what

has been reported in the news magazines. Pseudo-events begin to provide that "common discourse" which some of my old-fashioned friends have hoped to find in the Great Books.

(8) Finally, pseudo-events spawn other pseudo-events in geometric progression. They dominate our consciousness simply because there are more of them, and ever more.

By this new Gresham's law of American public life, counterfeit happenings tend to drive spontaneous happenings out of circulation. The rise in the power and prestige of the Presidency is due not only to the broadening powers of the office and the need for quick decisions, but also to the rise of centralized news gathering and broadcasting, and the increase of the Washington press corps. The President has an ever more ready, more frequent, and more centralized access to the world of pseudo-events. A similar explanation helps account for the rising prominence in recent years of the Congressional investigating committees. In many cases these committees have virtually no legislative impulse, and sometimes no intelligible legislative assignment. But they do have an almost unprecedented power, possessed now by no one else in the Federal government except the President, to make news. Newsmen support the committees because the committees feed the newsmen: they live together in happy symbiosis. The battle for power among Washington agencies becomes a contest to dominate the citizen's information of the government. This can most easily be done by fabricating pseudo-events.

A perfect example of how pseudo-events can dominate is the recent popularity of the quiz show format. Its original appeal came less from the fact that such shows were tests of intelligence (or of dissimulation) than from the fact that the situations were elaborately contrived—with isolation booths, armed bank guards, and all the rest—and they purported to inform the public.

The application of the quiz show format to the so-called "Great Debates" between Presidential candidates in the election of 1960 is only another example. These four campaign programs, pompously and self-righteously advertised by the broadcasting networks, were remarkably successful in reducing great national issues to trivial dimensions. With appropriate vulgarity, they might have been called the $400,000 Question (Prize: a $100,000-a-year job for four years). They were a clinical example of the pseudo-event, of how it is made, why it appeals, and of its consequences for democracy in America.

In origin the Great Debates were confusedly collaborative between politicians and news makers. Public interest centered around the pseudo-event itself: the lighting, make-up, ground rules, whether notes would be allowed, etc. Far more interest was shown in the performance than in what was said. The pseudo-events spawned in turn by the Great Debates were numberless. People who had seen the shows read about them the more avidly, and listened eagerly for interpretations by news commentators. Representatives of both parties made "statements" on the probable effects of the debates. Numerous interviews and discussion programs were broadcast exploring their meaning. Opinion polls kept us informed on the nuances of our own and other people's reactions. Topics of speculation multiplied. Even the question whether there should be a fifth debate became for a while a lively "issue."

The drama of the situation was mostly specious, or at least had an extremely ambiguous relevance to the main (but forgotten) issue: which participant was better qualified for the Presidency. Of course, a man's ability, while standing under klieg lights, without notes, to answer in two and a half minutes a question kept secret until that moment, had only the most dubious relevance—if any at all—to his real qualifications to make deliberate Presidential decisions on longstanding public questions after being instructed by a corps of advisers. The great Presidents in our history (with the possible exception of F.D.R.) would have done miserably, but our most notorious demagogues would have shone. A number of exciting pseudo-events were created—for example, the Quemoy–Matsu issue. But that, too, was a good example of a pseudo-event: it was created to be reported, it concerned a then-quiescent problem, and it put into the most factitious and trivial terms the great and real issue of our relation to Communist China.

The television medium shapes this new kind of political quiz-show spectacular in many crucial ways. Theodore H. White has proven this with copious detail in his *The Making of the President: 1960* (1961). All the circumstances of this particular competition for votes were far more novel than the old word "debate" and the comparisons with the Lincoln–Douglas Debates suggested. Kennedy's great strength in the critical first debate, according to White, was that he was in fact not "debating" at all, but was seizing the opportunity to address the whole nation; while Nixon stuck close to the issues raised by his opponent, rebutting them one by one. Nixon, moreover, suffered a handicap that was serious only on television: he has a light, naturally transparent skin. On an ordinary camera that takes pictures by optical projection, this skin photographs well. But a television camera projects electronically, by an "image-orthicon tube" which has an x-ray effect. This camera penetrates Nixon's transparent skin and brings out (even just after a shave) the tiniest hair growing in the follicles beneath the surface. For the decisive first program Nixon wore a make-up called "Lazy Shave" which was ineffective under these conditions. He therefore looked haggard and heavy-bearded by contrast to Kennedy, who looked pert and clean-cut.

This greatest opportunity in American history to educate the voters by debating the large issues of the campaign failed. The main reason, as White points out, was the compulsions of the medium. "The nature of both TV and radio is that they abhor silence and 'dead time.' All TV and radio discussion programs are compelled to snap question and answer back and forth as if the contestants were adversaries in an intellectual tennis match. Although every experienced newspaperman and inquirer knows that the most thoughtful and responsive answers to any difficult question come after long pause, and that the longer the pause the more illuminating the thought that follows it, nonetheless the electronic media cannot bear to suffer a pause of more than five seconds;

a pause of thirty seconds of dead time on air seems interminable. Thus, snapping their two-and-a-half-minute answers back and forth, both candidates could only react for the cameras and the people, they could not think." Whenever either candidate found himself touching a thought too large for two-minute exploration, he quickly retreated. Finally the television-watching voter was left to judge, not on issues explored by thoughtful men, but on the relative capacity of the two candidates to perform under television stress.

Pseudo-events thus lead to emphasis on pseudo-qualifications. Again the self-fulfilling prophecy. If we test Presidential candidates by their talents on TV quiz performances, we will, of course, choose Presidents for precisely these qualifications. In a democracy, reality tends to conform to the pseudo-event. Nature imitates art.

We are frustrated by our very efforts publicly to unmask the pseudo-event. Whenever we describe the lighting, the make-up, the studio setting, the rehearsals, etc., we simply arouse more interest. One newsman's interpretation makes us more eager to hear another's. One commentator's speculation that the debates may have little significance makes us curious to hear whether another commentator disagrees.

Pseudo-events do, of course, increase our illusion of grasp on the world, what some have called the American illusion of omnipotence. Perhaps, we come to think, the world's problems can really be settled by "statements," by "Summit" meetings, by a competition of "prestige," by overshadowing images, and by political quiz shows.

Once we have tasted the charm of pseudo-events, we are tempted to believe they are the only important events. Our progress poisons the sources of our experience. And the poison tastes so sweet that it spoils our appetite for plain fact. Our seeming ability to satisfy our exaggerated expectations makes us forget that they are exaggerated.

MURRAY EDELMAN

50. POLITICAL SYMBOLS

To political scientist Murray Edelman, the central political activity is the manipulation of symbols. Inasmuch as the mass public experiences the political world as a "passing parade of symbols," public perception of political events necessarily depends on communications about those

---

Source: From *The Symbolic Uses of Politics*. Copyright 1964, 1985 by Board of Trustees of the University of Illinois. Used with permission of the University of Illinois Press.

events. Edelman argues that the president and other national leaders use symbols to cue the public as to how to react to world events—when to feel threatened and when to feel reassured that all is well. Edelman was one of the first American political scientists to systematically analyze politics from a symbolic perspective.

Edelman's view is exemplified in the process of "spinning," the term commonly used to describe how political leaders attempt to manipulate public perceptions. Washington Post *reporter Howard Kurtz's 1998 book,* Spin Cycle, *argues that the Clinton White House is "arguably the most successful team of White House spin doctors in history." Though earlier administrations were cognizant of the need to control the flow of information to the public, produce appealing photo opportunities for reporters, and generally to manage perceptions of the president, by 1998 Bill Clinton was widely regarded as having elevated the art of spinning to a new level.*

A civil lawsuit alleging sexual harassment filed against the president by Paula Jones and the ensuing revelation that he had engaged in an 18-month sexual liaison with a former White House intern, Monica Lewinsky, and lied about it under oath and to the American people, however, tested even Bill Clinton's ability to "spin" the story so as to minimize political damage. In his brief August 17, 1998, speech to the American people following his appearance before a grand jury investigating charges that he may have committed perjury, subornation of perjury, and obstruction of justice in his efforts to cover up the Lewinsky affair, President Clinton took "complete responsibility" for all his actions.

Claiming to assume full responsibility is the classic tactic of a chief executive under fire. Richard Nixon employed a similar approach when he first addressed the nation concerning the Watergate scandals in the spring of 1973 when he accepted full responsibility for the illegal actions of White House officials. Ronald Reagan similarly accepted full responsibility for the Iran–Contra Affair of 1986. Unlike Richard Nixon and Ronald Reagan, who were accepting responsibility for the actions of others, Bill Clinton was accepting responsibility for his own actions. But just like his predecessors', Bill Clinton's acceptance of full responsibility was at heart symbolic—intended only to pinpoint where responsibility lay, not to suggest that he should be punished for his transgressions.

Basic to the recognition of symbolic forms in the political process is a distinction between politics as a spectator sport and political activity as utilized by organized groups to get quite specific, tangible benefits for themselves. For most men most of the time politics is a series of pictures in the mind, placed there by television news, newspapers, magazines, and discussions. The pictures create a moving panorama taking place in a world the mass public never quite touches, yet one its members come to fear or cheer, often with passion and sometimes with action. They are told of legislatures passing laws, foreign political figures threatening or offering trade agreements, wars starting and ending, candidates for public office losing or winning, decisions made to spend unimaginable sums of money to go to the moon.

There is, on the other hand, the immediate world in which people make and do things that have directly observable consequences. In these activities men can check their acts and assumptions against the consequences and correct errors. There is feedback. Some men, relatively few, are involved in politics in this direct way.

Politics is for most of us a passing parade of abstract symbols, yet a parade which our experience teaches us to be a benevolent or malevolent force that can be close to omnipotent. Because politics does visibly confer wealth, take life, imprison and free people, and represent a history with strong emotional and ideological associations, its processes become easy objects upon which to displace private emotions, especially strong anxieties and hopes.[1]

But it could not serve as conveyor of these fears and aspirations if it were simply a tool or mechanism which we all had the power and knowledge to manipulate for our own advantage. It is central to its potency as a symbol that it is remote, set apart, omnipresent as the ultimate threat or means of succor, yet not susceptible to effective influence through any act we as individuals can perform.

Research in a number of different sciences has pointed to the key function of remoteness as an influence upon symbolic meanings. One element involved here is the distinction between referential and condensation symbols. Every symbol stands for something other than itself, and it also evokes an attitude, a set of impressions, or a pattern of events associated through time, through space, through logic, or through imagination with the symbol. Students of this subject have noticed a fundamental distinction among symbols that groups them into two quite separate types. Referential symbols are economical ways of referring to the objective elements in objects or situations: the elements identified in the same way by different people. Such symbols are useful because they help in logical thinking about the situation and in manipulating it. Industrial accident statistics and cost figures in cost plus contracts are referential political symbols, though they may also be condensation symbols. Condensation symbols evoke the emotions associated with the situation. They condense into one symbolic event, sign, or act patriotic pride, anxieties, remembrances of past glories or humiliations, promises of future greatness: some one of these or all of them.[2]

Where condensation symbols are involved, the constant check of the immediate environment is lacking. A traffic policeman at a busy corner may grow entranced momentarily with himself or his stick as representative of the august majesty of the state and indulge in the luxury of arbitrary power, perhaps by favoring traffic on one street; but the lengthening line of cars in front of him and some irate honking will soon remind him that he must face reality: drivers and a prosaic chief of police. There is no such check on the fantasies and conceptualizing of those who never can test objectively their conviction that the government and their home towns abound in communist spies and dupes and that John Birch symbolizes resistance to the threat. Nor is there the check of reality and feedback upon those to whom Adlai Stevenson or Barry Goldwater or Dwight Eisenhower are symbols of reason, intelligence, and virtue in public policy. Conclusive demonstrations that their heroes' policies may often be futile or misconceived are impossible simply because the link between dramatic political announcements and their impact on people is so long and so tangled. These people may be right or they may be wrong. The point is that there is no necessity, and often no possibility, of continuously checking their convictions against real conditions.

No example can ever be wholly free of either referential or of condensation symbols; but the distinction between the two types of behavior is fundamental in realistic political analysis.

Practically every political act that is controversial or regarded as really important is bound to serve in part as a condensation symbol. It evokes a quiescent or an aroused mass response because it symbolizes a threat or reassurance. Because the meaning of the act in these cases depends only partly or not at all upon its objective consequences, which the mass public cannot know, the meaning can only come from the psychological needs of the respondents; and it can only be known from their responses.

One type of research that supports this view appears in the work of Smith, Bruner, and White,[3] who have explored the tie between personality and opinions. They conclude that political opinions serve three different functions for the personality. One of these, object appraisal, or help in understanding the world, can only be performed by those political opinions that are fairly realistic: opinions which, in our terms, are based upon referential symbols and are constantly checked against the objects to which they refer. An opinion that the chief function of a party platform is to attract votes and not to forecast public policy would presumably further object appraisal.

NOTES

1. Harold D. Lasswell, *Psychopathology and Politics* (New York, 1930), 75–76.
2. Edward Sapir, "Symbolism," in *Encyclopedia of the Social Sciences* (New York, 1934), 492–495.
3. M. Brewster Smith, J. S. Bruner, and R. W. White, *Opinions and Personality* (New York, 1956).

SECTION IX
REVIEW QUESTIONS

1. What evidence does George Orwell offer to show that "political speech and writing are largely the defence of the indefensible"? Do you think that he is correct? If so, is there any solution to this problem?

2. Do televised debates between presidential candidates help to clarify the positions of the candidates on major issues? How have presidential television debates changed since the Kennedy–Nixon debates of 1960?

3. How does Daniel Boorstin define a "pseudo-event"? Can you identify some recent political events that fit the definition? Can you identify a political event that Boorstin would agree was a "real" event?

4. How does Murray Edelman distinguish a "condensation" from a "referential" symbol? Do you agree that most Americans most of the time have very little objective information about the consequences of political decisions and events? What are the implications of this perspective for democratic theory?

X

The Congress

EDMUND BURKE

51. Representing the Nation

The basic problem of how an elected member of Congress should best "represent" the voters continues to puzzle congressional observers along with members themselves. The debate has changed little since Edmund Burke first criticized the British Parliament as a "congress of ambassadors from different and hostile interests." In his speech to the electors of Bristol, Burke argued that elected representatives should do more than merely count heads in their districts and vote accordingly. As Burke told his supporters, an elected representative owes his constituents "his unbiased opinion, his mature judgment, [and] his enlightened conscience."

In Burke's view of representation, an elected official should use the knowledge acquired on the job in the legislature to cast votes that the representative believes to be in the best interests of the nation. To Burke, elected leaders represent best when they work to educate and persuade their constituents on questions of public policy. Legislators must be careful, however, in following Burke's advice. After all, many ex-members of Congress have been defeated because they insisted on voting in the interest of the nation as a whole; their constituents felt sufficiently betrayed to throw them out of office!

Certainly, gentlemen, it ought to be the happiness and glory of a representative to live in the strictest union, the closest correspondence, and the most unreserved communication with his constituents. Their wishes ought to have great weight with him; their opinion, high respect; their business, unremitted attention. It is his duty to sacrifice his repose, his pleasures, his satisfactions, to theirs; and above all, ever, and in all cases, to prefer their interest to his own. But his unbiased opinion, his mature judgment, his enlightened conscience, he ought not to sacrifice to you, to any man, or to any set of men living. These he does not derive from your pleasure; no, nor from the law and the constitution. They are a trust from Providence, for the abuse of which he is deeply answerable. Your representative owes you, not his industry only, but his judgment; and he betrays, instead of serving you, if he sacrifices it to your opinion.

Source: From Edmund Burke, "Speech to the Electors of Bristol on Being Elected" (November 1774).

My worthy colleague says, his will ought to be subservient to yours. If that be all, the thing is innocent. If government were a matter of will upon any side, yours, without question, ought to be superior. But government and legislation are matters of reason and judgment, and not of inclination; and what sort of reason is that, in which the determination precedes the discussion; in which one set of men deliberate, and another decide; and where those who form the conclusion are perhaps three hundred miles distant from those who hear the arguments?

To deliver an opinion, is the right of all men; that of constituents is a weighty and respectable opinion, which a representative ought always to rejoice to hear; and which he ought always most seriously to consider. But *authoritative* instructions; *mandates* issued, which the member is bound blindly and implicitly to obey, to vote, and to argue for, though contrary to the clearest conviction of his judgment and conscience,—these are things utterly unknown to the laws of this land, and which arise from a fundamental mistake of the whole order and tenor of our constitution.

Parliament is not a *congress* of ambassadors from different and hostile interests; which interests each must maintain, as an agent and advocate, against other agents and advocates; but parliament is a *deliberative* assembly of *one* nation, with *one* interest, that of the whole; where, not local purposes, not local prejudices, ought to guide, but the general good, resulting from the general reason of the whole. You choose a member indeed; but when you have chosen him, he is not a member of Bristol, but he is a member of *parliament*. If the local constituent should have an interest, or should form an hasty opinion, evidently opposite to the real good of the rest of the community, the member for that place ought to be as far, as any other, from any endeavor to give it effect. I beg pardon for saying so much on this subject. I have been unwillingly drawn into it; but I shall ever use a respectful frankness of communication with you. Your faithful friend, your devoted servant, I shall be to the end of my life: a flatterer you do not wish for. On this point of instruction, however, I think it scarcely possible we ever can have any sort of difference. Perhaps I may give you too much, rather than too little, trouble.

From the first hour I was encouraged to court your favour, to this happy day of obtaining it, I have never promised you anything but humble and persevering endeavors to do my duty. The weight of that duty, I confess, makes me tremble; and whoever well considers what it is, of all things in the world, will fly from what has the least likeness to a positive and precipitate engagement. To be a good member of parliament is, let me tell you, no easy task; especially at this time, when there is so strong a disposition to run into the perilous extreme of servile compliance or wild popularity. To unite circumspection with vigour, is absolutely necessary; but it is extremely difficult. We are now members for a rich commercial *city;* this city, however, is but a part of a rich commercial *nation,* the interests of which are various, multiform, and intricate. We are members for that great nation, which however is itself but part of a great *empire,* extended by our virtue and our fortune to the farthest limits of the east and of the west. All these wide-spread interests must be considered; must be compared; must be reconciled, if possible. We are members for a *free* country; and surely we all know, that the machine of a free constitution is no simple thing; but as intricate and as delicate as it is valuable. We are members in a great and ancient *monarchy;* and we must preserve religiously the true legal rights of the sovereign, which form the key-stone that binds together the noble and well-constructed arch of our empire and our constitution. A constitution made up of balanced powers must ever be a critical thing. As such I mean to touch that part of it which comes within my reach. I know my inability, and I wish for support from every quarter. In particular I shall aim at the friendship, and shall cultivate the best correspondence, of the worthy colleague you have given me.

I trouble you no further than once more to thank you all; you, gentlemen, for your favours; the candidates, for their temperate and polite behavior; and the sheriffs, for a conduct which may give a model for all who are in public stations.

JAMES MADISON

52. THE FRAMERS' VIEW OF REPRESENTATION

Critics of the Constitution argued that the House of Representatives was not large enough to include members of all social classes. Therefore, they believed that the views of the excluded classes would not be adequately represented in the newly created House of Representatives. But James Madison in Federalist, No. 35 *dismissed the idea of "actual representation of all classes of the people, by persons of each class" as "altogether visionary." While acknowledging that the newly created House would include mostly businessmen, professionals, and landowners, Madison was convinced that these representatives, motivated by the need to win votes from all members of their districts, would adequately represent the interests of all groups. In contrast to Burke's emphasis on representation of the national interest,*

Source: From *The Federalist,* No. 35 (1788).

> *Madison asked, "Is it not natural that a man who is a candidate for the favor of the people . . . should take care to inform himself of their dispositions and inclinations?" Therefore, their concerns would find "their proper degree of influence upon his conduct."*

Let us now return to the examination of objections.

One which, if we may judge from the frequency of its repetition, seems most to be relied on, is, that the House of Representatives is not sufficiently numerous for the reception of all the different classes of citizens, in order to combine the interests and feelings of every part of the community, and to produce a due sympathy between the representative body and its constituents. This argument presents itself under a very specious and seducing form; and is well calculated to lay hold of the prejudices of those to whom it is addressed. But when we come to dissect it with attention, it will appear to be made up of nothing but fair-sounding words. The object it seems to aim at is, in the first place, impracticable, and in the sense in which it is contended for, is unnecessary. I reserve for another place the discussion of the question which relates to the sufficiency of the representative body in respect to numbers, and shall content myself with examining here the particular use which has been made of a contrary supposition, in reference to the immediate subject of our inquiries.

The idea of an actual representation of all classes of the people, by persons of each class, is altogether visionary. Unless it were expressly provided in the Constitution, that each different occupation should send one or more members, the thing would never take place in practice. Mechanics and manufacturers will always be inclined, with few exceptions, to give their votes to merchants, in preference to persons of their own professions or trades. Those discerning citizens are well aware that the mechanic and manufacturing arts furnish the materials of mercantile enterprise and industry. Many of them, indeed, are immediately connected with the operations of commerce. They know that the merchant is their natural patron and friend; and they are aware, that however great the confidence they may justly feel in their own good sense, their interests can be more effectually promoted by the merchant than by themselves. They are sensible that their habits in life have not been such as to give them those acquired endowments, without which, in a deliberate assembly, the greatest natural abilities are for the most part useless; and that the influence and weight, and superior acquirements of the merchants render them more equal to a contest with any spirit which might happen to infuse itself into the public councils, unfriendly to the manufacturing and trading interests. These considerations, and many others that might be mentioned, prove, and experience confirms it, that artisans and manufacturers will commonly be disposed to bestow their votes upon merchants and those whom they recommend. We must therefore consider merchants as the natural representatives of all these classes of the community.

With regard to the learned professions, little need be observed; they truly form no distinct interest in society, and according to their situation and talents, will be indiscriminately the objects of the confidence and choice of each other, and of other parts of the community.

Nothing remains but the landed interest; and this, in a political view, and particularly in relation to taxes, I take to be perfectly united, from the wealthiest landlord down to the poorest tenant. No tax can be laid on land which will not affect the proprietor of millions of acres as well as the proprietor of a single acre. Every landholder will therefore have a common interest to keep the taxes on land as low as possible; and common interest may always be reckoned upon as the surest bond of sympathy. But if we even suppose a distinction of interest between the opulent landholder and the middling farmer, what reason is there to conclude, that the first would stand a better chance of being deputed to the national legislature than the last? If we take fact as our guide, and look into our own senate and assembly, we shall find that moderate proprietors of land prevail in both; nor is this less the case in the senate, which consists of a smaller number, than in the assembly, which is composed of a greater number. Where the qualifications of the electors are the same, whether they have to choose a small or a large number, their votes will fall upon those in whom they have most confidence; whether these happen to be men of large fortunes, or of moderate property, or of no property at all.

It is said to be necessary, that all classes of citizens should have some of their own number in the representative body, in order that their feelings and interests may be the better understood and attended to. But we have seen that this will never happen under any arrangement that leaves the votes of the people free. Where this is the case, the representative body, with too few exceptions to have any influence on the spirit of the government, will be composed of landholders, merchants, and men of the learned professions. But where is the danger that the interests and feelings of the different classes of citizens will not be understood or attended to by these three descriptions of men? Will not the landholder know and feel whatever will promote or insure the interest of landed property? And will he not, from his own interest in that species of property, be sufficiently prone to resist every attempt to prejudice or encumber it? Will not the merchant understand and be disposed to cultivate, as far as may be proper, the interest of the mechanic and manufacturing arts, to which his commerce is so nearly allied? Will not the man of the learned profession, who will feel a neutrality to the rivalships between the different branches of industry, be likely to prove an impartial arbiter between them, ready to promote either, so far as it shall appear to him conducive to the general interests of the society?

If we take into the account the momentary humors or dispositions which may happen to prevail in particular parts of the society, and to which a wise administration will never be inattentive, is the man whose situation leads to extensive inquiry and information less likely to be a competent judge of their nature, extent, and foundation than one whose observation does not travel beyond the circle of his neighbors and acquaintances? Is it not natural that a man who is a candidate for the favor of the people, and who is dependent on the suffrages of his fellow-citizens for the continuance of his public honors, should take care to inform himself of their dispositions and inclinations, and should be willing to allow them their proper degree of influence upon his conduct? This dependence, and the necessity of being bound himself, and his posterity, by the laws to which he gives his assent, are the true, and they are the strong chords of sympathy between the representative and the constituent.

There is no part of the administration of government that requires extensive information and a thorough knowledge of the principles of political economy, so much as the business of taxation. The man who understands those principles best will be least likely to resort to oppressive expedients, or to sacrifice any particular class of citizens to the procurement of revenue. It might be demonstrated that the most productive system of finance will always be the least burdensome. There can be no doubt that in order to a judicious exercise of the power of taxation, it is necessary that the person in whose hands it is should be acquainted with the general genius, habits, and modes of thinking of the people at large, and with the resources of the country. And this is all that can be reasonably meant by a knowledge of the interests and feelings of the people. In any other sense the proposition has either no meaning, or an absurd one. And in that sense let every considerate citizen judge for himself where the requisite qualification is most likely to be found.

WOODROW WILSON

53. CONGRESSIONAL GOVERNMENT

Before being elected president of the United States in 1912, Woodrow Wilson (1856–1924) had served as president of Princeton University and as president of the American Political Science Association. But it was his becoming the reforming governor of New Jersey in 1911 that made him a credible candidate for the Democratic Party's nomination for president in 1912. He then won the presidency with a plurality of the vote when the incumbent Republican president, William Howard Taft,

Source: From Woodrow Wilson, *Congressional Government,* 1885, Chapter 3.

split the majority Republican vote with former Republican president Theodore Roosevelt who, after losing the nomination to Taft, ran as in independent on the Progressive or "Bull Moose" Party ticket. Wilson would serve two terms as president (1913–1921) and would lead the nation through World War I.

As a college professor, Wilson published the now classic account of the congressional legislative process, Congressional Government: A Study in American Politics (1885). *Wilson's analysis describes how the various committees, subcommittees, select committees, and conference committees result in a complex and decentralized distribution of power. The influence of the standing committees of the Congress cannot be overstated. As Woodrow Wilson declared more than a century ago, "I know not how better to describe our form of government in a single phrase than by calling it a government by the Chairmen of the Standing Committees of Congress." Because of the various subcommittees, select committees, and conference committees, overall authority "is perplexingly subdivided and distributed, and responsibility has to be hunted down in out-of-the-way corners." As a result, Wilson wrote, in perhaps the most famous statement from* Congressional Government, *"Congress in session is Congress on public exhibition, whilst Congress in its committee-rooms is Congress at work." Despite periodic bursts of congressional reform, Wilson's insights continue to provide us with an amazingly accurate picture of what he termed the "dance of legislation."*

Like a vast picture thronged with figures of equal prominence and crowded with elaborate and obtrusive details, Congress is hard to see satisfactorily and appreciatively at a single view and from a single stand-point. Its complicated forms and diversified structure confuse the vision, and conceal the system which underlies its composition. It is too complex to be understood without an effort, without a careful and systematic process of analysis. Consequently, very few people do understand it, and its doors are practically shut against the comprehension of the public at large. If Congress had a few authoritative leaders whose figures were very distinct and very conspicuous to the eye of the world, and who could represent and stand for the national legislature in the thoughts of that very numerous, and withal very respectable, class of persons who must think specifically and in concrete forms when they think at all, those persons who can make something out of men but very little out of intangible generalizations, it would be quite within the region of possibilities for the majority of the nation to follow the course of legislation without any very serious confusion of thought. I suppose that almost everybody who just now gives any heed to the policy of Great Britain, with regard even to the reform of the franchise and other like strictly legislative questions, thinks of Mr. Gladstone and his colleagues rather than of the House of Commons, whose servants they are. The question is not, What will Parliament do? but, What will Mr. Gladstone do? And there is even less doubt that it is easier and more natural to look upon the legislative designs of Germany as locked up behind Bismarck's heavy brows than to think of them as dependent upon the determinations of the Reichstag, although as a matter of fact its consent is indispensable even to the plans of the imperious and domineering Chancellor.

But there is no great minister or ministry to represent the will and being of Congress in the common thought. The Speaker of the House of Representatives stands as near to leadership as any one; but his will does not run as a formative and imperative power in legislation much beyond the appointment of the committees who are to lead the House and do its work for it, and it is, therefore, not entirely satisfactory to the public mind to trace all legislation to him. He may have a controlling hand in starting it; but he sits too still in his chair, and is too evidently not on the floor of the body over which he presides, to make it seem probable to the ordinary judgment that he has much immediate concern in legislation after it is once set afoot. Everybody knows that he is a staunch and avowed partisan, and that he likes to make smooth, whenever he can, the legislative paths of his party; but it does not seem likely that all important measures originate with him, or that he is the author of every distinct policy. And in fact he is not. He is a great party chief, but the hedging circumstances of his official position as presiding officer prevent his performing the part of active leadership. He appoints the leaders of the House, but he is not himself its leader.

The leaders of the House are the chairmen of the principal Standing Committees. Indeed, to be exactly accurate, the House has as many leaders as there are subjects of legislation; for there are as many Standing Committees as there are leading classes of legislation, and in the consideration of every topic of business the House is guided by a special leader in the person of the chairman of the Standing Committee, charged with the superintendence of measures of the particular class to which that topic belongs. It is this multiplicity of leaders, this many-headed leadership, which makes the organization of the House too complex to afford uninformed people and unskilled observers any easy clue to its methods of rule. For the chairmen of the Standing Committees do not constitute a cooperative body like a ministry. They do not consult and concur in the adoption of homogeneous and mutually helpful measures; there is no thought of acting in concert. Each Committee goes its own way as its own pace. It is impossible to discover any unity or method in the disconnected and therefore unsystematic, confused, and desultory action of the House, or any common purpose in the measures which its Committees from time to time recommend.

And it is not only to the unanalytic thought of the common observer who looks at the House from the outside that its doings seem helter-skelter, and without comprehensible rule; it is not at once easy to understand them when they are scrutinized in their daily headway through open session by one who is inside the House. The newly-elected member, entering its doors for the first time, and with no more knowledge of its rules and customs than the more intelligent of his constituents possess, always experiences great difficulty in adjusting his preconceived ideas of congressional life to the strange and unlooked-for conditions by which he finds himself surrounded after he has been sworn in and has become a part of the great legislative machine. Indeed there are generally many things connected with his career in Washington to disgust and dispirit, if not to aggrieve, the new member. In the first place, his local reputation does not follow him to the federal capital. Possibly the members from his own State know him, and receive him into full fellowship; but no one else knows him, except as an adherent of this or that party, or as a newcomer from this or that State. He finds his station insignificant, and his identity indistinct. But this social humiliation which he experiences in circles in which to be a congressman does not of itself confer distinction, because it is only to be one among many, is probably not to be compared with the chagrin and disappointment which come in company with the inevitable discovery that he is equally without weight or title to consideration in the House itself. No man, when chosen to the membership of a body possessing great powers and exalted prerogatives, likes to find his activity repressed, and himself suppressed, by imperative rules and precedents which seem to have been framed for the deliberate purpose of making usefulness unattainable by individual members. Yet such the new member finds the rules and precedents of the House to be. It matters not to him, because it is not apparent on the face of things, that those rules and precedents have grown, not out of set purpose to curtail the privileges of new members as such, but out of the plain necessities of business; it remains the fact that he suffers under their curb, and it is not until "custom hath made it in him a property of easiness" that he submits to them with anything like good grace.

Not all new members suffer alike, of course, under this trying discipline; because it is not every new member that comes to his seat with serious purposes of honest, earnest, and duteous work. There are numerous tricks and subterfuges, soon learned and easily used, by means of which the most idle and self-indulgent members may readily make such show of exemplary diligence as will quite satisfy, if it does not positively delight, constituents in Buncombe. But the number of congressmen who deliberately court uselessness and counterfeit well-doing is probably small. The great majority doubtless have a keen enough sense of their duty, and a sufficiently unhesitating desire to do it; and it may safely be taken for granted that the zeal of new members is generally hot and insistent. If it be not hot to begin with, it is like to become so by reason of friction with the rules, because such men must inevitably be chafed by the bonds of restraint drawn about them by the inexorable observances of the House.

Often the new member goes to Washington as the representative of a particular line of policy, having been elected, it may be, as an advocate of free trade, or as a champion of protection; and it is naturally his first care upon entering on his duties to seek immediate opportunity for the expression of his views and immediate means of giving them definite shape and thrusting them upon the attention of Congress. His disappointment is, therefore, very keen when he finds both opportunity and means denied him. He can introduce his bill; but that is all he can do, and he must do that at a particular time and in a particular manner. This he is likely to learn through rude experience, if he be not cautious to inquire beforehand the details of practice. He is likely to make a rash start, upon the supposition that Congress observes the ordinary rules of parliamentary practice to which he has become accustomed in the debating clubs familiar to his youth, and in the mass-meetings known to his later experience. His bill is doubtless ready for presentation early in the session, and some day, taking advantage of a pause in the proceedings, when there seems to be no business before the House, he rises to read it and move its adoption. But he finds getting the floor an arduous and precarious undertaking. There are certain to be others who want it as well as he; and his indignation is stirred by the fact that the Speaker does not so much as turn towards him, though he must have heard his call, but recognizes some one else readily and as a matter of course. If he be obstreperous and persistent in his cries of "Mr. Speaker," he may get that great functionary's attention for a moment,—only to be told, however, that he is out of order, and that his bill can be introduced at that stage only by unanimous consent: immediately there are mechanically-uttered but emphatic exclamations of objection, and he is forced to sit down confused and disgusted. He has, without knowing it, obtruded himself in the way of the "regular order of business," and been run over in consequence; without being quite clear as to how the accident occurred.

Moved by the pain and discomfiture of this first experience to respect, if not to fear, the rules, the new member casts about, by study or inquiry, to find out, if possible, the nature and occasion of his privileges. He learns that his only safe day is Monday. On that day the roll of the States is called, and members may introduce bills as their States are reached in the call. So on Monday he essays another bout with the rules, confident this time of being on their safe side,—but mayhap indiscreetly and unluckily over-confident. For if he supposes, as he naturally will, that after his bill has been sent up to be read by the clerk he may say a few words in its behalf, and in that belief sets out upon his long-considered remarks, he will be knocked down by the rules as surely as he was on the first occasion when he gained the floor for a brief moment. The rap of Mr. Speaker's gavel is sharp, immediate, and peremptory. He is curtly informed that no debate is in order; the bill can only be referred to the appropriate Committee.

This is, indeed, disheartening; it is his first lesson in committee government, and the master's rod smarts; but the sooner he learns the prerogatives and powers of the Standing Committees the sooner will he penetrate the mysteries of the rules and avoid the pain of further contact with their thorny side. The privileges of the Standing Committees are the beginning and the end of the rules. Both the House of Representatives and the Senate conduct their business by what may figuratively, but not inaccurately, be called an odd device of *disintegration.* The House virtually both deliberates and legislates in small sections. Time would fail it to discuss all the bills brought in, for they every session number thousands; and it is to be doubted whether, even if time allowed, the ordinary processes of debate and amendment would suffice to sift the chaff from the wheat in the bushels of bills every week piled upon the clerk's desk. Accordingly, no futile attempt is made to do anything of the kind. The work is parceled out, most of it to the forty-seven Standing Committees which constitute the regular organization of the House, some of it to select committees appointed for special and temporary purposes. Each of the almost numberless bills that come pouring in on Mondays is "read a first and second time,"—simply perfunctorily read, that is, by its title, by the clerk, and passed by silent assent through its first formal courses, for the purpose of bringing it to the proper stage for commitment,—and referred without debate to the appropriate Standing Committee. Practically, no bill escapes commitment—save, of course, bills introduced by committees, and a few which may now and then be crowded through under a suspension of the rules, granted by a two-thirds vote—though the exact disposition to be made of a bill is not always determined easily and as a matter of course. Besides the great Committee of Ways and Means and the equally great Committee on Appropriations, there are Standing Committees on Banking and Currency, on Claims, on Commerce, on the Public Lands, on Post-Offices and Post-Roads, on the Judiciary, on Public Expenditures, on Manufactures, on Agriculture, on Military Affairs, on Naval Affairs, on Mines and Mining, on Education and Labor, on Patents, and on a score of other branches of legislative concern; but careful and differential as is the topical division of the subjects of legislation which is represented in the titles of these Committees, it is not always evident to which Committee each particular bill should go. Many bills affect subjects which may be regarded as lying as properly within the jurisdiction of one as of another of the Committees; for no hard and fast lines separate the various classes of business which the Committees are commissioned to take in charge. Their jurisdictions overlap at many points, and it must frequently happen that bills are read which cover just this common ground. Over the commitment of such bills sharp and interesting skirmishes often take place. There is active competition for them, the ordinary, quiet routine of matter-of-course reference being interrupted by rival motions seeking to give very different directions to the disposition to be made of them. To which Committee should a bill "to fix and establish the maximum rates of fares of the Union Pacific and Central Pacific Railroads" be sent,—to the Committee on Commerce or to the Committee on the Pacific Railroads? Should a bill which prohibits the mailing of certain classes of letters and circulars go to the Committee on Post-Offices and Post-Roads, because it relates to the mails, or to the Committee on the Judiciary, because it proposes to make any transgression of its prohibition a crime? What is the proper disposition of any bill which thus seems to lie within two distinct committee jurisdictions?

The fate of bills committed is generally not uncertain. As a rule, a bill committed is a bill doomed. When it goes from the clerk's desk to a committee-room it crosses a parliamentary bridge of sighs to dim dungeons of silence whence it will never return. The means and time of its death are unknown, but its friends never see it again. Of course no Standing Committee is privileged to take upon itself the full powers of the House it represents, and formally and decisively reject a bill referred to it; its disapproval, if it disapproves, must be reported to the House in the form of a recommendation that the bill "do not pass." But it is easy, and therefore common, to let the session pass without making any report at all upon bills deemed objectionable or unimportant, and to substitute for reports upon them a few bills of the Committee's own drafting; so that thousands of bills expire with the expiration of each Congress, not having been rejected, but having been simply neglected. There was not time to report upon them.

Of course it goes without saying that the practical effect of this Committee organization of the House is to consign to each of the Standing Committees the entire direction of legislation upon those subjects which properly come to its consideration. As to those subjects it is entitled to the initiative, and all legislative action with regard to them is under its overruling guidance. It gives shape and course to the determinations of the House. In one respect, however, its initiative is limited. Even a Standing Committee cannot report a bill whose subject-matter has not been referred to it by the House, "by the rules or otherwise"; it cannot volunteer advice on questions upon which its advice has not been asked. But this is not a serious, not even an operative, limitation upon its functions of suggestion and leadership; for it is a very simple matter to get referred to it any subject it wishes to introduce to the attention of the House. Its chairman, or one of its leading members, frames a bill covering the point upon which the Committee wishes to suggest legislation; brings it in, in his capacity as a private member, on Monday, when the call of States is made; has it referred to his Committee; and thus secures an opportunity for the making of the desired report.

It is by this imperious authority of the Standing Committees that the new member is stayed and thwarted whenever he seeks to take an active part in the business of the House. Turn which way he may, some privilege of the Committees stands in his path. The rules are so framed as to put all business under their management; and one of the discoveries which the new member is sure to make, albeit after many trying experiences and sobering adventures and as his first session draws towards its close, is, that under their sway freedom of debate finds no place of allowance, and that his long-delayed speech must remain unspoken. For even a long congressional session is too short to afford time for a full consideration of all the reports of the forty-seven Committees, and debate upon them must be rigidly cut short, if not altogether excluded, if any considerable part of the necessary business is to be gotten through with before adjournment. There are some subjects to which the House must always give prompt attention; therefore reports from the Committees on Printing and on Elections are always in order; and there are some subjects to which careful consideration must always be accorded; therefore the Committee of Ways and Means and the Committee on Appropriations are clothed with extraordinary privileges; and revenue and supply bills may be reported, and will ordinarily be considered, at any time. But these four are the only specially licensed Committees. The rest must take their turns in fixed order as they are called on by the Speaker, contenting themselves with such crumbs of time as fall from the tables of the four Committees of highest prerogative. . . .

These are some of the plainer points of the rules. They are full of complexity, and of confusion to the uninitiated, and the confusions of practice are greater than the confusions of the rules. For the regular order of business is constantly being interrupted by the introduction of resolutions offered "by unanimous consent," and of bills let in under a "suspension of the rules." Still, it is evident that there is one principle which runs through every stage of procedure, and which is never disallowed or abrogated,—the principle that the Committees shall rule without let or hindrance. And this is a principle of extraordinary formative power. It is the mould of all legislation. In the first place, the speeding of business under the direction of the Committees determines the character and the amount of the discussion to which legislation shall be subjected. The House is conscious that time presses. It knows that, hurry as it may, it will hardly get through with one eighth of the business laid out for the session, and that to pause for lengthy debate is to allow the arrears to accumulate. Besides, most of the members are individually anxious to expedite action on every pending measure, because each member of the House is a member of one or more of the Standing Committees, and is quite naturally desirous that the bills prepared by his Committees, and in which he is, of course, specially interested by reason of the particular attention which he has been compelled to give them, should reach a hearing and a vote as soon as possible. It must, therefore, invariably happen that the Committee holding the floor at any particular time is the Committee whose proposals the majority wish to dispose of as summarily as circumstances will allow, in order that the rest of the forty-two unprivileged Committees to which the majority belong may gain the earlier and the fairer chance of a hearing. A reporting Committee, besides, is generally as glad to be pushed as the majority are to push it. It probably has several bills matured, and wishes to see them disposed of before its brief hours of opportunity are passed and gone.

Consequently, it is the established custom of the House to accord the floor for one hour to the member of the reporting Committee who has charge of the business under consideration; and that hour is made the chief hour of debate. The reporting committee-man seldom, if ever, uses the whole of the hour himself for his opening remarks; he uses part of it, and retains control of the rest of it; for by undisputed privilege it is his to dispose of, whether he himself be upon the floor or not. No amendment is in order during that hour, unless he consent to its presentation; and he does not, of course, yield his time indiscriminately to any one who wishes to speak. He gives way, indeed, as in fairness he should, to opponents as well as to friends of the measure under his charge; but generally no one is accorded a share of his time who has not obtained his previous promise of the floor; and those who do speak must not run beyond the number of minutes he has agreed to allow them. He keeps the course both of debate and of amendment thus carefully under his own supervision, as a good tactician, and before he finally yields the floor, at the expiration of his hour, he is sure to move the previous question. To neglect to do so would be to lose all control of the business in hand; for unless the previous question is ordered the debate may run on at will, and his Committee's chance for getting its measures through slip quite away; and that would be nothing less than his disgrace. He would be all the more blameworthy because he had but to ask for the previous question to get it. As I have said, the House is as eager to hurry business as he can be, and will consent to almost any limitation of discussion that he may demand; though, probably, if he were to throw the reins upon its neck, it would run at large from very wantonness, in scorn of such a driver. The previous question once ordered, all amendments are precluded, and one hour remains for the summing-up of this same privileged committee-man before the final vote is taken and the bill disposed of.

These are the customs which baffle and perplex and astound the new member. In these precedents and usages, when at length he comes to understand them, the novice spies out the explanation of the fact, once so confounding and seemingly inexplicable, that when he leaped to his feet to claim the floor other members who rose after him were coolly and unfeelingly preferred before him by the Speaker. Of course it is plain enough now that Mr. Speaker knew beforehand to whom the representative of the reporting Committee had agreed to yield the floor; and it was no use for any one else to cry out for recognition. Whoever wished to speak should, if possible, have made some arrangement with the Committee before the business came to a hearing, and should have taken care to notify Mr. Speaker that he was to be granted the floor for a few moments.

Unquestionably this, besides being a very interesting, is a very novel and significant method of restricting debate and expediting legislative action,—a method of very serious import, and obviously fraught with far-reaching constitutional effects. The practices of debate which prevail in its legislative assembly are manifestly of the utmost importance to a self-governing people; for that legislation which is not thoroughly discussed by the legislating body is practically done in a corner. It is impossible for Congress itself to do wisely what it does so hurriedly; and the constituencies cannot understand what Congress does not itself stop to consider. The prerogatives of the Committees represent something more than a mere convenient division of labor. There is only one part of its business to which Congress, as a whole, attends,—that part, namely, which is embraced under the privileged subjects of revenue and supply. The House never accepts the proposals of the Committee of Ways and Means, or of the Committee on Appropriations, without due deliberation; but it allows almost all of its other Standing Committees virtually to legislate for it. In form, the Committees only digest the various matter introduced by individual members, and prepare it, with care, and after thorough investigation, for the final consideration and action of the House; but, in reality, they dictate the course to be taken, prescribing the decisions of the House not only, but measuring out, according to their own wills, its opportunities for debate and deliberation as well. The House sits, not for serious discussion, but to sanction the conclusions of its Committees as rapidly as possible. It legislates in its committee-rooms; not by the determinations of majorities, but by the resolutions of specially-commissioned minorities; so that it is not far from the truth to say that Congress in session is Congress on public exhibition, whilst Congress in its committee-rooms is Congress at work.

GLENN R. PARKER AND
ROGER H. DAVIDSON

54. POPULAR CONGRESSMEN AND UNPOPULAR CONGRESS

Americans paradoxically seem to love their own member of Congress while thinking little of Congress as a whole. Based on national survey data, Parker and Davidson conclude that Americans use one set of standards for evaluating Congress and another for evaluating individual members of Congress. The slowness of Congress along with dissatisfaction with the policy results of congressional action lead to negative evaluations of the institution as a whole. On the other hand, individual members are rarely held accountable for policy decisions of the Congress, but are evaluated according to their personal qualities and level of service to constituents.

The past decade has witnessed the spread of public cynicism concerning established political institutions. The available evidence suggests that alienation

Source: From Glenn R. Parker and Roger H. Davidson, "Why Do Americans Love Their Congressmen So Much More Than Their Congress?" *Legislative Studies Quarterly,* IV, 1, February 1979. Comparative Legislative Research Center. Reprinted by permission of the publisher and the authors.

from the polity is a fairly widespread phenomenon, penetrating all countries, and bringing to the surface fundamental questions about the legitimacy of political institutions and authorities.

A recurring theme in critiques of the American political system is the citizen's dismay at the inability of the government to perform, an impediment that Seymour Lipset (1963, pp. 64–70) singles out as detrimental to political stability. Felix Frankfurter (1930, p. 3) characterized distrust of Depression-era government as an indication that people felt that government was unable to satisfy the needs of a modern society. In a later and presumably more benign era, Morris Rosenberg (1951, p. 14) contended that politics meant "very little to people because it literally does little for them," and that governmental action was considered by many as "irrelevant to their lives" (1954, p. 364). Such a posture toward government probably affects the public's image of political officials. In fact, William C. Mitchell (1959, p. 693) has suggested that such officials are not viewed as performing vital services because political functions themselves are not considered as providing a societal contribution.

Public assessments of governmental performance can be described in terms of three components: confidence, impact, and evaluation. *Confidence* reflects the degree to which individuals have faith in the actions of their officials and/or institutions. The extent to which governmental activity is perceived as affecting an individual's life is a measure of the *impact* of governmental performance. *Evaluations* are explicit judgments of the value the individual assigns to that impact. In this research note we focus on the last-mentioned component—the content of public evaluations of one political institution, the United States Congress.

Citizens' evaluations are certainly important in and of themselves. But in reporting these assessments, we too often overlook the bases of their judgments—that is, the criteria individuals use in forming their evaluations. Thus, the objective of this analysis is to describe the standards used in appraising Congress and its membership and to examine response categories in an effort to gauge the likelihood that certain standards generate favorable evaluations.

The findings are based on opinion surveys administered to national population samples (Harris, 1968; U.S. House of Representatives, 1977). Of particular interest are the responses elicited from two open-ended survey items concerning evaluations of Congress and the respondent's representative. In both surveys, individuals were first asked how they would evaluate the performance of Congress—excellent, pretty good, only fair, or poor. Respondents were then queried about the criteria upon which they based their evaluation. Later in the interview sessions, the same questioning was used to ascertain respondent's judgment of their representative's performance in the U.S. House of Representatives. The multiple-response nature of the open-ended questionnaire items allowed individuals the opportunity to provide as many different criteria as they desired. The responses to the above items were then coded and categorized on the basis of the criteria volunteered and, if discernible, the favorable or unfavorable nature of the responses.[1]

ANALYSIS

Domestic policy is the most frequently mentioned criterion for evaluating Congress (Table 1). Although the centrality of domestic policy appears to have declined somewhat since late 1968, it still is the most frequently cited basis for evaluating Congress. The valence associated with domestic policy has also changed in the last several years. While in 1968 domestic policy seemed to divide the electorate equally into those satisfied and dissatisfied with congressional actions, such policy actions had a distinctly negative effect in 1977; 93 percent of those citing domestic policy as a basis for their evaluations of Congress were negative in their assessments of congressional performance.

In late 1968, the Vietnam War's salience took its toll on the popularity of Congress: of those who cited foreign policy as a basis for evaluation, nearly two-thirds had negative evaluations. Several years later, in the absence of major American involvement in a foreign war, few people mentioned foreign policy considerations in evaluating Congress. As the Vietnam War and other foreign ventures began to fade from media attention and public consciousness, domestic policy conflicts gained greater saliency with the public. The ideological and partisan differences between those controlling the White House and Congress served to exacerbate the natural conflicts that the "sharing of power" produces. The resulting policy statements generated negative evaluations of congressional performance: in 1977, three of every four mentions of legislative–executive relations as a basis for evaluating Congress were negative.

Another frequently mentioned basis for assessing Congress is the style and pace of the legislative process. In fact, there appears to be an increase in the saliency of the congressional environment as a basis for congressional evaluations: In 1977, one of every three responses made reference to the congressional environment, and these references were distinctly negative. It seems clear that the congressional environment, like legislative–executive relations, tends to foster negative evaluations of Congress.

In light of the saliency of the various criteria, it is not too surprising that evaluations of Congress are often negative. The range and volume of policies and problems for which Congress is held accountable—by the media and the public—create numerous opportunities for dissatisfaction with congressional performance. The cumbersome legislative process, which often gives the appearance of delay and inaction, may be a necessary evil for the constitutional system, but it is not an attribute that appeals to the public. Further, both domestic policy and the legislative environment are frequently mentioned as bases for evaluating Congress. In short, the most salient concerns of the public appear to be those that frequently generate negative impressions of congressional performance.

The criteria for evaluating Congress and those applied in evaluating individual representatives show few parallels. Evaluations of representatives tend to be based upon constituency service provided the district and the personal attributes of incumbents (Table 2). In addition, these criteria tend to place incumbent House members in a favorable light: most of what people hear (or retain) about

TABLE 1 **Bases of Evaluations of Congress (in percentages)**

	1968[a]			1977[b]		
BASES OF EVALUATION	PERCENT OF ALL RESPONSES (N = 1370)	FAVORABLE	UNFAVORABLE	PERCENT OF ALL RESPONSES (N = 1813)	FAVORABLE	UNFAVORABLE
Policy	51.8			30.8		
Domestic	46.3	54	46	30.1	7	93
Foreign-Defense	5.5	35	65	0.7	100	—
Legislative–Executive Relations	6.5			19.6		
Presidential Support	3.1	72	28	—	—	—
Presidential Opposition	3.4	56	44	19.6	25	75
Congressional Environment	16.0			37.1		
Congressional Style and Pace	10.2	38	62	23.1	30	70
Congressional Ethics	2.4	—	100	4.9	—	100
Congressional Self-Seeking	3.4	—	100	9.1	—	100
Group Treatment	4.2	66	34	1.4	50	50
Other	6.4	27	73	8.4	33	67
Repeat of Closed-Ended Question	12.0					
Don't Know/Not Ascertained	3.0			2.8		
Total	99.9			100.1		

[a] *Question:* "How would you rate the job Congress did this past year in 1968—excellent, pretty good, only fair, or poor? Why do you feel this way? Any other reasons?"

[b] *Question:* "Overall, how would you rate the job Congress as a whole—that is the House of Representatives—has done during the past 2 or 3 years—would you say Congress has done an excellent job, a pretty good job, only a fair job, or a poor job? Why do you feel this way? Any other reasons?"

TABLE 2 **Bases of Evaluations of Members of Congress (in percentages)**

	1968[a]			1977[b]		
BASES OF EVALUATION	PERCENT OF ALL RESPONSES (N = 1258)	FAVORABLE	UNFAVORABLE	PERCENT OF ALL RESPONSES (N = 1232)	FAVORABLE	UNFAVORABLE
Policy	11.2			3.0		
Vague Reference	7.9	69	31	1.5	—	100
Specific Reference	3.3	46	54	1.5	—	100
Constituency Service	49.8			37.7		
District Service	28.1	74	26	13.3	100	—
Constituent Assistance	2.1	100	—	12.6	100	—
Direct Conditions	2.7	91	9	3.7	100	—
Informs Constituents	16.9	18	82	8.1	82	18
Personal Attributes	26.9			35.6		
Personal Characteristics	16.5	84	16	6.7	100	—
Reputation	9.4	95	5	28.9	67	33
Personal Acquaintance	1.0	—	—	—	—	—
Group Treatment	6.4	58	42	3.7	100	—
Other	0.3	50	50	10.4	57	43
Repeat of Closed-Ended Question	2.7					
Don't Know/Not Ascertained	2.7			9.7		
Total	100.0			100.1		

[a] *Question:* "How would you rate the service your representative gives in looking after this district in Washington—excellent, pretty good, only fair, or poor? Why do you feel this way? Any other reasons?"

[b] *Question:* "Overall, how would your rate the job the congressman who has been representing this area during the past 2 or 3 years has done—would you say your congressman has done an excellent job, a pretty good job, a fair job, or a poor job? Why do you feel this way? Any other reasons?"

incumbents is favorable. In fact, the reputation of House members was the most frequently mentioned criterion for evaluating the performance of incumbents: more than 70 percent of the responses refer to some aspect of the incumbents' constituency service or personal attributes.

Policy actions, in contrast, are infrequently cited as criteria for evaluating the representative. This may be a blessing to House members, inasmuch as references to public policy tend to be negative in content. The infrequent use of policy criteria and the emphasis on personal characteristics and district service promote positive evaluations of the incumbent. Rarely are the latter elements viewed in a negative light. In sum, evaluations of Congress and of individual members are apt to differ in valence because of the disparate criteria that are applied to each. Congress is held responsible for policy and for management of the legislative environment, while individual representatives are evaluated in terms of their personal characteristics or constituency service.

CONCLUSIONS

Clearly, quite disparate criteria are used in evaluating Congress and individual representatives. Furthermore, one's evaluative criteria influence the nature of one's appraisal: *certain criteria are associated with positive evaluations, while other criteria are identified with negative appraisals.* That is, the features of congressional activity that attract the concern and attention of individuals affect how congressional performance is evaluated. It also seems clear that evaluations of representatives rest more on service to the district than on policy concerns; moreover, such service generally is perceived in a favorable light by constituents. It is no wonder, then, that members of Congress pay so much attention to constituency service—it generates a positive image. Congress, on the other hand, is assessed more in terms of its policy actions, which tend to produce mixed (or negative) evaluations of the institution.

These findings cast new light on a paradox posed by Richard F. Fenno, Jr.: How can we account for the contrast in the popularity of Congress on the one hand, and individual representatives on the other? "If our congressmen are so good," he asks (1975, p. 278), "how can our Congress be so bad? If it is the individuals that make up the institution, why should there be such a disparity in our judgments?"

One possible explanation for this disparity is that people simply apply divergent standards of judgment to Congress as an institution and to individual legislators. Fenno speculates (1975, pp. 278–280) that individual legislators are judged on the basis of personal style and policy views. Stylistically, we expect our legislators to display a solicitous attitude toward constituents—to appear frequently in the district, to maintain contact through the media, and to work on local projects and individual cases. As for policy views, we ask merely that our legislators not stray too far from the norm as expressed by a majority of constituents.

Our data support Fenno's speculations, and they further indicate how much precedence stylistic considerations take over policy concerns. No more than 15 percent of our respondents, by the most generous reckoning, cited policies in explaining how they rated their representative. Unless they were specific, these policy references tended to tilt in the incumbents' favor. Fortunately for incumbents, few voters voice specific policy concerns—indeed, few voice policy concerns of any kind—in evaluating members' performance.

For Congress as an institution, in contrast, citizens enunciate the task of resolving national problems. This is a far more hazardous assignment than citizens set for individual representatives. Many problems are virtually insoluble on a national scale; even if they were solved, would we be able to ascertain that fact? As we have seen, in assessing Congress, respondents mention policy factors more frequently than any other considerations. In the late 1960s, domestic policy concerns tended to produce favorable assessments, while foreign policy concerns yielded critical assessments by almost a two-to-one margin. A decade later, the valences were reversed. Legislative–executive relations also produce mixed reviews: some people expect Congress to fall into line behind the president; others want it to resist White House initiatives and act as a watchdog. Finally, what citizens read and hear of Capitol Hill style carries an overwhelmingly negative message. Scandal and venality are highly visible features of legislative institutions; expertise or courage are less well publicized.

The present data, in short, give eloquent testimony to the reasons why we "love our congressmen so much" yet denigrate the institution of Congress. Individual legislators are evaluated in terms of personal style and district service—attributes upon which few voters are able to make comparisons with other legislators. But Congress-as-institution is evaluated largely on the basis of policies—which tend to be intractable and divisive.

In view of the divergence we have found in the public's premises in assessing congressmen and Congress, incumbents are entirely rational in emphasizing constituency service and equipping themselves with the necessary staff and perquisites to do the job. Members of the U.S. House have historically had a firm grassroots base, cultivated by constituency service as well as by localist legislative roles. There is nothing novel about this: indeed, the House was designed to operate in this fashion (*Wesberry v. Sanders,* 1964). Yet, students of Congress agree that recently legislative roles have shifted perceptibly in the direction of constituency service. As Fiorina (1977, p. 61) puts it:

> Congressmen are going home more, pressing the flesh, getting around. They are building a personal base of support, one dependent on personal contacts and favors.

The present emphasis upon constituency errand-running, which appears to date from the mid-1960s, contrasts with at least some of the dominant House norms of the previous generation or two.

If the push toward errand-running is conceded, there remains a critical issue of cause and effect. Put bluntly, the question is: In erecting the machinery for constituency communication and service, did legislators mainly contrive to ensure their own re-election, or did they simply respond to what they assumed the public demanded?

Perhaps this question will never be answered with certainty. At the very least, we need to review carefully the sequence of events that produced the present congressional establishment, with special attention to the decade of the 1960s. Survey data should be re-analyzed to determine legislators' and citizens' states of mind during this period of time, even though such data are bound to yield a fragmentary and inconclusive picture.

The present findings nonetheless leave little room for doubt concerning the public's expectations for legislators' performance. The data indicate that, whereas citizens' expectations for Congress are vague and anchored to generalized policy and stylistic concerns, their expectations for their own representatives are unmistakable. Legislators are judged very largely on the way they serve their districts and communicate with them. Successful performance of this aspect of the representative's job typically pays off handsomely, as indicated by incumbents' high rates of re-election. Yet such judgments on the part of voters imply sanctions as well: legislators who lose touch or who seem preoccupied with national issues may be disciplined by declining support or even defeat. A few "lessons" of this type will suffice to persuade other legislators, who after all are politicians, to shift their job priorities.

Is it possible then that public expectation, rather than legislative connivance, is the cause of the bureaucratic establishment that supports constituency-oriented policy making? If so, we may wish to modify the currently popular notion (Fiorina, 1977, p. 3) that congressmen are to blame for this state of affairs. The public may well be the key to the Washington establishment. If the public did not create this establishment, they have inspired and sustained it, and are apt to continue to do so.

NOTES

1. The data for the open-ended congressional evaluation questions in the 1977 survey were obtained from: U.S. House of Representatives (1977). We have recoded these data into the categories utilized in coding the 1968 data in order to facilitate comparisons and sharpen patterns of congressional evaluations. A description of the recoding scheme is available from the authors.

REFERENCES

Fenno, Richard F., Jr., 1975. "If, as Ralph Nader Says, Congress Is 'The Broken Branch,' How Come We Love Our Congressmen So Much?" in Norman J. Ornstein, ed., *Congress in Change: Evolution and Reform*. New York: Praeger, pp. 277–287.

Fiorina, Morris P. 1977. *Congress: Keystone of the Washington Establishment*. New Haven: Yale University Press.

Frankfurter, Felix. 1930. *The Public and Its Government.* New Haven: Yale University Press.
Harris, Louis & Associates. 1968. Study No. 1900, contracted by Roger H. Davidson, under a grant from the Committee on Governmental and Legal Services, Social Science Research Council.
Lipset, Seymour M. 1963. *Political Man.* New York: Anchor Books.
Mitchell, William C. 1959. "The Ambivalent Social Status of the American Politician," *Western Political Quarterly* 12 (September, 1959): 683–698.
Rosenberg, Morris. 1951. "The Meaning of Politics in Mass Society," *Public Opinion Quarterly* 15 (Spring, 1951): 5–15.
____________. 1954. "Some Determinants of Political Apathy," *Public Opinion Quarterly* 18 (Winter, 1954): 349–366.
U.S. House of Representatives, Commission on Administrative Review. 1977. *Final Report: Survey Materials.* H. Doc. 95–272 (95th Congress, 1st session): Vol. 2, pp. 817–819.

Section X
Review Questions

1. On what basis does Edmund Burke conclude that members of an elected legislative body would better represent the voters by relying on their own judgment than by mirroring the views of their constituents? Do you want your member of Congress to follow Burke's advice?

2. In *Federalist* No. 35 James Madison argues that the need to win votes will assure that all people will be adequately represented in Congress. Do you think history has proven him right? What groups might now agree with his optimistic prediction about how representatives would behave?

3. Although there have been many reforms in Congress since Wilson's book was published, do you think that Congress has really changed?

4. Do the findings of Glenn Parker and Roger Davidson reflect your perceptions of Congress? How do Parker and Davidson explain the apparent contradictory views held by the public regarding individual members versus the Congress as an institution?

XI

The Presidency

ALEXANDER HAMILTON

55. CREATING THE PRESIDENCY

Alexander Hamilton, George Washington's aide and first Secretary of the Treasury, used Federalist No. 69 *to defend the powers of the president proposed in the Constitution. He explained that although executive powers were to be in the hands of a single chief executive as they had been in Great Britain, the similarities to King George ended right there. Unlike the British monarch, the president was severely limited: He could be impeached for treason, bribery, and other crimes and misdemeanors; his veto of legislation could be overridden by strong majorities in the Congress; and the president could not even agree to a treaty without the advice and consent of the U.S. Senate. Hamilton wanted it unambiguously understood that the essential difference between the King of England and the proposed President of the United States was that "one can perform alone what the other can do only with the concurrence of a branch of the legislature."*

I proceed now to trace the real characters of the proposed Executive, as they are marked out in the plan of the convention. This will serve to place in a strong light the unfairness of the representations which have been made in regard to it.

The first thing which strikes our attention is, that the executive authority, with few exceptions, is to be vested in a single magistrate. This will scarcely, however, be considered as a point upon which any comparison can be grounded; for if, in this particular, there be a resemblance to the King of Great Britain, there is not less a resemblance to the Grand Seignior, to the khan of Tartary, to the Man of the Seven Mountains, or to the governor of New York.

That magistrate is to be elected for *four* years; and is to be reëligible as often as the people of the United States shall think him worthy of their confidence. In these circumstances there is a total dissimilitude between *him* and a king of Great Britain, who is an *hereditary* monarch, possessing the crown as a patrimony descendible to his heirs forever; but there is a close analogy between *him* and a governor of New York, who is elected for *three* years, and is reëligible without limitation or intermission. If we consider how much less

---

Source: From *The Federalist,* No. 69 (1788).

time would be requisite for establishing a dangerous influence in a single State, than for establishing a like influence throughout the United States, we must conclude that a duration of *four* years for the Chief Magistrate of the Union is a degree of permanency far less to be dreaded in that office, than a duration of *three* years for a corresponding office in a single state.

The President of the United States would be liable to be impeached, tried, and, upon conviction of treason, bribery, or other high crimes or misdemeanors, removed from office; and would afterwards be liable to prosecution and punishment in the ordinary course of law. The person of the king of Great Britain is sacred and inviolable; there is no constitutional tribunal to which he is amenable; no punishment to which he can be subjected without involving the crisis of a national revolution. In this delicate and important circumstance of personal responsibility, the President of Confederated America would stand upon no better ground than a governor of New York, and upon worse ground than the governors of Maryland and Delaware.

The President of the United States is to have power to return a bill, which shall have passed the two branches of the legislature, for reconsideration; and the bill so returned is to become a law, if, upon that reconsideration, it be approved by two thirds of both houses. The king of Great Britain, on his part, has an absolute negative upon the acts of the two houses of Parliament. The disuse of that power for a considerable time past does not affect the reality of its existence; and is to be ascribed wholly to the crown's having found the means of substituting influence to authority, or the art of gaining a majority in one or the other of the two houses, to the necessity of exerting a prerogative which could seldom be exerted without hazarding some degree of national agitation. The qualified negative of the President differs widely from this absolute negative of the British sovereign. . . .

The President is to be the "commander-in-chief of the army and navy of the United States, and of the militia of the several States, when called into the actual service of the United States. He is to have power to grant reprieves and pardons for offences against the United States, *except in cases of impeachment;* to recommend to the consideration of Congress such measures as he shall judge necessary and expedient; to convene, on extraordinary occasions, both houses of the legislature, or either of them, and, in case of disagreement between them *with respect to the time of adjournment,* to adjourn them to such time as he shall think proper; to take care that the laws be faithfully executed; and to commission all officers of the United States." In most of these particulars, the power of the President will resemble equally that of the king of Great Britain and of the governor of New York. The most material points of difference are these:—*First.* The President will have only the occasional command of such part of the militia of the nation as by legislative provision may be called into the actual service of the Union. The king of Great Britain and the governor of New York have at all times the entire command of all the militia within their several jurisdictions. In this article, therefore, the power of the President would be inferior to that of either the monarch or the governor. *Secondly.* The

President is to be commander-in-chief of the army and navy of the United States. In this respect his authority would be nominally the same with that of the king of Great Britain, but in substance much inferior to it. . . . *Thirdly.* The power of the President, in respect to pardons, would extend to all cases, *except those of impeachment.* . . . The better to judge of this matter, it will be necessary to recollect, that, by the proposed Constitution, the offence of treason is limited "to levying war upon the United States, and adhering to their enemies, giving them aid and comfort"; and that by the law of New York it is confined within similar bounds. *Fourthly.* The President can only adjourn the national legislature in the single case of disagreement about the time of adjournment. The British monarch may prorogue or even dissolve the Parliament. The governor of New York may also prorogue the legislature of this State for a limited time; a power which, in certain situations, may be employed to very important purposes.

The President is to have power, with the advice and consent of the Senate, to make treaties, provided two thirds of the senators present concur. The king of Great Britain is the sole and absolute representative of the nation in all foreign transactions. He can of his own accord make treaties of peace, commerce, alliance, and of every other description. It has been insinuated, that his authority in this respect is not conclusive, and that his conventions with foreign powers are subject to the revision, and stand in need of the ratification, of Parliament. But I believe this doctrine was never heard of, until it was broached upon the present occasion. Every jurist of that kingdom, and every other man acquainted with its Constitution, knows, as an established fact, that the prerogative of making treaties exists in the crown in its utmost plenitude; and that the compacts entered into by the royal authority have the most legal validity and perfection, independent of any other sanction. The Parliament, it is true, is sometimes seen employing itself in altering the existing laws to conform them to the stipulations in a new treaty; and this may have possibly given birth to the imagination, that its coöperation was necessary to the obligatory efficacy of the treaty. But this parliamentary interposition proceeds from a different cause: from the necessity of adjusting a most artificial and intricate system of revenue and commercial laws, to the changes made in them by the operation of the treaty; and of adapting new provisions and precautions to the new state of things, to keep the machine from running into disorder. In this respect, therefore, there is no comparison between the intended power of the President and the actual power of the British sovereign. The one can perform alone what the other can do only with the concurrence of a branch of the legislature. It must be admitted, that, in this instance, the power of the federal Executive would exceed that of any State Executive. But this arises naturally from the sovereign power which relates to treaties. If the Confederacy were to be dissolved, it would become a question whether the Executives of the several States were not solely invested with that delicate and important prerogative.

The President is also authorized to receive ambassadors and other public ministers. This, though it has been a rich theme of declamation, is more a matter of dignity than of authority. It is a circumstance which will be without consequence in the administration of the government; and it was far more convenient that it should be arranged in this manner, than that there should be a necessity of convening the legislature, or one of its branches, upon every arrival of a foreign minister, though it were merely to take the place of a departed predecessor.

The President is to nominate, and, *with the advice and consent of the Senate,* to appoint ambassadors and other public ministers, judges of the Supreme Court, and in general all officers of the United States established by law, and whose appointments are not otherwise provided for by the Constitution. . . .

Hence it appears that, except as to the concurrent authority of the President in the article of treaties, it would be difficult to determine whether that magistrate would in the aggregate, possess more or less power than the governor of New York. And it appears yet more unequivocally, that there is no pretence for the parallel which has been attempted between him and the king of Great Britain. But to render the contrast in this respect still more striking, it may be of use to throw the principal circumstances of dissimilitude into a closer group.

The President of the United States would be an officer elected by the people for *four* years; the king of Great Britain is a perpetual and *hereditary* prince. The one would be amenable to personal punishment and disgrace; the person of the other is sacred and inviolable. The one would have a *qualified* negative upon the acts of the legislative body; the other has an *absolute* negative. The one would have a right to command the military and naval forces of the nation; the other, in addition to this right, possesses that of *declaring* war, and of *raising* and *regulating* fleets and armies by his own authority. The one would have a concurrent power with a branch of the legislature in the formation of treaties; the other is the *sole possessor* of the power of making treaties. The one would have a like concurrent authority in appointing to offices; the other is the sole author of all appointments. The one can confer no privileges whatever: the other can make denizens of aliens, noblemen of commoners: can erect corporations with all the rights incident to corporate bodies. The one can prescribe no rules concerning the commerce or currency of the nation; the other is in several respects the arbiter of commerce, and in his capacity can establish markets and fairs, can regulate weights and measures, can lay embargoes for a limited time, can coin money, can authorize or prohibit the circulation of foreign coin. The one has no particle of spiritual jurisdiction; the other is the supreme head and governor of the national church! What answer shall we give to those who would persuade us that things so unlike resemble each other? The same that ought to be given to those who tell us that a government, the whole power of which would be in the hands of the elective and periodical servants of the people, is an aristocracy, a monarchy, and a despotism.

ABRAHAM LINCOLN

56. THE PREROGATIVE THEORY OF THE PRESIDENCY

President Abraham Lincoln's "prerogative" approach to presidential powers was first stated by English political theorist John Locke in his Second Treatise of Government *(1690)—that there must be "a latitude left to the executive power to do many things of choice which the laws do not prescribe." In this letter to the editor of a Kentucky newspaper, Lincoln recognizes that his election to the office of president of the United States did not automatically give him the authority to impose his strong personal opposition to slavery on the nation as a whole. On the other hand, having taken an oath "to preserve, protect, and defend the Constitution of the United States," Lincoln believed that extraordinary steps were justified in order to save the union. These steps included violating some provisions of the Constitution if it was necessary to save the country from being split apart over the issue of slavery. Lincoln believed that it would have been a breach of his oath of office not to have taken all necessary steps to save the union. His claim that he could violate the Constitution in order to save the Constitution remains the strongest assertion of presidential power ever made by a U.S. president.*

LETTER TO A. G. HODGES EXECUTIVE MANSION, APRIL 4, 1864

My dear Sir: You ask me to put in writing the substance of what I verbally said the other day in your presence, to Governor Bramlett and Senator Dixon. It was about as follows:

"I am naturally antislavery. If slavery is not wrong, nothing is wrong. I cannot remember when I did not so think and feel, and yet I have never understood that the presidency conferred upon me an unrestricted right to act

---

Source: From John Nicolay and John Hay, eds., *The Complete Works of Abraham Lincoln,* Vol. 10 (New York: Francis D. Tandy Co., 1894), pp. 65–68. This letter to Albert G. Hodges, editor of the Frankfort, Kentucky, *Commonwealth* was used as a campaign document in the election of 1864.

officially upon this judgment and feeling. It was in the oath I took that I would, to the best of my ability, preserve, protect, and defend the Constitution of the United States. I could not take the office without taking the oath. Nor was it my view that I might take an oath to get power, and break the oath in using the power. I understood, too, that in ordinary civil administration this oath even forbade me to practically indulge my primary abstract judgment on the moral question of slavery. I had publicly declared this many times, and in many ways. And I aver that, to this day, I have done no official act in mere deference to my abstract judgment and feeling on slavery. I did understand, however, that my oath to preserve the Constitution to the best of my ability imposed upon me the duty of preserving, by every indispensable means, that government—that nation, of which that Constitution was the organic law. Was it possible to lose the nation and yet preserve the Constitution? By general law, life and limb must be protected, yet often a limb must be amputated to save a life; but a life is never wisely given to save a limb. I felt that measures otherwise unconstitutional might become lawful by becoming indispensable to the preservation of the Constitution through the preservation of the nation. Right or wrong, I assume this ground, and now avow it. I could not feel that, to the best of my ability, I had even tried to preserve the Constitution, if, to save slavery or any minor matter, I should permit the wreck of government, country, and Constitution all together. When, early in the war, General Frémont attempted military emancipation, I forbade it, because I did not then think it an indispensable necessity. When, a little later, General Cameron, then Secretary of War, suggested the arming of blacks, I objected because I did not yet think it an indispensable necessity. When, still later, General Hunter attempted military emancipation, I again forbade it, because I did not yet think the indispensable necessity had come. When in March and May and July, 1862, I made earnest and successive appeals to the border States to favor compensated emancipation, I believed the indispensable necessity for military emancipation and arming the blacks would come unless averted by that measure. They declined the proposition, and I was, in my best judgment, driven to the alternative of either surrendering the Union, and with it the Constitution, or of laying strong hand upon the colored element. I chose the latter. In choosing it, I hoped for greater gain than loss; but of this, I was not entirely confident. More than a year of trial now shows no loss by it in our foreign relations, none in our home popular sentiment, none in our white military force—no loss by it anyhow or anywhere. On the contrary it shows a gain of quite a hundred and thirty thousand soldiers, seamen, and laborers. These are palpable facts, about which, as facts, there can be no caviling. We have the men; and we could not have had them without the measure.

"And now let any Union man who complains of the measure test himself by writing down in one line that he is for subduing the rebellion by force of arms; and in the next, that he is for taking these hundred and thirty thousand men from the Union side, and placing them where they would be but for the measure he condemns. If he cannot face his case so stated, it is only because he cannot face the truth."

I add a word which was not in the verbal conversation. In telling this tale I attempt no compliment to my own sagacity. I claim not to have controlled events, but confess plainly that events have controlled me. Now, at the end of three years' struggle, the nation's condition is not what either party, or any man, devised or expected. God alone can claim it. Whither it is tending seems plain. If God now wills the removal of a great wrong, and wills also that we of the North, as well as you of the South, shall pay fairly for our complicity in that wrong, impartial history will find therein new cause to attest and revere the justice and goodness of God. *Yours truly,*

A. Lincoln

THEODORE ROOSEVELT

57. THE STEWARDSHIP THEORY OF THE PRESIDENCY

President Theodore Roosevelt expressed his thoughts on the powers of the presidency in an autobiography published after he left office. He forcefully argued that the job of the president was to act as "a steward of the people" who could do anything that wasn't "forbidden by the Constitution or by the laws." According to Roosevelt, the president needed to consult with Congress only when explicitly required to do so under the Constitution. In all other cases—whether involving foreign policy or allegations of wrongdoing within his administration—the president was empowered to act on his own. Roosevelt's view allowed the president to exercise power so long as there was no clear constitutional prohibition on doing so. Note that Lincoln had gone even further and justified his exercising power even where the Constitution and laws prohibited him from doing so.

My view was that every executive officer, and above all every executive officer in high position, was a steward of the people bound actively and affirmatively to do all he could for the people, and not to content himself with the negative merit of keeping his talents undamaged in a napkin. I declined to adopt the view that what was imperatively necessary for the nation could not be done by

---

Source: From Theodore Roosevelt, *The Autobiography of Theodore Roosevelt* (New York: Charles Scribner's Sons, 1913).

the President unless he could find some specific authorization to do it. My belief was that it was not only his right but his duty to do anything that the needs of the nation demanded unless such action was forbidden by the Constitution or by the laws. Under this interpretation of executive power I did and caused to be done many things not previously done by the President and the heads of departments. I did not usurp power, but I did greatly broaden the use of executive power. In other words, I acted for the public welfare, I acted for the common well-being of all our people, whenever and in whatever manner was necessary, unless prevented by direct constitutional or legislative prohibition. . . .

The course I followed, of regarding the Executive as subject only to the people, and, under the Constitution, bound to serve the people affirmatively in cases where the Constitution does not explicitly forbid him to render the service, was substantially the course followed by both Andrew Jackson and Abraham Lincoln. Other honorable and well-meaning Presidents, such as James Buchanan, took the opposite and, as it seems to me, narrowly legalistic view that the President is the servant of Congress rather than of the people, and can do nothing, no matter how necessary it be to act, unless the Constitution explicitly commands the action. Most able lawyers who are past middle age take this view, and so do large numbers of well-meaning, respectable citizens. My successor in office took this, the Buchanan, view of the President's powers and duties.

For example, under my administration we found that one of the favorite methods adopted by the men desirous of stealing the public domain was to carry the decision of the secretary of the interior into court. By vigorously opposing such action, and only by so doing, we were able to carry out the policy of properly protecting the public domain. My successor not only took the opposite view, but recommended to Congress the passage of a bill which would have given the courts direct appellate power over the secretary of the interior in these land matters. . . . Fortunately, Congress declined to pass the bill. Its passage would have been a veritable calamity.

I acted on the theory that the President could at any time in his discretion withdraw from entry any of the public lands of the United States and reserve the same for forestry, for water-power sites, for irrigation, and other public purposes. Without such action it would have been impossible to stop the activity of the land-thieves. No one ventured to test its legality by lawsuit. My successor, however, himself questioned it, and referred the matter to Congress. Again Congress showed its wisdom by passing a law which gave the President the power which he had long exercised, and of which my successor had shorn himself.

Perhaps the sharp difference between what may be called the Lincoln-Jackson and the Buchanan-Taft schools, in their views of the power and duties of the President, may be best illustrated by comparing the attitude of my successor toward the Secretary of the Interior, Mr. Ballinger, when the latter was accused of gross misconduct in office, with my attitude toward my chiefs of department and other subordinate officers. More than once while I was President my officials were attacked by Congress, generally because these officials did their duty well and fearlessly. In every such case I stood by the official and refused to recognize the right of Congress to interfere with me excepting by impeachment or in other constitutional manner. On the other hand, wherever I found the officer unfit for his position, I promptly removed him, even although the most influential men of Congress fought for his retention. The Jackson-Lincoln view is that a President who is fit to do good work should be able to form his own judgment as to his own subordinates, and, above all, of the subordinates standing highest and in closest and most intimate touch with him. My secretaries and their subordinates were responsible to me, and I accepted the responsibility for all their deeds. As long as they were satisfactory to me I stood by them against every critic or assailant, within or without Congress; and as for getting Congress to make up my mind for me about them, the thought would have been inconceivable to me. My successor took the opposite, or Buchanan, view when he permitted and requested Congress to pass judgment on the charges made against Mr. Ballinger as an executive officer. These charges were made to the President; the President had the facts before him and could get at them at any time, and he alone had power to act if the charges were true. However, he permitted and requested Congress to investigate Mr. Ballinger. The party minority of the committee that investigated him, and one member of the majority, declared that the charges were well-founded and that Mr. Ballinger should be removed. The other members of the majority declared the charges ill-founded. The President abode by the view of the majority. Of course believers in the Jackson-Lincoln theory of the presidency would not be content with this townmeeting majority and minority method of determining by another branch of the government what it seems the especial duty of the President himself to determine for himself in dealing with his own subordinate in his own department. . . .

WILLIAM HOWARD TAFT

58. The Literalist Theory of the Presidency

President William Howard Taft's "literalist" view of presidential power offers a clear contrast with the views of Lincoln and Roosevelt. Taft feared that allowing presidents to act on behalf of the people in violation of the

---

Source: From William Howard Taft, *Our Chief Magistrate and His Powers* (New York: Columbia University Press, 1916).

> *Constitution, or where not clearly prohibited by the Constitution, could lead them to broad and unlimited presidential power and that could result in "irremediable injustice." Whereas Lincoln and Roosevelt were comfortable in seizing powers not clearly held out of their grasp by the Constitution, Taft argued that "the president can exercise no power which cannot be fairly and reasonably traced to some specific grant of power or justly implied."*

While it is important to mark out the exclusive field of jurisdiction of each branch of the government, Legislative, Executive and Judicial, it should be said that in the proper working of the government there must be coöperation of all branches, and without a willingness of each branch to perform its function, there will follow a hopeless obstruction to the progress of the whole government. Neither branch can compel the other to affirmative action, and each branch can greatly hinder the other in the attainment of the object of its activities and the exercise of its discretion.

The true view of the Executive functions is, as I conceive it, that the President can exercise no power which cannot be fairly and reasonably traced to some specific grant of power or justly implied and included within such express grant as proper and necessary to its exercise. Such specific grant must be either in the Federal Constitution or in an act of Congress passed in pursuance thereof. There is no undefined residuum of power which he can exercise because it seems to him to be in the public interest, and there is nothing in the Neagle case and its definition of a law of the United States, or in other precedents, warranting such an inference. The grants of Executive power are necessarily in general terms in order not to embarrass the Executive within the field of action plainly marked for him, but his jurisdiction must be justified and vindicated by affirmative constitutional or statutory provision, or it does not exist. There have not been wanting, however, eminent men in high public office holding a different view and who have insisted upon the necessity for an undefined residuum of Executive power in the public interest. They have not been confined to the present generation. We may learn this from the complaint of a Virginia statesman, Abel P. Upshur, a strict constructionist of the old school, who succeeded Daniel Webster as Secretary of State under President Tyler. He was aroused by Story's commentaries on the Constitution to write a monograph answering and criticizing them, and in the course of this he comments as follows on the Executive power under the Constitution:

> The most defective part of the Constitution beyond all question, is that which related to the Executive Department. It is impossible to read that instrument, without being struck with the loose and unguarded terms in which the powers and duties of the President are pointed out. So far as the legislature is concerned, the limitations of the Constitution, are, perhaps, as precise and strict as they could safely have been made; but in regard to the Executive, the Convention appears to have studiously selected such loose and general expressions, as

> would enable the President, by implication and construction either to neglect his duties or to enlarge his powers. We have heard it gravely asserted in Congress that whatever power is neither legislative nor judiciary, is of course executive, and, as such, belongs to the President under the Constitution. How far a majority of that body would have sustained a doctrine so monstrous, and so utterly at war with the whole genius of our government, it is impossible to say, but this, at least, we know, that it met with no rebuke from those who supported the particular act of Executive power, in defense of which it was urged. Be this as it may, it is a reproach to the Constitution that the Executive trust is so ill-defined, as to leave any plausible pretense even to the insane zeal of party devotion, for attributing to the President of the United States the powers of a despot; powers which are wholly unknown in any limited monarchy in the world.

The view that he takes as a result of the loose language defining the Executive powers seems exaggerated. But one must agree with him in his condemnation of the view of the Executive power which he says was advanced in Congress. In recent years there has been put forward a similar view by executive officials and to some extent acted on. Men who are not such strict constructionists of the Constitution as Mr. Upshur may well feel real concern if such views are to receive the general acquiescence. Mr. Garfield, when Secretary of the Interior, under Mr. Roosevelt, in his final report to Congress in reference to the power of the Executive over the public domain, said:

> Full power under the Constitution was vested in the Executive Branch of the Government and the extent to which that power may be exercised is governed wholly by the discretion of the Executive unless any specific act has been prohibited either by the Constitution or by legislation.

In pursuance of this principle, Mr. Garfield, under an act for the reclamation of arid land by irrigation, which authorized him to make contracts for irrigation works and incur liability equal to the amount on deposit in the Reclamation Fund, made contracts with associations of settlers by which it was agreed that if these settlers would advance money and work, they might receive certificates from the government engineers of the labor and money furnished by them, and that such certificates might be received in the future in the discharge of their legal obligations to the government for water rent and other things under the statute. It became necessary for the succeeding administration to pass on the validity of these government certificates. They were held by Attorney-General Wickersham to be illegal, on the ground that no authority existed for their issuance. He relied on the Floyd acceptances in 7th Wallace, in which recovery was sought in the Court of Claims on commercial paper in the form of acceptances signed by Mr. Floyd when Secretary of War and delivered to certain contractors. The Court held that they were void because the Secretary of War had no statutory authority to issue them. Mr. Justice Miller, in deciding the case, said:

> The answer which at once suggests itself to one familiar with the structure of our government, in which all power is delegated, and is defined by law, constitutional or statutory, is, that to one or both of these sources we must resort in

> every instance. We have no officers in this government, from the President down to the most subordinate agent, who does not hold office under the law, with prescribed duties and limited authority. And while some of these, as the President, the Legislature, and the Judiciary, exercise powers in some sense left to the more general definitions necessarily incident to fundamental law found in the Constitution, the larger portion of them are the creation of statutory law, with duties and powers prescribed and limited by that law.

My judgment is that the view of Mr. Garfield and Mr. Roosevelt, ascribing an undefined residuum of power to the President is an unsafe doctrine and that it might lead under emergencies to results of an arbitrary character, doing irremediable injustice to private right. The mainspring of such a view is that the Executive is charged with responsibility for the welfare of all the people in a general way, that he is to play the part of a Universal Providence and set all things right, and that anything that in his judgment will help the people he ought to do, unless he is expressly forbidden not to do it. The wide field of action that this would give to the Executive one can hardly limit.

RICHARD E. NEUSTADT

59. THE PRESIDENTIAL POWER TO PERSUADE

While presidents have written about when they should exercise power, scholars who observe presidents from a distance have tried to better understand how that power is exercised. The general debate has been between those who argue that the power of the president comes from the many roles associated with the office—commander in chief, legislative leader, chief executive, foreign policy marker—and those who have argued that presidential power is really nothing more than the "power to persuade" others to go along. Richard Neustadt's influential book Presidential Power, *first published in 1960, advised presidents that in order to accomplish anything, they must carefully use the prestige of the Oval Office*

Source: Reprinted with the permission of The Free Press, a division of Simon & Schuster Adult Publishing Group, from *Presidential Power and the Modern Presidents: The Politics of Leadership from Roosevelt to Reagan* by Richard E. Neustadt. Copyright © 1990 by Richard E. Neustadt. All rights reserved.

> *and their own negotiating skills to bargain with legislators and bureaucrats. Neustadt's message is clear: The constitutional powers granted to the president mean little to a president unable to persuade others to go along.*

The limits on command suggest the structure of our government. The constitutional convention of 1787 is supposed to have created a government of "separated powers." It did nothing of the sort. Rather, it created a government of separated institutions *sharing* powers.[1] "I am part of the legislative process," Eisenhower often said in 1959 as a reminder of his veto.[2] Congress, the dispenser of authority and funds, is no less part of the administrative process. Federalism adds another set of separated institutions. The Bill of Rights adds others. Many public purposes can only be achieved by voluntary acts of private institutions; the press, for one, in Douglass Cater's phrase, is a "fourth branch of government."[3] And with the coming of alliances abroad, the separate institutions of a London, or a Bonn, share in the making of American public policy.

What the Constitution separates our political parties do not combine. The parties are themselves composed of separated organizations sharing public authority. The authority consists of nominating powers. Our national parties are confederations of state and local party institutions, with a headquarters that represents the White house, more or less, if the party has a President in office. These confederacies manage presidential nominations. All other public offices depend upon electorates confined within the state.[4] All other nominations are controlled within the states. The President and congressmen who bear one party's label are divided by dependence upon different sets of voters. The differences are sharpest at the stage of nomination. The White House has too small a share in nominating congressmen, and Congress has too little weight in nominating Presidents for party to erase their constitutional separation. Party links are stronger than is frequently supposed, but nominating processes assure the separation.[5]

The separateness of institutions and the sharing of authority prescribe the terms on which a President persuades. When one man shares authority with another, but does not gain or lose his job upon the other's whim, his willingness to act upon the urging of the other turns on whether he conceives the action right for him. The essence of a President's persuasive task is to convince such men that what the White House wants of them is what they ought to do for their sake and on their authority.

Persuasive power, thus defined, amounts to more than charm or reasoned argument. These have their uses for a President, but these are not the whole of his resources. For the men he would induce to do what he wants done on their own responsibility will need or fear some acts by him on his responsibility. If they share his authority, he has some share in theirs. Presidential "powers" may be inconclusive when a President commands, but always remain relevant as he persuades. The status and authority inherent in his office reinforce his logic and his charm.

Status adds something to persuasiveness; authority adds still more. When Truman urged wage changes on his Secretary of Commerce while the latter was administering the steel mills, he and Secretary Sawyer were not just two men reasoning with one another. Had they been so, Sawyer probably would never have agreed to act. Truman's status gave him special claims to Sawyer's loyalty, or at least attention. In Walter Bagehot's charming phrase "No man can *argue* on his knees." Although there is no kneeling in this country, few men—and exceedingly few Cabinet officers—are immune to the impulse to say "yes" to the President of the United States. It grows harder to say "no" when they are seated in his oval office at the White House, or in his study on the second floor, where almost tangibly he partakes of the aura of his physical surroundings. In Sawyer's case, moreover, the President possessed formal authority to intervene in many matters of concern to the Secretary of Commerce. These matters ranged from jurisdictional disputes among the defense agencies to legislation pending before Congress and, ultimately, to the tenure of the Secretary, himself. There is nothing in the record to suggest that Truman voiced specific threats when they negotiated over wage increases. But given his *formal* powers and their relevance to Sawyer's other interests, it is safe to assume that Truman's very advocacy of wage action conveyed an implicit threat.

A President's authority and status give him great advantages in dealing with the men he would persuade. Each "power" is a vantage point for him in the degree that other men have use for his authority. From the veto to appointments, from publicity to budgeting, and so down a long list, the White House now controls the most encompassing array of vantage points in the American political system. With hardly an exception, the men who share in governing this country are aware that at some time, in some degree, the doing of *their* jobs, the furthering of *their* ambitions, may depend upon the President of the United States. Their need for presidential action, or their fear of it, is bound to be recurrent if not actually continuous. Their need or fear is his advantage.

A President's advantages are greater than mere listing of his "powers" might suggest. The men with whom he deals must deal with him until the last day of his term. Because they have continuing relationships with him, his future, while it lasts, supports his present influence. Even though there is no need or fear of him today, what he could do tomorrow may supply today's advantage. Continuing relationships may convert any "power," any aspect of his status, into vantage points in almost any case. When he induces other men to do what he wants done, a President can trade on their dependence now *and* later.

The President's advantages are checked by the advantages of others. Continuing relationships will pull in both directions. These are relationships of mutual dependence. A President depends upon the men he would persuade; he has to reckon with his need or fear of them. They too will possess status, or authority, or both, else they would be of little use to him. Their vantage points confront his own; their power tempers his.

Persuasion is a two-way street. Sawyer, it will be recalled, did not respond at once to Truman's plan for wage increases at the steel mills. On the contrary, the Secretary hesitated and delayed and only acquiesced when he was satisfied that publicly he would not bear the onus of decision. Sawyer had some points of vantage all his own from which to resist presidential pressure. If he had to reckon with coercive implications in the President's "situations of strength," so had Truman to be mindful of the implications underlying Sawyer's place as a department head, as steel administrator, and as a Cabinet spokesman for business. Loyalty is reciprocal. Having taken on a dirty job in the steel crisis, Sawyer had strong claims to loyal support. Besides, he had authority to do some things that the White House could ill afford. Emulating Wilson, he might have resigned in a huff (the removal power also works two ways). Or emulating Ellis Arnall, he might have declined to sign necessary orders. Or, he might have let it be known publicly that he deplored what he was told to do and protested its doing. By following any of these courses Sawyer almost surely would have strengthened the position of management, weakened the position of the White House, and embittered the union. But the whole purpose of a wage increase was to enhance White House persuasiveness in urging settlement upon union and companies alike. Although Sawyer's status and authority did not give him the power to prevent an increase outright, they gave him capability to undermine its purpose. If his authority over wage rates had been vested by a statute, not by revocable presidential order, his power of prevention might have been complete. So Harold Ickes demonstrated in the famous case of helium sales to Germany before the Second World War.[6]

The power to persuade is the power to bargain. Status and authority yield bargaining advantages. But in a government of "separated institutions sharing powers," they yield them to all sides. With the array of vantage points at his disposal, a President may be far more persuasive than his logic or his charm could make him. But outcomes are not guaranteed by his advantages. There remain the counter pressures those whom he would influence can bring to bear on him from vantage points at their disposal. Command has limited utility; persuasion becomes give-and-take. It is well that the White House holds the vantage points it does. In such a business any President may need them all—and more.

NOTES

1. The reader will want to keep in mind the distinction between two senses in which the word *power* is employed. When I have used the word (or its plural) to refer to formal constitutional, statutory, or customary authority, it is either qualified by the adjective "formal" or placed in quotation marks as "power(s)." Where I have used it in the sense of effective influence upon the conduct of others, it appears without quotation marks (and always in the singular). Where clarity and convenience permit, *authority* is substituted for "power" in the first sense and *influence* for power in the second sense.
2. See, for example, his press conference of July 22, 1959, as reported in the *New York Times,* July 23, 1959.
3. See Douglass Cater, *The Fourth Branch of Government* (Boston: Houghton-Mifflin, 1959.)

4. With the exception of the Vice-Presidency, of course.
5. See David B. Truman's illuminating study of party relationships in the 81st Congress, *The Congressional Party,* New York: Wiley, 1959, especially chaps. 4, 6, and 8.
6. As Secretary of the Interior in 1939, Harold Ickes refused to approve the sale of helium to Germany despite the insistence of the State Department and the urging of President Roosevelt. Without the Secretary's approval, such sales were forbidden by statute. See *The Secret Diaries of Harold L. Ickes,* New York: Simon and Schuster, 1954, Vol. 2, especially pp. 391–393, 396–399. See also Michael J. Reagan. "The Helium Controversy," in the forthcoming case book on civil–military relations prepared for the Twentieth Century Fund under the editorial direction of Harold Stein.

In this instance the statutory authority ran to the Secretary as a matter of *his* discretion. A President is unlikely to fire Cabinet officers for the conscientious exercise of such authority. If the president did so, their successors might well be embarrassed both publicly and at the Capitol were they to reverse decisions previously taken. As for a President's authority to set aside discretionary determinations of this sort, it rests, if it exists at all, on shaky legal ground not likely to be trod save in the gravest of situations.

AARON B. WILDAVSKY

60. THE TWO PRESIDENCIES

Presidents wield considerably more power when making decisions in the area of foreign policy than in domestic policy. After reviewing the exercise of presidential power in the post–World War II period, Aaron Wildavsky concluded that while the United States has one president, "it has two presidencies: one presidency is for domestic affairs, and the other is concerned with defense and foreign policy."

This observation, first published in 1966, continues to describe a basic truth about the presidency. All presidents have been able to exercise more power in foreign than domestic policy areas. Because of the greater need for speed in dealing with foreign policy problems, the constitutionally mandated power of the president to command the armed forces, the lower level of public understanding about international problems, the general unwillingness of Congress to stand up to the president

Source: From Aaron B. Wildavsky, "The Two Presidencies," *Transaction* 4, no. 2 (December, 1966). Reproduced by permission of Transaction Publishers.

on foreign policy issues—any president is going to be more successful in foreign than domestic policy.

The United States has one President, but it has two presidencies; one presidency is for domestic affairs, and the other is concerned with defense and foreign policy. Since World War II, Presidents have had much greater success in controlling the nation's defense and foreign policies than in dominating its domestic policies. Even Lyndon Johnson has seen his early record of victories in domestic legislation diminish as his concern with foreign affairs grows.

What powers does the President have to control defense and foreign policies and so completely overwhelm those who might wish to thwart him?

The President's normal problem with domestic policy is to get congressional support for the programs he prefers. In foreign affairs, in contrast, he can almost always get support for policies that he believes will protect the nation—but his problem is to find a viable policy.

Whoever they are, whether they begin by caring about foreign policy like Eisenhower and Kennedy or about domestic policies like Truman and Johnson, Presidents soon discover they have more policy preferences in domestic matters than in foreign policy. The Republican and Democratic parties possess a traditional roster of policies, which can easily be adopted by a new President—for example, he can be either for or against Medicare and aid to education. Since existing domestic policy usually changes in only small steps, Presidents find it relatively simple to make minor adjustments. However, although any President knows he supports foreign aid and NATO, the world outside changes much more rapidly than the nation inside—Presidents and their parties have no prior policies on Argentina and the Congo. The world has become a highly intractable place with a whirl of forces we cannot or do not know how to alter.

THE RECORD OF PRESIDENTIAL CONTROL

It takes great crises, such as Roosevelt's hundred days in the midst of the depression, or the extraordinary majorities that Barry Goldwater's candidacy willed to Lyndon Johnson, for Presidents to succeed in controlling domestic policy. From the end of the 1930s to the present (what may roughly be called the modern era), Presidents have often been frustrated in their domestic programs. From 1938, when conservatives regrouped their forces, to the time of his death, Franklin Roosevelt did not get a single piece of significant domestic legislation passed. Truman lost out on most of his intense domestic preferences, except perhaps for housing. Since Eisenhower did not ask for much domestic legislation, he did not meet consistent defeat, yet he failed in his general policy of curtailing governmental commitments. Kennedy, of course, faced great difficulties with domestic legislation.

TABLE 1 **Congressional Action on Presidential Proposals from 1948 to 1964**

POLICY AREA	CONGRESSIONAL ACTION		NUMBER OF PROPOSALS
	% PASS	% FAIL	
Domestic policy (natural resources, labor, agriculture, taxes, etc.)	40.2	59.8	2,499
Defense policy (defense, disarmament, manpower, misc.)	73.3	26.7	90
Foreign policy	58.5	41.5	655
Immigration, refugees	13.2	86.0	129
Treaties, general foreign relations, State Department, foreign aid	70.8	29.2	445

SOURCE: Congressional Quarterly Service, *Congress and the Nation,* 1945–1964 (Washington, 1965).

In the realm of foreign policy there has not been a single major issue on which Presidents, when they were serious and determined, have failed. The list of their victories is impressive: entry into the United Nations, the Marshall Plan, NATO, the Truman Doctrine, the decisions to stay out of Indochina in 1954 and to intervene in Vietnam in the 1960s, aid to Poland and Yugoslavia, the test-ban treaty, and many more. Serious setbacks to the President in controlling foreign policy are extraordinary and unusual.

Table 1, compiled from the Congressional Quarterly Service tabulation of presidential initiative and congressional response from 1948 through 1964, shows that Presidents have significantly better records in foreign and defense matters than in domestic policies. When refugees and immigration—which Congress considers primarily a domestic concern—are removed from the general foreign policy area, it is clear that Presidents prevail about 70 percent of the time in defense and foreign policy, compared with 40 percent in the domestic sphere.

WORLD EVENTS AND PRESIDENTIAL RESOURCES

Power in politics is control over governmental decisions. How does the President manage his control of foreign and defense policy? The answer does not reside in the greater constitutional power in foreign affairs that Presidents have possessed since the founding of the Republic. The answer lies in the changes that have taken place since 1945.

The number of nations with which the United States has diplomatic relations has increased from 53 in 1939 to 113 in 1966. But sheer numbers do not tell enough; the world has also become a much more dangerous place. However remote it may seem at times, our government must always be aware of the possibility of nuclear war.

Yet the mere existence of great powers with effective thermonuclear weapons would not, in and of itself, vastly increase our rate of interaction with most other nations. We see events in Assam or Burundi as important because they are also part of a larger worldwide contest, called the cold war, in which great powers are rivals for the control or support of other nations. Moreover, the reaction against the blatant isolationism of the 1930s has led to a concern with foreign policy that is worldwide in scope. We are interested in what happens everywhere because we see these events as connected with larger interests involving, at the worst, the possibility of ultimate destruction.

Given the overriding fact that the world is dangerous and that small causes are perceived to have potentially great effects in an unstable world, it follows that Presidents must be interested in relatively "small" matters. So they give Azerbaijan or Lebanon or Vietnam huge amounts of their time. Arthur Schlesinger, Jr., wrote of Kennedy that "in the first two months of his administration he probably spent more time on Laos than on anything else." Few failures in domestic policy, Presidents soon realize, could have as disastrous consequences as any one of dozens of mistakes in the international arena.

The result is that foreign policy concerns tend to drive out domestic policy. Except for occasional questions of domestic prosperity and for civil rights, foreign affairs have consistently higher priority for Presidents. Once, when trying to talk to President Kennedy about natural resources, Secretary of the Interior Stewart Udall remarked, "He's imprisoned by Berlin."

The importance of foreign affairs to Presidents is intensified by the increasing speed of events in the international arena. The event and its consequences follow closely on top of one another. The blunder at the Bay of Pigs is swiftly followed by the near catastrophe of the Cuban missile crisis. Presidents can no longer count on passing along their most difficult problems to their successors. They must expect to face the consequences of their actions—or failure to act—while still in office.

Domestic policy-making is usually based on experimental adjustments to an existing situation. Only a few decisions, such as those involving large dams, irretrievably commit future generations. Decisions in foreign affairs, however, are often perceived to be irreversible. This is expressed, for example, in the fear of escalation or the various "spiral" or "domino" theories of international conflict.

If decisions are perceived to be both important and irreversible, there is every reason for Presidents to devote a great deal of resources to them. Presidents have to be oriented toward the future in the use of their resources. They serve a fixed term in office, and they cannot automatically count on support from the populace, Congress, or the administrative apparatus. They have to be careful, therefore, to husband their resources for pressing future needs. But because the consequences of events in foreign affairs are potentially more grave, faster to manifest themselves, and less easily reversible than in domestic affairs, Presidents are more willing to use up their resources.

THE POWER TO ACT

Their formal powers to commit resources in foreign affairs and defense are vast. Particularly important is their power as Commander-in-Chief to move troops. Faced with situations like the invasion of South Korea or the emplacement of missiles in Cuba, fast action is required. Presidents possess both the formal power to act and the knowledge that elites and the general public expect them to act. Once they have committed American forces, it is difficult for Congress or anyone else to alter the course of events. The Dominican venture is a recent case in point.

Presidential discretion in foreign affairs also makes it difficult (though not impossible) for Congress to restrict their actions. Presidents can use executive agreements instead of treaties, enter into tacit agreements instead of written ones, and otherwise help create *de facto* situations not easily reversed. Presidents also have far greater ability than anyone else to obtain information on developments abroad through the Departments of State and Defense. The need for secrecy in some aspects of foreign and defense policy further restricts the ability of others to compete with Presidents. These things are well known. What is not so generally appreciated is the growing presidential ability to *use* information to achieve goals.

In the past Presidents were amateurs in military strategy. They could not even get much useful advice outside of the military. As late as the 1930s the number of people outside the military establishment who were professionally engaged in the study of defense policy could be numbered on the fingers. Today there are hundreds of such men. The rise of the defense intellectuals has given the President of the United States enhanced ability to control defense policy. He is no longer dependent on the military for advice. He can choose among defense intellectuals from the research corporations and the academies for alternative sources of advice. He can install these men in his own office. He can play them off against each other or use them to extend spheres of coordination.

Even with these advisers, however, Presidents and Secretaries of Defense might still be too bewildered by the complexity of nuclear situations to take action—unless they had an understanding of the doctrine and concepts of deterrence. But knowledge of the doctrine about deterrence has been widely diffused; it can be picked up by any intelligent person who will read books or listen to enough hours of conversation. Whether or not the doctrine is good is a separate question; the point is that civilians can feel they understand what is going on in defense policy. Perhaps the most extraordinary feature of presidential action during the Cuban missile crisis was the degree to which the Commander-in-Chief of the Armed Forces insisted on controlling even the smallest moves. From the positioning of ships to the methods of boarding, to the precise words and actions to be taken by individual soldiers and sailors, the President and his civilian advisers were in control.

Although Presidents have rivals for power in foreign affairs, the rivals do not usually succeed. Presidents prevail not only because they may have superior resources but because their potential opponents are weak, divided, or believe that they should not control foreign policy. Let us consider the potential rivals—the general citizenry, special interest groups, the Congress, the military, the so-called military-industrial complex, and the State Department.

COMPETITORS FOR CONTROL OF POLICY

The Public

The general public is much more dependent on Presidents in foreign affairs than in domestic matters. While many people know about the impact of social security and Medicare, few know about the politics in Malawi. So it is not surprising that people expect the President to act in foreign affairs and reward him with their confidence. Gallup Polls consistently show that presidential popularity rises after he takes action in a crisis—whether the action is disastrous as in the Bay of Pigs or successful as in the Cuban missile crisis. Decisive action, such as the bombing of oil fields near Haiphong, resulted in a sharp (though temporary) increase in Johnson's popularity.

The Vietnam situation illustrates another problem of public opinion in foreign affairs: it is extremely difficult to get operational policy directions from the general public. It took a long time before any sizable public interest in the subject developed. Nothing short of the large scale involvement of American troops under fire probably could have brought about the current high level of concern. Yet this relatively well developed popular opinion is difficult to interpret. While a majority appear to support President Johnson's policy, it appears that they could easily be persuaded to withdraw from Vietnam if the administration changed its line. Although a sizable majority would support various initiatives to end the war, they would seemingly be appalled if this action led to Communist encroachments elsewhere in Southeast Asia. (See "The President, the Polls, and Vietnam" by Seymour Martin Lipset, *Trans-action,* Sept/Oct 1966.)

Although Presidents lead opinion in foreign affairs, they know they will be held accountable for the consequences of their actions. President Johnson has maintained a large commitment in Vietnam. His popularity shoots up now and again in the midst of some imposing action. But the fact that a body of citizens do not like the war comes back to damage his overall popularity. We will support your initiatives, the people seem to say, but we will reserve the right to punish you (or your party) if we do not like the results.

Special Interest Groups

Opinions are easier to gauge in domestic affairs because, for one thing, there is a stable structure of interest groups that covers virtually all matters of concern. The farm, labor, business, conservation, veteran, civil rights, and other interest groups provide cues when a proposed policy affects them. Thus people who identify with these groups may adopt their views. But in foreign policy matters the interest group structure is weak, unstable, and thin rather than dense. In many matters affecting Africa and Asia, for example, it is hard to think of well-known interest groups. While ephemeral groups arise from time to time to support or protest particular policies, they usually disappear when the immediate problem is resolved. In contrast, longer-lasting elite groups like the Foreign Policy Association and Council on Foreign Relations are composed of people of diverse views; refusal to take strong positions on controversial matters is a condition of their continued viability.

The strongest interest groups are probably the ethnic associations whose members have strong ties with a homeland, as in Poland or Cuba, so they are rarely activated simultaneously on any specific issue. They are most effective when most narrowly and intensely focused—as in the fierce pressure from Jews to recognize the state of Israel. But their relatively small numbers limits their significance to Presidents in the vastly more important general foreign policy picture—as continued aid to the Arab countries shows. Moreover, some ethnic groups may conflict on significant issues such as American acceptance of the Oder-Neisse line separating Poland from what is now East Germany.

The Congress

Congressmen also exercise power in foreign affairs. Yet they are ordinarily not serious competitors with the President because they follow a self-denying ordinance. They do not think it is their job to determine the nation's defense policies. Lewis A. Dexter's extensive interviews with members of the Senate Armed Services Committee, who might be expected to want a voice in defense policy, reveal that they do not desire for men like themselves to run the nation's defense establishment. Aside from a few specific conflicts among the armed services which allow both the possibility and desirability of direct intervention, the Armed Services Committee constitutes a sort of real estate committee dealing with the regional economic consequences of the location of military facilities.

The congressional appropriations power is potentially a significant resource, but circumstances since the end of World War II have tended to reduce its effectiveness. The appropriations committees and Congress itself might make their will felt by refusing to allot funds unless basic policies were altered. But this has not happened. While Congress makes its traditional small cuts in the military budget, Presidents have mostly found themselves warding off congressional attempts to increase specific items still further.

Most of the time, the administration's refusal to spend has not been seriously challenged. However, there have been occasions when individual legislators or committees have been influential. Senator Henry Jackson in his campaign (with the aid of colleagues on the Joint Committee on Atomic Energy) was able to gain acceptance for the Polaris weapons system and Senator Arthur H. Vandenberg played a part in determining the shape of the Marshall Plan and so on. The few congressmen who are expert in defense policy act, as Samuel P. Huntington says, largely as lobbyists with the executive branch. It is apparently more fruitful for these congressional experts to use their resources in order to get a hearing from the executive than to work on other congressmen.

When an issue involves the actual use or threat of violence, it takes a great deal to convince congressmen not to follow the President's lead. James Robinson's tabulation of foreign and defense policy issues from the late 1930s to 1961 (Table 2) shows dominant influence by Congress in only one case out of seven—the 1954 decision not to intervene with armed force in Indochina. In that instance President Eisenhower deliberately sounded out congressional opinion and, finding it negative, decided not to intervene—against the advice of Admiral Radford, chairman of the Joint Chiefs of Staff. This attempt to abandon responsibility did not succeed, as the years of American involvement demonstrate.

THE MILITARY

The outstanding feature of the military's participation in making defense policy is their amazing weakness. Whether the policy decisions involve the size of the armed forces, the choice of weapons systems, the total defense budget, or its division into components, the military have not prevailed. Let us take budgetary decisions as representative of the key choices to be made in defense policy. Since the end of World War II the military has not been able to achieve significant (billion dollar) increases in appropriations by their own efforts. Under Truman and Eisenhower defense budgets were determined by what Huntington calls the remainder method: the two Presidents estimated revenues, decided what they could spend on domestic matters, and the remainder was assigned to defense. The usual controversy was between some military and congressional groups supporting much larger expenditures while the President and his executive allies refused. A typical case, involving the desire of the Air Force to increase the number of groups of planes is described by Huntington in *The Common Defense:*

> The FY [fiscal year] 1949 budget provided 48 groups. After the Czech coup, the Administration yielded and backed an Air Force of 55 groups in its spring rearmament program. Congress added additional funds to aid Air Force expansion to 70 groups. The Administration refused to utilize them, however, and in the gathering economy wave of the summer and fall of 1948, the Air Force goal was cut back again to 48 groups. In 1949 the House of Representatives picked up

Table 2 **Congressional Involvement in Foreign and Defense Policy Decisions**

Issue	Congressional Involvement (High, Low, None)	Initiator (Congress or Executive)	Predominant Influence (Congress or Executive)	Legislation or Resolution (Yes or No)	Violence at Stake (Yes or No)	Decision Time (Long or Short)
Neutrality legislation, the 1930s	High	Exec	Cong	Yes	No	Long
Lend-lease, 1941	High	Exec	Exec	Yes	Yes	Long
Aid to Russia, 1941	Low	Exec	Exec	No	No	Long
Repeal of Chinese exclusion, 1943	High	Cong	Cong	Yes	No	Long
Fulbright Resolution, 1943	High	Cong	Cong	Yes	No	Long
Building the atomic bomb, 1944	Low	Exec	Exec	Yes	Yes	Long
Foreign Services Act of 1946	High	Exec	Exec	Yes	No	Long
Truman Doctrine, 1947	High	Exec	Exec	Yes	No	Long
The Marshall Plan, 1947–48	High	Exec	Exec	Yes	No	Long
Berlin airlift, 1948	None	Exec	Exec	No	Yes	Long
Vandenberg Resolution, 1948	High	Exec	Cong	Yes	No	Long
North Atlantic Treaty, 1947–49	High	Exec	Exec	Yes	No	Long
Korean decision, 1950	None	Exec	Exec	No	Yes	Short
Japanese peace treaty, 1952	High	Exec	Exec	Yes	No	Long
Bohlen Nomination, 1953	High	Exec	Exec	Yes	No	Long
Indo-China, 1954	High	Exec	Cong	No	Yes	Short
Formosan Resolution, 1955	High	Exec	Exec	Yes	Yes	Long
International Finance Corporation, 1956	Low	Exec	Exec	Yes	No	Long
Foreign aid, 1957	High	Exec	Exec	Yes	No	Long
Reciprocal trade agreements, 1958	High	Exec	Exec	Yes	No	Long
Monroney Resolution, 1958	High	Cong	Cong	Yes	No	Long
Cuban decision, 1961	Low	Exec	Exec	No	Yes	Long

Source: James A. Robinson, *Congress and Foreign Policy-Making* (Homewood, Ill.: Dorsey Press, 1962).

the challenge and appropriated funds for 58 groups. The President impounded the money. In June, 1950, the Air Force had 48 groups.

The great increases in the defense budget were due far more to Stalin and modern technology than to the military. The Korean War resulted in an increase from $12 to 44 billion and much of the rest followed Sputnik and the huge costs of missile programs. Thus modern technology and international conflict put an end to the one major effort to subordinate foreign affairs to domestic policies through the budget.

It could be argued that the President merely ratifies the decisions made by the military and their allies. If the military and/or Congress were united and insistent on defense policy, it would certainly be difficult for Presidents to resist these forces. But it is precisely the disunity of the military that has characterized the entire postwar period. Indeed, the military have not been united on any major matter of defense policy. The apparent unity of the Joint Chiefs of Staff turns out to be illusory. The vast majority of their recommendations appear to be unanimous and are accepted by the Secretary of Defense and the President. But this facade of unity can only be achieved by methods that vitiate the impact of the recommendations. Genuine disagreements are hidden by vague language that commits no one to anything. Mutually contradictory plans are strung together so everyone appears to get something, but nothing is decided. Since it is impossible to agree on really important matters, all sorts of trivia are brought in to make a record of agreement. While it may be true, as Admiral Denfield, a former Chief of Naval Operations, said, that "On nine-tenths of the matters that come before them the joint Chiefs of Staff reach agreement themselves," the vastly more important truth is that "normally the *only* disputes are on strategic concepts, the size and composition of forces, and budget matters."

MILITARY-INDUSTRIAL

But what about the fabled military-industrial complex? If the military alone is divided and weak, perhaps the giant industrial firms that are so dependent on defense contracts play a large part in making policy.

First, there is an important distinction between the questions "Who will get a given contract?" and "What will our defense policy be?" It is apparent that different answers may be given to these quite different questions. There are literally tens of thousands of defense contractors. They may compete vigorously for business. In the course of this competition, they may wine and dine military officers, use retired generals, seek intervention by their congressmen, place ads in trade journals, and even contribute to political campaigns. The famous TFX controversy—should General Dynamics or Boeing get the expensive contract?—is a larger than life example of the pressure brought to bear in search of lucrative contracts.

But neither the TFX case nor the usual vigorous competition for contracts is involved with the making of substantive defense policy. Vital questions like the size of the defense budget, the choice of strategic programs, massive retaliation vs. a counter-city strategy, and the like were far beyond the policy aims of any company. Industrial firms, then, do not control such decisions, nor is there much evidence that they actually try. No doubt a precipitous and drastic rush to disarmament would meet with opposition from industrial firms among other interests. However, there has never been a time when any significant element in the government considered a disarmament policy to be feasible.

It may appear that industrial firms had no special reason to concern themselves with the government's stance on defense because they agree with the national consensus on resisting communism, maintaining a large defense establishment, and rejecting isolationism. However, this hypothesis about the climate of opinion explains everything and nothing. For every policy that is adopted or rejected can be explained away on the grounds that the cold war climate of opinion dictated what happened. Did the United States fail to intervene with armed force in Vietnam in 1954? That must be because the climate of opinion was against it. Did the United States send troops to Vietnam in the 1960s? That must be because the cold war climate demanded it. If the United States builds more missiles, negotiates a test-ban treaty, intervenes in the Dominican Republic, fails to intervene in a dozen other situations, all these actions fit the hypothesis by definition. The argument is reminiscent of those who defined the Soviet Union as permanently hostile and therefore interpreted increases of Soviet troops as menacing and decreases of troop strength as equally sinister.

If the growth of the military establishment is not directly equated with increasing military control of defense policy, the extraordinary weakness of the professional soldier still requires explanation. Huntington has written about how major military leaders were seduced in the Truman and Eisenhower years into believing that they should bow to the judgment of civilians that the economy could not stand much larger military expenditures. Once the size of the military pie was accepted as a fixed constraint, the military services were compelled to put their major energies into quarreling with one another over who should get the larger share. Given the natural rivalries of the military and their traditional acceptance of civilian rule, the President and his advisers—who could claim responsibility for the broader picture of reconciling defense and domestic policies—had the upper hand. There are, however, additional explanations to be considered.

The dominant role of the congressional appropriations committee is to be guardian of the treasury. This is manifested in the pride of its members in cutting the President's budget. Thus it was difficult to get this crucial committee to recommend even a few hundred million increase in defense; it was practically impossible to get them to consider the several billion jump that might really have made a difference. A related budgetary matter concerned the planning, programming, and budgetary system introduced by Secretary of Defense McNamara. For if the defense budget contained major categories that crisscrossed the services, only the Secretary of Defense could put it together. Whatever the other debatable consequences of program budgeting, its major consequence was to grant power to the secretary and his civilian advisers.

The subordination of the military through program budgeting is just one symptom of a more general weakness of the military. In the past decade the military has suffered a lack of intellectual skills appropriate to the nuclear age. For no one has (and no one wants) direct experience with nuclear war. So the usual military talk about being the only people to have combat experience is not very impressive. Instead, the imaginative creation of possible future wars—in order to avoid them—requires people with a high capacity for abstract thought combined with the ability to manipulate symbols using quantitative methods. West Point has not produced many such men.

THE STATE DEPARTMENT

Modern Presidents expect the State Department to carry out their policies. John F. Kennedy felt that State was "in some particular sense 'his' department." If a Secretary of State forgets this, as was apparently the case with James Byrnes under Truman, a President may find another man. But the State Department, especially the Foreign Service, is also a highly professional organization with a life and momentum of its own. If a President does not push hard, he may find his preferences somehow dissipated in time. Arthur Schlesinger fills his book on Kennedy with laments about the bureaucratic inertia and recalcitrance of the State Department.

Yet Schlesinger's own account suggests that State could not ordinarily resist the President. At one point, he writes of "the President, himself, increasingly the day-to-day director of American foreign policy." On the next page, we learn that "Kennedy dealt personally with almost every aspect of policy around the globe. He knew more about certain areas than the senior officials at State and probably called as many issues to their attention as they did to his." The President insisted on his way in Laos. He pushed through his policy on the Congo against strong opposition with the State Department. Had Kennedy wanted to get a great deal more initiative out of the State Department, as Schlesinger insists, he could have replaced the Secretary of State, a man who did not command special support in the Democratic party or in Congress. It may be that Kennedy wanted too strongly to run his own foreign policy. Dean Rusk may have known far better than Schlesinger that the one thing Kennedy did not want was a man who might rival him in the field of foreign affairs.

Schlesinger comes closest to the truth when he writes that "the White House could always win any battle it chose over the [Foreign] Service; but the prestige and proficiency of the Service limited the number of battles any White House would find it profitable to fight." When the President knew what he wanted, he got it. When he was doubtful and perplexed, he sought good advice and frequently did not get that. But there is no evidence that the people on his staff came up with better ideas. The real problem may have been a lack of good ideas anywhere. Kennedy undoubtedly encouraged his staff to prod the State Department. But the President was sufficiently cautious not to push so hard that he got his way when he was not certain what that way should be. In this context Kennedy appears to have played his staff off against elements in the State Department.

The growth of a special White House staff to help Presidents in foreign affairs expresses their need for assistance, their refusal to rely completely on the regular executive agencies, and their ability to find competent men. The deployment of this staff must remain a presidential prerogative, however, if its members are to serve Presidents and not their opponents. Whenever critics do not like existing foreign and defense policies, they are likely to complain that the White House staff is screening out divergent views from the President's attention. Naturally, the critics recommend introducing many more different viewpoints. If the critics could maneuver the President into counting hands all day ("on the one hand and on the other"), they would make it impossible for him to act. Such a viewpoint is also congenial to those who believe that action rather than inaction is the greatest present danger in foreign policy. But Presidents resolutely refuse to become prisoners of their advisers by using them as other people would like. Presidents remain in control of their staff as well as of major foreign policy decisions.

HOW COMPLETE IS THE CONTROL?

Some analysts say that the success of Presidents in controlling foreign policy decisions is largely illusory. It is achieved, they say, by anticipating the reactions of others, and eliminating proposals that would run into severe opposition. There is some truth in this objection. In politics, where transactions are based on a high degree of mutual interdependence, what others may do has to be taken into account. But basing presidential success in foreign and defense policy on anticipated reactions suggests a static situation which does not exist. For if Presidents propose only those policies that would get support in Congress, and Congress opposes them only when it knows that it can muster overwhelming strength, there would never be any conflict. Indeed, there might never be any action.

How can "anticipated reaction" explain the conflict over policies like the Marshall Plan and the test-ban treaty in which severe opposition was overcome only by strenuous efforts? Furthermore, why doesn't "anticipated reaction" work in domestic affairs? One would have to argue that for some reason presidential perception of what would be successful is consistently confused on domestic issues and most always accurate on major foreign policy issues. But the role of "anticipated reactions" should be greater in the more familiar domestic situations, which provide a backlog of experience for forecasting, than in foreign policy with many novel situations such as the Suez crisis or the Rhodesian affair.

Are there significant historical examples which might refute the thesis of presidential control of foreign policy? Foreign aid may be a case in point. For many years, Presidents have struggled to get foreign aid appropriations because of hostility from public and congressional opinion. Yet several billion dollars a year are appropriated regularly despite the evident unpopularity of the program. In the aid programs to Communist countries like Poland and Yugoslavia, the Congress attaches all sorts of restrictions to the aid, but Presidents find ways of getting around them.

What about the example of recognition of Communist China? The sentiment of the country always has been against recognizing Red China or admitting it to the United Nations. But have Presidents wanted to recognize Red China and been hamstrung by opposition? The answer, I suggest, is a qualified "no." By the time recognition of Red China might have become a serious issue for the Truman administration, the war in Korea effectively precluded its consideration. There is no evidence that President Eisenhower or Secretary Dulles ever thought it wise to recognize Red China or help admit her to the United Nations. The Kennedy administration viewed the matter as not of major importance and, considering the opposition, moved cautiously in suggesting change. Then came the war in Vietnam. If the advantages for foreign policy had been perceived to be much higher, then Kennedy or Johnson might have proposed changing American policy toward recognition of Red China.

One possible exception, in the case of Red China, however, does not seem sufficient to invalidate the general thesis that Presidents do considerably better in getting their way in foreign and defense policy than in domestic policies.

THE WORLD INFLUENCE

The forces impelling Presidents to be concerned with the widest range of foreign and defense policies also affect the ways in which they calculate their power stakes. As Kennedy used to say, "Domestic policy . . . can only defeat us; foreign policy can kill us."

It no longer makes sense for Presidents to "play politics" with foreign and defense policies. In the past, Presidents might have thought that they could gain by prolonged delay or by not acting at all. The problem might disappear or be passed on to their successors. Presidents must now expect to pay the high costs themselves if the world situation deteriorates. The advantages of pursuing a policy that is viable in the world, that will not blow up on Presidents or their fellow citizens, far outweigh any temporary political disadvantages accrued in supporting an initially unpopular policy. Compared with domestic affairs, Presidents engaged in world politics are immensely more concerned with meeting problems on their own terms. Who supports and opposes a policy, though a matter of considerable interest, does not assume the crucial importance that it does in domestic affairs. The best policy Presidents can find is also the best politics.

The fact that there are numerous foreign and defense policy situations competing for a President's attention means that it is worthwhile to organize political activity in order to effect his agenda. For if a President pays more attention to certain problems he may develop different preferences; he may seek and receive different advice; his new calculations may lead him to devote greater resources to seeking a solution. Interested congressmen may exert influence not by directly determining a presidential decision, but indirectly by making it costly for a President to avoid reconsidering the basis for his action. For example, citizen groups, such as those concerned with a change in China policy, may have an impact simply by keeping their proposals on the public agenda. A President may be compelled to reconsider a problem even though he could not overtly be forced to alter the prevailing policy.

In foreign affairs we may be approaching the stage where knowledge is power. There is a tremendous receptivity to good ideas in Washington. Most anyone who can present a convincing rationale for dealing with a hard world finds a ready audience. The best way to convince Presidents to follow a desired policy is to show that it might work. A man like McNamara thrives because he performs; he comes up with answers he can defend. It is, to be sure, extremely difficult to devise good policies or to predict their consequences accurately. Nor is it easy to convince others that a given policy is superior to other alternatives. But it is the way to influence with Presidents. For if they are convinced that the current policy is best, the likelihood of gaining sufficient force to compel a change is quite small. The man who can build better foreign policies will find Presidents beating a path to his door.

UNITED STATES V. NIXON

61. EXECUTIVE PRIVILEGE

As is true of most major questions in American government, the Supreme Court was finally forced to enter the debate over presidential power when President Richard M. Nixon claimed that presidents have an absolute executive privilege—that they could determine for themselves what information they would release to

Source: U.S. Supreme Court, *United States v. Nixon* (1974).

the courts. At issue were tapes secretly made in the White House that had been subpoenaed for use in the Watergate scandal criminal prosecution. In United States v. Nixon *the Supreme Court unanimously disagreed with President Nixon, stating that "neither the separation of powers, nor the need for confidentiality of high-level communications, without more, can sustain an absolute, unqualified, presidential immunity from judicial process under all circumstances." This decision literally forced the resignation of Nixon a few days later—because the tapes were so incriminating that Nixon's impeachment by the House and conviction by the Senate seemed certain with their release.*

Chief Justice BURGER delivers the opinion of the Court.

[W]e turn to the claim that the subpoena should be quashed because it demands "confidential conversations between a President and his close advisors that it would be inconsistent with the public interest to produce." The first contention is a broad claim that the separation of powers doctrine precludes judicial review of a President's claim of privilege. The second contention is that if he does not prevail on the claim of absolute privilege, the court should hold as a matter of constitutional law that the privilege prevails over the subpoena *duces tecum.*

In the performance of assigned constitutional duties each branch of the Government must initially interpret the Constitution, and the interpretation of its powers by any branch is due great respect from the others. The President's counsel, as we have noted, reads the Constitution as providing an absolute privilege of confidentiality for all Presidential communications. Many decisions of this Court, however, have unequivocally reaffirmed the holding of *Marbury v. Madison,* [1 Cr. 137 (1803)], that "[i]t is emphatically the province and duty of the judicial department to say what the law is."

Our system of government "requires that federal courts on occasion interpret the Constitution in a manner at variance with the construction given the document by another branch." *Powell v. McCormack,* [395 U.S. 486 (1969)]. And in *Baker v. Carr,* [369 U.S. 186 (1962)], the Court stated:

> "[D]eciding whether a matter has in any measure been committed by the Constitution to another branch of government, or whether the action of that branch exceeds whatever authority has been committed, is itself a delicate exercise in constitutional interpretation, and is a responsibility of this Court as ultimate interpreter of the Constitution."

Notwithstanding the deference each branch must accord the others, the "judicial Power of the United States" vested in the federal courts by Art. III, §1, of the

Constitution can no more be shared with the Executive Branch than the Chief Executive, for example, can share with the Judiciary the veto power, or the Congress share with the Judiciary the power to override a Presidential veto. Any other conclusion would be contrary to the basic concept of separation of powers and the checks and balances that flow from the scheme of a tripartite government. We therefore reaffirm that it is the province and duty of this Court "to say what the law is" with respect to the claim of privilege presented in this case. *Marbury v. Madison.* . . .

In support of his claim of absolute privilege, the President's counsel urges two grounds, one of which is common to all governments and one of which is peculiar to our system of separation of powers. The first ground is the valid need for protection of communications between high Government officials and those who advise and assist them in the performance of their manifold duties: the importance of this confidentiality is too plain to require further discussion. Human experience teaches that those who expect public dissemination of their remarks may well temper candor with a concern for appearances and for their own interests to the detriment of the decisionmaking process. Whatever the nature of the privilege of confidentiality of Presidential communications in the exercise of Art. II powers, the privilege can be said to derive from the supremacy of each branch within its own assigned area of constitutional duties. Certain powers and privileges flow from the nature of enumerated powers; the protection of the confidentiality of Presidential communications has similar constitutional underpinnings.

The second ground asserted by the President's counsel in support of the claim of absolute privilege rests on the doctrine of separation of powers. Here it is argued that the independence of the Executive Branch within its own sphere, *Humphrey's Executor v. United States,* 295 U.S. 602 (1935); *Kilbourn v. Thompson,* 103 U.S. 168 (1881), insulates a President from a judicial subpoena in an ongoing criminal prosecution, and thereby protects confidential Presidential communications.

However, neither the doctrine of separation of powers, nor the need for confidentiality of high-level communications, without more, can sustain an absolute, unqualified Presidential privilege of immunity from judicial process under all circumstances. The President's need for complete candor and objectivity from advisers calls for great deference from the courts. However, when the privilege depends solely on the broad, undifferentiated claim of public interest in the confidentiality of such conversations, a confrontation with other values arises. Absent a claim of need to protect military, diplomatic, or sensitive national security secrets, we find it difficult to accept the argument that even the very important interest in confidentiality of Presidential communications is significantly diminished by production of such material for *in camera* inspection with all the protection that a district court will be obliged to provide.

The impediment that an absolute, unqualified privilege would place in the way of the primary constitutional duty of the Judicial Branch to do justice in criminal prosecutions would plainly conflict with the function of the courts under Art. III. In designing the structure of our Government and dividing and allocating the sovereign power among three co-equal branches, the Framers of the Constitution sought to provide a comprehensive system, but the separate powers were not intended to operate with absolute independence. . . .

To read the Art. II powers of the President as providing an absolute privilege as against a subpoena essential to enforcement of criminal statutes on no more than a generalized claim of the public interest in confidentiality of nonmilitary and nondiplomatic discussions would upset the constitutional balance of "a workable government" and gravely impair the role of the courts under Art. III.

Since we conclude that the legitimate needs of the judicial process may outweigh Presidential privilege, it is necessary to resolve those competing interests in a manner that preserves the essential functions of each branch. The right and indeed the duty to resolve that question does not free the Judiciary from according high respect to the representations made on behalf of the President. *United States v. Burr,* [4 Cr. (8 U.S.) 470 (1807)].

The expectation of a President to the confidentiality of his conversations and correspondence, like the claim of confidentiality of judicial deliberations, for example, has all the values to which we accord deference for the privacy of all citizens and, added to those values, is the necessity for protection of the public interest in candid, objective, and even blunt or harsh opinions in Presidential decisionmaking. A President and those who assist him must be free to explore alternatives in the process of shaping policies and making decisions and to do so in a way many would be unwilling to express except privately. These are the considerations justifying a presumptive privilege for Presidential communications. The privilege is fundamental to the operation of Government and inextricably rooted in the separation of powers under the Constitution. In *Nixon v. Sirica,* 159 U.S. App. D.C. 58 (1973), the Court of Appeals held that such Presidential communications are "presumptively privileged" and this position is accepted by both parties in the present litigation. We agree with Chief Justice MARSHALL's observation, therefore, that "[i]n no case of this kind would a court be required to proceed against the president as against an ordinary individual." *United States v. Burr. . . .*

But this presumptive privilege must be considered in light of our historic commitment to the rule of law. This is nowhere more profoundly manifest than in our view that "the twofold aim [of criminal justice] is that guilt shall not escape or innocence suffer." *Berger v. United States* [295 U.S. 78 (1935)]. We have elected to employ an adversary system of criminal justice in which the parties contest all issues before a court of law. The need to develop all relevant facts in the adversary system is both fundamental and comprehensive. The ends of criminal justice would be defeated if judgments were to be founded on a partial or speculative presentation of the facts. The very integrity of the judicial system and public confidence in the system depend on full disclosure of all the facts, within the framework of the rules of evidence. To ensure that justice is done, it is imperative to the function of courts that compulsory process be available for the production of evidence needed either by the prosecution or by the defense.

Only recently the Court restated the ancient proposition of law, albeit in the context of a grand jury inquiry rather than a trial.

> "that 'the public . . . has a right to every man's evidence,' except for those persons protected by a constitutional, common-law, or statutory privilege. . . . "

The privileges referred to by the Court are designed to protect weighty and legitimate competing interests. Thus, the Fifth Amendment to the Constitution provides that no man "shall be compelled in any criminal case to be a witness against himself." And, generally, an attorney or a priest may not be required to disclose what has been revealed in professional confidence. These and other interests are recognized in law by privileges against forced disclosure, established in the Constitution, by statute, or at common law. Whatever their origins, these exceptions to the demand for every man's evidence are not lightly created nor expansively construed, for they are in derogation of the search for truth.

In this case the President challenges a subpoena served on him as a third party requiring the production of materials for use in a criminal prosecution on the claim that he has a privilege against disclosure of confidential communications. He does not place his claim of privilege on the ground they are military or diplomatic secrets. As to these areas of Art. II duties the courts have traditionally shown the utmost deference to presidential responsibilities. No case of the Court, however, has extended this high degree of deference to a President's generalized interest in confidentiality. Nowhere in the Constitution, as we have noted earlier, is there any explicit reference to a privilege of confidentiality, yet to the extent this interest relates to the effective discharge of a President's powers, it is constitutionally based. . . .

In this case we must weigh the importance of the general privilege of confidentiality of presidential communications in performance of his responsibilities against the inroads of such a privilege on the fair administration of criminal justice. The interest in preserving confidentiality is weighty indeed and entitled to great respect. However we cannot conclude that advisers will be moved to temper the candor of their remarks by the infrequent occasions of disclosure because of the possibility that such conversations will be called for in the context of a criminal prosecution.

On the other hand, the allowance of the privilege to withhold evidence that is demonstrably relevant in a criminal trial could cut deeply into the guarantee of the process of law and gravely impair the basic function of the courts. A President's acknowledged need for confidentiality in the communications of his office is general in nature, whereas the constitutional need for production of relevant evidence in a criminal proceeding is specific and central to the fair adjudication of a particular criminal case in the administration of justice. Without access to specific facts a criminal prosecution may be totally frustrated. The President's broad interest in confidentiality of communications will not be violated by disclosure of a limited number of conversations preliminarily shown to have some bearing on the pending criminal cases.

We conclude that when the ground for asserting privilege as to subpoenaed materials sought for use in a criminal trial is based only on the generalized interest in confidentiality, it cannot prevail over the fundamental demands of due process of law in the fair administration of criminal justice. The generalized assertion of privilege must yield to the demonstrated, specific need for evidence in a pending criminal trial. We have earlier determined that the District Court did not err in authorizing the issuance of the subpoena. If a president concludes that compliance with a subpoena would be injurious to the public interest he may properly, as was done here, invoke a claim of privilege on the return of the subpoena. Upon receiving a claim of privilege from the Chief Executive, it became the further duty of the District Court to treat the subpoenaed material as presumptively privileged and to require the Special Prosecutor to demonstrate that the presidential material was "essential to the justice of the [pending criminal] case." *United States v. Burr.* Here the District Court treated the material as presumptively privileged, proceeded to find that the Special Prosecutor had made a sufficient showing to rebut the presumption and ordered an *in camera* examination of the subpoenaed material. On the basis of our examination of the record we are unable to conclude that the District Court erred in ordering the inspection. Accordingly we affirm the order of the District Court that subpoenaed materials be transmitted to that court. We now turn to the important question of the District Court's responsibilities in conducting the *in camera* examination of presidential materials or communications delivered under the compulsion of the subpoena *duces tecum.*

It is elementary that *in camera* inspection of evidence is always a procedure calling for scrupulous protection against any release or publication of material not found by the court, at that stage, probably admissable in evidence and relevant to the issues of the trial for which it is sought. That being true of an ordinary situation, it is obvious that the District Court has a very heavy responsibility to see to it that Presidential conversations, which are either not relevant or not admissible, are accorded that high degree of respect due the President of the United States. Chief Justice MARSHALL, sitting as a trial judge in the *Burr* case was extraordinarily careful to point out that

> "[i]n no case of this kind would a court be required to proceed against the president as against an ordinary individual." . . .

MARSHALL's statement cannot be read to mean in any sense that a President is above the law, but relates to the singularly unique role under Art. II of a President's communications and activities related to the performance of duties under that Article. Moreover, a President's communications and activities encompass a vastly wider range of sensitive material than would be true of any "ordinary individual." It is therefore necessary in the public interest to afford Presidential confidentiality the greatest protection consistent with the fair administration of justice. The need for confidentiality even as to idle conversations with associates in which casual reference might be made concerning political leaders within the country or foreign statesmen is too obvious to call for further treatment. We have no doubt that the District Judge will at all times accord to Presidential records that high degree of deference suggested in *United States v. Burr, supra* and will discharge his responsibility to see to it that until released to the Special Prosecutor no *in camera* material is revealed to anyone. This burden applies with even greater force to excised material; once the decision is made to excise, the material is restored to its privileged status and should be returned under seal to its lawful custodians.

Since this matter came before the Court during the pendency of a criminal prosecution, and on representations that time is of the essence, the mandate shall issue forthwith.

Affirmed.

WILLIAM JEFFERSON CLINTON
V. PAULA CORBIN JONES

62. SUING THE PRESIDENT

In what could turn out to be one of the most important modern Supreme Court decisions about the presidency, the U.S. Supreme Court ruled in 1998 that a sitting president could be sued by a private citizen seeking money damages in a civil suit for conduct alleged to have occurred before the president took office. President Clinton urged the Court to delay the suit until he left office, claiming that the chief executive should not be burdened and distracted by having to defend against civil suits except in exceptional circumstances. The sexual harassment claim brought by Paula Jones, based on Clinton's alleged conduct while serving as governor of Arkansas years earlier would not, he argued, be such a suit.

Writing for the majority, Justice John Paul Stevens rejected Clinton's argument and concluded that it would be highly unlikely that allowing the Jones case to proceed would generate a flood of other suits against this or other presidents and, in any event, Stevens noted, the lower court judge could always defer such a case where

Source: U.S. Supreme Court, *William Jefferson Clinton v. Paula Corbin Jones* (1997).

it appears that to proceed would hamper a president's ability to do his job. What neither the members of the Court nor the public knew at the time was that President Clinton's testimony about Monica Lewinsky in a sworn deposition in the Jones case would set off a political firestorm powerful enough to threaten Clinton's presidency. Whether the Supreme Court's decision to permit civil actions against sitting presidents will result in future political and legal battles for presidents cannot be known. It is possible that the very nature of the presidency and the ever-present existence of powerful and well-funded political opponents anxious to "trap" presidents in sworn statements in civil suits were underestimated by the Court.

This case raises a constitutional and a prudential question concerning the Office of the President of the United States. Respondent, a private citizen, seeks to recover damages from the current occupant of that office based on actions allegedly taken before his term began. The President submits that in all but the most exceptional cases the Constitution requires federal courts to defer such litigation until his term ends and that, in any event, respect for the office warrants such a stay. Despite the force of the arguments supporting the President's submissions, we conclude that they must be rejected.

Petitioner, William Jefferson Clinton, was elected to the Presidency in 1992, and re-elected in 1996. His term of office expires on January 20, 2001. In 1991 he was the Governor of the State of Arkansas. Respondent, Paula Corbin Jones, is a resident of California. In 1991 she lived in Arkansas, and was an employee of the Arkansas Industrial Development Commission.

On May 6, 1994, she commenced this action in the United States District Court for the Eastern District of Arkansas by filing a complaint naming petitioner and Danny Ferguson, a former Arkansas State Police officer, as defendants. The complaint alleges two federal claims, and two state law claims over which the federal court has jurisdiction because of the diverse citizenship of the parties. As the case comes to us, we are required to assume the truth of the detailed—but as yet untested—factual allegations in the complaint.

Those allegations principally describe events that are said to have occurred on the afternoon of May 8, 1991, during an official conference held at the Excelsior Hotel in Little Rock, Arkansas. The Governor delivered a speech at the conference; respondent—working as a state employee—staffed the registration desk. She alleges that Ferguson persuaded her to leave her desk and to visit the Governor in a business suite at the hotel, where he made "abhorrent" sexual advances that she vehemently rejected. She further claims that her superiors at work subsequently dealt with her in a hostile and rude manner, and changed her duties to punish her for rejecting those advances. Finally, she alleges that after petitioner was elected President, Ferguson defamed her by making a statement to a reporter that implied she had accepted petitioner's alleged overtures, and that various persons authorized to speak for the President publicly branded her a liar by denying that the incident had occurred. . . .

The District Judge denied the motion to dismiss on immunity grounds and ruled that discovery in the case could go forward, but ordered any trial stayed until the end of petitioner's Presidency. Although she recognized that a "thin majority" in *Nixon v. Fitzgerald,* had held that "the President has absolute immunity from civil damage actions arising out of the execution of official duties of office," she was not convinced that "a President has absolute immunity from civil causes of action arising prior to assuming the office." She was, however, persuaded by some of the reasoning in our opinion in *Fitzgerald* that deferring the trial if one were required would be appropriate. Relying in part on the fact that respondent had failed to bring her complaint until two days before the 3 year period of limitations expired, she concluded that the public interest in avoiding litigation that might hamper the President in conducting the duties of his office outweighed any demonstrated need for an immediate trial.

Both parties appealed. A divided panel of the Court of Appeals affirmed the denial of the motion to dismiss, but because it regarded the order postponing the trial until the President leaves office as the "functional equivalent" of a grant of temporary immunity, it reversed that order. Writing for the majority, Judge Bowman explained that "the President, like all other government officials, is subject to the same laws that apply to all other members of our society," that he could find no "case in which any public official ever has been granted any immunity from suit for his unofficial acts," and that the rationale for official immunity "is inapposite where only personal, private conduct by a President is at issue." The majority specifically rejected the argument that, unless immunity is available, the threat of judicial interference with the Executive Branch through scheduling orders, potential contempt citations, and sanctions would violate separation of powers principles. Judge Bowman suggested that "judicial case management sensitive to the burdens of the presidency and the demands of the President's schedule," would avoid the perceived danger. . . .

The President, represented by private counsel, filed a petition for certiorari. The Solicitor General, representing the United States, supported the petition, arguing that the decision of the Court of Appeals was "fundamentally mistaken" and created "serious risks for the institution of the Presidency." In her brief in opposition to certiorari, respondent argued that this "one of a kind case is singularly inappropriate" for the exercise of our certiorari jurisdiction because it did not create any conflict among the Courts of Appeals, it "does not pose any conceivable threat to the functioning of the Executive Branch," and there is no precedent supporting the President's position. . . .

Petitioner's principal submission—that "in all but the most exceptional cases," the Constitution affords the President temporary immunity from civil damages litigation arising out of events that occurred before he took office—cannot be sustained on the basis of precedent.

Only three sitting Presidents have been defendants in civil litigation involving their actions prior to taking office. Complaints against Theodore Roosevelt and Harry Truman had been dismissed before they took office; the dismissals were affirmed after their respective inaugurations. Two companion cases arising out of an automobile accident were filed against John F. Kennedy in 1960 during the Presidential campaign. After taking office, he unsuccessfully argued that his status as Commander in Chief gave him a right to stay under the Soldiers' and Sailors' Civil Relief Act of 1940. The motion for a stay was denied by the District Court, and the matter was settled out of court. Thus, none of those cases sheds any light on the constitutional issue before us.

The principal rationale for affording certain public servants immunity from suits for money damages arising out of their official acts is inapplicable to unofficial conduct. In cases involving prosecutors, legislators, and judges we have repeatedly explained that the immunity serves the public interest in enabling such officials to perform their designated functions effectively without fear that a particular decision may give rise to personal liability. We explained in *Ferri v. Ackerman:*

> As public servants, the prosecutor and the judge represent the interest of society as a whole. The conduct of their official duties may adversely affect a wide variety of different individuals, each of whom may be a potential source of future controversy. The societal interest in providing such public officials with the maximum ability to deal fearlessly and impartially with the public at large has long been recognized as an acceptable justification for official immunity. The point of immunity for such officials is to forestall an atmosphere of intimidation that would conflict with their resolve to perform their designated functions in a principled fashion.

That rationale provided the principal basis for our holding that a former President of the United States was "entitled to absolute immunity from damages liability predicated on his official acts." Our central concern was to avoid rendering the President "unduly cautious in the discharge of his official duties."

This reasoning provides no support for an immunity for *unofficial* conduct. As we explained in *Fitzgerald,* "the sphere of protected action must be related closely to the immunity's justifying purposes." Because of the President's broad responsibilities, we recognized in that case an immunity from damages claims arising out of official acts extending to the "outer perimeter of his authority." But we have never suggested that the President, or any other official, has an immunity that extends beyond the scope of any action taken in an official capacity. . . .

Petitioner's strongest argument supporting his immunity claim is based on the text and structure of the Constitution. He does not contend that the occupant of the Office of the President is "above the law," in the sense that his conduct is entirely immune from judicial scrutiny. The President argues merely for a postponement of the judicial proceedings that will determine whether he violated any law. His argument is grounded in the character of the office that was created by Article II of the Constitution, and relies on separation of powers principles that have structured our constitutional arrangement since the founding.

As a starting premise, petitioner contends that he occupies a unique office with powers and responsibilities so vast and important that the public interest demands that he devote his undivided time and attention to his public duties. He submits that—given the nature of the office—the doctrine of separation of powers places limits on the authority of the Federal Judiciary to interfere with the Executive Branch that would be transgressed by allowing this action to proceed.

We have no dispute with the initial premise of the argument. Former presidents, from George Washington to George Bush, have consistently endorsed petitioner's characterization of the office. After serving his term, Lyndon Johnson observed: "Of all the 1,886 nights I was President, there were not many when I got to sleep before 1 or 2 A.M., and there were few mornings when I didn't wake up by 6 or 6:30." In 1967, the Twenty-fifth Amendment to the Constitution was adopted to ensure continuity in the performance of the powers and duties of the office; one of the sponsors of that Amendment stressed that importance of providing that "at all times" there be a President "who has complete control and will be able to perform" those duties. As Justice Jackson has pointed out, the Presidency concentrates executive authority "in a single head in whose choice the whole Nation has a part, making him the focus of public hopes and expectations. In drama, magnitude and finality his decisions so far overshadow any others that almost alone he fills the public eye and ear." We have, in short, long recognized the "unique position in the constitutional scheme" that this office occupies. . . .

It does not follow, however, that separation of powers principles would be violated by allowing this action to proceed. The doctrine of separation of powers is concerned with the allocation of official power among the three coequal branches of our Government. The Framers "built into the tripartite Federal Government . . . a self executing safeguard against the encroachment or aggrandizement of one branch at the expense of the other." . . .

Of course the lines between the powers of the three branches are not always neatly defined. But in this case there is no suggestion that the Federal Judiciary is being asked to perform any function that might in some way be described as "executive." Respondent is merely asking the courts to exercise their core Article III jurisdiction to decide cases and controversies. Whatever the outcome of this case, there is no possibility that the decision will curtail the scope of the official powers of the Executive Branch. The litigation of questions that relate entirely to the unofficial conduct of the individual who happens to be the President poses no perceptible risk of misallocation of either judicial power or executive power.

Rather than arguing that the decision of the case will produce either an aggrandizement of judicial power or a narrowing of executive power, petitioner contends that—as a by-product of an otherwise traditional exercise of judicial power—burdens will be placed on the President that will hamper the performance of his official duties. We have recognized that "[e]ven when a branch does not arrogate power to itself . . . the separation of powers doctrine requires that a branch not impair another in the performance of its constitutional duties." As a factual matter, petitioner contends that this particular case—as well as the potential additional litigation that an affirmance of the Court of Appeals judgment might spawn—may impose an unacceptable burden on the President's time and energy, and thereby impair the effective performance of his office.

Petitioner's predictive judgment finds little support in either history or the relatively narrow compass of the issues raised in this particular case. As we have already noted, in the more than 200 year history of the Republic, only three sitting Presidents have been subjected to suits for their private actions. If the past is any indicator, it seems unlikely that a deluge of such litigation will ever engulf the Presidency. As for the case at hand, if properly managed by the District Court, it appears to us highly unlikely to occupy any substantial amount of petitioner's time.

Of greater significance, petitioner errs by presuming that interactions between the Judicial Branch and the Executive, even quite burdensome interactions, necessarily rise to the level of constitutionally forbidden impairment of the Executive's ability to perform its constitutionally mandated functions. "[O]ur . . . system imposes upon the Branches a degree of overlapping responsibility, a duty of interdependence as well as independence the absence of which 'would preclude the establishment of a Nation capable of governing itself effectively.'" As Madison explained, separation of powers does not mean that the branches "ought to have no *partial agency* in, or no *controul* over the acts of each other." The fact that a federal court's exercise of its traditional Article III jurisdiction may significantly burden the time and attention of the Chief Executive is not sufficient to establish a violation of the Constitution. Two long settled propositions, first announced by Chief Justice Marshall, support that conclusion.

First, we have long held that when the President takes official action, the Court has the authority to determine whether he has acted within the law. . . .

Second, it is also settled that the President is subject to judicial process in appropriate circumstances. . . .

In sum, "[i]t is settled law that the separation of powers doctrine does not bar every exercise of jurisdiction over the President of the United States." If the Judiciary may severely burden the Executive Branch by reviewing the legality of the President's official conduct, and if it may direct appropriate process to the President himself, it must follow that the federal courts have power to determine the legality of his unofficial conduct. The burden on the President's time and energy that is a mere by-product of such review surely cannot be considered as onerous as the direct burden imposed by judicial review and the occasional invalidation of his official actions. We therefore hold that the doctrine of separation of powers does not require federal courts to stay all private actions against the President until he leaves office.

The reasons for rejecting such a categorical rule apply as well to a rule that would require a stay "in all but the most exceptional cases." Indeed, if the

Framers of the Constitution had thought it necessary to protect the President from the burdens of private litigation, we think it far more likely that they would have adopted a categorical rule than a rule that required the President to litigate the question whether a specific case belonged in the "exceptional case" subcategory. In all events, the question whether a specific case should receive exceptional treatment is more appropriately the subject of the exercise of judicial discretion than an interpretation of the Constitution. Accordingly, we turn to the question whether the District Court's decision to stay the trial until after petitioner leaves office was an abuse of discretion.

The Court of Appeals described the District Court's discretionary decision to stay the trial as the "functional equivalent" of a grant of temporary immunity. Concluding that petitioner was not constitutionally entitled to such an immunity, the court held that it was error to grant the stay. Although we ultimately conclude that the stay should not have been granted, we think the issue is more difficult than the opinion of the Court of Appeals suggests. . . .

The decision to postpone the trial was . . . premature. The proponent of a stay bears the burden of establishing its need. In this case, at the stage at which the District Court made its ruling, there was no way to assess whether a stay of trial after the completion of discovery would be warranted. Other than the fact that a trial may consume some of the President's time and attention, there is nothing in the record to enable a judge to assess the potential harm that may ensue from scheduling the trial promptly after discovery is concluded. We think the District Court may have given undue weight to the concern that a trial might generate unrelated civil actions that could conceivably hamper the President in conducting the duties of his office. If and when that should occur, the court's discretion would permit it to manage those actions in such fashion (including deferral of trial) that interference with the President's duties would not occur. But no such impingement upon the President's conduct of his office was shown here.

We add a final comment on two matters that are discussed at length in the briefs: the risk that our decision will generate a large volume of politically motivated harassing and frivolous litigation, and the danger that national security concerns might prevent the President from explaining a legitimate need for a continuance.

We are not persuaded that either of these risks is serious. Most frivolous and vexatious litigation is terminated at the pleading stage or on summary judgment, with little if any personal involvement by the defendant. Moreover, the availability of sanctions provides a significant deterrent to litigation directed at the President in his unofficial capacity for purposes of political gain or harassment. History indicates that the likelihood that a significant number of such cases will be filed is remote. Although scheduling problems may arise, there is no reason to assume that the District Courts will be either unable to accommodate the President's needs or unfaithful to the tradition—especially in matters involving national security—of giving "the utmost deference to Presidential responsibilities." Several Presidents, including petitioner, have given testimony without jeopardizing the Nation's security. In short, we have confidence in the ability of our federal judges to deal with both of these concerns.

If Congress deems it appropriate to afford the President stronger protection, it may respond with appropriate legislation. As petitioner notes in his brief, Congress has enacted more than one statute providing for the deferral of civil litigation to accommodate important public interests. If the Constitution embodied the rule that the President advocates, Congress, of course, could not repeal it. But our holding today raises no barrier to a statutory response to these concerns.

The Federal District Court has jurisdiction to decide this case. Like every other citizen who properly invokes that jurisdiction, respondent has a right to an orderly disposition of her claims. Accordingly, the judgment of the Court of Appeals is affirmed.

It is so ordered.

Section XI
Review Questions

1. According to Alexander Hamilton, what are the major limitations on the powers of the president that distinguish the office from that of the British monarch? Do you think Hamilton would be surprised at how the power of the presidency has grown? Would he approve?

2. Summarize how Presidents Abraham Lincoln, Theodore Roosevelt, and William Howard Taft defined the role of the president. Which is closest to Hamilton's vision of the office? In your view, how should the office of president evolve to best serve the interests of the United States in the twenty-first century?

3. If Richard Neustadt is correct, then the power of the presidency derives from the president's ability to persuade the public and the Congress to go along with him. What are some of the resources available to help a president be persuasive? What are some of the limits on this ability? Can you apply your analysis to the efforts of President Bill Clinton to resist impeachment in the wake of the report of Special Prosecutor Kenneth Starr?

4. To what extent do you believe Aaron Wildavsky's theory of the "two presidencies" has held up since it was first published in 1966? Can you think of any reasons to anticipate that the president's power in domestic affairs might grow or his power in foreign affairs might decline?

5. What is the rationale for permitting a chief executive to invoke the principle of executive privilege? How did the Supreme Court's decision in *United States v. Nixon* limit executive privilege?

6. In retrospect, did the Supreme Court's decision in *Clinton v. Jones* set a dangerous precedent? What harm would there have been in requiring Paula Jones to wait until Mr. Clinton left office before having her "day in court"? What harm did the Court see in making her wait?

XII

The Supreme Court

ALEXANDER HAMILTON

63. DEFENDING THE JUDICIARY

In The Federalist, *No. 78, Alexander Hamilton argued that inasmuch as the newly designed judicial branch of government controlled neither the purse strings nor the military, there was no reason to fear its powers. He assured skeptics that the newly proposed judicial branch of government would be the "least dangerous to the political rights of the Constitution" and would not even be able to enforce its judgments without the assistance of the executive branch.*

Hamilton's persuasive defense of the judiciary provided the theoretical basis for the doctrine of judicial review later announced by the Supreme Court in Marbury v. Madison *(1803). As stated in No. 78, the basic principle was that the Constitution should be seen as "fundamental law" and that the role of the courts was to "ascertain its meaning, as well as the meaning of any particular act proceeding from the legislative body."*

Although it took the words of Chief Justice John Marshall in Marbury *to give legal effect to this idea, it was Hamilton who first clearly stated the view that the Constitution as interpreted by the Supreme Court should prevail over any legislative enactment.*

To the People of the State of New York:

We proceed now to an examination of the judiciary department of the proposed government.

In unfolding the defects of the existing Confederation, the utility and necessity of a federal judicature have been clearly pointed out. It is the less necessary to recapitulate the considerations there urged, as the propriety of the institution in the abstract is not disputed; the only questions which have been raised being relative to the manner of constituting it, and to its extent. To these points, therefore, our observations shall be confined.

The manner of constituting it seems to embrace these several objects: 1st. The mode of appointing the judges. 2d. The tenure by which they are to hold their places. 3d. The partition of the judiciary authority between different courts, and their relations to each other.

Source: From *The Federalist,* No. 78 (1788).

First. As to the mode of appointing the judges; this is the same with that of appointing the officers of the Union in general, and has been so fully discussed in the two last numbers, that nothing can be said here which would not be useless repetition.

Second. As to the tenure by which the judges are to hold their places: this chiefly concerns their duration in office; the provisions for their support; the precautions for their responsibility.

According to the plan of the convention, all judges who may be appointed by the United States are to hold their offices *during good behavior;* which is conformable to the most approved of the State constitutions, and among the rest, to that of this State. Its propriety having been drawn into question by the adversaries of that plan, is no light symptom of the rage for objection, which disorders their imaginations and judgments. The standard of good behavior for the continuance in office of the judicial magistracy, is certainly one of the most valuable of the modern improvements in the practice of government. In a monarchy it is an excellent barrier to the despotism of the prince; in a republic it is a no less excellent barrier to the encroachments and oppressions of the representative body. And it is the best expedient which can be devised in any government, to secure a steady, upright, and impartial administration of the laws.

Whoever attentively considers the different departments of power must perceive, that, in a government in which they are separated from each other, the judiciary, from the nature of its functions, will always be the least dangerous to the political rights of the Constitution; because it will be least in a capacity to annoy or injure them. The Executive not only dispenses the honors, but holds the sword of the community. The legislature not only commands the purse, but prescribes the rules by which the duties and rights of every citizen are to be regulated. The judiciary, on the contrary, has no influence over either the sword or the purse; no direction either of the strength or of the wealth of the society; and can take no active resolution whatever. It may truly be said to have neither force nor will, but merely judgment; and must ultimately depend upon the aid of the executive arm even for the efficacy of its judgments.

This simple view of the matter suggests several important consequences. It proves incontestably, that the judiciary is beyond comparison the weakest of the three departments of power; that it can never attack with success either of the other two; and that all possible care is requisite to enable it to defend itself against their attacks. It equally proves, that though individual oppression may now and then proceed from the courts of justice, the general liberty of the people can never be endangered from that quarter; I mean so long as the judiciary remains truly distinct from both the legislature and the Executive. For I agree, that "there is no liberty, if the power of judging be not separated from the legislative and executive powers." And it proves, in the last place, that as liberty can have nothing to fear from the judiciary alone, but would have every thing to fear from its union with either of the other departments; that as all the effects of such a union must ensue from a dependence of the former on the latter, notwithstanding a nominal and apparent separation; that as, from the natural feebleness of the judiciary, it is in continual jeopardy of being overpowered, awed, or influenced by its coördinate branches; and that as nothing can contribute so much to its firmness and independence as permanency in office, this quality may therefore be justly regarded as an indispensable ingredient in its constitution, and, in a great measure, as the citadel of the public justice and the public security.

The complete independence of the courts of justice is peculiarly essential in a limited Constitution. By a limited Constitution, I understand one which contains certain specified exceptions to the legislative authority; such, for instance, as that it shall pass no bills at attainder, no *ex-post-facto* laws, and the like. Limitations of this kind can be preserved in practice no other way than through the medium of courts of justice, whose duty it must be to declare all acts contrary to the manifest tenor of the Constitution void. Without this, all the reservations of particular rights and privileges would amount to nothing.

Some perplexity respecting the rights of the courts to pronounce legislative acts void, because contrary to the Constitution, has arisen from an imagination that the doctrine would imply a superiority of the judiciary to the legislative power. It is urged that the authority which can declare the acts of another void, must necessarily be superior to the one whose acts may be declared void. As this doctrine is of great importance in all the American constitutions, a brief discussion of the ground on which it rests cannot be unacceptable.

There is no position which depends on clearer principles, than that every act of a delegated authority, contrary to the tenor of the commission under which it is exercised, is void. No legislative act, therefore, contrary to the Constitution, can be valid. To deny this, would be to affirm, that the deputy is greater than his principal; that the servant is above his master; that the representatives of the people are superior to the people themselves; that men acting by virtue of powers, may do not only what their powers do not authorize, but what they forbid.

If it be said that the legislative body are themselves the constitutional judges of their own powers, and that the construction they put upon them is conclusive upon the other departments, it may be answered, that this cannot be the natural presumption, where it is not to be collected from any particular provisions in the Constitution. It is not otherwise to be supposed, that the Constitution could intend to enable the representatives of the people to substitute their *will* to that of their constituents. It is far more rational to suppose, that the courts were designed to be an intermediate body between the people and the legislature, in order, among other things, to keep the latter within the limits assigned to their authority. The interpretation of the laws is the proper and peculiar province of the courts. A constitution is, in fact, and must be regarded by the judges, as a fundamental law. It therefore belongs to them to ascertain its meaning, as well as the meaning of any particular act proceeding from the legislative body. If there should happen to be an irreconcilable variance between the two, that which has the superior obligation and validity ought, of course, to be preferred; or, in other words, the Constitution ought to be preferred to the statute, the intention of the people to the intention of their agents.

Nor does this conclusion by any means suppose a superiority of the judicial to the legislative power. It only supposes that the power of the people is superior to both; and that where the will of the legislature, declared in its statutes, stands in opposition to that of the people, declared in the Constitution, the judges ought to be governed by the latter rather than the former. They ought to regulate their decisions by the fundamental laws, rather than by those which are not fundamental.

This exercise of judicial discretion, in determining between two contradictory laws, is exemplified in a familiar instance. It not uncommonly happens, that there are two statutes existing at one time, clashing in whole or in part with each other, and neither of them containing any repealing clause or expression. In such a case, it is the province of the courts to liquidate and fix their meaning and operation. So far as they can, by any fair construction, be reconciled to each other, reason and law conspire to dictate that this should be done; where this is impracticable, it becomes a matter of necessity to give effect to one, in exclusion of the other. The rule which has obtained in the courts for determining their relative validity is, that the last in order of time shall be preferred to the first. But there is a mere rule of construction, not derived from any positive law, but from the nature and reason of the thing. It is a rule not enjoined upon the courts by legislative provision, but adopted by themselves, as consonant to truth and propriety, for the direction of their conduct as interpreters of the law. They thought it reasonable, that between the interfering acts of an *equal* authority, that which was the last indication of its will should have the preference.

But in regard to the interfering acts of a superior and subordinate authority, of an original and derivative power, the nature and reason of the thing indicate the converse of that rule as proper to be followed. They teach us that the prior act of a superior ought to be preferred to the subsequent act of an inferior and subordinate authority; and that accordingly, whenever a particular statute contravenes the Constitution, it will be the duty of the judicial tribunals to adhere to the latter and disregard the former.

It can be of no weight to say that the courts, on the pretence of a repugnancy, may substitute their own pleasure to the constitutional intentions of the legislature. This might as well happen in the case of two contradictory statutes; or it might as well happen in every adjudication upon any single statute. The courts must declare the sense of the law; and if they should be disposed to exercise will instead of judgment, the consequence would equally be the substitution of their pleasure to that of the legislative body. The observation, if it prove any thing, would prove that there ought to be no judges distinct from that body.

If, then, the courts of justice are to be considered as the bulwarks of a limited Constitution against legislative encroachments, this consideration will afford a strong argument for the permanent tenure of judicial offices, since nothing will contribute so much as this to that independent spirit in the judges which must be essential to the faithful performance of so arduous a duty.

This independence of the judges is equally requisite to guard the Constitution and the rights of individuals from the effects of those ill humors, which the arts of designing men, or the influence of particular conjectures, sometimes disseminate among the people themselves, and which, though they speedily give place to better information, and more deliberate reflection, have a tendency, in the meantime, to occasion dangerous innovations in the government, and serious oppressions of the minor party in the community. Though I trust the friends of the proposed Constitution will never concur with its enemies, in questioning that fundamental principle of republican government, which admits the right of the people to alter or abolish the established Constitution, whenever they find it inconsistent with their happiness, yet it is not to be inferred from this principle, that the representatives of the people, whenever a momentary inclination happens to lay hold of a majority of their constituents, incompatible with the provisions in the existing Constitution, would, on that account, be justifiable in a violation of those provisions; or that the courts would be under a greater obligation to connive at infractions in this shape, than when they had proceeded wholly from the cabals of the representative body. Until the people have, by some solemn and authoritative act, annulled or changed the established form, it is binding upon themselves collectively, as well as individually; and no presumption, or even knowledge, of their sentiments, can warrant their representatives in a departure from it, prior to such an act. But it is easy to see, that it would require an uncommon portion of fortitude in the judges to do their duty as faithful guardians of the Constitution, where legislative invasions of it had been instigated by the major voice of the community.

But it is not with a view to infractions of the Constitution only, that the independence of the judges may be an essential safeguard against the effects of occasional ill humors in the society. These sometimes extend no farther than to the injury of the private rights of particular classes of citizens, by unjust and partial laws. Here also the firmness of the judicial magistracy is of vast importance in mitigating the severity and confining the operation of such laws. It not only serves to moderate immediate mischiefs of those which may have been passed, but it operates as a check upon the legislative body in passing them; who, perceiving that obstacles to the success of iniquitous intention are to be expected from the scruples of the courts, are in a manner compelled, by the very motives of the injustice they mediate, to qualify their attempts. This is a circumstance calculated to have more influence upon the character of our governments, than but few may be aware of. The benefits of the integrity and moderation of the judiciary have already been felt in more States than one; and though they may have displeased those whose sinister expectations they may have disappointed, they must have commanded the esteem and applause of all the virtuous and disinterested. Considerate men, of every description, ought to prize whatever will tend to beget or fortify that temper in the courts; as no man can be sure that he may not be to-morrow the victim of a spirit of injustice, by which he may be a gainer today. And every man must now feel, that the inevitable tendency of such a spirit is to sap the foundations of public and private confidence, and to introduce in its stead universal distrust and distress.

That inflexible and uniform adherence to the rights of the Constitution, and of individuals, which we perceive to be indispensable in the courts of justice, can certainly not be expected from judges who hold their offices by a temporary commission. Periodical appointments, however regulated, or by whomsoever made, would, in some way or other, be fatal to their necessary independence. If the power of making them was committed either to the Executive or legislature, there would be danger of an improper complaisance to the branch which possessed it; if to both, there would be an unwillingness to hazard the displeasure of either; if to the people, or to persons chosen by them for the special purpose, there would be too great a disposition to consult popularity, to justify a reliance that nothing would be consulted but the Constitution and the laws.

There is yet a further and a weightier reason for the permanency of the judicial offices, which is deducible from the nature of the qualifications they require. It has been frequently remarked, with great propriety, that a voluminous code of laws is one of the inconveniences necessarily connected with the advantages of a free government. To avoid an arbitrary discretion in the courts, it is indispensable that they should be bound down by strict rules and precedents, which serve to define and point out their duty in every particular case that comes before them; and it will readily be conceived from the variety of controversies which grow out of the folly and wickedness of mankind, that the records of those precedents must unavoidably swell to a very considerable bulk, and must demand long and laborious study to acquire a competent knowledge of them. Hence it is, that there can be but few men in the society who will have sufficient skill in the laws to qualify them for the stations of judges. And making the proper deductions for the ordinary depravity of human nature, the number must be still smaller of those who unite the requisite integrity with the requisite knowledge. These considerations apprise us, that the government can have no great option between fit character; and that a temporary duration in office, which would naturally discourage such characters from quitting a lucrative line of practice to accept a seat on the bench, would have a tendency to throw the administration of justice into hands less able, and less well qualified, to conduct it with utility and dignity. In the present circumstances of this country, and in those in which it is likely to be for a long time to come, the disadvantages on this score would be greater than they may at first sight appear; but it must be confessed, that they are far inferior to those which present themselves under the other aspects of the subject.

Upon the whole, there can be no room to doubt that the convention acted wisely in copying from the models of those constitutions which have established *good behavior* as the tenure of their judicial offices, in point of duration; and that so far from being blamable on this account, their plan would have been inexcusably defective, if it had wanted this important feature of good government. The experience of Great Britain affords an illustrious comment on the excellence of the institution.

MARBURY V. MADISON

64. ESTABLISHING JUDICIAL REVIEW

In this landmark decision, Chief Justice John Marshall declared that the Supreme Court had the power of judicial review, which is the power to declare actions of the president, the Congress, or any other government agency at any level to be invalid or unconstitutional. In the 1803 case of Marbury v. Madison *the Court held that it was the duty of the judiciary to say what the law is, including expounding and interpreting that law. The law contained in the Constitution, Marshall said, was paramount, and laws repugnant to its provisions must fall. He concluded that it was the province of the courts to decide when other laws were in violation of the basic law of the Constitution and, where this was found to occur, to declare such laws null and void. This power of judicial review, first asserted in this case, has given the United States the most powerful judiciary in the world.*

Chief Justice MARSHALL delivers the opinion of the Court.

At the last term on the affidavits then read and filed with the clerk, a rule was granted in this case, requiring the secretary of state to show cause why a mandamus should not issue, directing him to deliver to William Marbury his commission as a justice of the peace for the county of Washington, in the District of Columbia.

No cause has been shown, and the present motion is for a *mandamus*. The peculiar delicacy of this case, the novelty of some of its circumstances, and the

---

Source: U.S. Supreme Court, *Marbury v. Madison* (1803).

real difficulty attending the points which occur in it, require a complete exposition of the principles on which the opinion to be given by the court is founded.

These principles have been, on the side of the applicant very ably argued at the bar. In rendering the opinion of the court, there will be some departure in form, though not in substance, from the points stated in that argument.

In the order in which the court has viewed this subject, the following questions have been considered and decided.

1st. Has the applicant a right to the commission he demands?

2d. If he has a right, and that right has been violated, do the laws of his country afford him a remedy?

3d. If they do afford him a remedy, is it a *mandamus* issuing from this court?

The first object of inquiry is,

1st. Has the applicant a right to the commission he demands?

His right originates in an act of congress passed in February, 1801, concerning the District of Columbia.

After dividing the district into two counties, the 11th section of this law enacts, "that there shall be appointed in and for each of the said counties, such number of discreet persons to be justices of the peace as the president of the United States shall, from time to time, think expedient, to continue in office for five years."

It appears, from the affidavits, that in compliance with this law, a commission for William Marbury, as a justice of the peace for the county of Washington, was signed by John Adams, then President of the United States; after which the seal of the United States was affixed to it; but the commission has never reached the person for whom it was made out. . . .

Mr. Marbury, then, since his commission was signed by the president, and sealed by the secretary of state, was appointed; and as the law creating the office, gave the officer a right to hold for five years, independent of the executive, the appointment was not revocable, but vested in the officer legal rights, which are protected by the laws of his country.

To withhold his commission, therefore, is an act deemed by the court not warranted by law, but violative of a vested legal right.

This brings us to the second inquiry; which is,

2d. If he has a right, and that right has been violated, do the laws of this country afford him a remedy?

The very essence of civil liberty certainly consists in the right of every individual to claim the protection of the laws, whenever he receives an injury. One of the first duties of government is to afford that protection. In Great Britain the king himself is sued in the respectful form of a petition, and he never fails to comply with the judgment of his court. . . .

By the constitution of the United States, the president is invested with certain important political powers, in the exercise of which he is to use his own discretion, and is accountable only to his country in his political character and to his own conscience. To aid him in the performance of these duties, he is authorized to appoint certain officers, who act by his authority, and in conformity with his orders.

In such cases, their acts are his acts; and whatever opinion may be entertained of the manner in which executive discretion may be used, still there exists, and can exist, no power to control that discretion. The subjects are political. They respect the nation, not individual rights, and being intrusted to the executive, the decision of the executive is conclusive. . . .

But when the legislature proceeds to impose on that officer other duties; when he is directed peremptorily to perform certain acts; when the rights of individuals are dependent on the performance of those acts; he is so far the officer of the law; is amenable to the laws for his conduct; and cannot at his discretion sport away the vested rights of others.

The conclusion from this reasoning is, that where the heads of departments are the political or confidential agents of the executive, merely to execute the will of the president, or rather to act in cases in which the executive possesses a constitutional or legal discretion, nothing can be more perfectly clear than that their acts are only politically examinable. But where a specific duty is assigned by law, and individual rights depend upon the performance of that duty, it seems equally clear that the individual who considers himself injured, has a right to resort to the laws of his country for a remedy. . . .

It is, then, the opinion of the Court,

1st. That by signing the commission of Mr. Marbury, the President of the United States appointed him a justice of peace for the county of Washington, in the District of Columbia; and that the seal of the United States, affixed thereto by the secretary of state, is conclusive testimony of the verity of the signature, and of the completion of the appointment; and that the appointment conferred on him a legal right to the office for the space of five years.

2d. That, having this legal title to the office, he has a consequent right to the commission; a refusal to deliver which is a plain violation of that right, for which the laws of his country afford him a remedy.

It remains to be inquired whether,

3d. He is entitled to the remedy for which he applies. This depends on,

1st. The nature of the writ applied for; and

2d. The power of this court.

1st. The nature of the writ. . . .

[T]o render the *mandamus* a proper remedy, the officer to whom it is to be directed, must be one to whom, on legal principles, such writ may be directed; and the person applying for it must be without any other specific and legal remedy. . . .

The act to establish the judicial courts of the United States authorizes the Supreme Court "to issue writs of *mandamus* in cases warranted by the principles and usages of law, to any courts appointed, or persons holding office, under the authority of the United States."

The secretary of state, being a person holding an office under the authority of the United States, is precisely within the letter of the description, and if this court is not authorized to issues a writ of mandamus to such an officer, it must be because the law is unconstitutional, and therefore absolutely incapable of conferring the authority, and assigning the duties which its words purport to confer and assign.

The constitution vests the whole judicial power of the United States in one supreme court, and such inferior courts as congress shall, from time to time, ordain and establish. This power is expressly extended to all cases arising under the laws of the United States; and, consequently, in some form, may be exercised over the present case; because the right claimed is given by a law of the United States.

In the distribution of this power it is declared that "the supreme court shall have original jurisdiction in all cases affecting ambassadors, other public ministers and consuls, and those in which a state shall be a party. In all other cases, the supreme court shall have appellate jurisdiction."

It has been insisted, at the bar, that as the original grant of jurisdiction, to the supreme and inferior courts, is general, and the clause, assigning original jurisdiction to the supreme court, contains no negative or restrictive words, the power remains to the legislature, to assign original jurisdiction to that court in other cases than those specified in the article which has been recited; provided those cases belong to the judicial power of the United States.

If it had been intended to leave it in the discretion of the legislature to apportion the judicial power between the supreme and inferior courts according to the will of that body, it would certainly have been useless to have proceeded further than to have defined the judicial power, and the tribunals in which it should be vested. The subsequent part of the section is mere surplusage, is entirely without meaning, if such is to be the construction. If congress remains at liberty to give this court appellate jurisdiction, where the constitution has declared their jurisdiction shall be original; and original jurisdiction where the constitution has declared it shall be appellate; the distribution of jurisdiction, made in the constitution, is form without substance. . . .

To enable this court, then, to issue a *mandamus,* it must be shown to be an exercise of appellate jurisdiction, or to be necessary to enable them to exercise appellate jurisdiction.

It has been stated at the bar that the appellate jurisdiction may be exercised in a variety of forms, and that if it be the will of the legislature that a *mandamus* should be used for that purpose, that will must be obeyed. This is true, yet the jurisdiction must be appellate, not original.

It is the essential criterion of appellate jurisdiction, that it revises and corrects the proceedings in a cause already instituted, and does not create that cause. Although, therefore, a mandamus may be directed to courts, yet to issue such a writ to an officer for the delivery of a paper, is in effect the same as to sustain an original action for that paper, and, therefore, seems not to belong to appellate, but to original jurisdiction. Neither is it necessary in such a case as this, to enable the court to exercise its appellate jurisdiction.

The authority, therefore, given to the supreme court, by the act establishing the judicial courts of the United States, to issue writs of *mandamus* to public officers, appears not to be warranted by the constitution; and it becomes necessary to inquire whether a jurisdiction so conferred can be exercised. . . .

The distinction between a government with limited and unlimited powers is abolished, if those limits do not confine the persons on whom they are imposed, and if acts prohibited and acts allowed, are of equal obligation. It is a proposition too plain to be contested, and the constitution controls any legislative act repugnant to it; or, that the legislature may alter the constitution by an ordinary act.

Between these alternatives there is no middle ground. The constitution is either a superior paramount law, unchangeable by ordinary means, or it is on a level with ordinary legislative acts, and, like other acts, is alterable when the legislature shall please to alter it.

If the former part of the alternative be true, then a legislative act contrary to the constitution is not law: if the latter part be true, then written constitutions are absurd attempts, on the part of the people, to limit a power in its own nature illimitable.

Certainly all those who have framed written constitutions contemplate them as forming the fundamental and paramount law of the nation, and consequently, the theory of every such government must be, that an act of the legislature, repugnant to the constitution, is void.

This theory is essentially attached to a written constitution, and, is consequently, to be considered, by this court, as one of the fundamental principles of our society. It is not therefore to be lost sight of in the further consideration of this subject.

If an act of the legislature, repugnant to the constitution, is void, does it, notwithstanding its invalidity, bind the courts, and oblige them to give it effect? Or, in other words, though it be not law, does it constitute a rule as operative as if it was a law? This would be to overthrow in fact what was established in theory; and would seem, at first view, an absurdity too gross to be insisted on. It shall, however, receive a more attentive consideration.

It is emphatically the province and duty of the judicial department to say what the law is. Those who apply the rule to particular cases, must of necessity expound and interpret that rule. If two laws conflict with each other, the courts must decide on the operation of each.

So if a law be in opposition to the constitution; if both the law and the constitution apply to a particular case, so that the court must either decide that case conformably to the law, disregarding the constitution; or conformably to the constitution, disregarding the law; the court must determine which of these conflicting rules governs the case. This is of the very essence of judicial duty.

If, then, the courts are to regard the constitution, and the constitution is superior to any ordinary act of the legislature, the constitution, and not such ordinary act, must govern the case to which they both apply.

Those, then, who controvert the principle that the constitution is to be considered, in court, as a paramount law, are reduced to the necessity of maintaining that courts must close their eyes on the constitution, and see only the law.

This doctrine would subvert the very foundation of all written constitutions. It would declare that an act which, according to the principles and theory of our government, is entirely void, is yet, in practice, completely obligatory. It would declare that if the legislature shall do what is expressly forbidden, such act, notwithstanding the express prohibition, is in reality effectual. It would be given to the legislature a practical and real omnipotence, with the same breath which professes to restrict their powers within narrow limits. It is prescribing limits, and declaring that those limits may be passed at pleasure.

That it thus reduces to nothing what we have deemed the greatest improvement on political institutions, a written constitution, would of itself be sufficient, in America, where written constitutions have been viewed with so much reverence, for rejecting the construction. But the peculiar expressions of the constitution of the United States furnish additional arguments in favour of its rejection.

The judicial power of the United States is extended to all cases arising under the constitution.

Could it be the intention of those who gave this power, to say that in using it the constitution should not be looked into? That a case arising under the constitution should be decided without examining the instrument under which it arises?

This is too extravagant to be maintained.

In some cases, then, the constitution must be looked into by the judges. And if they can open it at all, what part of it are they forbidden to read or to obey?

There are many other parts of the constitution which serve to illustrate this subject.

It is declared that "no tax or duty shall be laid on articles exported from any state." Suppose a duty on the export of cotton, of tobacco, or of flour; and a suit instituted to recover it. Ought judgment to be rendered in such a case? Ought the judges to close their eyes on the constitution, and only see the law?

The constitution declares "that no bill of attainder or *ex post facto* law shall be passed."

If, however, such a bill should be passed, and a person should be prosecuted under it; must the court condemn to death those victims whom the constitution endeavors to preserve?

"No person," says the constitution, "shall be convicted of treason unless on the testimony of two witnesses to the same overt act, or on confession in open court."

Here the language of the constitution is addressed especially to the courts. It prescribes, directly for them, a rule of evidence not to be departed from. If the legislature should change that rule, and declare one witness, or a confession out of court, sufficient for conviction, must the constitutional principle yield to the legislative act?

From these, and many other selections which might be made, it is apparent, that the framers of the constitution contemplated that instrument as a rule for the government of courts, as well as of the legislature.

Why otherwise does it direct the judges to take an oath to support it? This oath certainly applies in an especial manner, to their conduct in their official character. How immoral to impose it on them, if they were to be used as the instruments, and the knowing instruments, for violating what they swear to support!

The oath of office, too, imposed by the legislature, is completely demonstrative of the legislative opinion on this subject. It is in these words: "I do solemnly swear that I will administer justice without respect to persons, and do equal right to the poor and to the rich; and that I will faithfully and impartially discharge all the duties incumbent on me as ————, according to the best of my abilities and understanding agreeably to the constitution and laws of the United States."

Why does a judge swear to discharge his duties agreeably to the constitution of the United States, if that constitution forms no rule for his government? if it is closed upon him, and cannot be inspected by him?

If such be the real state of things, this is worse than solemn mockery. To prescribe, or to take this oath, becomes equally a crime.

It is also not entirely unworthy of observation, that in declaring what shall be the *supreme law* of the land, *the constitution* itself is first mentioned; and not the laws of the United States generally, but those only which shall be made in *pursuance* of the constitution, have that rank.

Thus, the particular phraseology of the constitution of the United States confirms and strengthens the principle, supposed to be essential to all written constitutions, that a law repugnant to the constitution is void; and that *courts,* as well as other departments, are bound by that instrument.

The rule must be discharged.

ASHWANDER V. TENNESSEE VALLEY AUTHORITY

65. DEFINING THE COURT'S JURISDICTION

Associate Justice Louis Brandeis's concurring opinion in this case set forth a widely accepted view of when and how the Supreme Court should exercise its jurisdiction.

Source: U.S. Supreme Court, *Ashwander v. Tennessee Valley Authority* (1936).

Brandeis asserted that the Court should not decide constitutional questions unless they are absolutely essential and should avoid constitutional questions if other legal grounds can be found. Further, he argued that the Court should not make a constitutional ruling broader than required to decide the case at hand. This particular case upheld the construction of dams and the selling of electric power by the federal government. Despite Brandeis's efforts to restrain the Supreme Court by adopting what have become known as Ashwander *rules, the constitutional decisions of the modern Supreme Court continue to touch on and frequently dominate the major political questions of our time.*

Mr. Justice BRANDEIS, concurring. . . .

The Court developed, for its own governance in the cases confessedly within its jurisdiction, a series of rules under which it has avoided passing upon a large part of all the constitutional questions pressed upon it for decision. They are:

1. The Court will not pass upon the constitutionality of legislation in a friendly, non-adversary, proceeding, declining because to decide such questions "is legitimate only in the last resort, and as a necessity in the determination of real, earnest and vital controversy between individuals. It never was the thought that, by means of a friendly suit, a party beaten in the legislature could transfer to the courts an inquiry as to the constitutionality of the legislative act." *Chicago & Grand Trunk Ry. v. Wellman,* 143 U.S. 339, 345. . . .

2. The Court will not "anticipate a question of constitutional law in advance of the necessity of deciding it." *Liverpool, N. Y. & P. S. S. Co. v. Emigration Commissioners,* 113 U.S. 33, 39; . . . "It is not the habit of the court to decide questions of a constitutional nature unless absolutely necessary to a decision of the case." *Burton v. United States,* 196 U.S. 283, 295.

3. The Court will not "formulate a rule of constitutional law broader than is required by the precise facts to which it is to be applied." *Liverpool, N. Y. & P. S. S. Co. v. Emigration Commissioners, supra. . . .*

4. The Court will not pass upon a constitutional question although properly presented by the record, if there is also present some other ground upon which the case may be disposed of. This rule has found most varied application. Thus, if a case can be decided on either of two grounds, one involving a constitutional question, the other a question of statutory construction or general law, the court will decide only the latter. *Siler v. Lousiville & Nashville R. Co.,* 213 U.S. 175, 191; *Light v. United States,* 220 U.S. 523, 538. Appeals from the highest court of a state challenging its decision of a question under the Federal Constitution are frequently dismissed because the judgement can be sustained on an independent state ground. *Berea College v. Kentucky,* 211 U.S. 45, 53.

5. The Court will not pass upon the validity of a statute upon complaint of one who fails to show that he is injured by its operation. *Tyler v. The Judges,* 179 U.S. 405; *Hendrick v. Maryland,* 235 U.S. 610, 621. Among the many applications of this rule, none is more striking than the denial of the right of challenge to one who lacks a personal or property right. Thus, the challenge by a public official interested only in the performance of his official duty will not be entertained. . . . In *Fairchild v. Hughes,* 258 U.S. 126, the Court affirmed the dismissal of a suit brought by a citizen who sought to have the Nineteenth Amendment declared unconstitutional. In *Massachusetts v. Mellon,* 262, U.S. 447, the challenge of the federal Maternity Act was not entertained although made by the Commonwealth on behalf of all its citizens.

6. The Court will not pass upon the constitutionality of a statute at the instance of one who has availed himself of its benefits. *Great Falls Mfg. Co. v. Attorney General,* 124 U.S. 581. . . .

7. "When the validity of an act of the Congress is drawn in question, and even if a serious doubt of constitutionality is raised, it is a cardinal principle that this Court will first ascertain whether a construction of the statute is fairly possible by which the question may be avoided." *Cromwell v. Benson,* 285 U.S. 22, 62.

EUGENE V. ROSTOW

66. The Democratic Character of Judicial Review

Think about it: The Congress or your state legislature passes a law that is signed by the president or the governor. As few as five appointed judges on the U.S. Supreme Court can declare the law to be "unconstitutional," thereby vetoing the decisions of your popularly elected public officials. Is this not profoundly "undemocratic"? This question has troubled Americans—both scholars and the public at large—since the founding of the republic.

Eugene Rostow's defense of "judicial review," or the power of the Supreme Court to rule that the laws,

---

Source: From "The Democratic Character of Judicial Review," by Eugene V. Rostow in *Harvard Law Review,* Vol. 66, no. 2 (1952). Copyright © 1952 by the Harvard Law Review Association. Reprinted by permission of Harvard Law School.

decisions, and acts of elected governmental officials are in violation of the Constitution, stands as one of the classic statements of why such a power is quite consistent with democratic theory and democratic politics. Rostow argues that a constitution that outlines the powers of the government would be meaningless without a means of identifying "cases of conflicting action by different branches of government or constitutionally unauthorized governmental action against individuals." In effect, he reasons that if elected officials could simply alter the meaning of the Constitution at any time by their actions, the Constitution would provide no real limitation on them at all. Nonetheless, even if one accepts the democratic legitimacy of judicial review, the debate will rage on as to when and how the Supreme Court should exercise this awesome power to limit majority rule.

A theme of uneasiness, and even of guilt, colors the literature about judicial review. Many of those who have talked, lectured, and written about the Constitution have been troubled by a sense that judicial review is undemocratic. Why should a majority of nine Justices appointed for life be permitted to outlaw as unconstitutional the acts of elected officials or of officers controlled by elected officials? Judicial review, they have urged, is an undemocratic show on an otherwise respectable tree. It should be cut off, or at least kept pruned and inconspicuous. The attack has gone further. Reliance on bad political doctrine, they say, has produced bad political results. The strength of the courts has weakened other parts of the government. The judicial censors are accused of causing laxness and irresponsibility in the state and national legislatures, and political apathy in the electorate. At the same time, we are warned, the participation of the courts in this essentially political function will inevitably lead to the destruction of their independence and thus compromise all other aspects of their work.

The idea that judicial review is undemocratic is not an academic issue of political philosophy. Like most abstractions, it has far-reaching practical consequences. I suspect that for some judges it is the mainspring of decision, inducing them in many cases to uphold legislative and executive action which would otherwise have been condemned. Particularly in the multiple opinions of recent years, the Supreme Court's self-searching often boils down to a debate within the bosoms of the Justices over the appropriateness of judicial review itself.

The attack on judicial review as undemocratic rests on the premise that the Constitution should be allowed to grow without a judicial check. The proponents of this view would have the Constitution mean what the President, the Congress, and the state legislatures say it means. . . .

It is a grave oversimplification to contend that no society can be democratic unless its legislature has sovereign powers. The social quality of democracy cannot be defined by so rigid a formula. Government and politics are after all the arms, not the end, of social life. The purpose of the Constitution is to assure the people a free and democratic society. The final aim of that society is as much freedom as possible for the individual human being. The Constitution provides society with a mechanism of government fully competent to its task, but by no means universal in its powers. The power to govern is parcelled out between the states and the nation and is further divided among the three main branches of all governmental units. By custom as well as constitutional practice, many vital aspects of community life are beyond the direct reach of government—for example, religion, the press, and, until recently at any rate, many phases of educational and cultural activities. The separation of powers under the Constitution serves the end of democracy in society by limiting the roles of the several branches of government and protecting the citizen, and the various parts of the state itself, against encroachments from any source. The root idea of the Constitution is that man can be free because the state is not.

The power of constitutional review, to be exercised by some part of the government, is implicit in the conception of a written constitution delegating limited powers. A written constitution would promote discord rather than order in society if there were no accepted authority to construe it, at the least in cases of conflicting action by different branches of government or of constitutionally unauthorized governmental action against individuals. The limitation and separation of powers, if they are to survive, require a procedure for independent mediation and construction to reconcile the inevitable disputes over the boundaries of constitutional power which arise in the process of government. . . .

So far as the American Constitution is concerned, there can be little real doubt that the courts were intended from the beginning to have the power they have exercised. The Federalist Papers are unequivocal; the Debates as clear as debates normally are. The power of judicial review was commonly exercised by the courts of the states, and the people were accustomed to judicial construction of the authority derived from colonial charters. Constitutional interpretation by the courts, Hamilton said, does not

> by any means suppose a superiority of the judicial to the legislative power. It only supposes that the power of the people is superior to both; and that where the will of the legislature, declared in its statutes, stands in opposition to that of the people, declared in the Constitution, the judges ought to be governed by the latter rather than the former. They ought to regulate their decisions by the fundamental laws, rather than by those which are not fundamental.

Hamilton's statement is sometimes criticized as a verbal legalism. But it has an advantage too. For much of the discussion has complicated the problem without clarifying it. Both judges and their critics have wrapped themselves so successfully in the difficulties of particular cases that they have been able to evade the ultimate issue posed in the Federalist Papers.

Whether another method of enforcing the Constitution could have been devised, the short answer is that no such method has developed. The argument over the constitutionality of judicial review has long since been settled by history. The power and duty of the Supreme Court to declare statutes or executive action unconstitutional in appropriate cases is part of the living Constitution. "The course of constitutional history," Mr. Justice Frankfurter recently remarked, has cast responsibilities upon the Supreme Court which it would be "stultification" for it to evade. The Court's power has been exercised differently at different times: sometimes with reckless and doctrinaire enthusiasm; sometimes with great deference to the status and responsibilities of other branches of the government; sometimes with a degree of weakness and timidity that comes close to the betrayal of trust. But the power exists, as an integral part of the process of American government. The Court has the duty of interpreting the Constitution in many of its most important aspects, and especially in those which concern the relations of the individual and the state. The political proposition underlying the survival of the power is that there are some phases of American life which should be beyond the reach of any majority, save by constitutional amendment. In Mr. Justice Jackson's phrase, "One's right to life, liberty, and property, to free speech, a free press, freedom of worship and assembly, and other fundamental rights may not be submitted to vote; they depend on the outcome of no elections." Whether or not this was the intention of the Founding Fathers, the unwritten Constitution is unmistakable.

If one may use a personal definition of the crucial word, this way of policing the Constitution is not undemocratic. True, it employs appointed officials, to whom large powers are irrevocably delegated. But democracies need not elect all the officers who exercise crucial authority in the name of the voters. Admirals and generals can win or lose wars in the exercise of their discretion. The independence of judges in the administration of justice has been the pride of communities which aspire to be free. Members of the Federal Reserve Board have the lawful power to plunge the country into depression or inflation. The list could readily be extended. Government by referendum or town meeting is not the only possible form of democracy. The task of democracy is not to have the people vote directly on every issue, but to assure their ultimate responsibility for the acts of their representatives, elected or appointed. For judges deciding ordinary litigation, the ultimate responsibility of the electorate has a special meaning. It is a responsibility for the quality of the judges and for the substance of their instructions, never a responsibility for their decisions in particular cases. It is hardly characteristic of law in democratic society to encourage bills of attainder, or to allow appeals from the courts in particular cases to legislatures or to mobs. Where the judges are carrying out the function of constitutional review, the final responsibility of the people is appropriately guaranteed by the provisions for amending the Constitution itself, and by the benign influence of time, which changes the personnel of courts. Given the possibility of constitutional amendment, there is nothing undemocratic in having responsible and independent judges act as important constitutional mediators. Within the narrow limits of their capacity to act, their great task is to help maintain a pluralist equilibrium in society. They can do much to keep it from being dominated by the states or the Federal Government, by Congress or the President, by the purse or the sword.

In the execution of this crucial but delicate function, constitutional review by the judiciary has an advantage thoroughly recognized in both theory and practice. The power of the courts, however final, can only be asserted in the course of litigation. Advisory opinions are forbidden, and reefs of self-limitation have grown up around the doctrine that the courts will determine constitutional questions only in cases of actual controversy, when no lesser ground of decision is available, and when the complaining party would be directly and personally injured by the assertion of the power deemed unconstitutional. Thus the check of judicial review upon the elected branches of government must be a mild one, limited not only by the detachment, integrity, and good sense of the Justices, but by the structural boundaries implicit in the fact that the power is entrusted to the courts. Judicial review is inherently adapted to preserving broad and flexible lines of constitutional growth, not to operating as a continuously active factor in legislative or executive decisions. . . .

Democracy is a slippery term. I shall make no effort at a formal definition here. Certainly as a matter of historical fact some societies with parliamentary governments have been and are "democratic" by standards which Americans would accept, although it is worth noting that almost all of them employ second chambers, with powers at least of delay, and indirect devices for assuring continuity in the event of a parliamentary collapse, either through the crown or some equivalent institution, like the presidency in France. But it would be scholastic pedantry to define democracy in such a way as to deny the title of "democrat" to Jefferson, Madison, Lincoln, Brandeis, and others who have found the American constitutional system, including its tradition of judicial review, well adapted to the needs of a free society. As Mr. Justice Brandeis said,

> the doctrine of the separation of powers was adopted by the Convention of 1787, not to promote efficiency but to preclude the exercise of arbitrary power. The purpose was, not to avoid friction, but, by means of the inevitable friction incident to the distribution of governmental powers among three departments, to save the people from autocracy.

It is error to insist that no society is democratic unless it has a government of unlimited powers, and that no government is democratic unless its legislature has unlimited powers. Constitutional review by an independent judiciary is a tool of proven use in the American quest for an open society of widely dispersed powers. In a vast country, of mixed population, with widely different regional problems, such an organization of society is the surest base for the hopes of democracy.

ALEXANDER M. BICKEL

67. THE LEAST DANGEROUS BRANCH INDEED

Alexander Bickel (1924–1974), one of the leading constitutional scholars of the twentieth century, insisted that if the basis of American government rests on the principle of majority rule, then the power of judicial review requires considerable justification. Bickel's starting point was Alexander Hamilton's argument in Federalist *No. 78 that the separation of judicial, executive, and legislative powers in the American system virtually guaranteed that "the judiciary, from the nature of its functions, will always be the least dangerous to the political rights of the Constitution; because it will be least in a capacity to annoy or injure them." Bickel believed that because the Supreme Court lacks any significant enforcement powers, "the Supreme Court's law could not in our system prevail . . . if it ran counter to deeply felt popular needs or convictions." For Bickel, the mere fact that the democratically chosen branches of government accept and enforce the Court's rulings means that judicial review is consistent with democratic theory. In a later book,* The Morality of Consent *(1975), Bickel strongly criticizes the Supreme Court for deciding cases more on the basis of expediency than principle.*

THE COUNTER-MAJORITARIAN DIFFICULTY

The root difficulty is that judicial review is a counter-majoritarion force in our system. There are various ways of sliding over this ineluctable reality. Marshall did so when he spoke of enforcing, in behalf of "the people," the limits that they have ordained for the institutions of a limited government. And it has been done ever since in much the same fashion by all too many commentators. Marshall himself followed Hamilton, who in the 78th *Federalist* denied that judicial review implied a superiority of the judicial over the legislative power—denied, in other words, that judicial review constituted control by an unrepresentative

---

Source: From Alexander M. Bickel, *The Least Dangerous Branch* (Indianapolis: Bobbs-Merrill Company Inc., 1962). Copyright © by Josephine A. Bickel. Reproduced by permission.

minority of an elected majority. "It only supposes," Hamilton went on, "that the power of the people is superior to both; and that where the will of the legislature, declared in its statutes, stands in opposition to that of the people, declared in the Constitution, the judges ought to be governed by the latter rather than the former." But the word "people" so used is an abstraction. Not necessarily a meaningless or a pernicious one by any means; always charged with emotion, but nonrepresentational—an abstraction obscuring the reality that when the Supreme Court declares unconstitutional a legislative act or the action of an elected executive, it thwarts the will of representatives of the actual people of the here and now; it exercises control, not in behalf of the prevailing majority, but against it. That, without mystic overtones, is what actually happens. It is an altogether different kettle of fish, and it is the reason the charge can be made that judicial review is undemocratic. . . .

It is true, of course, that the process of reflecting the will of a popular majority in the legislature is deflected by various inequalities of representation and by all sorts of institutional habits and characteristics, which perhaps tend most often in favor of inertia. Yet it must be remembered that statutes are the product of the legislature and the executive acting in concert, and that the executive represents a very different constituency and thus tends to cure inequities of over- and underrepresentation. Reflecting a balance of forces in society for purposes of stable and effective government is more intricate and less certain than merely assuring each citizen his equal vote. Moreover, impurities and imperfections, if such they be, in one part of the system are no argument for total departure from the desired norm in another part. A much more important complicating factor—first adumbrated by Madison in the 10th *Federalist* and lately emphasized by Professor David B. Truman and others—is the proliferation and power of what Madison foresaw as "faction," what Mr. Truman calls "groups," and what in popular parlance has always been deprecated as the "interests" or the "pressure groups."

No doubt groups operate forcefully on the electoral process, and no doubt they seek and gain access to and an effective share in the legislative and executive decisional process. Perhaps they constitute also, in some measure, an impurity or imperfection. But no one has claimed that they have been able to capture the governmental process except by combining in some fashion, and thus capturing or constituting (are not the two verbs synonymous?) a majority. They often tend themselves to be majoritarian in composition and to be subject to broader majoritarian influences. And the price of what they sell or buy in the legislature is determined in the biennial or quadrennial electoral marketplace. It may be, as Professor Robert A. Dahl has written, that elections themselves, and the political competition that renders them meaningful, "do not make for government by majorities in any very significant way," for they do not establish a great many policy preferences. However, "they are a crucial device for controlling leaders." And if the control is exercised by "groups of various types and sizes, all seeking in various ways to advance their goals," so that we have "minorities rule" rather than majority rule, it remains true nevertheless that only those minorities rule which can command the votes of a majority of individuals in the legislature who can command the votes of a majority of individuals in the electorate. In one fashion or another, both in the legislative process and at elections, the minorities must coalesce into a majority. Although, as Mr. Dahl says, "it is fashionable in some quarters to suggest that everything believed about democratic politics prior to World War I, and perhaps World War II, was nonsense," he makes no bones about his own belief that "the radical democrats who, unlike Madison, insist upon the decisive importance of the election process in the whole grand strategy of democracy are essentially correct."

The insights of Professor Truman and other writers into the role that groups play in our society and our politics have a bearing on judicial review. They indicate that there are other means than the electoral process, though subordinate and subsidiary ones, of making institutions of government responsive to the needs and wishes of the governed. Hence one may infer that judicial review, although not responsible, may have ways of being responsive. But nothing can finally depreciate the central function that is assigned in democratic theory and practice to the electoral process; nor can it be denied that the policy-making power of representative institutions, born of the electoral process, is the distinguishing characteristic of the system. Judicial review works counter to this characteristic. . . .

Besides being a counter-majoritarian check on the legislature and the executive, judicial review may, in a larger sense, have a tendency over time seriously to weaken the democratic process. Judicial review expresses, of course, a form of distrust of the legislature. "The legislatures," wrote James Bradley Thayer at the turn of the century,

> are growing accustomed to this distrust and more and more readily inclined to justify it, and to shed the considerations of constitutional restraints,—certainly as concerning the exact extent of these restrictions,—turning that subject over to the courts; and what is worse, they insensibly fall into a habit of assuming that whatever they could constitutionally do they may do,—as if honor and fair dealing and common honesty were not relevant to their inquiries. The people, all this while, become careless as to whom they send to the legislature; too often they cheerfully vote for men whom they would not trust with an important private affair, and when these unfit persons are found to pass foolish and bad laws, and the courts step in and disregard them, the people are glad that these few wiser gentlemen on the bench are so ready to protect them against their more immediate representatives. . . . [I]t should be remembered that the exercise of it [the power of judicial review] even when unavoidable, is always attended with a serious evil, namely, that the correction of legislative mistakes comes from the outside, and the people thus lose the political experience, and the moral education and stimulus that comes from fighting the question out in the ordinary way, and correcting their own errors. The tendency of a common and easy resort to this great function, now lamentably too common, is to dwarf the political capacity of the people, and to deaden its sense of moral responsibility. It is no light thing to do that.

To this day, on how many hundreds of occasions does Congress enact a measure that it deems expedient, having essayed consideration of its constitutionality (that is to say, of its acceptability on principle), only to abandon the attempt in the declared confidence that the Court will correct errors of principle, if any? It may well be, as has been suggested, that any lowering of the level of legislative performance is attributable to many factors other than judicial review. Yet there is no doubt that what Thayer observed remains observable. . . .

Finally, another, though related, contention has been put forward. It is that judicial review runs so fundamentally counter to democratic theory that in a society which in all other respects rests on that theory, judicial review cannot ultimately be effective. We pay the price of a grave inner contradiction in the basic principle of our government, which is an inconvenience and a dangerous one; and in the end to no good purpose, for when the great test comes, judicial review will be unequal to it. The most arresting expression of this thought is in a famous passage from a speech of Judge Learned Hand, a passage, Dean Eugene V. Rostow has written, "of Browningesque passion and obscurity," voicing a "gloomy and apocalyptic view." Absent the institution of judicial review, Judge Hand said:

> I do not think that anyone can say what will be left of those [fundamental principles of equity and fair play which our constitutions enshrine]; I do not know whether they will serve only as counsels; but this much I think I do know—that a society so riven that the spirit of moderation is gone, no court can save; that a society where that spirit flourishes, no court need save; that in a society which evades its responsibility by thrusting upon the courts the nurture of that spirit, that spirit in the end will perish. . . .

Such, in outline, are the chief doubts that must be met if the doctrine of judicial review is to be justified on principle. Of course, these doubts will apply with lesser or greater force to various forms of the exercise of the power. For the moment the discussion is at wholesale, and we are seeking a justification on principle, quite aside from supports in history and the continuity of practice. The search must be for a function which might (indeed, must) involve the making of policy, yet which differs from the legislative and executive functions; which is peculiarly suited to the capabilities of the courts; which will not likely be performed elsewhere if the courts do not assume it; which can be so exercised as to be acceptable in a society that generally shares Judge Hand's satisfaction in a "sense of common venture"; which will be effective when needed; and whose discharge by the courts will not lower the quality of the other departments' performance by denuding them of the dignity and burden of their own responsibility. It will not be possible fully to meet all that is said against judicial review. Such is not the way with questions of government. We can only fill the other side of the scales with countervailing judgments on the real needs and the actual workings of our society and, of course, with our own portions of faith and hope. Then we may estimate how far the needle has moved.

The point of departure is a truism; perhaps it even rises to the unassailability of a platitude. It is that many actions of government have two aspects: their immediate, necessarily intended, practical effects, and their perhaps unintended or unappreciated bearing on values we hold to have more general and permanent interest. It is a premise we deduce not merely from the fact of a written constitution but from the history of the race, and ultimately as a moral judgment of the good society, that government should serve not only what we conceive from time to time to be our immediate material needs but also certain enduring values. This in part is what is meant by government under law. But such values do not present themselves ready-made. They have a past always, to be sure, but they must be continually derived, enunciated, and seen in relevant application. And it remains to ask which institution of our government—if any single one in particular—should be the pronouncer and guardian of such values.

Men in all walks of public life are able occasionally to perceive this second aspect of public questions. Sometimes they are also able to base their decisions on it; that is one of the things we like to call acting on principle. Often they do not do so, however, particularly when they sit in legislative assemblies. There, when the pressure for immediate results is strong enough and emotions ride high enough, men will ordinarily prefer to act on expediency rather than take the long view. Possibly legislators—everything else being equal—are as capable as other men of following the path of principle, where the path is clear or at any rate discernible. Our system, however, like all secular systems, calls for the evolution of principle in novel circumstances, rather than only for its mechanical application. Not merely respect for the rule of established principles but the creative establishment and renewal of a coherent body of principled rules—that is what our legislatures have proven themselves ill equipped to give us.

Initially, great reliance for principled decision was placed in the Senators and the President, who have more extended terms of office and were meant to be elected only indirectly. Yet the Senate and the President were conceived of as less closely tied to, not as divorced from, electoral responsibility and the political marketplace. And so even then the need might have been felt for an institution which stands altogether aside from the current clash of interests, and which, insofar as is humanly possible, is concerned only with principle. We cannot know whether, as Thayer believed, our legislatures are what they are because we have judicial review, or whether we have judicial review and consider it necessary because legislatures are what they are. Yet it is arguable also that the partial separation of the legislative and judicial functions—and it is not meant to be absolute—is beneficial in any event, because it makes it possible for the desires of various groups and interests concerning immediate results to be heard clearly and unrestrainedly in one place. It may be thought fitting that somewhere in government, at some stage in the process of law-making, such felt needs should find unambiguous expression. Moreover, and more importantly, courts have certain capacities for dealing with matters of principle that legislatures and executives do not possess. Judges have, or should have, the leisure, the training, and the insulation to follow the ways of the scholar in pursuing the ends of government. This is crucial in sorting out the enduring values of a society, and it is not something that institutions can do well occasionally, while operating for the most part with a different set of gears. It calls for a habit of mind, and for undeviating institutional customs. Another advantage that courts have is that questions of principle never carry the same aspect for them as they did for the legislature or the executive. Statutes, after all, deal typically with abstract or dimly foreseen problems. The courts are concerned with the flesh and blood of an actual case. This tends to modify, perhaps to lengthen, everyone's view. It also provides an extremely salutary proving ground for all abstractions; it is conducive, in a phrase of Holmes, to thinking things, not words, and thus to the evolution of principle by a process that tests as it creates.

Their insulation and the marvelous mystery of time give courts the capacity to appeal to men's better natures, to call forth their aspirations, which may have been forgotten in the moment's hue and cry. This is what Justice Stone called the opportunity for "the sober second thought." Hence it is that the courts, although they may somewhat dampen the people's and the legislatures' efforts to educate themselves, are also a great and highly effective educational institution. Judge Gibson, in the very opinion mentioned earlier, highly critical as he was, took account of this. "In the business of government," he wrote, "a recurrence to first principles answers the end of an observation at sea with a view to correct the dead reckoning; and, for this purpose, a written constitution is an instrument of inestimable value. It is of inestimable value also, in rendering its principles familiar to the mass of the people. . . . " The educational institution that both takes the observation to correct the dead reckoning and makes it known is the voice of the Constitution: the Supreme Court exercising judicial review. The Justices, in Dean Rostow's phrase, "are inevitable teachers in a vital national seminar." No other branch of the American government is nearly so well equipped to conduct one. And such a seminar can do a great deal to keep our society from becoming so riven that no court will be able to save it. Of course, we have never quite been that society in which the spirit of moderation is so richly in flower that no court need save it.

Section XII
Review Questions

1. On what basis did Alexander Hamilton seek to persuade Americans that the newly created Supreme Court posed no threat to the people of the United States? Do you think Hamilton would approve of the Supreme Court's role in contemporary American life? Why? Why not?

2. Trace the reasoning of Chief Justice Marshall in *Marbury v. Madison.* What is the irony in the Court's decision to strike down the particular section of an Act of Congress that was involved in this case?

3. Was Justice Brandeis' opinion in *Ashwander v. Tennessee Valley Authority* a plea for expanding or limiting the Supreme Court? In your opinion, if the Court actually believes that a governmental action is unconstitutional, is there a good reason the Court should not rule on this question?

4. Can you think of a response to Eugene Rostow's claim that without judicial review the Congress could simply change the Constitution at will? Did you know that this is exactly how the British system works? Is Britain not a democratic nation?

5. What does Alexander Bickel see as the "root difficulty" regarding judicial review? How does he resolve the problem?

XIII

Public Policy

E. PENDLETON HERRING

68. Bureaucracy and the Public Interest

E. Pendleton Herring was one of the most influential of the pre–World War II scholars in the field of public administration. His analysis of the relations between government agencies and their formal and informal constituencies remains one of the major contributions to an understanding of how bureaucracies function in the real world.

Herring examined the problems posed by the dramatic increase in the scope of government and the influence of administrative discretion. He argued that the bureaucrat, by default, had the job of providing definition to the general principles embodied in legislative enactments. In "making effective and workable the economic and social compromises arrived at through the legislative process," Herring argued, the bureaucrat really has the job of defining the public interest.

Upon the shoulders of the bureaucrat has been placed in large part the burden of reconciling group differences and making effective and workable the economic and social compromises arrived at through the legislative process. Thus Congress passes a statute setting forth a general principle. The details must be filled in by supplemental regulation. The bureaucrat is left to decide as to the conditions that necessitate the law's application. He is in a better position than the legislators to perform these duties. His daily occupation brings him into direct contact with the situation the law is intended to meet. He knows what can be enforced and he can better envisage the limits of legislative fiats. This increase in administrative discretion, while making possible the more understanding application of rules to concrete situations, nevertheless places a heavy duty on the administrator. The words of the statute delimit his scope, but within the margin of his discretion he must write his interpretation of state purpose.

The social and economic aspects of this process must be left to others. The political result has been the preservation thus far of the liberal democratic state as the agency of control and the transfer from Congress of much of the

---

Source: From E. Pendleton Herring, *Public Administration and the Public Interest* (McGraw-Hill, 1936).

direct superintendence of reconciling the conflicting groups within the state. The governmental result has been the creation of a great bureaucracy with wide powers to carry on these functions. Great public services are needed all the way from the primary functions relating to police, sanitation, and the care of paupers to official enterprises that compete with private business. There are huge public-relief projects financed by taxing one class in order to alleviate the hunger pangs of another. The extent to which these activities are carried cannot be fixed but will vary in accordance with the character of the economic groups that have succeeded in attaining control of the government at any given time. There persists, nevertheless, a residue of responsibility no matter what combination is in control of the government. The mere existence of a great administrative organization necessitates a certain continuity that has little reference to political overturns. Groups must be willing to recognize that the state has a purpose which transcends their own immediate ends. The bureaucracy cannot assert a state purpose against the united hostility of groups that basically comprise the source whence authority springs.

In the United States the bureaucracy suffers for want of a hierarchical organization and a personnel united by a harmonious concept of state service. But a bureaucracy in these terms arouses the suspicion and criticism of interest groups, who regard the administration as designed to serve them or at least *not to interfere* with their group purposes. And it is these interest groups that wield political authority under a representative system. Such interests criticize "bureaucracy" as inimical to popular government. Yet only through developing a proper administrative organization can democracy survive.

We conclude, then, that the purpose of the democratic state is the free reconciliation of group interests and that the attainment of this end necessitates the development of a great administrative machine. Thus, paradoxical as it may seem to Jeffersonian Democrats, the liberal democratic state must be sustained by a huge bureaucracy. This viewpoint, however, has not won general acceptance.

Groups of citizens, seeking to advance their own interests or to protect themselves from the onslaughts of rivals, have turned to the government for aid. Yet the citizen distrusts the state at the same time that he appeals to it for help. He desires to use the facilities of the government; but he does not wish the government to direct or control his activities. As a result the federal administrative services have not been fused into a unified and responsible whole. They are a conglomeration of service agencies, independent regulatory commissions, and ill-proportioned bureaus and departments.

The present tangle of alphabetical monstrosities is not a new phenomenon. The confusion is greater because the variety of federal functions is greater. If the government is to become responsible for the economic security of various classes, the administrative machinery must be made adequate to the burden imposed. This does not mean creating more bureaus and commissions but rather reorganizing those that exist. The federal administration must be viewed as a whole: it must be developed into an institution for executing policy in the public interest and for promoting the general welfare. This will require a change in attitude on the part of most citizens. Groups have demanded special consideration from the federal government for themselves while condemning the general encroachment of the state into private affairs. The establishment of an adequate administrative structure and personnel must be undertaken if the state is to carry its ever-increasing load. The problem of bureaucracy must be faced directly.

No civil servant, however, wrapt in the bindings of official red tape, can regard himself as insulated from the currents of opinion generated by the groups with which his bureau comes into contact. The citizen for his part must feel that his experience and his special competence have some place in governance. How can a mutually advantageous connection be made?

The adjustment is not easy. "In every country," Herman Finer states, "the public is hostile to the official because at some time or other, as an inspector or a tax collector or a medical officer, or what not, he comes to take away, not to give—it is in the nature of his task to limit one's freedom and property." The suspicion of bureaucracy is particularly keen in the United States, and not without just cause. "Political pull" remains the citizen's chief defense against officialdom in this country. This faulty resource is all the more necessary under a system where ministerial responsibility is lacking and public integrity is often wanting in official circles. Moreover, we have a tradition of distrust for government that harks back to Colonial and Revolutionary days. Official interference has long been regarded as irksome and unfriendly. Conditions of pioneer life doubtless intensified this feeling. We accepted bureaucratic incompetence as an inevitable characteristic of an institution from which little good was to be expected in any case. Our confidence was placed in the courts where the justice of the rule of the law would protect us, we hoped, from the caprice of a government by men.

The courts are often found taking the part of the citizen against the powers of officialdom. Their verdict time and again delimits or restricts bureaucratic competence. In the elected executive and legislature the citizen feels that some degree of control is attainable through political channels. The tradition of a rule of law gives him confidence in the courts. But how can he affect the course of administrative action? Underlying such criticism is the uneasy feeling that the force of the government is turned to purposes contrary to those of his group. It often happens that a regulatory measure is enacted over the urgent protest of those thereby affected. The legislature, supported by a momentary public enthusiasm, discharges its duty in passing the law and turns to other matters. The bureaucrat is left to enforce the law over the disgruntled group thus brought under his jurisdiction. Governmental activity is unobjectionable to special interests when in accord with their aims, but when it is directed to other ends the cry of bureaucratic interference is raised.

The legislature, often because of a fortuitous combination of political factors, enacts a law. An administrative agency becomes responsible for its execution, and the legislative will is thus in a sense institutionalized and personified. Except for the relatively rare instances where a statute is rendered innocuous by nonenforcement, the legislative will is "frozen" until the law is changed. Meanwhile, a change of economic or political conditions may alter the alignment of social forces in the community and thereby bring the statute into disfavor, without necessarily forcing legislative amendment in response to criticisms. The legal responsibility of the official remains the same and the censure he incurs is the price of discharging his manifest duties. . . .

Government today is largely a matter of expert administration. Increasing authority and discretion are granted the executive branch. The state has undertaken a great number of services left in the past to private enterprise or scarcely attempted at all. These activities have given special interests a stake in the government. The actual point at which their right to pursue freely their own aims comes into conflict with the fulfillment of the broader aims of the community is a matter for judgment as particular cases arise. But the civil servant has no clear standard upon which to act. In a word, our present bureaucracy has accumulated vast authority but it lacks direction and coördination.

The President is nominal head of the "administration," but under present conditions the task of coördination is beyond the capacities of the transient occupants of this position. A system of administrative law might in time indicate the limits of bureaucratic responsibility and develop the conception of public interest. But the official today finds himself largely isolated except for the presence of those interests directly affected by the consequences of his action. These loom largest in the context of his administrative surroundings.

What criteria are to guide him? The *public interest* is the standard that guides the administrator in executing the law. This is the verbal symbol designed to introduce unity, order, and objectivity into administration.

This concept is to the bureaucracy what the "due process" clause is to the judiciary. Its abstract meaning is vague but its application has far-reaching effects. The radio commissioners were to execute the law in the "public interest, convenience or necessity." The trade commissioners are to apply the law when they deem such action "to the interest of the public." Congress has frequently authorized boards and quasi-judicial commissions to determine the public interest.

Although it is clear that the official must balance the interests of the conflicting groups before him, by what standards is he to weigh their demands? To hold out the public interest as a criterion is to offer an imponderable. Its value is psychological and does not extend beyond the significance that each responsible civil servant must find in the phrase for himself. Acting in accordance with this subjective conception and bounded by his statutory competence, the bureaucrat selects from the special interests before him a combination to which he gives official sanction. Thus inescapably in practice the concept of public interest is given substance by its identification with the interests of certain groups. The bureaucrat is placed in a situation similar to the plight of Rousseau's citizen.

The latter was to vote in accordance with the general will. If he found himself in the minority when the votes were counted, he knew that he had guessed incorrectly as to the *volonté générale.* The official, however, must endeavor to act in the public interest, but without the consolation of testing his judgment in a bureaucratic plebiscite. He must follow his star with but little light on the immediate pitfalls in his path.

The administrator has certain guiding criteria supplied by statutes, but inevitably a margin of discretion remains inherent in the administrative process. He can build up support for his policies and to some extent choose his adversaries. The choice may be of crucial importance. By supporting the groups demanding a strict interpretation of the law, he may bring about an ultimate effect quite different to the outcome resulting from coöperation with those who favor a liberal reading of the statute. He may even reach out for the opinions held by groups less well organized or aggressively directed.

The predicament of the bureaucrat now becomes clear. Special interests cannot be denied a voice in the councils of state since it is their concerns that provide substance out of which the public welfare is formulated. On the other hand, a well-coördinated and responsible bureaucracy is essential if the purpose of the state is to be attained. The solution of the liberal democratic state must lie in establishing a working relationship between the bureaucrats and special interests—a relationship that will enable the former to carry out the purpose of the state and the latter to realize their own ends.

Such a harmonious relationship is made all the more difficult in the United States by the diversity of conditions over the country and by the variety of activities undertaken by the government. Moreover, federal officials concern themselves with some problems over which they can exercise no coercive authority. The successful administration of many federal services depends upon the cooperation of state and local authorities with the national government. The ties between the community and the federal bureaucracy can best be described and evaluated in terms of the particular situations they are designed to meet. It is difficult to discuss these developments in general terms. Officials working in their own domains have used their ingenuity and found their own solutions.

Public administration in actual practice is a process whereby one individual acting in an official capacity and in accordance with his interpretation of his legal responsibility applies a statute to another individual who is in a legally subordinate position. The public as such is not concerned in this process.

To the officer executing the law, the public is simply an abstraction. Law is applied by one man to another. In the realm of discussion, the public is treated as a reality and words are directed to the populace. But this is a one-sided relationship. Officials receive many responses from individuals but the only reaction they receive from the public is that which they may choose to read into a collection of individual reactions.

Generally these responses may be arranged in more precise categories built around an occupational or economic interest. When this happens, the official finds it possible to negotiate with groups articulate and self-conscious because of a common concern.

Thus law is not administered in a vacuum, but in an environment composed of all those who have an interest in the application or the nonenforcement of the statute. The official is surrounded by a web of interests—and a web often dominated by an unpredictable spider. This ultimate determinator may be the courts, the legislature, an administrative superior, or a powerful economic interest. The administrator is one strand in a complicated mesh of forces, political, social, and economic. The public, viewed in the mass, is of relatively little importance in this context.

FRANKLIN D. ROOSEVELT

69. THE CASE FOR LIBERALISM

Classical liberalism espoused freedom of the individual from governmental interference and laissez-faire economic policies, but the stock market crash of 1929 and the ensuing Great Depression gave birth to a new strain of liberalism. Democratic President Franklin D. Roosevelt (1882–1945) came to office in 1933 with plans for a New Deal, a set of polices that saw government as having responsibility for minimizing economic inequalities, regulating business and the free market, and promoting programs for the welfare of individuals. Consequently, a term that meant small government and low taxation in the nineteenth century came to mean big government and high taxation in the twentieth century.

Roosevelt argued in a 1935 speech to the Young Democratic Clubs of America that unrestrained free enterprise could no longer be assumed to produce acceptable social and economic outcomes. Government would have to invest resources to achieve social change and to help the economically disadvantaged achieve a decent standard of living. While not opposing the free enterprise model, Roosevelt clearly urged his young audience to understand that "The freedom and opportunity that have

---

Source: From Franklin D. Roosevelt, Address to Young Democratic Clubs of America, August 24, 1935.

characterized American development in the past can be maintained if we recognize the fact that the individual system of our day calls for the collaboration of all of us to provide, at the least, security for all of us." The New Deal policies of the Roosevelt administration (1933–1945), supplemented by the Great Society programs of Lyndon B. Johnson's administration (1963–1969), resulted in the welfare state as we know it today. This is one of the main reasons why, at the beginning of the twenty-first century, the Republican Party positions itself as the party of classical liberalism and seeks to portray the Democratic Party as an irresponsible advocate of liberal "tax and spend" policies. But irresponsibility, as with beauty, is in the eyes of the beholder.

You doubtless know everything that I am going to say to you, because starting as early as last Monday certain special writers of a few papers have given you a complete outline of my remarks. I have been interested and somewhat amused by these clairvoyants who put on the front page many days ago this speech, which, because of pressure of time, I could only think out and dictate this very morning.

Whatever his party affiliations may be, the President of the United States, in addressing the youth of the country—even when speaking to the younger citizens of his own party—should speak as President of the whole people. It is true that the Presidency carries with it, for the time being, the leadership of a political party as well. But the Presidency carries with it a far higher obligation than this—the duty of analyzing and setting forth national needs and ideals which transcend and cut across all lines of party affiliation. Therefore, what I am about to say to you, members of the Young Democratic Clubs, is precisely—word for word—what I would say were I addressing a convention of the youth of the Republican Party.

A man of my generation comes to the councils of the younger warriors in a very different spirit from that in which the older men addressed the youth of my time. Party or professional leaders who talked to us twenty-five or thirty years ago almost inevitably spoke in a mood of achievement and of exultation. They addressed us with the air of those who had won the secret of success for themselves and of permanence of achievement for their country for all generations to come. They assumed that there was a guarantee of final accomplishment for the people of this country and that the grim specter of insecurity and want among the great masses would never haunt this land of plenty as it had widely visited other portions of the world. And so the elders of that day used to tell us, in effect, that the job of youth was merely to copy them and thereby to preserve the great things they had won for us.

I have no desire to underestimate the achievements of the past. We have no right to speak slightingly of the heritage, spiritual and material, that comes down to us. There are lessons that it teaches that we abandon only at our own peril. "Hold fast to that which is permanently true" is still a counsel of wisdom.

While my elders were talking to me about the perfection of America, I did not know then of the lack of opportunity, the lack of education, the lack of many of the essential needs of civilization which existed among millions of our people who lived not alone in the slums of the great cities and in the forgotten corners of rural America but even under the very noses of those who had the advantages and the power of Government of those days.

I say from my heart that no man of my generation has any business to address youth unless he comes to that task not in a spirit of exultation, but in a spirit of humility. I cannot expect you of a newer generation to believe me, of an older generation, if I do not frankly acknowledge that had the generation that brought you into the world been wiser and more provident and more unselfish, you would have been saved from needless difficult problems and needless pain and suffering. We may not have failed you in good intentions but we have certainly not been adequate in results. Your task, therefore, is not only to maintain the best in your heritage, but to labor to lift from the shoulders of the American people some of the burdens that the mistakes of a past generation have placed there.

There was a time when the formula for success was the simple admonition to have a stout heart and willing hands. A great, new country lay open. When life became hard in one place it was necessary only to move on to another. But circumstances have changed all that. Today we can no longer escape into virgin territory: we must master our environment. The youth of this generation finds that the old frontier is occupied, but that science and invention and economic evolution have opened up a new frontier—one not based on geography but on the resourcefulness of men and women applied to the old frontier.

The cruel suffering of the recent depression has taught us unforgettable lessons. We have been compelled by stark necessity to unlearn the too comfortable superstition that the American soil was mystically blessed with every kind of immunity to grave economic maladjustments, and that the American spirit of individualism—all alone and unhelped by the cooperative efforts of Government—could withstand and repel every form of economic disarrangement or crisis. The severity of the recent depression, toward which we had been heading for a whole generation, has taught us that no economic or social class in the community is so richly endowed and so independent of the general community that it can safeguard its own security, let alone assure security for the general community.

The very objectives of young people have changed. In the older days a great financial fortune was too often the goal. To rule through wealth, or through the power of wealth, fired our imagination. This was the dream of the golden ladder—each individual for himself.

It is my firm belief that the newer generation of America has a different dream. You place emphasis on sufficiency of life, rather than on a plethora of riches. You think of the security for yourself and your family that will give you good health, good food, good education, good working conditions, and the opportunity for normal recreation and occasional travel. Your advancement, you hope, is along a broad highway on which thousands of your fellow men and women are advancing with you.

You and I know that this modern economic world of ours is governed by rules and regulations vastly more complex than those laid down in the days of Adam Smith or John Stuart Mill. They faced simpler mechanical processes and social needs. It is worth remembering, for example, that the business corporation, as we know it, did not exist in the days of Washington and Hamilton and Jefferson. Private businesses then were conducted solely by individuals or by partnerships in which every member was immediately and wholly responsible for success or failure. Facts are relentless. We must adjust our ideas to the facts of today.

Our concepts of the regulation of money and credit and industrial competition, of the relation of employer and employee, created for the old civilization, are being modified to save our economic structure from confusion, destruction and paralysis. The rules that governed the relationship between an employer and employee in the blacksmith's shop in the days of Washington cannot, of necessity, govern the relationship between the fifty thousand employees of a great corporation and the infinitely complex and diffused ownership of that corporation. If fifty thousand employees spoke with fifty thousand voices, there would be a modern Tower of Babel. That is why we insist on their right to choose their representatives to bargain collectively in their behalf with their employer. In the case of the employees, every individual employee will know in his daily work whether he is adequately represented or not. In the case of the hundreds of thousands of stockholders in the present-day ownership of great corporations, however, their knowledge of the success of the management is based too often solely on a financial balance sheet. Things may go wrong in the management without their being aware of it for a year, or for many years to come. Without their day-to-day knowledge they may be exploited and their investments jeopardized. Therefore, we have come to the recognition of the need of simple but adequate public protection for the rights of the investing public.

A rudimentary concept of credit control appropriate for financing the economic life of a Nation of 3,000,000 people can hardly be urged as a means of directing and protecting the welfare of our twentieth-century industrialism. The simple banking rules of Hamilton's day, when all the transactions of a fair-sized bank could be kept in the neat penmanship of a clerk in one large ledger, fail to protect the millions of individual depositors of a great modern banking institution. And so it goes through all the range of economic life. Aggressive enterprise and shrewd invention have been at work on our economic machine. Our rules of conduct for the operation of that machine must be subjected to the same constant development.

And so in our social life. Forty years ago, slum conditions in our great cities were much worse than today. Living conditions on farms and working conditions in mines and factories were primitive. But they were taken for granted. Few people considered that the Government had responsibility for sanitation, for safety devices, for preventing child labor and night work for women. In 1911, twenty-four years ago, when I was first a member of the New York State Legislature, a number of the younger members of the Legislature worked against these old conditions and called for laws governing factory inspection, for workmen's compensation and for the limitation of work for women and children to fifty-four hours, with one day's rest in seven. Those of us who joined in this movement in the Legislature were called reformers, socialists, and wild men. We were opposed by many of the same organizations and the same individuals who are now crying aloud about the socialism involved in social security legislation, in bank deposit insurance, in farm credit, in the saving of homes, in the protection of investors and the regulation of public utilities. The reforms, however, for which we were condemned twenty-four years ago are taken today as a matter of course. And so, I believe, will be regarded the reforms that now cause such concern to the reactionaries of 1935. We come to an understanding of these new ways of protecting people because our knowledge enlarges and our capacity for organized action increases. People have learned that they can carry their burdens effectively only by cooperation. We have found out how to conquer the ravages of diseases that years ago were regarded as unavoidable and inevitable. We must learn that many other social ills can be cured.

Let me emphasize that serious as have been the errors of unrestrained individualism, I do not believe in abandoning the system of individual enterprise. The freedom and opportunity that have characterized American development in the past can be maintained if we recognize the fact that the individual system of our day calls for the collaboration of all of us to provide, at the least, security for all of us. Those words "freedom" and "opportunity" do not mean a license to climb upwards by pushing other people down.

Any paternalistic system which tries to provide for security for everyone from above only calls for an impossible task and a regimentation utterly uncongenial to the spirit of our people. But Government cooperation to help make the system of free enterprise work, to provide that minimum security without which the competitive system cannot function, to restrain the kind of individual action which in the past has been harmful to the community—that kind of governmental cooperation is entirely consistent with the best tradition of America.

MILTON FRIEDMAN

70. THE CASE FOR CONSERVATISM

Prior to the 1960s the premises of national economic policy established thirty years earlier by the New Deal were largely unchallenged. Indeed, they would soon be reinforced by the Great Society programs of the Lyndon B. Johnson Administration. But high rates of federal taxation and seemingly ever increasing federal involvement with more and more aspects of life in the United States caused the revival of classical liberalism.

All national economies other than totalitarian tyrannies are necessarily a mixture of capitalism and socialism. It is the emphasis of the mix that tilts the subsequent doctrine and ensuing policies one way or the other. Even the staunchest libertarian believes in the necessity of public programs for police, fire, and military protection. The economic liberalism of even the most conservative Republicans would still allow welfare state programs but at a minimal level.

The current debate over economic policy is one of degree. Since a mixed economy is a given, the doctrinal question is not whether there should be an economic safety net, but how large it should be; not whether there should be government regulation of business, but how much of it. Deregulation is the lifting of restrictions on business, industry, and other professional activities for which government rules have been established, with bureaucracies created to administer them. The modern movement toward deregulation, which really began during the Jimmy Carter administration, was supported by both parties in the United States, but for different reasons. Republicans tended to support it because they were inclined to be philosophically hostile toward government interference with business in the first place. Democrats tended to support it because they believed that greater market competition would bring down prices for the consumer.

Source: From Milton Friedman, *Capitalism and Freedom*. Copyright © 1962 by The University of Chicago. Reprinted by permission of the University of Chicago Press and the author.

Milton Friedman (1912–) is the conservative economist generally considered the leading proponent of deregulation and a return to laissez-faire economics. A 1976 Nobel Prize winner, he has had a major influence on thinking about monetary policy, consumption, and the proper role of government in regulating the economy. Friedman advocated government deregulation, the lifting of restrictions on business, industry, and other professional activities, and the elimination or downsizing of the bureaucracies that had grown up to administer these regulations.

In Capitalism and Freedom *(1962), Friedman presents his highly influential argument for deregulation and also explains the evolution of the word* liberal *as it reversed its meaning from the nineteenth to the twentieth century. The central thrust of his work is to defend "the role of competitive capitalism—the organization of the bulk of economic activity through private enterprise operating in a free market—as a system of economic freedom and a necessary condition for political freedom."*

In a much quoted passage in his inaugural address, President Kennedy said, "Ask not what your country can do for you—ask what you can do for your country." It is a striking sign of the temper of our times that the controversy about this passage centered on its origin and not on its content. Neither half of the statement expresses a relation between the citizen and his government that is worthy of the ideals of free men in a free society. The paternalistic "what your country can do for you" implies that government is the patron, the citizen the ward, a view that is at odds with the free man's belief in his own responsibility for his own destiny. The organismic "what you can do for your country" implies that government is the master or the deity, the citizen, the servant or the votary. To the free man, the country is the collection of individuals who compose it, not something over and above them. He is proud of a common heritage and loyal to common traditions. But he regards government as a means, an instrumentality, neither a grantor of favors and gifts, nor a master or god to be blindly worshipped and served. He recognizes no national goal except as it is the consensus of the goals that the citizens severally serve. He recognizes no national purpose except as it is the consensus of the purposes for which the citizens severally strive.

The free man will ask neither what his country can do for him nor what he can do for his country. He will ask rather "What can I and my compatriots do through government" to help us discharge our individual responsibilities, to achieve our several goals and purposes, and above all, to protect our freedom? And he will accompany this question with another: How can we keep the government we create from becoming a Frankenstein that will destroy the very freedom we establish it to protect? Freedom is a rare and delicate plant. Our minds tell us, and history confirms, that the great threat to freedom is the concentration of power. Government is necessary to preserve our freedom, it is an instrument through which we can exercise our freedom; yet by concentrating power in political hands, it is also a threat to freedom. Even though the men who wield this power initially be of good will and even though they be not corrupted by the power they exercise, the power will both attract and form men of a different stamp.

How can we benefit from the promise of government while avoiding the threat to freedom? Two broad principles embodied in our Constitution give an answer that has preserved our freedom so far, though they have been violated repeatedly in practice while proclaimed as precept.

First, the scope of government must be limited. Its major function must be to protect our freedom both from the enemies outside our gates and from our fellow-citizens: to preserve law and order, to enforce private contracts, to foster competitive markets. Beyond this major function, government may enable us at times to accomplish jointly what we would find it more difficult or expensive to accomplish severally. However, any such use of government is fraught with danger. We should not and cannot avoid using government in this way. But there should be a clear and large balance of advantages before we do. By relying primarily on voluntary co-operation and private enterprise, in both economic and other activities, we can insure that the private sector is a check on the powers of the governmental sector and an effective protection of freedom of speech, of religion, and of thought.

The second broad principle is that government power must be dispersed. If government is to exercise power, better in the county than in the state, better in the state than in Washington. If I do not like what my local community does, be it in sewage disposal, or zoning, or schools, I can move to another local community, and though few may take this step, the mere possibility acts as a check. If I do not like what my state does, I can move to another. If I do not like what Washington imposes, I have few alternatives in this world of jealous nations.

The very difficulty of avoiding the enactments of the federal government is of course the great attraction of centralization to many of its proponents. It will enable them more effectively, they believe, to legislate programs that—as they see it—are in the interest of the public, whether it be the transfer of income from the rich to the poor or from private to governmental purposes. They are in a sense right. But this coin has two sides. The power to do good is also the power to do harm; those who control the power today may not tomorrow; and, more important, what one man regards as good, another may regard as harm. The great tragedy of the drive to centralization, as of the drive to extend the scope of government in general, is that it is mostly led by men of good will who will be the first to rue its consequences.

The preservation of freedom is the protective reason for limiting and decentralizing governmental power. But there is also a constructive reason. The great advances of civilization, whether in architecture or painting, in science or literature, in industry or agriculture, have never come from centralized government. Columbus did not set out to seek a new route to China in response to a majority directive of a parliament, though he was partly financed by an absolute monarch. Newton and Leibnitz; Einstein and Bohr; Shakespeare, Milton, and Pasternak; Whitney, McCormick, Edison, and Ford; Jane Addams, Florence Nightingale, and Albert Schweitzer; no one of these opened new frontiers in human knowledge and understanding, in literature, in technical possibilities, or in the relief of human misery in response to governmental directives. Their achievements were the product of individual genius, of strongly held minority views, of a social climate permitting variety and diversity.

Government can never duplicate the variety and diversity of individual action. At any moment in time, by imposing uniform standards in housing, or nutrition, or clothing, government could undoubtedly improve the level of living of many individuals; by imposing uniform standards in schooling, road construction, or sanitation, central government could undoubtedly improve the level of performance in many local areas and perhaps even on the average of all communities. But in the process, government would replace progress by stagnation, it would substitute uniform mediocrity for the variety essential for that experimentation which can bring tomorrow's laggards above today's mean.

This book discusses some of these great issues. Its major theme is the role of competitive capitalism—the organization of the bulk of economic activity through private enterprise operating in a free market—as a system of economic freedom and a necessary condition for political freedom. Its minor theme is the role that government should play in a society dedicated to freedom and relying primarily on the market to organize economic activity.

The first two chapters deal with these issues on an abstract level, in terms of principles rather than concrete application. The later chapters apply these principles to a variety of particular problems.

An abstract statement can conceivably be complete and exhaustive, though this ideal is certainly far from realized in the two chapters that follow. The application of the principles cannot even conceivably be exhaustive. Each day brings new problems and new circumstances. That is why the role of the state can never be spelled out once and for all in terms of specific functions. It is also why we need from time to time to re-examine the bearing of what we hope are unchanged principles on the problems of the day. A by-product is inevitably a retesting of the principles and a sharpening of our understanding of them.

It is extremely convenient to have a label for the political and economic viewpoint elaborated in this book. The rightful and proper label is liberalism. Unfortunately, "As a supreme, if unintended compliment, the enemies of the system of private enterprise have thought it wise to appropriate its label",[1] so that liberalism has, in the United States, come to have a very different meaning than it did in the nineteenth century or does today over much of the Continent of Europe.

As it developed in the late eighteenth and early nineteenth centuries, the intellectual movement that went under the name of liberalism emphasized freedom as the ultimate goal and the individual as the ultimate entity in the society. It supported laissez faire at home as a means of reducing the role of the state in economic affairs and thereby enlarging the role of the individual; it supported free trade abroad as a means of linking the nations of the world together peacefully and democratically. In political matters, it supported the development of representative government and of parliamentary institutions, reduction in the arbitrary power of the state, and protection of the civil freedoms of individuals.

Beginning in the late nineteenth century, and especially after 1930 in the United States, the term liberalism came to be associated with a very different emphasis, particularly in economic policy. It came to be associated with a readiness to rely primarily on the state rather than on private voluntary arrangements to achieve objectives regarded as desirable. The catchwords became welfare and equality rather than freedom. The nineteenth-century liberal regarded an extension of freedom as the most effective way to promote welfare and equality; the twentieth-century liberal regards welfare and equality as either prerequisites of or alternatives to freedom. In the name of welfare and equality, the twentieth-century liberal has come to favor a revival of the very policies of state intervention and paternalism against which classical liberalism fought. In the very act of turning the clock back to seventeenth-century mercantilism, he is fond of castigating true liberals as reactionary!

The change in the meaning attached to the term liberalism is more striking in economic matters than in political. The twentieth-century liberal, like the nineteenth-century liberal, favors parliamentary institutions, representative government, civil rights, and so on. Yet even in political matters, there is a notable difference. Jealous of liberty, and hence fearful of centralized power, whether in governmental or private hands, the nineteenth-century liberal favored political decentralization. Committed to action and confident of the beneficence of power so long as it is in the hands of a government ostensibly controlled by the electorate, the twentieth-century liberal favors centralized government. He will resolve any doubt about where power should be located in favor of the state instead of the city, of the federal government instead of the state, and of a world organization instead of a national government.

Because of the corruption of the term liberalism, the views that formerly went under that name are now often labeled conservatism. But this is not a satisfactory alternative. The nineteenth-century liberal was a radical, both in the etymological sense of going to the root of the matter, and in the political sense of favoring major changes in social institutions. So too must be his modern heir. We do not wish to conserve the state interventions that have interfered so greatly with our freedom, though, of course, we do wish to conserve those that have promoted it. Moreover, in practice, the term conservatism has come to cover so wide a range of views, and views so incompatible with one another, that we shall no doubt see the growth of hyphenated designations, such as libertarian-conservative and aristocratic-conservative.

Partly because of my reluctance to surrender the term to proponents of measures that would destroy liberty, partly because I cannot find a better alternative, I shall resolve these difficulties by using the word liberalism in its original sense—as the doctrines pertaining to a free man.

NOTE

1. Joseph Schumpeter, *History of Economic Analysis* (New York: Oxford University Press, 1954), p. 394.

MICHAEL LIPSKY

71. Street-Level Bureaucrats

Michael Lipsky's central premise is that the public sector employees who deliver goods and services are in many cases the true policy makers. Their range of discretion, their extensive level of contact with the public, and their control of the resource base of many public organizations make them the central force in public sector decision making. Lipsky wrote about the implications of this situation for accountability, equity, and citizen access as well as the resulting controversy implicit in this reality. His arguments are even more important when one considers the impact of nonprofit organizations that have taken over major shares of human assistance and social services and have even fewer political controls.

Public service workers currently occupy a critical position in American society. Although they are normally regarded as low-level employees, the actions of most public service workers actually constitute the services "delivered" by government. Moreover, when taken together the individual decisions of these workers become, or add up to, agency policy. Whether government policy is to

---

Source: Reprinted from *Street-Level Bureaucracy: Dilemmas of the Individual in Public Services,* by Michael Lipsky. © 1980, Russell Sage Foundation. Used with permission of the Russell Sage Foundation.

deliver "goods"—such as welfare or public housing—or to confer status—such as "criminal" or "mentally ill"—the discretionary actions of public employees are the benefits and sanctions of government programs or determine access to government rights and benefits.

Most citizens encounter government (if they encounter it at all) not through letters to congressmen or by attendance at school board meetings but through their teachers and their children's teachers and through the policeman on the corner or in the patrol car. Each encounter of this kind represents an instance of policy delivery.

Public service workers who interact directly with citizens in the course of their jobs, and who have substantial discretion in the execution of their work, are called *street-level bureaucrats* in this study. Public service agencies that employ a significant number of street-level bureaucrats in proportion to their work force are called *street-level bureaucracies.* Typical street-level bureaucrats are teachers, police officers and other law enforcement personnel, social workers, judges, public lawyers and other court officers, health workers, and many other public employees who grant access to government programs and provide services with them. People who work in these jobs tend to have much in common because they experience analytically similar work conditions.[1]

The ways in which street-level bureaucrats deliver benefits and sanctions structure and delimit people's lives and opportunities. These ways orient and provide the social (and political) contexts in which people act. Thus every extension of service benefits is accompanied by an extension of state influence and control. As providers of public benefits and keepers of public order, street-level bureaucrats are the focus of political controversy. They are constantly torn by the demands of service recipients to improve effectiveness and responsiveness and by the demands of citizen groups to improve the efficacy and efficiency of government services. Since the salaries of street-level bureaucrats comprise a significant proportion of nondefense governmental expenditures, any doubts about the size of government budgets quickly translate into concerns for the scope and content of these public services. Moreover, public service workers have expanded and increasingly consolidated their collective strength so that in disputes over the scope of public services they have become a substantial independent force in the resolution of controversy affecting their status and position.

Street-level bureaucrats dominate political controversies over public services for two general reasons. First, debates about the proper scope and focus of governmental services are essentially debates over the scope and function of these public employees. Second, street-level bureaucrats have considerable impact on people's lives. This impact may be of several kinds. They socialize citizens to expectations of government services and a place in the political community. They determine the eligibility of citizens for government benefits and sanctions. They oversee the treatment (the service) citizens receive in those programs. Thus, in a sense street-level bureaucrats implicitly mediate aspects of the constitutional relationship of citizens to the state. In short, they hold the keys to a dimension of citizenship.

CONFLICT OVER THE SCOPE AND SUBSTANCE OF PUBLIC SERVICES

In the world of experience we perceive teachers, welfare workers, and police officers as members of separately organized and motivated public agencies. And so they are from many points of view. But if we divide public employees according to whether they interact with citizens directly and have discretion over significant aspects of citizens' lives, we see that a high proportion and enormous number of public workers share these job characteristics. They comprise a great portion of all public employees working in domestic affairs. State and local governments employ approximately 3.7 million in local schools, more than 500,000 people in police operations, and over 300,000 people in public welfare. Public school employees represent more than half of all workers employed in local governments. Instructional jobs represent about two-thirds of the educational personnel, and many of the rest are former teachers engaged in administration, or social workers, psychologists, and librarians who provide direct services in the schools. Of the 3.2 million local government public employees not engaged in education, approximately 14 percent work as police officers. One of every sixteen jobs in state and local government outside of education is held by a public welfare worker.[2] In this and other areas the majority of jobs are held by people with responsibility for involvement with citizens.

Other street-level bureaucrats comprise an important part of the remainder of local government personnel rolls. Although the U.S. Census Bureau does not provide breakdowns of other job classifications suitable for our purposes, we can assume that many of the 1.1 million health workers,[3] most of the 5,000 public service lawyers,[4] many of the employees of the various court systems, and other public employees also perform as street-level bureaucrats. Some of the nation's larger cities employ a staggering number of street-level bureaucrats. For example, the 26,680 school teachers in Chicago are more numerous than the populations of many of the Chicago suburbs.[5]

Another measure of the significance of street-level bureaucrats in public sector employment is the amount of public funds allocated to pay them. Of all local government salaries, more than half went to public education in 1973. Almost 80 percent of these monies was used to pay instructional personnel. Police salaries comprised approximately one-sixth of local public salaries not assigned to education.[6]

Much of the growth in public employment in the past 25 years has occurred in the ranks of street-level bureaucrats. From 1955 to 1975 government employment more than doubled, largely because the baby boom of the postwar years and the growing number of elderly, dependent citizens increased state and local activity in education, health, and public welfare.[7]

Street-level bureaucracies are labor-intensive in the extreme. Their business is providing service through people, and the operating costs of such agencies reflect their dependence upon salaried workers. Thus most of whatever is spent by government on education, police, or other social services (aside, of course, from income maintenance, or in the case of jails and prisons, inmate upkeep) goes directly to pay street-level bureaucrats. For example, in large cities over 90 percent of police expenditures is used to pay for salaries.[8]

Not only do the salaries of street-level bureaucrats constitute a major portion of the cost of public services, but also the scope of public services employing street-level bureaucrats has increased over time. Charity was once the responsibility of private agencies. The federal government now provides for the income needs of the poor. The public sector has absorbed responsibilities previously discharged by private organizations in such diverse and critical areas as policing, education, and health. Moreover, in all these fields government not only has supplanted private organizations but also has expanded the scope of responsibility of public ones. This is evident in increased public expectations for security and public safety, the extension of responsibilities in the schools to concerns with infant as well as postadolescent development, and public demands for affordable health care services.[9]

Public safety, public health, and public education *may* still be elusive social objectives, but in the past century they have been transformed into areas for which there is active governmental responsibility. The transformation of public responsibility in the area of social welfare has led some to recognize that what people "have" in modern American society often may consist primarily of their claims on government "largesse," and that claims to this "new property" should be protected as a right of citizens.[10] Street-level bureaucrats play a critical role in these citizen entitlements. Either they directly provide public benefits through services, or they mediate between citizens and their new but by no means secure estates.

The poorer people are, the greater the influence street-level bureaucrats tend to have over them. Indeed, these public workers are so situated that they may well be taken to be part of the problem of being poor. Consider the welfare recipient who lives in public housing and seeks the assistance of a legal services lawyer in order to reinstate her son in school. He has been suspended because of frequent encounters with the police. She is caught in a net of street-level bureaucrats with conflicting orientations toward her, all acting in what they call her "interest" and "the public interest."[11]

People who are not able to purchase services in the private sector must seek them from government if they are to receive them at all. Indeed, it is taken as a sign of social progress that poor people are granted access to services if they are too poor to pay for them.

Thus, when social reformers seek to ameliorate the problems of the poor, they often end up discussing the status of street-level bureaucrats. Welfare reformers move to separate service provision from decisions about support payments, or they design a negative income tax system that would eliminate social workers in allocating welfare. Problems of backlog in the courts are met with proposals to increase the number of judges. Recognition that early-childhood development largely established the potential for later achievement results in the development of new programs (such as Head Start) in and out of established institutions, to provide enriched early-childhood experiences.

In the 1960s and early 1970s the modal governmental response to social problems was to commission a corps of street-level bureaucrats to attend to them. Are poor people deprived of equal access to the courts? Provide them with lawyers. Equal access to health care? Establish neighborhood clinics. Educational opportunity? Develop preschool enrichment programs. It is far easier and less disruptive to develop employment for street-level bureaucrats than to reduce income inequalities.

In recent years public employees have benefited considerably from the growth of public spending on street-level bureaucracies.[12] Salaries have increased from inadequate to respectable and even desirable. Meanwhile, public employees, with street-level bureaucrats in the lead, have secured unprecedented control over their work environments through the development of unions and union-like associations.[13] For example, teachers and other instructional personnel have often been able to maintain their positions and even increase in number, although schools are more frequently under attack for their cost to taxpayers. The ratio of instructional personnel in schools has continued to rise despite the decline in the number of school-age children.[14] This development supplements general public support for the view that some street-level bureaucrats, such as teachers and police officers, are necessary for a healthy society.[15]

The fiscal crisis that has affected many cities, notably New York and more recently Cleveland and Newark, has provided an opportunity to assess the capacity of public service workers to hold onto their jobs in the face of enormous pressures. Since so much of municipal budgets consists of inflexible, mandated costs—for debt service, pension plans and other personnel benefits, contractually obligated salary increases, capital expenditure commitments, energy purchases, and so on—the place to find "fat" to eliminate from municipal budgets is in the service sector, where most expenditures tend to be for salaries. While many public employees have been fired during this crisis period, it is significant that public service workers often have been able to lobby, bargain, and cajole to minimize this attrition.[16] They are supported in their claims by a public fearful of a reduced police force on the street and resentful of dirtier streets resulting from fewer garbage pickups. They are supported by families whose children will receive less instruction from fewer specialists than in the past if teachers are fired. And it does not hurt their arguments that many public employees and their relatives vote in the city considering force reductions.[17]

The growth of the service sector represents the furthest reaches of the welfare state. The service sector penetrates every area of human needs as they are recognized and defined, and it grows within each recognized area. This is not to say that the need is met, but only that the service state breaches the barriers between public responsibility and private affairs.

The fiscal crisis of the cities focuses on the service sector, fundamentally challenging the priorities of the service state under current perceptions of scarcity. Liberals have now joined fiscal conservatives in challenging service provision. They do not do so directly, by questioning whether public services and responsibilities developed in this century are appropriate. Instead, they do it backhandedly, arguing that the accretion of public employees and their apparently irreversible demands upon revenues threaten the autonomy, flexibility, and prosperity of the political order. Debates over the proper scope of services face the threat of being overwhelmed by challenges to the entire social service structure as seen from the perspective of unbalanced public budgets.

CONFLICT OVER INTERACTIONS WITH CITIZENS

I have argued that street-level bureaucrats engender controversy because they must be dealt with if policy is to change. A second reason street-level bureaucrats tend to be the focus of public controversy is the immediacy of their interactions with citizens and their impact on people's lives. The policy delivered by street-level bureaucrats is most often immediate and personal. They usually make decisions on the spot (although sometimes they try not to) and their determinations are focused entirely on the individual. In contrast, an urban renewal program might destroy a neighborhood and replace and substitute new housing and different people, but the policy was prolonged, had many different stages, and was usually played out in arenas far removed from the daily life of neighborhood residents.

The decisions of street-level bureaucrats tend to be redistributive as well as allocative. By determining eligibility for benefits they enhance the claims of some citizens to governmental goods and services at the expense of general taxpayers and those whose claims are denied. By increasing or decreasing benefits availability to low-income recipient populations they implicitly regulate the degree of redistribution that will be paid for by more affluent sectors.

In another sense, in delivering policy street-level bureaucrats make decisions about people that affect their life chances. To designate or treat someone as a welfare recipient, a juvenile delinquent, or a high achiever affects the relationships of others to that person and also affects the person's self-evaluation. Thus begins (or continues) the social process that we infer accounts for so many self-fulfilling prophecies. The child judged to be a juvenile delinquent develops such a self-image and is grouped with other "delinquents," increasing the chances that he or she will adopt the behavior thought to have been incipient in the first place. Children thought by their teacher to be richly endowed in learning ability learn more than peers of equal intelligence who were not thought to be superior.[18] Welfare recipients find or accept housing inferior to those with equal disposable incomes who are not recipients.[19]

A defining facet of the working environment of street-level bureaucrats is that they must deal with clients' personal reactions to their decisions, however they cope with their implications. To say that people's self-evaluation is affected by the actions of street-level bureaucrats is to say that people are reactive to the policy. This is not exclusively confined to subconscious processes. Clients of street-level bureaucracies respond angrily to real or perceived injustices, develop strategies to ingratiate themselves with workers, act grateful and elated or sullen and passive in reaction to street-level bureaucrats' decisions. It is one thing to be treated neglectfully and routinely by the telephone company, the motor vehicle bureau, or other government agencies whose agents know nothing of the personal circumstances surrounding a claim or request. It is quite another thing to be shuffled, categorized, and treated "bureaucratically" (in the pejorative sense) by someone to whom one is directly talking and from whom one expects at least an open and sympathetic hearing. In short, the reality of the work of street-level bureaucrats could hardly be farther from the bureaucratic ideal of impersonal detachment in decision making.[20] On the contrary, in street-level bureaucracies the objects of critical decisions—*people*—actually change as a result of the decisions.

Street-level bureaucrats are also the focus of citizen reactions because their discretion opens up the possibility that they will respond favorably on behalf of people. Their general and diffuse obligation to the "public interest" permits hope to flourish that the individual worker will adopt a benign or favorable orientation toward the client. Thus, in a world of large and impersonal agencies that apparently hold the keys to important benefits, sanctions, and opportunities, the ambiguity of work definitions sustains hope for a friend in court.

This discussion helps explain continued controversy over street-level bureaucracies at the level of individual service provision. At the same time, the peculiar nature of government service delivery through street-level bureaucrats helps explain why street-level bureaucracies are apparently the primary focus of community conflict in the current period, and why they are likely to remain the focus of such conflict in the foreseeable future. It is no accident that the most heated community conflicts since 1964 have focused on schools and police departments, and on the responsiveness of health and welfare agencies and institutions.[21] These are the sites of the provision of public benefits and sanctions. They are the locus of individual decisions about and treatment of citizens, and thus are primary targets of protest. As Frances Fox Piven and Richard Cloward explain:

> . . . people experience deprivation and oppression within a concrete setting, not as the end product of large and abstract processes, and it is the concrete experience that molds their discontent into specific grievances against specific targets. . . . People on relief [for example] experience the shabby waiting rooms, the overseer or caseworker and the dole. They do not experience American social welfare policy. . . . In other words, it is the daily experience of people that shapes their grievances, establishes the measure of their demands, and points out the targets of their anger.[22]

While people may experience these bureaucracies as individuals, schools, precinct houses, or neighborhood clinics are places where policy about individuals is organized collectively. These administrative arrangements suggest to citizens the possibility that controlling, or at least affecting, their structures will influence the quality of individual treatment. Thus we have two preconditions for successful community organization efforts: the hope and plausibility that individual benefits may accrue to those taking part in group action and a visible, accessible, and blamable collective target.[23]

Community action focused on street-level bureaucracies is also apparently motivated by concerns for community character. The dominant institutions in communities help shape community identity. They may be responsive to the dominant community group (this has been the traditional role of high schools in Boston) or they may be unresponsive and opposed to conceptions of community and identity favored by residents, as in the case of schools that neglect the Spanish heritage of a significant minority. Whether people are motivated by specific grievances or more diffuse concerns that become directed at community institutions, their focus in protesting the actions of street-level bureaucracies may be attributed to the familiarity of the agency, its critical role in community welfare, and a perception at some level that these institutions are not sufficiently accountable to the people they serve.

Finally, street-level bureaucrats play a critical role in regulating the degree of contemporary conflict by virtue of their role as agents of social control. Citizens who receive public benefits interact with public agents who require certain behaviors of them. They must anticipate the requirements of these public agents and claimants must tailor their actions and develop "suitable" attitudes both toward the services they receive and toward the street-level bureaucrats themselves. Teachers convey and enforce expectations of proper attitudes toward schooling, self, and efficacy in other interactions. Policemen convey expectations about public behavior and authority. Social workers convey expectations about public benefits and the status of recipients.

The social control function of street-level bureaucrats requires comment in a discussion of the place of public service workers in the larger society. The public service sector plays a critical part in softening the impact of the economic system on those who are not its primary beneficiaries and inducing people to accept the neglect or inadequacy of primary economic and social institutions. Police, courts, and prisons obviously play such a role in processing the junkies, petty thieves, muggers, and others whose behavior toward society is associated with their economic position. It is a role equally played by schools in socializing the population to the economic order and the likely opportunities for different strata of the population. Public support and employment programs expand to ameliorate the impact of unemployment or reduce the incidence of discontent; they contract when employment opportunities improve. Moreover, they are designed and implemented to convey the message that welfare status is to be avoided and that work, however poorly rewarded, is preferable to public assistance. One can also see the two edges of public policy in the "war on poverty" where the public benefits of social service and community action invested neighborhood institutions with benefits for which potential dissidents could compete and ordinary citizens could develop dependency.[24]

What to some are the highest reaches of the welfare state are to others the furthest extension of social control. Street-level bureaucrats are partly the focus of controversy because they play this dual role. Welfare reform founders on disagreements over whether to eliminate close scrutiny of welfare applications in order to reduce administrative costs and harassment of recipients, or to increase the scrutiny in the name of controlling abuses and preventing welfare recipients from taking advantage. Juvenile corrections and mental health policy founder on disputes over the desirability of dismantling large institutions in the name of cost effectiveness and rehabilitation, or retaining close supervision in an effort to avoid the costs of letting unreconstructed "deviants" loose. In short, street-level bureaucrats are also at the center of controversy because a divided public perceives that social control in the name of public order and acceptance of the status quo are social objectives with which proposals to reduce the role of street-level bureaucrats (eliminating welfare checkups, reducing parole personnel, decriminalizing marijuana) would interfere.

Public controversy also focuses on the proper kind of social control. Current debates in corrections policy, concerning automatic sentencing and a "hard-nosed" view of punishment or more rehabilitative orientations, reflect conflict over the degree of harshness in managing prison populations. In educational practice the public is also divided as to the advisability of liberal disciplinary policies and more flexible instruction or punitive discipline and more rigid, traditional approaches. The "medicalization" of deviance, in which disruptive behavior is presumed cause for intervention by a doctor rather than a disciplinarian, is another area in which there is controversy over the appropriate kind of social control.

From the citizen's viewpoint, the roles of street-level bureaucrats are as extensive as the functions of government and intensively experienced as daily routines require them to interact with the street ministers of education, dispute settlement, and health services. Collectively, street-level bureaucrats absorb a high share of public resources and become the focus of society's hopes for a healthy balance between provision of public services and a reasonable burden of public expenditures. As individuals, street-level bureaucrats represent the hopes of citizens for fair and effective treatment by government even as they are positioned to see clearly the limitations on effective intervention and the constraints on responsiveness engendered by mass processing.

NOTES

1. These definitions are analytical. They focus not on nominal occupational roles but on the characteristics of the particular work situations. Thus not every street-level bureaucrat works for a street-level bureaucracy [for example, a relocation specialist (a type of street-level bureaucrat) may work for an urban renewal agency whose employees are mostly planners, builders, and other technicians]. Conversely, not all employees of street-level bureaucracies are street-level bureaucrats (for example, file clerks in a welfare department or police officers on routine clerical assignments).

The conception of street-level bureaucracy was originally proposed in a paper prepared for the Annual Meeting of the American Political Science Association in 1969, "Toward a Theory of Street-Level Bureaucracy." It was later revised and published in Willis Hawley and Michael Lipsky, eds., *Theoretical Perspectives on Urban Politics* (Englewood Cliffs, N.J.: Prentice-Hall, 1977), pp. 196–213.

2. U.S. Bureau of the Census, Public Employment in 1973, Series GE No. 1 (Washington, D.C.: Government Printing Office, 1974), p. 9. Presented in Alan Baker and Barbara Grouby, "Employment and Payrolls of State and Local Governments, by Function: October 1973," *Municipal Year Book, 1975* (Washington, D.C.: International City Managers Association, 1975), pp. 109–112, table 4/3. Also, Marianne Stein Kah, "City Employment and Payrolls: 1975," *Municipal Year Book, 1977* (Washington, D.C.: International City Managers Association, 1977), pp. 173–179. These figures have been adjusted to represent full-time equivalents. For purposes of assessing public commitments to providing services, full-time equivalents are more appropriate statistics than total employment figures, which count many part-time employees.

3. Jeffry H. Galper, *The Politics of Social Services* (Englewood Cliffs, N.J.: Prentice-Hall, 1975), p. 56.

4. Lois Forer, *Death of the Law* (New York: McKay, 1975), p. 191.

5. *New York Times,* April 4, 1976, p. 22.

6. Baker and Grouby, "Employment and Payrolls of State and Local Governments."

7. *New York Times,* July 10, 1977, p. F13.

8. Of four cities with populations over one million responding to a *Municipal Year Book* survey, the proportion of personnel expenditures to total expenditures in police departments averaged 94 percent and did not go below 86 percent. Cities with smaller populations showed similar tendencies. These observations are derived from David Lewin, "Expenditure, Compensation, and Employment Data in Police, Fire and Refuse Collection and Disposal Departments," *Municipal Year Book, 1975,* pp. 39–98, table 1/21. However, the variation was much greater in the less populous cities because of smaller base figures and the fact that when cities with smaller bases make capital investments, the ratio of personnel to total expenditures changes more precipitously.

That public expenditures for street-level bureaucracies go to individuals primarily as salaries may also be demonstrated in the case of education. For example, more than 73 percent of all noncapital education expenditures inside Standard Metropolitan Statistical Areas goes toward personal services (i.e., salaries). See Government Finances, Number 1, Finances of School Districts, 1972 U.S. Census of Government (Bureau of the Census, Social and Economic Statistics Administration, U.S. Department of Commerce), table 4.

9. Many analysts have discussed the increasing role of services in the economy. See Daniel Bell, *The Coming of the Post-Industrial Society: A Venture in Social Forecasting* (New York: Basic Books, 1973); Alan Gartner and Frank Reissman, *The Service Society and the Consumer Vanguard* (New York: Harper & Row, 1974); Victor Fuchs, *The Service Economy* (New York: Columbia University Press, 1968). On transformations in public welfare, see Gilbert Steiner, *Social Insecurity* (Chicago: Rand McNally, 1966), chap. 1; on public safety, see Allan Silver, "The Demand for Order in Civil Society," in David Bordua, ed., *The Police: Six Sociological Essays* (New York: John Wiley, 1967), pp. 1–24.

10. Charles Reich, "The New Property," *Yale Law Journal,* vol. 72 (April, 1964): 733–787.

11. Carl Hosticka, "Legal Services Lawyers Encounter Clients: A Study in Street-Level Bureaucracy" (Ph.D. diss., Massachusetts Institute of Technology, 1976), pp. 11–13.

12. See Frances Piven's convincing essay in which she argues that social service workers were the major beneficiaries of federal programs concerned with cities and poor people in the 1960s. Piven, "The Urban Crisis: Who Got What and Why," in Richard Cloward

and Frances Piven, *The Politics of Turmoil* (New York: Vintage Books, 1972), pp. 314–351.

13. J. Joseph Loewenberg and Michael H. Moskow, eds., *Collective Bargaining in Government* (Englewood Cliffs, N.J.: Prentice-Hall, 1972); A. Laurence Chickering, ed., *Public Employee Unions* (Lexington, Mass.: Lexington Books, 1976); and Margaret Levi, *Bureaucratic Insurgency* (Lexington, Mass.: Lexington Books, 1977).

14. The decline is a function of the lower birthrate and periodicity in the size of the school-age population originally resulting from the birth explosion following World War II. See Baker and Grouby, *Municipal Year Book, 1975*, pp. 109 ff., on serviceability ratios.

15. This perspective remains applicable in the current period. However, in reaction to this tendency, programs that would eliminate service mediators and service providers, such as negative income taxation and housing allowances, have gained support. Fiscal scarcity has brought to public attention questions concerning the marginal utility of some of these service areas.

16. Consider the New York City policemen who, in October 1976, agreed to work overtime without pay so that a crop of rookie patrolmen would not be eliminated. *New York Times,* October 24, 1976, p. 24.

17. There can be no better illustration of the strength of the organized service workers and their support by relevant interests then the New York State Assembly's overriding of Gov. Hugh Carey's veto of the so-called Stavisky bill. This legislation, written in a period of massive concern for cutting the New York City budget, required the city to spend no less on education in the three years following the fiscal collapse than in the three years before the crisis, thus tying the hands of the city's financial managers even more. *New York Times,* April 4, 1976, p. E6; April 18, 1976, p. E6.

18. The seminal work here is Robert Rosenthal and Lenore Jacobson, *Pygmalion in the Classroom* (New York: Holt, Rinehart and Winston, 1968).

19. Martin Rein, "Welfare and Housing," Joint Center Working Paper Series, no. 4 (Cambridge, Mass.: Joint Center for Urban Studies, Spring, 1971, rev. Feb. 1972).

20. On the alleged importance of bureaucratic detachment in processing clients see Peter Blau, *Exchange and Power in Social Life* (New York: John Wiley, 1964), p. 66.

21. See National Advisory Commission on Civil Disorders, *Report* (New York: Bantam, 1968); Peter Rossi et al., *Roots of Urban Discontent* (New York: John Wiley, 1974).

22. Frances Fox Piven and Richard Cloward, *Poor People's Movements* (New York: Pantheon, 1977), pp. 20–21.

23. Michael Lipsky and Margaret Levi, "Community Organization as a Political Resource," in Harlan Hahn, ed., *People and Places in Urban Society* (Urban Affairs Annual Review, vol. 6) (Newbury Park, Calif.: Sage Publications, 1972), pp. 175–199.

24. See James O'Connor's discussion of "legitimation" and his general thesis concerning the role of the state service sector, in O'Connor, *The Fiscal Crisis of the State* (New York: St. Martin's, 1973). On social control functions in particular policy sectors see Samuel Bowles and Herbert Gintis, *Schooling in Capitalist America* (New York: Basic Books, 1976); Frances Fox Piven and Richard Cloward, *Regulating the Poor* (New York: Pantheon, 1971); Galper, *The Politics of Social Services;* Richard Quinney, *Criminology* (Boston: Little, Brown, 1975); Ira Katznelson, "Urban Counterrevolution," in Robert P. Wolff, ed., *1984 Revisited* (New York: Alfred Knopf, 1973), pp. 139–164.

JAMES Q. WILSON AND
GEORGE L. KELLING

72. POLICE BUREAUCRATS AND CRIME

Among all government bureaucrats, none has more constant and personal contact with citizens—with the possible exception of mail carriers—than the police officer on the street. In their classic "Broken Windows" article, Wilson and Kelling first articulated the theory that there is a link between disorder in a community and crime in that community. Police officers, they suggested, should be as concerned with maintaining order as with preventing crime.

The authors draw on the argument that where a community permits a few broken windows to remain unrepaired and a few unsightly instances of graffiti to remain unpainted, more broken windows and more graffiti are inevitable. By analogy, Wilson and Kelling suggest that the police should pay more attention to the small disruptions in communities—"the ill-smelling drunk, the rowdy teenager, or the importuning beggar." According to the theory, by "repairing" these "broken windows," the police will create an atmosphere where criminals feel uncomfortable and move on to other places. Urban police officials—including New York City's William Bratton—relied on this theory to reduce crime successfully and significantly in their cities during the decade of the 1990s. As recently as 1997, New York City Police Commissioner Howard Safir wrote in Police Chief Magazine *(December, 1997): "The merits of the 'Broken Windows' theory have clearly demonstrated the fact that police agencies that aggressively address quality-of-life issues are also those that achieve the greatest reductions in crime."*

In the mid-1970s the State of New Jersey announced a "Safe and Clean Neighborhoods Program," designed to improve the quality of community life in

Source: From "Broken Windows" by James Q. Wilson and George L. Kelling, *The Atlantic Monthly*, March 1982. Reprinted by permission of the authors.

twenty-eight cities. As part of that program, the state provided money to help cities take police officers out of their patrol cars and assign them to walking beats. The governor and other state officials were enthusiastic about using foot patrol as a way of cutting crime, but many police chiefs were skeptical. Foot patrol, in their eyes, had been pretty much discredited. It reduced the mobility of the police, who thus had difficulty responding to citizen calls for service, and it weakened headquarters control over patrol officers.

Many police officers also disliked foot patrol, but for different reasons: it was hard work, it kept them outside on cold, rainy nights, and it reduced their chances for making a "good pinch." In some departments, assigning officers to foot patrol had been used as a form of punishment. And academic experts on policing doubted that foot patrol would have any impact on crime rates; it was, in the opinion of most, little more than a sop to public opinion. But since the state was paying for it, the local authorities were willing to go along.

Five years after the program started, the Police Foundation, in Washington, D.C., published an evaluation of the foot-patrol project. Based on its analysis of a carefully controlled experiment carried out chiefly in Newark, the foundation concluded, to the surprise of hardly anyone, that foot patrol had not reduced crime rates. But residents of the foot patrolled neighborhoods seemed to feel more secure than persons in other areas, tended to believe that crime had been reduced, and seemed to take fewer steps to protect themselves from crime (staying at home with the doors locked, for example). Moreover, citizens in the foot-patrol areas had a more favorable opinion of the police than did those living elsewhere. And officers walking beats had higher morale, greater job satisfaction, and a more favorable attitude toward citizens in their neighborhoods than did officers assigned to patrol cars.

These findings may be taken as evidence that the skeptics were right—foot patrol has no effect on crime; it merely fools the citizens into thinking that they are safer. But in our view, and in the view of the authors of the Police Foundation study (of whom Kelling was one), the citizens of Newark were not fooled at all. They knew what the foot-patrol officers were doing, they knew it was different from what motorized officers do, and they knew that having officers walk beats did in fact make their neighborhoods safer.

But how can a neighborhood be "safer" when the crime rate has not gone down—in fact, may have gone up? Finding the answer requires first that we understand what most often frightens people in public places. Many citizens, of course, are primarily frightened by crime, especially crime involving a sudden, violent attack by a stranger. This risk is very real, in Newark as in many large cities. But we tend to overlook another source of fear—the fear of being bothered by disorderly people. Not violent people, nor, necessarily, criminals, but disreputable or obstreperous or unpredictable people: panhandlers, drunks, addicts, rowdy teenagers, prostitutes, loiterers, the mentally disturbed.

What foot-patrol officers did was to elevate, to the extent they could, the level of public order in these neighborhoods. Though the neighborhoods were predominantly black and the foot patrolmen were mostly white, this "order-maintenance" function of the police was performed to the general satisfaction of both parties.

One of us (Kelling) spent many hours walking with Newark foot-patrol officers to see how they defined "order" and what they did to maintain it. One beat was typical: a busy but dilapidated area in the heart of Newark, with many abandoned buildings, marginal shops (several of which prominently displayed knives and straight-edged razors in their windows), one large department store, and, most important, a train station and several major bus stops. Though the area was run-down, its streets were filled with people, because it was a major transportation center. The good order of this area was important not only to those who lived and worked there but also to many others, who had to move through it on their way home, to supermarkets, or to factories.

The people on the street were primarily black; the officer who walked the street was white. The people were made up of "regulars" and "strangers." Regulars included both "decent folk" and some drunks and derelicts who were always there but who "knew their place." Strangers were, well, strangers, and viewed suspiciously, sometimes apprehensively. The officer—call him Kelly—knew who the regulars were, and they knew him. As he saw his job, he was to keep an eye on strangers, and make certain that the disreputable regulars observed some informal but widely understood rules. Drunks and addicts could sit on the stoops, but could not lie down. People could drink on side streets, but not at the main intersection. Bottles had to be in paper bags. Talking to, bothering, or begging from people waiting at the bus stop was strictly forbidden. If a dispute erupted between a businessman and a customer, the businessman was assumed to be right, especially if the customer was a stranger. If a stranger loitered, Kelly would ask him if he had any means of support and what his business was; if he gave unsatisfactory answers, he was sent on his way. Persons who broke the informal rules, especially those who bothered people waiting at bus stops, were arrested for vagrancy. Noisy teenagers were told to keep quiet.

These rules were defined and enforced in collaboration with the "regulars" on the street. Another neighborhood might have different rules, but these, everybody understood, were the rules for *this* neighborhood. If someone violated them, the regulars not only turned to Kelly for help but also ridiculed the violator. Sometimes what Kelly did could be described as "enforcing the law," but just as often it involved taking informal or extralegal steps to help protect what the neighborhood had decided was the appropriate level of public order. Some of the things he did probably would not withstand a legal challenge.

A determined skeptic might acknowledge that a skilled foot-patrol officer can maintain order but still insist that this sort of "order" has little to do with the real sources of community fear—that is with violent crime. To a degree, that is true. But two things must be borne in mind. First, outside observers should not assume that they know how much of the anxiety now endemic in many big-city neighborhoods stems from a fear of "real" crime and how much from a sense that the street is disorderly, a source of distasteful, worrisome encounters.

The people of Newark, to judge from their behavior and their remarks to interviewers, apparently assign a high value to public order, and feel relieved and reassured when the police help them maintain that order.

Second, at the community level, disorder and crime are usually inextricably linked, in a kind of developmental sequence. Social psychologists and police officers tend to agree that if a window in a building is broken and is left unrepaired, all the rest of the windows will soon be broken. This is as true in nice neighborhoods as in rundown ones. Window-breaking does not necessarily occur on a large scale because some areas are inhabited by determined window-breakers whereas others are populated by window-lovers; rather, one unrepaired broken window is a signal that no one cares, and so breaking more windows costs nothing. (It has always been fun.)

Philip Zimbardo, a Stanford psychologist, reported in 1969 on some experiments testing the broken-window theory. He arranged to have an automobile without license plates parked with its hood up on a street in the Bronx and a comparable automobile on a street in Palo Alto, California. The car in the Bronx was attacked by "vandals" within ten minutes of its "abandonment." The first to arrive were a family—father, mother, and young son—who removed the radiator and battery. Within twenty-four hours, virtually everything of value had been removed. Then random destruction began—windows were smashed, parts torn off, upholstery ripped. Children began to use the car as a playground. Most of the adult "vandals" were well-dressed, apparently clean-cut whites. The car in Palo Alto sat untouched for more than a week. Then Zimbardo smashed part of it with a sledgehammer. Soon, passersby were joining in. Within a few hours, the car had been turned upside down and utterly destroyed. Again, the "vandals" appeared to be primarily respectable whites.

Untended property becomes fair game for people out for fun or plunder and even for people who ordinarily would not dream of doing such things and who probably consider themselves law-abiding. Because of the nature of community life in the Bronx—its anonymity, the frequency with which cars are abandoned and things are stolen or broken, the past experience of "no one caring"—vandalism begins much more quickly than it does in staid Palo Alto, where people have come to believe that private possessions are cared for, and that mischievous behavior is costly. But vandalism can occur anywhere once communal barriers—the sense of mutual regard and the obligations of civility—are lowered by actions that seem to signal that "no one cares."

We suggest that "untended" behavior also leads to the breakdown of community controls. A stable neighborhood of families who care for their homes, mind each other's children, and confidently frown on unwanted intruders can change, in a few years or even a few months, to an inhospitable and frightening jungle. A piece of property is abandoned, weeds grow up, a window is smashed. Adults stop scolding rowdy children; the children, emboldened, become more rowdy. Families move out, unattached adults move in. Teenagers gather in front of the corner store. The merchant asks them to move; they refuse. Fights occur. Litter accumulates. People start drinking in front of the grocery; in time, an inebriate slumps to the sidewalk and is allowed to sleep it off. Pedestrians are approached by panhandlers.

At this point it is not inevitable that serious crime will flourish or violent attacks on strangers will occur. But many residents will think that crime, especially violent crime, is on the rise, and they will modify their behavior accordingly. They will use the streets less often, and when on the streets will stay apart from their fellows, moving with averted eyes, silent lips, and hurried steps. "Don't get involved." For some residents, this growing atomization will matter little, because the neighborhood is not their "home" but "the place where they live." Their interests are elsewhere; they are cosmopolitans. But it will matter greatly to other people, whose lives derive meaning and satisfaction from local attachments rather than worldly involvement; for them, the neighborhood will cease to exist except for a few reliable friends whom they arrange to meet.

Such an area is vulnerable to criminal invasion. Though it is not inevitable, it is more likely that here, rather than in places where people are confident they can regulate public behavior by informal controls, drugs will change hands, prostitutes will solicit, and cars will be stripped. That the drunks will be robbed by boys who do it as a lark, and the prostitutes' customers will be robbed by men who do it purposefully and perhaps violently. That muggings will occur.

Among those who often find it difficult to move away from this are the elderly. Surveys of citizens suggest that the elderly are much less likely to be the victims of crime than younger persons, and some have inferred from this that the well-known fear of crime voiced by the elderly is an exaggeration: perhaps we ought not to design special programs to protect older persons; perhaps we should even try to talk them out of their mistaken fears. This argument misses the point. The prospect of a confrontation with an obstreperous teenager or a drunken panhandler can be as fear-inducing for defenseless persons as the prospect of meeting an actual robber; indeed, to a defenseless person, the two kinds of confrontation are often indistinguishable. Moreover, the lower rate at which the elderly are victimized is a measure of the steps they have already taken—chiefly, staying behind locked doors—to minimize the risks they face. Young men are more frequently attacked than older women, not because they are easier or more lucrative targets but because they are on the streets more.

Nor is the connection between disorderliness and fear made only by the elderly. Susan Estrich, of the Harvard Law School, has recently gathered together a number of surveys on the sources of public fear. One, done in Portland, Oregon, indicated that three fourths of the adults interviewed cross to the other side of a street when they see a gang of teenagers; another survey, in Baltimore, discovered that nearly half would cross the street to avoid even a single strange youth. When an interviewer asked people in a housing project where the most dangerous spot was, they mentioned a place where young persons gathered to drink and play music, despite the fact that not a single crime had occurred there. In Boston public housing projects, the greatest fear was expressed by persons living in the buildings where disorderliness and incivility, not crime, were the greatest. Knowing this helps one understand the significance of such otherwise harmless displays as subway graffiti. As Nathan Glazer has written, the proliferation of graffiti, even when not obscene, confronts the subway rider with the inescapable knowledge that the environment he must endure for an hour or more a day is uncontrolled and uncontrollable, and that anyone can invade it to do whatever damage and mischief the mind suggests.

In response to fear people avoid one another, weakening controls. Sometimes they call the police. Patrol cars arrive, an occasional arrest occurs but crime continues and disorder is not abated. Citizens complain to the police chief, but he explains that his department is low on personnel and that the courts do not punish petty or first-time offenders. To the residents, the police who arrive in squad cars are either ineffective or uncaring: to the police, the residents are animals who deserve each other. The citizens may soon stop calling the police, because "they can't do anything."

The process we call urban decay has occurred for centuries in every city. But what is happening today is different in at least two important respects. First, in the period before, say, World War II, city dwellers—because of money costs, transportation difficulties, familial and church connections—could rarely move away from neighborhood problems. When movement did occur, it tended to be along public-transit routes. Now mobility has become exceptionally easy for all but the poorest or those who are blocked by racial prejudice. Earlier crime waves had a kind of built-in self-correcting mechanism: the determination of a neighborhood or community to reassert control over its turf. Areas in Chicago, New York, and Boston would experience crime and gang wars, and then normalcy would return, as the families for whom no alternative residences were possible reclaimed their authority over the streets.

Second, the police in this earlier period assisted in that reassertion of authority by acting, sometimes violently, on behalf of the community. Young toughs were roughed up, people were arrested "on suspicion" or for vagrancy, and prostitutes and petty thieves were routed. "Rights" were something enjoyed by decent folk, and perhaps also by the serious professional criminal, who avoided violence and could afford a lawyer.

This pattern of policing was not an aberration or the result of occasional excess. From the earliest days of the nation, the police function was seen primarily as that of a night watchman: to maintain order against the chief threats to order—fire, wild animals, and disreputable behavior. Solving crimes was viewed not as a police responsibility but as a private one. In the March, 1969, *Atlantic,* one of us (Wilson) wrote a brief account of how the police role had slowly changed from maintaining order to fighting crimes. The change began with the creation of private detectives (often ex-criminals), who worked on a contingency-fee basis for individuals who had suffered losses. In time, the detectives were absorbed in municipal agencies and paid a regular salary simultaneously, the responsibility for prosecuting thieves was shifted from the aggrieved private citizen to the professional prosecutor. This process was not complete in most places until the twentieth century.

In the 1960s, when urban riots were a major problem, social scientists began to explore carefully the order maintenance function of the police, and to suggest ways of improving it—not to make streets safer (its original function) but to reduce the incidence of mass violence. Order maintenance became, to a degree, coterminous with "community relations." But, as the crime wave that began in the early 1960s continued without abatement throughout the decade and into the 1970s, attention shifted to the role of the police as crime-fighters. Studies of police behavior ceased, by and large, to be accounts of the order-maintenance function and became, instead, efforts to propose and test ways whereby the police could solve more crimes, make more arrests, and gather better evidence. If these things could be done, social scientists assumed, citizens would be less fearful.

A great deal was accomplished during this transition, as both police chiefs and outside experts emphasized the crime-fighting function in their plans, in the allocation of resources, and in deployment of personnel. The police may well have become better crime-fighters as a result. And doubtless they remained aware of their responsibility for order. But the link between order-maintenance and crime-prevention, so obvious to earlier generations, was forgotten.

That link is similar to the process whereby one broken window becomes many. The citizen who fears the ill-smelling drunk, the rowdy teenager, or the importuning beggar is not merely expressing his distaste for unseemly behavior; he is also giving voice to a bit of folk wisdom that happens to be a correct generalization—namely, that serious street crime flourishes in areas in which disorderly behavior goes unchecked. The unchecked panhandler is, in effect, the first broken window. Muggers and robbers, whether opportunistic or professional, believe they reduce their chances of being caught or even identified if they operate on streets where potential victims are already intimidated by prevailing conditions. If the neighborhood cannot keep a bothersome panhandler from annoying passersby, the thief may reason, it is even less likely to call the police to identify a potential mugger or to interfere if the mugging actually takes place.

Some police administrators concede that this process occurs, but argue that motorized-patrol officers can deal with it as effectively as foot patrol officers. We are not so sure. In theory, an officer in a squad car can observe as much as an officer on foot; in theory, the former can talk to as many people as the latter. But the reality of police–citizen encounters is powerfully altered by the automobile. An officer on foot cannot separate himself from the street people; if he is approached, only his uniform and his personality can help him manage whatever is about to happen. And he can never be certain what that will be—a request for directions, a plea for help, an angry denunciation, a teasing remark, a confused babble, a threatening gesture.

In a car, an officer is more likely to deal with street people by rolling down the window and looking at them. The door and the window exclude the approaching citizen; they are a barrier. Some officers take advantage of this barrier, perhaps unconsciously, by acting differently if in the car than they would on foot. We have seen this countless times. The police car pulls up to a corner where teenagers are gathered. The window is rolled down. The officer stares at the youths. They stare back. The officer says to one, "C'mere." He saunters over, conveying to his friends by his elaborately casual style the idea that he is not intimidated by authority. "What's your name?" "Chuck." "Chuck who?" "Chuck Jones." "What'ya doing, Chuck?" "Nothin'." "Got a P.O. [parole officer]?" "Nah." "Sure?" "Yeah." "Stay out of trouble, Chuckie." Meanwhile, the other boys laugh and exchange comments among themselves, probably at the officer's expense. The officer stares harder. He cannot be certain what is being said, nor can he join in and, by displaying his own skill at street banter, prove that he cannot be "put down." In the process, the officer has learned almost nothing, and the boys have decided the officer is an alien force who can safely be disregarded, even mocked.

Our experience is that most citizens like to talk to a police officer. Such exchanges give them a sense of importance, provide them with the basis for gossip, and allow them to explain to the authorities what is worrying them (whereby they gain a modest but significant sense of having "done something" about the problem). You approach a person on foot more easily, and talk to him more readily, than you do a person in a car. Moreover, you can more easily retain some anonymity if you draw an officer aside for a private chat. Suppose you want to pass on a tip about who is stealing handbags, or who offered to sell you a stolen TV. In the inner city, the culprit, in all likelihood, lives nearby. To walk up to a marked patrol car and lean in the window is to convey a visible signal that you are a "fink."

The essence of the police role in maintaining order is to reinforce the informal control mechanisms of the community itself. The police cannot, without committing extraordinary resources, provide a substitute for that informal control. On the other hand, to reinforce those natural forces the police must accommodate them. And therein lies the problem.

Should police activity on the street be shaped, in important ways, by the standards of the neighborhood rather than by the rules of the state? Over the past two decades, the shift of police from order maintenance to law enforcement has brought them increasingly under the influence of legal restrictions, provoked by media complaints and enforced by court decisions and departmental orders. As a consequence, the order-maintenance functions of the police are now governed by rules developed to control police relations with suspected criminals. This is, we think, an entirely new development. For centuries, the role of the police as watchmen was judged primarily not in terms of its compliance with appropriate procedures but rather in terms of its attaining a desired objective. The objective was order, an inherently ambiguous term but a condition that people in a given community recognized when they saw it. The means were the same as those the community itself would employ, if its members were sufficiently determined, courageous, and authoritative. Detecting and apprehending criminals, by contrast, was a means to an end, not an end in itself; a judicial determination of guilt or innocence was the hoped-for result of the law-enforcement mode. From the first, the police were expected to follow rules defining that process, though states differed in how stringent the rules should be. The criminal-apprehension process was always understood to involve individual rights, the violation of which was unacceptable because it meant that the violating officer would be acting as a judge and jury—and that was not his job. Guilt or innocence was to be determined by universal standards under special procedures.

Ordinarily, no judge or jury ever sees the persons caught up in a dispute over the appropriate level of neighborhood order. That is true not only because most cases are handled informally on the street but also because no universal standards are available to settle arguments over disorder, and thus a judge may not be any wiser or more effective than a police officer. Until quite recently in many states, and even today in some places, the police made arrests on such charges as "suspicious person" or "vagrancy" or "public drunkenness"—charges with scarcely any legal meaning. These charges exist not because society wants judges to punish vagrants or drunks but because it wants an officer to have the legal tools to remove undesirable persons from a neighborhood when informal efforts to preserve order in the streets have failed.

Once we begin to think of all aspects of police work as involving the application of universal rules under special procedures, we inevitably ask what constitutes an "undesirable person" and why we should "criminalize" vagrancy or drunkenness. A strong and commendable desire to see that people are treated fairly makes us worry about allowing the police to rout persons who are undesirable by some vague or parochial standard. A growing and not-so-commendable utilitarianism leads us to doubt that any behavior that does not "hurt" another person should be made illegal. And thus many of us who watch over the police are reluctant to allow them to perform, in the only way they can, a function that every neighborhood desperately wants them to perform.

This wish to "decriminalize" disreputable behavior that "harms no one"—and thus remove the ultimate sanction the police can employ to maintain neighborhood order—is, we think, a mistake. Arresting a single drunk or a single vagrant who has harmed no identifiable person seems unjust, and in a sense it is. But failing to do anything about a score of drunks or a hundred vagrants may destroy an entire community. A particular rule that seems to make sense in the individual case makes no sense when it is made a universal rule and applied to all cases. It makes no sense because it fails to take into account the connection between one broken window left untended and a thousand broken windows. Of course, agencies other than the police could attend to the problems posed by drunks or the mentally ill, but in most communities—especially where the "deinstitutionalization" movement has been strong—they do not.

The concern about equity is more serious. We might agree that certain behavior makes one person more undesirable than another but how do we ensure that age or skin color or national origin or harmless mannerisms will not also become the basis for distinguishing the undesirable from the desirable? How do we ensure, in short, that the police do not become the agents of neighborhood bigotry?

We can offer no wholly satisfactory answer to this important question. We are not confident that there is a satisfactory answer except to hope that by their selection, training, and supervision, the police will be inculcated with a clear sense of the outer limit of their discretionary authority. That limit, roughly, is this—the police exist to help regulate behavior, not to maintain the racial or ethnic purity of a neighborhood.

Consider the case of the Robert Taylor Homes in Chicago, one of the largest public-housing projects in the country. It is home for nearly 20,000 people, all black, and extends over ninety-two acres along South State Street. It was named after a distinguished black who had been, during the 1940s, chairman of the Chicago Housing Authority. Not long after it opened, in 1962, relations between project residents and the police deteriorated badly. The citizens felt that the police were insensitive or brutal; the police, in turn, complained of unprovoked attacks on them. Some Chicago officers tell of times when they were afraid to enter the Homes. Crime rates soared.

Today, the atmosphere has changed. Police–citizen relations have improved—apparently, both sides learned something from the earlier experience. Recently, a boy stole a purse and ran off. Several young persons who saw the theft voluntarily passed along to the police information on the identity and residence of the thief, and they did this publicly, with friends and neighbors looking on. But problems persist, chief among them the presence of youth gangs that terrorize residents and recruit members in the project. The people expect the police to "do something" about this, and the police are determined to do just that.

But do what? Though the police can obviously make arrests whenever a gang member breaks the law, a gang can form, recruit, and congregate without breaking the law. And only a tiny fraction of gang-related crimes can be solved by an arrest; thus, if an arrest is the only recourse for the police, the residents' fears will go unassuaged. The police will soon feel helpless, and the residents will again believe that the police "do nothing." What the police in fact do is to chase known gang members out of the project. In the words of one officer, "We kick ass." Project residents both know and approve of this. The tacit police–citizen alliance in the project is reinforced by the police view that the cops and the gangs are the two rival sources of power in the area, and that the gangs are not going to win.

None of this is easily reconciled with any conception of due process or fair treatment. Since both residents and gang members are black, race is not a factor. But it could be. Suppose a white project confronted a black gang, or vice versa. We would be apprehensive about the police taking sides. But the substantive problem remains the same: how can the police strengthen the informal social-control mechanisms of natural communities in order to minimize fear in public places? Law enforcement, per se, is no answer: a gang can weaken or destroy a community by standing about in a menacing fashion and speaking rudely to passersby without breaking the law.

We have difficulty thinking about such matters, not simply because the ethical and legal issues are so complex but because we have become accustomed to thinking of the law in essentially individualistic terms. The law defines *my* rights, punishes *his* behavior and is applied by *that* officer because of *this* harm. We assume, in thinking this way, that what is good for the individual will be good for the community and what doesn't matter when it happens to one person won't matter if it happens to many. Ordinarily, those are plausible assumptions. But in cases where behavior that is tolerable to one person is intolerable to many others, the reactions of the others—fear, withdrawal, flight—may ultimately make matters worse for everyone, including the individual who first professed his indifference.

It may be their greater sensitivity to communal as opposed to individual needs that helps explain why the residents of small communities are more satisfied with their police than are the residents of similar neighborhoods in big cities. Elinor Ostrom and her co-workers at Indiana University compared the perception of police services in two poor, all-black Illinois towns—Phoenix and East Chicago Heights—with those of three comparable all-black neighborhoods in Chicago. The level of criminal victimization and the quality of police–community relations appeared to be about the same in the towns and the Chicago neighborhoods. But the citizens living in their own villages were much more likely than those living in the Chicago neighborhoods to say that they do not stay at home for fear of crime, to agree that the local police have "the right to take any action necessary" to deal with problems, and to agree that the police "look out for the needs of the average citizen." It is possible that the residents and the police of the small towns saw themselves as engaged in a collaborative effort to maintain a certain standard of communal life, whereas those of the big city felt themselves to be simply requesting and supplying particular services on an individual basis.

If this is true, how should a wise police chief deploy his meager forces? The first answer is that nobody knows for certain, and the most prudent course of action would be to try further variations on the Newark experiment, to see more precisely what works in what kinds of neighborhoods. The second answer is also a hedge—many aspects of order maintenance in neighborhoods can probably best be handled in ways that involve the police minimally if at all. A busy bustling shopping center and a quiet, well-tended suburb may need almost no visible police presence. In both cases, the ratio of respectable to disreputable people is ordinarily so high as to make informal social control effective.

Even in areas that are in jeopardy from disorderly elements, citizen action without substantial police involvement may be sufficient. Meetings between teenagers who like to hang out on a particular corner and adults who want to use that corner might well lead to an amicable agreement on a set of rules about how many people can be allowed to congregate, where, and when.

Where no understanding is possible—or if possible, not observed—citizen patrols may be a sufficient response. There are two traditions of communal involvement in maintaining order: One, that of the "community watchmen," is as old as the first settlement of the New World. Until well into the nineteenth century, volunteer watchmen, not policemen, patrolled their communities to keep order. They did so, by and large, without taking the law into their own hands—without, that is, punishing persons or using force. Their presence deterred disorder or alerted the community to disorder that could not be deterred. There are hundreds of such efforts today in communities all across the nation. Perhaps the best known is that of the Guardian Angels, a group of unarmed young persons in distinctive berets and T-shirts, who first came to public attention when they began patrolling the New York City subways but who claim now to have chapters in more than thirty American cities. Unfortunately, we have little information about the effect of these groups on crime. It is possible, however, that whatever their effect on crime, citizens find their presence reassuring, and that they thus contribute to maintaining a sense of order and civility.

The second tradition is that of the "vigilante." Rarely a feature of the settled communities of the East, it was primarily to be found in those frontier towns that grew up in advance of the reach of government. More than 350 vigilante groups are known to have existed; their distinctive feature was that their members did take the law into their own hands, by acting as judge, jury, and often executioner as well as policeman. Today, the vigilante movement is conspicuous by its rarity, despite the great fear expressed by citizens that the older cities are becoming "urban frontiers." But some community-watchmen groups have skirted the line, and others may cross it in the future. An ambiguous case, reported in *The Wall Street Journal,* involved a citizens' patrol in the Silver Lake area of Belleville, New Jersey. A leader told the reporter, "We look for outsiders." If a few teenagers from outside the neighborhood enter it, "we ask them their business," he said. "If they say they're going down the street to see Mrs. Jones, fine, we let them pass. But then we follow them down the block to make sure they're really going to see Mrs. Jones."

Though citizens can do a great deal, the police are plainly the key to order maintenance. For one thing, many communities, such as the Robert Taylor Homes, cannot do the job by themselves. For another, no citizen in a neighborhood, even an organized one, is likely to feel the sense of responsibility that wearing a badge confers. Psychologists have done many studies on why people fail to go to the aid of persons being attacked or seeking help, and they have learned that the cause is not "apathy" or "selfishness" but the absence of some plausible grounds for feeling that one must personally accept responsibility. Ironically, avoiding responsibility is easier when a lot of people are standing about. On streets and in public places, where order is so important, many people are likely to be "around," a fact that reduces the chance of any one person acting as the agent of the community. The police officer's uniform singles him out as a person who must accept responsibility if asked. In addition, officers, more easily than their fellow citizens, can be expected to distinguish between what is necessary to protect the safety of the street and what merely protects its ethnic purity.

But the police forces of America are losing, not gaining, members. Some cities have suffered substantial cuts in the number of officers available for duty. These cuts are not likely to be reversed in the near future. Therefore, each department must assign its existing officers with great care. Some neighborhoods are so demoralized and crime-ridden as to make foot patrol useless; the best the police can do with limited resources is respond to the enormous number of calls for service. Other neighborhoods are so stable and serene as to make foot patrol unnecessary. The key is to identify neighborhoods at the tipping point—where the public order is deteriorating but not unreclaimable, where the streets are used frequently but by apprehensive people, where a window is likely to be broken at any time, and must quickly be fixed if all are not to be shattered.

Most police departments do not have ways of systematically identifying such areas and assigning officers to them. Officers are assigned on the basis of crime rates (meaning that marginally threatened areas are often stripped so that police can investigate crimes in areas where the situation is hopeless) or on the basis of calls for service (despite the fact that most citizens do not call the police when they are merely frightened or annoyed). To allocate patrol wisely, the department must look at the neighborhoods and decide, from first-hand evidence, where an additional officer will make the greatest difference in promoting a sense of safety.

One way to stretch limited police resources is being tried in some public housing projects. Tenant organizations hire off-duty police officers for patrol work in their buildings. The costs are not high (at least not per resident), the officer likes the additional income, and the residents feel safer. Such arrangements are probably more successful than hiring private watchmen, and the Newark experiment helps us understand why. A private security guard may deter crime or misconduct by his presence, and he may go to the aid of persons needing help, but he may well not intervene—that is, control or drive away—someone challenging community standards. Being a sworn officer—a "real cop"—seems to give one the confidence, the sense of duty, and the aura of authority necessary to perform this difficult task.

Patrol officers might be encouraged to go to and from duty stations on public transportation and, while on the bus or subway car, enforce rules about smoking, drinking, disorderly conduct, and the like. The enforcement need involve nothing more than ejecting the offender (the offense, after all, is not one with which a booking officer or a judge wishes to be bothered). Perhaps the random but relentless maintenance of standards on buses would lead to conditions on buses that approximate the level of civility we now take for granted on airplanes.

But the most important requirement is to think that to maintain order in precarious situations is a vital job. The police know this is one of their functions, and they also believe, correctly, that it cannot be done to the exclusion of criminal investigation and responding to calls. We may have encouraged them to suppose, however, on the basis of our oft-repeated concerns about serious, violent crime, that they will be judged exclusively on their capacity as crime-fighters. To the extent that this is the case, police administrators will continue to concentrate police personnel in the highest-crime areas (though not necessarily in the areas most vulnerable to criminal invasion), emphasize their training in the law and criminal apprehension (and not their training in managing street life), and join too quickly in campaigns to decriminalize "harmless" behavior (though public drunkenness, street prostitution, and pornographic displays can destroy a community more quickly than any team of professional burglars).

Above all, we must return to our long-abandoned view that the police ought to protect communities as well as individuals. Our crime statistics and victimization surveys measure individual losses, but they do not measure communal losses. Just as physicians now recognize the importance of fostering health rather than simply treating illness, so the police—and the rest of us—ought to recognize the importance of maintaining, intact, communities without broken windows.

Section XIII
Review Questions

1. If E. Pendleton Herring is correct in his description of the role of the bureaucrat, doesn't this give an enormous amount of power to nonelected public employees? Too much power?

2. Do you think that Franklin Roosevelt's version of liberalism will ever again regain its position as the dominant political ideology of Americans? What did the presidential election of 2004 tell us about the current status of Roosevelt's liberalism in the United States?

3. Do you agree with Milton Friedman's classical liberal assumption that less government regulation of business remains the best way to protect political freedom and to encourage progress through individual entrepreneurial action?

4. How does Michael Lipsky make the case that the lowest-level bureaucrats are really the policy makers? Does his analysis conform to your experience with "street-level bureaucrats"?

5. Why do James Q. Wilson and George L. Kelling believe that if the police control minor crimes, major crimes will be reduced in the community as well? Has such a strategy been successful in your community? Can you find evidence that their theory has actually reduced crime anywhere? Is crime simply being displaced to another community by this strategy?

XIV

Foreign and Defense Policy

HARRY S. TRUMAN

73. The Case for the Cold War: The Truman Doctrine

Arguably the most significant single strategic plan of the twentieth century was the Truman Doctrine, President Harry S. Truman's now classic statement of the U.S. policy of taking the steps necessary to contain the expansion of the Soviet Union and the spread of Communism in the post–World War II world. Truman outlined a policy of extending military and economic aid to those countries (originally Greece and Turkey) seeking to resist "totalitarian aggression." The Truman Doctrine became the cornerstone of the U.S. policy of containing the Soviet Union, the underlying basis of U.S. foreign, military, and much of domestic policy for the half-century that followed World War II. The demise of the Soviet Union in 1991 can be seen as the ultimate vindication of the containment strategy.

Although there was broad agreement on the objective of containment, at least until the reaction against U.S. involvement in Vietnam in the late 1960s, different strategies were used to implement this objective. From 1947 until 1950, the emphasis was on rebuilding allies and former enemies in Western Europe; this massive infusion of economic aid became known as the Marshall Plan—so named by Truman to honor Secretary of State George C. Marshall, Jr., who headed the U.S. Army during World War II. During the Korean War (1950–1953), the emphasis moved to actual fighting on the borders of the free world to prevent the spread of Communism. The Eisenhower administration (1953–1961) emphasized the possibility of nuclear retaliation. Then the Kennedy and Johnson administrations (1961–1969) used containment as its rationale for massively escalating the limited war in Vietnam. The Nixon administration (1969–1974) did not abandon containment but tried instead to uphold it through greater reliance on allies and détente with the

Source: From Harry S. Truman, address to joint session of Congress, March 12, 1947.

Soviet Union. The Carter administration (1977–1981) initially tried to ignore containment, but embraced it after the Soviet invasion of Afghanistan. The Reagan administration (1981–1989) not only pursued a highly military containment policy but tried to go beyond it and roll back some of the Soviet gains of the 1970s in the Third World through support for anti-Communist revolutionary movements. The Bush administration (1989–1993) saw containment come to an end with the demise of the Soviet Union in 1991.

The Truman Doctrine provided the vision, the overall philosophy, for all of these efforts. Its strategic vision guided all of the details of the Cold War that followed—from the Marshall Plan to the Korean and Vietnam wars to the Reagan military buildup. President Truman made the initial statement of his doctrine to a joint session of Congress on March 12, 1947.

The gravity of the situation which confronts the world today necessitates my appearance before a joint session of the Congress. The foreign policy and the national security of this country are involved.

One aspect of the present situation, which I wish to present to you at this time for your consideration and decision, concerns Greece and Turkey.

The United States has received from the Greek Government an urgent appeal for financial and economic assistance. Preliminary reports from the American Economic Mission now in Greece and reports from the American Ambassador in Greece corroborate the statement of the Greek Government that assistance is imperative if Greece is to survive as a free nation.

I do not believe that the American people and the Congress wish to turn a deaf ear to the appeal of the Greek Government.

Greece is not a rich country. Lack of sufficient natural resources has always forced the Greek people to work hard to make both ends meet. Since 1940, this industrious and peace loving country has suffered invasion, four years of cruel enemy occupation, and bitter internal strife.

When forces of liberation entered Greece they found that the retreating Germans had destroyed virtually all the railways, roads, port facilities, communications, and merchant marine. More than a thousand villages had been burned. Eighty-five per cent of the children were tubercular. Livestock, poultry, and draft animals had almost disappeared. Inflation had wiped out practically all savings.

As a result of these tragic conditions, a militant minority, exploiting human want and misery, was able to create political chaos which, until now, has made economic recovery impossible.

Greece is today without funds to finance the importation of those goods which are essential to bare subsistence. Under these circumstances the people of Greece cannot make progress in solving their problems of reconstruction. Greece is in desperate need of financial and economic assistance to enable it to resume purchases of food, clothing, fuel and seeds. These are indispensable for the subsistence of its people and are obtainable only from abroad. Greece must have help to import the goods necessary to restore internal order and security, so essential for economic and political recovery.

The Greek Government has also asked for the assistance of experienced American administrators, economists and technicians to insure that the financial and other aid given to Greece shall be used effectively in creating a stable and self-sustaining economy and in improving its public administration.

The very existence of the Greek state is today threatened by the terrorist activities of several thousand armed men, led by Communists, who defy the government's authority at a number of points, particularly along the northern boundaries. A Commission appointed by the United Nations Security Council is at present investigating disturbed conditions in northern Greece and alleged border violations along the frontier between Greece on the one hand and Albania, Bulgaria, and Yugoslavia on the other.

Meanwhile, the Greek Government is unable to cope with the situation. The Greek army is small and poorly equipped. It needs supplies and equipment if it is to restore the authority of the government throughout Greek territory. Greece must have assistance if it is to become a self-supporting and self-respecting democracy.

The United States must supply that assistance. We have already extended to Greece certain types of relief and economic aid but these are inadequate.

There is no other country to which democratic Greece can turn.

No other nation is willing and able to provide the necessary support for a democratic Greek government.

The British Government, which has been helping Greece, can give no further financial or economic aid after March 31. Great Britain finds itself under the necessity of reducing or liquidating its commitments in several parts of the world, including Greece.

We have considered how the United Nations might assist in this crisis. But the situation is an urgent one requiring immediate action and the United Nations and its related organizations are not in a position to extend help of the kind that is required.

It is important to note that the Greek Government has asked for our aid in utilizing effectively the financial and other assistance we may give to Greece, and in improving its public administration. It is of the utmost importance that we supervise the use of any funds made available to Greece, in such a manner that each dollar spent will count toward making Greece self-supporting, and will help to build an economy in which a healthy democracy can flourish.

No government is perfect. One of the chief virtues of a democracy, however, is that its defects are always visible and under democratic processes can be pointed out and corrected. The Government of Greece is not perfect. Nevertheless it represents eighty-five per cent of the members of the Greek Parliament who were chosen in an election last year. Foreign observers, including 692 Americans, considered this election to be a fair expression of the views of the Greek people.

The Greek Government has been operating in an atmosphere of chaos and extremism. It has made mistakes. The extension of aid by this country does not mean that the United States condones everything that the Greek Government has done or will do. We have condemned in the past, and we condemn now, extremist measures of the right or the left. We have in the past advised tolerance, and we advise tolerance now.

Greece's neighbor, Turkey, also deserves our attention.

The future of Turkey as an independent and economically sound state is clearly no less important to the freedom-loving peoples of the world than the future of Greece. The circumstances in which Turkey finds itself today are considerably different from those of Greece. Turkey has been spared the disasters that have beset Greece. And during the war, the United States and Great Britain furnished Turkey with material aid.

Nevertheless, Turkey now needs our support.

Since the war Turkey has sought financial assistance from Great Britain and the United States for the purpose of effecting that modernization necessary for the maintenance of its national integrity.

That integrity is essential to the preservation of order in the Middle East.

The British government has informed us that, owing to its own difficulties it can no longer extend financial or economic aid to Turkey.

As in the case of Greece, if Turkey is to have the assistance it needs, the United States must supply it. We are the only country able to provide that help.

I am fully aware of the broad implications involved if the United States extends assistance to Greece and Turkey, and I shall discuss these implications with you at this time.

One of the primary objectives of the foreign policy of the United States is the creation of conditions in which we and other nations will be able to work out a way of life free from coercion. This was a fundamental issue in the war with Germany and Japan. Our victory was won over countries which sought to impose their will, and their way of life, upon other nations.

To ensure the peaceful development of nations, free from coercion, the United States has taken a leading part in establishing the United Nations. The United Nations is designed to make possible lasting freedom and independence for all its members. We shall not realize our objectives, however, unless we are willing to help free peoples to maintain their free institutions and their national integrity against aggressive movements that seek to impose upon them totalitarian regimes. This is no more than a frank recognition that totalitarian regimes imposed on free peoples, by direct or indirect aggression, undermine the foundations of international peace and hence the security of the United States.

The peoples of a number of countries of the world have recently had totalitarian regimes forced upon them against their will. The Government of the United States has made frequent protests against coercion and intimidation, in violation of the Yalta agreement, in Poland, Rumania, and Bulgaria. I must also state that in a number of other countries there have been similar developments.

At the present moment in world history nearly every nation must choose between alternative ways of life. The choice is too often not a free one.

One way of life is based upon the will of the majority, and is distinguished by free institutions, representative government, free elections, guarantees of individual liberty, freedom of speech and religion, and freedom from political oppression.

The second way of life is based upon the will of a minority forcibly imposed upon the majority. It relies upon terror and oppression, a controlled press and radio, fixed elections, and the suppression of personal freedoms.

I believe that it must be the policy of the United States to support free peoples who are resisting attempted subjugation by armed minorities or by outside pressures.

I believe that we must assist free peoples to work out their own destinies in their own way.

I believe that our help should be primarily through economic and financial aid which is essential to economic stability and orderly political processes.

The world is not static, and the status quo is not sacred. But we cannot allow changes in the status quo in violation of the Charter of the United Nations by such methods as coercion, or by such subterfuges as political infiltration. In helping free and independent nations to maintain their freedom, the United States will be giving effect to the principles of the Charter of the United Nations.

It is necessary only to glance at a map to realize that the survival and integrity of the Greek nation are of grave importance in a much wider situation. If Greece should fall under the control of an armed minority, the effect upon its neighbor, Turkey, would be immediate and serious. Confusion and disorder might well spread throughout the entire Middle East.

Moreover, the disappearance of Greece as an independent state would have a profound effect upon those countries in Europe whose peoples are struggling against great difficulties to maintain their freedoms and their independence while they repair the damages of war.

It would be an unspeakable tragedy if these countries, which have struggled so long against overwhelming odds, should lose that victory for which they sacrificed so much. Collapse of free institutions and loss of independence would be disastrous not only for them but for the world. Discouragement and possibly failure would quickly be the lot of neighboring peoples striving to maintain their freedom and independence.

Should we fail to aid Greece and Turkey in this fateful hour, the effect will be far reaching to the West as well as to the East.

We must take immediate and resolute action.

I therefore ask the Congress to provide authority for assistance to Greece and Turkey in the amount of $400,000,000 for the period ending June 30, 1948. In requesting these funds, I have taken into consideration the maximum amount of relief assistance which would be furnished to Greece out of the $350,000,000 which I recently requested that the Congress authorize for the prevention of starvation and suffering in countries devastated by the war.

In addition to funds, I ask the Congress to authorize the detail of American civilian and military personnel to Greece and Turkey, at the request of those countries, to assist in the tasks of reconstruction, and for the purpose of supervising the use of such financial and material assistance as may be furnished. I recommend that authority also be provided for the instruction and training of selected Greek and Turkish personnel.

Finally, I ask that the Congress provide authority which will permit the speediest and most effective use, in terms of needed commodities, supplies, and equipment, of such funds as may be authorized.

If further funds, or further authority, should be needed for purposes indicated in this message, I shall not hesitate to bring the situation before the Congress. On this subject the Executive and Legislative branches of the Government must work together.

This is a serious course upon which we embark.

I would not recommend it except that the alternative is much more serious. The United States contributed $341,000,000,000 toward winning World War II. This is an investment in world freedom and world peace.

The assistance that I am recommending for Greece and Turkey amounts to little more than 1 tenth of 1 per cent of this investment. It is only common sense that we should safeguard this investment and make sure that it was not in vain.

The seeds of totalitarian regimes are nurtured by misery and want. They spread and grow in the evil soil of poverty and strife. They reach their full growth when the hope of a people for a better life has died. We must keep that hope alive.

The free peoples of the world look to us for support in maintaining their freedoms.

If we falter in our leadership, we may endanger the peace of the world—and we shall surely endanger the welfare of our own nation.

Great responsibilities have been placed upon us by the swift movement of events.

I am confident that the Congress will face these responsibilities squarely.

GEORGE W. BUSH

74. THE CASE FOR PREEMPTIVE WAR: THE BUSH DOCTRINE

Historically, preemption *has been used as a nice word for a sneak attack. The most famous such attack in the twentieth century occurred at Pearl Harbor, the United States Pacific fleet headquarters in Hawaii, where, on Sunday, December 7, 1941, more than 350 aircraft from six Japanese aircraft carriers launched an attack against the U.S. Navy ships moored in the harbor. The Pearl Harbor attack incensed the American public not just because it was a surprise (which is to be expected in war), but because it was a sneak attack when there was no declared state of war. Indeed, Japanese emissaries were in Washington at the same time purportedly negotiating in good faith to resolve differences. The Japanese had intended to notify the Americans that a state of war existed one-half hour before the attack. But because of decoding difficulties, the war message was not delivered until after the attack was well under way. This time difference is the difference between honor and dishonor.*

Ever since Pearl Harbor the United States has scrupulously avoided any hint that its military would initiate a preemptive attack on any adversary. The idea of a preemptive war against Soviet nuclear installations was advocated when it was apparent that the United States was about to lose its nuclear monopoly, but the idea was rejected as inconsistent with the principles of a democratic state.

Preemption is traditionally related to the issue of survivability of military forces. The less survivable one's forces—the less able they are to ride out an enemy attack—the more incentive there is to strike preemptively. The temptation of preemptive action during a crisis between the nuclear superpowers was a cause for concern at various junctures during the Cold War. This explains the emphasis on making strategic nuclear forces invulnerable

---

Source: From George W. Bush, speech at West Point, June 1, 2002.

to a first strike by putting such weapons in underground hardened silos or on submarines. A preemptive strike is not necessarily illegal under international law. As far back as 1625 British statesman Francis Bacon (1561–1626) wrote in his Essays *("Of Empire"): "A just fear of imminent danger, though there be no blow given, is lawful cause of war."*

But traditional thinking about preemption changed after September 11, 2001, and the debate over the concept was conducted in the press and the political arena. There could be no "balance of terror" with the Islamic terrorists who had vowed to attack and kill Americans wherever and whenever they could. So, on June 1, 2002, President George W. Bush traveled to the United States Military Academy at West Point, New York, and told the assembled throng: "For much of the last century, America's defense relied on the Cold War doctrines of deterrence and containment. . . . But . . . deterrence—the promise of massive retaliation against nations—means nothing against shadowy terrorist networks with no nation or citizens to defend. Containment is not possible when unbalanced dictators with weapons of mass destruction can deliver those weapons on missiles or secretly provide them to terrorist allies."

The problem, Bush clearly implied in this commencement address, was that the United States needed a new doctrine for defense. "If we wait for threats to fully materialize, we will have waited too long. . . . The war on terror will not be won on the defensive. We must take the battle to the enemy, disrupt his plans, and confront the worst threats before they emerge." In the war on terror, "the only path to safety is the path of action. . . . Our security will require all Americans to be . . . ready for preemptive action when necessary to defend our liberty and to defend our lives."

What Bush said was truly radical. But only after Bush acted upon his new doctrine, with the initiation of the 2003 war with Iraq, did people realize how very serious he was about preemptive war during that peaceful graduation day. It is possible that Bush's West Point commencement address may parallel in significance the one that Secretary of State George C. Marshall gave at the Harvard University commencement in 1947 that led to the Marshall Plan for rebuilding Europe after

World War II. This goes to show that sometimes commencement addresses are very much worth listening to—but not often!

In every corner of America, the words "West Point" command immediate respect. This place where the Hudson River bends is more than a fine institution of learning. The United States Military Academy is the guardian of values that have shaped the soldiers who have shaped the history of the world. . . .

Every West Point class is commissioned to the Armed Forces. Some West Point classes are also commissioned by history, to take part in a great new calling for their country. Speaking here to the class of 1942—six months after Pearl Harbor—General Marshall said, "We're determined that before the sun sets on this terrible struggle, our flag will be recognized throughout the world as a symbol of freedom on the one hand, and of overwhelming power on the other." (Applause.)

Officers graduating that year helped fulfill that mission, defeating Japan and Germany, and then reconstructing those nations as allies. West Point graduates of the 1940s saw the rise of a deadly new challenge—the challenge of imperial communism—and opposed it from Korea to Berlin, to Vietnam, and in the Cold War, from beginning to end. And as the sun set on their struggle, many of those West Point officers lived to see a world transformed.

History has also issued its call to your generation. In your last year, America was attacked by a ruthless and resourceful enemy. You graduate from this Academy in a time of war, taking your place in an American military that is powerful and is honorable. Our war on terror is only begun, but in Afghanistan it was begun well. (Applause.)

I am proud of the men and women who have fought on my orders. America is profoundly grateful for all who serve the cause of freedom, and for all who have given their lives in its defense. This nation respects and trusts our military, and we are confident in your victories to come. (Applause.)

This war will take many turns we cannot predict. Yet I am certain of this: Wherever we carry it, the American flag will stand not only for our power, but for freedom. (Applause.) Our nation's cause has always been larger than our nation's defense. We fight, as we always fight, for a just peace—a peace that favors human liberty. We will defend the peace against threats from terrorists and tyrants. We will preserve the peace by building good relations among the great powers. And we will extend the peace by encouraging free and open societies on every continent.

Building this just peace is America's opportunity, and America's duty. From this day forward, it is your challenge, as well, and we will meet this challenge together. (Applause.) You will wear the uniform of a great and unique country. America has no empire to extend or utopia to establish. We wish for others only what we wish for ourselves—safety from violence, the rewards of liberty, and the hope for a better life.

In defending the peace, we face a threat with no precedent. Enemies in the past needed great armies and great industrial capabilities to endanger the American people and our nation. The attacks of September the 11th required a few hundred thousand dollars in the hands of a few dozen evil and deluded men. All of the chaos and suffering they caused came at much less than the cost of a single tank. The dangers have not passed. This government and the American people are on watch, we are ready, because we know the terrorists have more money and more men and more plans.

The gravest danger to freedom lies at the perilous crossroads of radicalism and technology. When the spread of chemical and biological and nuclear weapons, along with ballistic missile technology—when that occurs, even weak states and small groups could attain a catastrophic power to strike great nations. Our enemies have declared this very intention, and have been caught seeking these terrible weapons. They want the capability to blackmail us, or to harm us, or to harm our friends—and we will oppose them with all our power. (Applause.)

For much of the last century, America's defense relied on the Cold War doctrines of deterrence and containment. In some cases, those strategies still apply. But new threats also require new thinking. Deterrence—the promise of massive retaliation against nations—means nothing against shadowy terrorist networks with no nation or citizens to defend. Containment is not possible when unbalanced dictators with weapons of mass destruction can deliver those weapons on missiles or secretly provide them to terrorist allies.

We cannot defend America and our friends by hoping for the best. We cannot put our faith in the word of tyrants, who solemnly sign non-proliferation treaties, and then systemically break them. If we wait for threats to fully materialize, we will have waited too long. (Applause.)

Homeland defense and missile defense are part of stronger security, and they're essential priorities for America. Yet the war on terror will not be won on the defensive. We must take the battle to the enemy, disrupt his plans, and confront the worst threats before they emerge. (Applause.) In the world we have entered, the only path to safety is the path of action. And this nation will act. (Applause.)

Our security will require the best intelligence, to reveal threats hidden in caves and growing in laboratories. Our security will require modernizing domestic agencies such as the FBI, so they're prepared to act, and act quickly, against danger. Our security will require transforming the military you will lead—a military that must be ready to strike at a moment's notice in any dark corner of the world. And our security will require all Americans to be forward-looking and resolute, to be ready for preemptive action when necessary to defend our liberty and to defend our lives. (Applause.)

The work ahead is difficult. The choices we will face are complex. We must uncover terror cells in 60 or more countries, using every tool of finance, intelligence and law enforcement. Along with our friends and allies, we must oppose proliferation and confront regimes that sponsor terror, as each case requires. Some nations need military training to fight terror, and we'll provide it. Other nations oppose terror, but tolerate the hatred that leads to terror—and that must change. (Applause.) We will send diplomats where they are needed, and we will send you, our soldiers, where you're needed. (Applause.)

All nations that decide for aggression and terror will pay a price. We will not leave the safety of America and the peace of the planet at the mercy of a few mad terrorists and tyrants. (Applause.) We will lift this dark threat from our country and from the world.

Because the war on terror will require resolve and patience, it will also require firm moral purpose. In this way our struggle is similar to the Cold War. Now, as then, our enemies are totalitarians, holding a creed of power with no place for human dignity. Now, as then, they seek to impose a joyless conformity, to control every life and all of life.

America confronted imperial communism in many different ways—diplomatic, economic, and military. Yet moral clarity was essential to our victory in the Cold War. When leaders like John F. Kennedy and Ronald Reagan refused to gloss over the brutality of tyrants, they gave hope to prisoners and dissidents and exiles, and rallied free nations to a great cause.

Some worry that it is somehow undiplomatic or impolite to speak the language of right and wrong. I disagree. (Applause.) Different circumstances require different methods, but not different moralities. (Applause.) Moral truth is the same in every culture, in every time, and in every place. Targeting innocent civilians for murder is always and everywhere wrong. (Applause.) Brutality against women is always and everywhere wrong. (Applause.) There can be no neutrality between justice and cruelty, between the innocent and the guilty. We are in a conflict between good and evil, and America will call evil by its name. (Applause.) By confronting evil and lawless regimes, we do not create a problem, we reveal a problem. And we will lead the world in opposing it. (Applause.)

As we defend the peace, we also have an historic opportunity to preserve the peace. We have our best chance since the rise of the nation state in the 17th century to build a world where the great powers compete in peace instead of prepare for war. The history of the last century, in particular, was dominated by a series of destructive national rivalries that left battlefields and graveyards across the Earth. Germany fought France, the Axis fought the Allies, and then the East fought the West, in proxy wars and tense standoffs, against a backdrop of nuclear Armageddon.

Competition between great nations is inevitable, but armed conflict in our world is not. More and more, civilized nations find ourselves on the same side—united by common dangers of terrorist violence and chaos. America has, and intends to keep, military strengths beyond challenge—(applause)—thereby, making the destabilizing arms races of other eras pointless, and limiting rivalries to trade and other pursuits of peace.

Today the great powers are also increasingly united by common values, instead of divided by conflicting ideologies. The United States, Japan and our

Pacific friends, and now all of Europe, share a deep commitment to human freedom, embodied in strong alliances such as NATO. And the tide of liberty is rising in many other nations.

Generations of West Point officers planned and practiced for battles with Soviet Russia. I've just returned from a new Russia, now a country reaching toward democracy, and our partner in the war against terror. (Applause.) Even in China, leaders are discovering that economic freedom is the only lasting source of national wealth. In time, they will find that social and political freedom is the only true source of national greatness. (Applause.)

When the great powers share common values, we are better able to confront serious regional conflicts together, better able to cooperate in preventing the spread of violence or economic chaos. In the past, great power rivals took sides in difficult regional problems, making divisions deeper and more complicated. Today, from the Middle East to South Asia, we are gathering broad international coalitions to increase the pressure for peace. We must build strong and great power relations when times are good, to help manage crisis when times are bad. America needs partners to preserve the peace, and we will work with every nation that shares this noble goal. (Applause.)

And finally, America stands for more than the absence of war. We have a great opportunity to extend a just peace, by replacing poverty, repression, and resentment around the world with hope of a better day. Through most of history, poverty was persistent, inescapable, and almost universal. In the last few decades, we've seen nations from Chile to South Korea build modern economies and freer societies, lifting millions of people out of despair and want. And there's no mystery to this achievement.

The 20th century ended with a single surviving model of human progress, based on nonnegotiable demands of human dignity, the rule of law, limits on the power of the state, respect for women and private property and free speech and equal justice and religious tolerance. America cannot impose this vision—yet we can support and reward governments that make the right choices for their own people. In our development aid, in our diplomatic efforts, in our international broadcasting, and in our educational assistance, the United States will promote moderation and tolerance and human rights. And we will defend the peace that makes all progress possible.

When it comes to the common rights and needs of men and women, there is no clash of civilizations. The requirements of freedom apply fully to Africa and Latin America and the entire Islamic world. The peoples of the Islamic nations want and deserve the same freedoms and opportunities as people in every nation. And their governments should listen to their hopes. (Applause.)

A truly strong nation will permit legal avenues of dissent for all groups that pursue their aspirations without violence. An advancing nation will pursue economic reform, to unleash the great entrepreneurial energy of its people. A thriving nation will respect the rights of women, because no society can prosper while denying opportunity to half its citizens. Mothers and fathers and children across the Islamic world, and all the world, share the same fears and aspirations. In poverty, they struggle. In tyranny, they suffer. And as we saw in Afghanistan, in liberation they celebrate. (Applause.)

America has a greater objective than controlling threats and containing resentment. We will work for a just and peaceful world beyond the war on terror.

The bicentennial class of West Point now enters this drama. With all in the United States Army, you will stand between your fellow citizens and grave danger. You will help establish a peace that allows millions around the world to live in liberty and to grow in prosperity. You will face times of calm, and times of crisis. And every test will find you prepared—because you're the men and women of West Point. (Applause.) You leave here marked by the character of this Academy, carrying with you the highest ideals of our nation.

Toward the end of his life, Dwight Eisenhower recalled the first day he stood on the plain at West Point. "The feeling came over me," he said, "that the expression 'the United States of America' would now and henceforth mean something different than it had ever before. From here on, it would be the nation I would be serving, not myself."

Today, your last day at West Point, you begin a life of service in a career unlike any other. You've answered a calling to hardship and purpose, to risk and honor. At the end of every day you will know that you have faithfully done your duty. May you always bring to that duty the high standards of this great American institution. May you always be worthy of the long gray line that stretches two centuries behind you.

On behalf of the nation, I congratulate each one of you for the commission you've earned and for the credit you bring to the United States of America. May God bless you all. (Applause.)

Section XIV
Review Questions

1. President Truman argued for economic and military aid to Greece and Turkey in 1947 as an effective way to contain the Soviet Union. But he also believed that the United States should help spread freedom and democracy to other nations. Does this sound at all like President George W. Bush's defense of the U.S. invasion of Iraq in 2003?

2. President George W. Bush told the West Point graduates that containment and deterrence are inadequate theories on which to defend the United States in the face of nonstate terrorism such as the September 11th attack on New York City in 2001. But does his belief that the "only path to safety is the path of action" really tell us much about when he thinks that preemptive war is justified?

Credits

These pages constitute an extension of the copyright page. We have made every effort to trace the ownership of all copyrighted material and to secure permission from copyright holders. In the event of any question arising as to the use of any material, we will be pleased to make the necessary corrections in future printings. Thanks are due to the following authors, publishers, and agents for permission to use the material indicated.

Selection 8. 39–43: Thurgood Marshall, "The Constitution's Bicentennial: Commemorating the Wrong Document?" Volume 40, Vanderbilt Law Review (1987). Reprinted by permission of Vanderbilt Law Review. Footnotes omitted.

Selection 13. 63–67: From Morton Grodzins, "The Federal System," in Goals for Americans, The Committee on National Goals, pp. 365–282. New York, The American Assembly. Reprinted with permission.

Selection 27. 130–133: Reprinted with the permission of Scribner, an imprint of Simon & Schuster Adult Publishing Group, from Public Opinion by Walter Lippmann. Copyright © 1922 by Walter Lippmann; copyright renewed © 1950 by Walter Lippmann.

Selection 28. 134–140: From George Gallup, "Polling the Public" from Public Opinion in a Democracy. Copyright © 1944, 1948 by George Gallup, renewed 1976 by Princeton University Press. Reprinted by permission of Princeton University Press.

Selection 29. 141–149: From "Fundamental Principles of Democracy: Bases of Agreement and Disagreement," by James W. Prothro and Charles M. Grigg in Journal of Politics, Vol. 22 (1960). Reprinted by permission of Blackwell Publishing.

Selection 30. 150–153: From V. O. Key Jr., Public Opinion and American Democracy (New York: Alfred A. Knopf, 1961). Reprinted by permission of Sandra Gettys.

Selection 31. 154–165: From "The Paranoid Style in American Politics" by Richard Hofstadter, pp. 77–82, 85–86 in the November 1964 issue of Haper's. Copyright © 1964.

Selection 32. 168–174: From Harold F. Gosnell, Machine Politics: Chicago Model, Selection 9, pp. 183–193 (Chicago: The University of Chicago Press, 1937). Copyright © 1938 The University of Chicago Press. All rights reserved. Reprinted by permission.

Selection 33. 174–179: From American Political Science Association, "Toward a More Responsible Two-Party System: A Report of the Committee on Political Parties," American Political Science Review (September 1950). Reprinted by permission of Cambridge University Press.

Selection 34. 180–191: "The Decline of Collective Responsibility in American Politics" from Daedalus, Vol. 109, No. 3 (Summer 1980), pp. 25–46. © 1980 by the American Academy of Arts and Sciences. Reprinted by permission of MIT Press Journals.

Selection 35. 192–196: From Maurice Duverger, Political Parties: Their Organization and Activity in the Modern State (New York: John Wiley & Sons, Inc., 1951). Reprinted by permission of Armand Colin.

Selection 36. 197–200: "The Socialization of Conflict" from The Semisovereign People, copyright © 1960 by E. E. Schattschneider and renewed 1988 by Frank W. Schattschneider, reprinted by permission of Harcourt Brace & Company.

Selection 37. 201–205: From The Emerging Republican Majority by Kevin Phillips, copyright © 1969 by Arlington House, Inc. Used by permission of Arlington House, a division of Random House, Inc.

Selection 40. 212–217: Joe McGinniss, The Selling of the President. Copyright © 1969 by JoeMac, Inc. Reprinted by permission of Janklow & Nesbit Associates.

Selection 41. 217–220: From Critical Elections and the Mainstream of American Politics by Walter Dean Burnham. Copyright © 1970 by W. W. Norton & Company, Inc. Used by permission of W. W. Norton & Company, Inc.

Selection 42. 220–235: From Dirty Politics: Deceptions, Distraction, and Democracy by Kathleen Hall Jamieson, copyright © 1993 by Kathleen Hall Jamieson. Used by permission of Oxford University Press, Inc.

Selection 45. 248–253: From David B. Truman, The Governmental Process (New York: Alfred A. Knopf, 1951). Reprinted by permission of the author.

Selection 46. 253–257: From The End of Liberalism, First edition by Theodore J. Lowi. Copyright © 1969 by W. W. Norton & Company, Inc. Used by permission of W. W. Norton & Company, Inc.

Selection 47. 260–264: Excerpt from "Politics and the English Language" by George Orwell, copyright 1946 by Sonia Brownwell Orwell and renewed 1974 by Sonia Orwell, reprinted from his volume Shooting an Elephant and Other Essays by permission of Harcourt Brace & Company.

Selection 48. 264–270: From The Making of the President: 1960 by Theodore White. Copyright © 1961 by Atheneum Publishers. Reprinted by permission of Atheneum Publishers and the estate of Theodore White.

Selection 49. 271–276: Reprinted with the permission of Scribner, an imprint of Simon & Schuster Adult Publishing Group, from The Image: A Guide to Pseudo-Events in America by Daniel J. Boorstin. Copyright © 1961 by Daniel J. Boorstin; copyright renewed © 1989.

Selection 50. 276–279: From The Symbolic Uses of Politics. Copyright 1964, 1985 by Board of Trustees of the University of Illinois. Used with permission of the University of Illinois Press.

Selection 54. 296–304: From Glenn R. Parker and Roger H. Davidson, "Why Do Americans Love Their Congressmen So Much More Than Their Congress?" Legislative Studies Quarterly, IV, 1, February 1979. Comparative Legislative Research Center. Reprinted by permission of the publisher and the authors.

Selection 59. 319–323: Reprinted with the permission of The Free Press, a division of Simon & Schuster Adult Publishing Group, from Presidential Power and the Modern Presidents: The Politics of Leadership from Roosevelt to Reagan by Richard E. Neustadt. Copyright © 1990 by Richard E. Neustadt. All rights reserved.

Selection 60. 323–337: From Aaron B. Wildavsky, "The Two Presidencies," Transaction 4, no. 2 (December, 1966). Reproduced by permission of Transaction Publishers.

Selection 66. 368–372: From "The Democratic Character of Judicial Review," by Eugene V. Rostow in Harvard Law Review, Vol. 66, no. 2 (1952). Copyright © 1952 by the Harvard Law Review Association. Reprinted by permission of Harvard Law School.

Selection 67. 373–378: From Alexander M. Bickel, The Least Dangerous Branch (Indianapolis: Bobbs-Merrill Company, Inc., 1962). Copyright © by Josephine A. Bickel. Reproduced by permission.

Selection 70. 392–397: From Capitalism and Freedom. Copyright © 1962 by The University of Chicago Press. Reprinted by permission of the University of Chicago Press and the author.

Selection 71. 397–407: Reprinted from Street-Level Bureaucracy: Dilemmas of the Individual in Public Services, by Michael Lipsky. © 1980, Russell Sage Foundation. Used with permission of the Russell Sage Foundation.

Selection 72. 408–421: From "Broken Windows" by James Q. Wilson and George L. Kelling, The Atlantic Monthly, March 1982. Reprinted by permission of the authors.